The Great Globe Itself

A History of the Eighteenth and Nineteenth Century

Part 1: The Years of George Washington

PETER HARDY

ISBN 979-8-89309-340-7 (Paperback)
ISBN 979-8-89309-341-4 (Digital)

Copyright © 2024 Peter Hardy
All rights reserved
First Edition

All rights reserved. No part of this publication may be reproduced, distributed, or transmitted in any form or by any means, including photocopying, recording, or other electronic or mechanical methods without the prior written permission of the publisher. For permission requests, solicit the publisher via the address below.

Covenant Books
11661 Hwy 707
Murrells Inlet, SC 29576
www.covenantbooks.com

CONTENTS

Part 1: The Years of George Washington
Chapter 1: The Dawn of the World as We Know It......................3
  The Columbian Epoch...3
    Evolution and revolution 3
    England 5
    Western Europe 6
    The House of Orleans.......................................8
    Poland and Russia...10
    Freemasonry and the Enlightenment.........................12
  Colonization in North America 16
    New Spain 16
    Brazil 19
    New France..20
    New England, Virginia, Maryland, and the
    Dutch colonies 21
  1700–1754: Europe and North America............................22
    The War of the Spanish Succession, 1701–1714 22
    The War of the Austrian Succession, 1740–1748 25
    North America at the start of the French and
    Indian War 31
    Young George Washington..................................32
  1754–1763: The Nine Years of the Seven Years' War.............32
    Fort Necessity, 1754.....................................32
    Reversal of alliances, 1755..............................34
    Opening moves, 1756......................................35
    Pitt the Great Commoner, 1757 37

Louisbourg, 1758..40
White House plantation..43
Annus Mirabilis, 1759 44
George III, 1760...48
Bourbon family compact, 1761.......................................50
The last battles, 1762...52
Chief Pontiac, 1763 56
Chapter 2: Revolution in America, 1764–1783.........................60
1764–1774: Striking at Their Chains 60
Great Britain and North America, 1764–1774.................60
The Industrial Revolution in Great Britain 71
France, 1764 to 1774...73
Central Europe, 1764–1774 77
1775–1777: Potemkin and the Greek Project 84
The American Revolution, 1775–1777............................84
Great Britain, 1775–1777..97
France, 1775–1777..99
Russia, 1775–1777 101
1778–1779: Great Britain against the World 104
The American Revolution, 1778–1779..........................104
Benedict Arnold in Philadelphia, West Point,
and with the British Army 111
The Coalition War against Great Britain, 1778– 1779.....114
Central and Eastern Europe, 1778–1779 118
1780–1783: Solid as the Rock of Gibraltar.........................121
The American Revolution, 1780–1781 121
Other theaters of war, 1780–1783 127
The United States, 1781–1783 128
Great Britain, 1780–1783..136
France, 1780–1783..140
Central and Eastern Europe, 1780–1783 143
Chapter 3: Assemblies, Congresses, and Conventions,
1784–1791 146
1784–1786: The Blood of Patriots and Tyrants..................146
The United States, 1784–1786 146
Shays' Rebellion, 1786 153

The second British Empire..157
France, 1784–1786...160
Central and Eastern Europe, 1784–1786 164
1787–1788: If the King Does It, It's Not Illegal.................166
The United States, 1787–1788 166
Great Britain, 1787–1788.......................................171
France, Great Britain, and the Netherlands,
1787–1788...173
Central and Eastern Europe, 1787–1788 177
1789: A Tocsin for the Saint Bartholomew of the Patriots....180
The United States, 1789 180
France, 1789...184
Austria, Russia, and the Ottomans, 1789 202
1790: "Ca Ira" (It'll Be Fine)...204
The United States, 1790 204
Great Britain, 1790...206
France, 1790...207
Central and Eastern Europe, 1790 212
1791: A Sham of Royalty..214
The United States, 1791 214
Great Britain, 1791...216
Eastern Europe, 1791...218
France and Austria, 1791 220
Chapter 4: The French Convention, 1792–1794 233
1792: L'Audace, et Encore de l'Audace, et Toujours
de l'Audace 233
The United States 233
Eastern Europe...235
Europe goes to war, 1792......................................236
The overthrow of the monarchy in France 241
Military operations and political developments
in France, July to December 253
1793: Tambours (Drums)...260
The United States, 1793 260
Eastern Europe, 1793...264

France, Flanders, Mainz, and the Pyrenees,
January to June 1793 267
France, June to October 1793 276
The Reign of Terror begins, October 1793....................286
1794: Terror Is the Order of the Day 294
The United States 294
Eastern Europe..302
France, 1794 305
Chapter 5: The Directory, 1795–1799 323
1795–1796: Young Bonaparte 323
The United States, 1795–1796 323
Eastern and Central Europe 330
France 332
1797: God Save Emperor Francis 362
The United States, 1797 362
Eastern and Central Europe 366
Western Europe, 1797 370
1798: The Principle of Population 386
The United States, 1798 386
Egypt, 1798 391
Italy, 1798..397
Switzerland, the bridge between Italy and France, 1798 ...400
Great Britain and Ireland, 1798 401
France, Eastern and Central Europe, 1798 408
1799: Let's Throw All the Lawyers in the River...................410
The United States, 1799 410
Egypt, 1799 415
Italy, 1799..418
Eastern and Central Europe, 1799 425
Great Britain, 1799...428
France, 1799 431
An Afterword to Part 1: The Years of George Washington 439
Index...445

PART 1

The Years of George Washington

CHAPTER 1

The Dawn of the World as We Know It

The Columbian Epoch

Evolution and revolution

Halford Mackinder, director of the London School of Economics from 1903 to 1908, predicted in 1904 that in the distant future, historians would dub the period of time that he was living in as the Columbian epoch and that they would say it lasted from 1492 to sometime soon after the year 1904. Mackinder called himself a geographer and wrote on topics that would, these days, be called geopolitics, although that word hadn't been coined yet. Two words that Mackinder did coin were *heartland* and *manpower*, concepts that had been very important to the study of the geopolitics of Europe and their colonies since 1492.

As the forces of the Renaissance and the Reformation were at work shaping Europe, about 1600, the center of gravity of geopolitics in Western Europe was between the great powers of France, Spain, and Austria, with England and the Ottoman Empire on the fringes. At the same date, the center of gravity in Eastern Europe was between the powers of Russia, Poland, and Sweden, with Austria and the Ottomans on the fringes. Prussia, with a combination of strenuous effort and incredible luck, pushed itself into the front ranks of nations right in between these centers of gravity starting in 1740.

3

The two centers of gravity began converging into one, with Russia, Austria, Great Britain, France, and Prussia forming a five-sided structure of international intrigue, politics, diplomacy, and war. Alliances shifted as nations considered where their interests lay. As Lord Palmerston later said, nations have permanent interests, not allies.

There was also an increase in scientific and technological knowledge as Newton, Galileo, Pascal, and many others lived and worked during this time. Human intelligence, which is to say the capacity of the human brain, hasn't changed since the dawn of recorded history. We can be sure that even the earliest periods had produced thinkers who were just as smart as now, the difference in the Columbian epoch being the ability to publish their findings for a wide audience. For example, we read about a scientist in Alexandria in the days of the Egyptian Ptolemies who built a steam engine consisting of a hollow ball on a swivel with two angled tubes extending from it. When steam was run through the ball, it twirled, thus converting heat energy to mechanical energy. The inventor may or may not have had ideas on applications for this device, but because there was no way to widely disseminate the information, it didn't reach the people who could have put it to a million and one uses.

There is a relationship between a nation's history and the science that arises from that history. For example, the history of France is that of a country that has a long period of stable regimes, followed by a short period of upheaval and turmoil, followed by another long period of stable regimes. In science, France produced paleontologist Georges Cuvier, who developed the fossil record, showing sudden appearance of forms, long periods of stasis, and then catastrophic extinction, paralleling the country's history. Cuvier referred to these cycles as "revolutions." The history of England is that of a country that adapts their political institutions to meet changing circumstances. The crown, the Parliament, and the church remain as institutions, adapted to survive as the environment changes; the country even adapts its name from England to Great Britain to the United Kingdom. They produced biologist Charles Darwin, who developed theories on the adaptation of simple organisms to more complex ones in response to the environment. Darwin referred to these adaptations as "evolution."

England

In 1649, the English finished their civil war by beheading Charles I. To justify the beheading, Oliver Cromwell quoted Numbers 35:33, "For blood it defileth the land: and the land cannot be cleansed of the blood that is shed therein, but by the blood of him that shed it." The purpose of the passage was not to encourage retribution for land defilement but to discourage it in the first place, and Cromwell's interpretation was the kind of cherry-picking of scripture that the Catholic Church had warned about when they opposed translation of the Bible into the common tongue. Charles's father, James I had authorized the translation in 1611, which is why it is called the King James Bible. Cromwell spent the next four years subjugating the Scots and the Irish, the first steps in creating that more complex organism known today as the United Kingdom. When he returned to London in 1653, he was displeased to find that Parliament had failed to write a constitution, so he forcibly dissolved it and called an election that voted in a new Parliament that made Cromwell lord protector, a position differing only in name from that of military dictator. He died in 1658 and was succeeded by his son Richard, who lacked the political base, military experience, energy, and ruthlessness of his father and resigned after a year. The British found they could not carry on without a legitimate monarch and brought back the ruling dynasty, the House of Stuart. Adaptation rather than extinction.

During the years that Cromwell was lord protector, his policies were found onerous to his former opponents, the supporters of Charles I, also known as the Cavaliers. George Washington's great-grandfather John was the son of a Cavalier, and he emigrated from England to Virginia in 1657. George Washington's father died in 1743, when George was eleven. George's older half-brother Lawrence was able to step up and be a surrogate father to him until he died in 1752. However, his father's death prevented George from obtaining an education or at even broadening himself by travel. As a result, he was a genuine homespun American with no trace of the European about him, a fact that would be crucial to his success as the commander in chief of the Continental Army.

The Cavaliers all seemed to want to live in the south, and the Puritans, as the followers of Cromwell were called, all seemed to want to live in the north. It's strange that the descendants of the Cavaliers and the descendants of the Puritans would once again engage in a civil war over two hundred years after the execution of Charles I. It makes you think that maybe two strains of DNA just have it in for each other, and questions like aristocrats versus Parliament, or free states versus slave states, are just excuses for them to fight.

Western Europe

In 1649 in Central Europe, the Thirty Years' War had just ended. It had started in 1618 as a war in Germany between Catholics and Protestants when an official in Prague had been defenestrated, which is a fancy word for being thrown out of a window. Austria got the upper hand in 1635, and so France got involved on the anti-Austria side, even though both countries were Catholic. The result of the war was a slight weakening of Austria's position in Europe. Unfortunately for the Austrians, this came just at the time that English and the Scots to the west and the Russians and the Ukrainians to the east were making common cause to get their countries more directly involved in European affairs.

Louis XIV was eleven in 1649, and the government was run by his mother and Cardinal Mazarin. Louis was in peril because of the Fronde, a civil war in France from 1649 to 1653, which was an attempt on the part of the nobles to curb the power of the king. The cause of the war was an attempt by the crown to impose taxes that the nobles resisted. In France, the royalist faction was ultimately successful, while in England, the royalists had to make some concessions to Parliament. Because of the Fronde, Louis XIV distrusted Paris and, in 1671, moved his residence from the Tuileries Palace to Versailles, ten miles away. He didn't ignore Paris, building many monuments

THE GREAT GLOBE ITSELF

there during his long reign, but there was an estrangement, and from 1671 to 1715, he only visited the city an average of once every two years, never staying more than twenty-four hours.

By the 1680s the trend toward royal absolutism in France was clear, while the opposite trend was just as clear in Great Britain. In 1682 Louis XIV moved the court permanently to Versailles, making it easier to keep the nobles under his thumb. The year 1682 was a good one for France, as they were able to lay claim to the entire Mississippi, Missouri, Ohio River Valleys as well as the Great Lakes. Then in 1685, for reasons that seemed good to Louis, he revoked the Edict of Nantes, a 1598 proclamation from Louis XIV's grandfather Henry IV that proclaimed toleration of Protestants in France. A year later, Louis was proud to report that of a population of eight hundred thousand Huguenots in France, all but one thousand had converted or emigrated. France doesn't seem to have suffered much from the loss. Louis was solidly in place as an absolute monarch and would go down in history as one of the ablest men ever to sit on a throne. His ability to mobilize the wealth of France for the glory and enrichment of himself and of the nobles was truly impressive. His successors would sustain it for most of the eighteenth century, until it was suddenly swept away in 1789. The period of 107 years, from 1682 to 1789, that the French court spent in Versailles is known as *le grand siècle.*

Having chopped off the head of Charles I in 1649, Britain deposed his son James II in 1688, an event known as the Glorious Revolution. James II was Catholic and in his fifties, so the Parliament was willing to put up with him for the sake of legitimacy, as his daughter and heir, Mary Stuart, had been raised Protestant. But in 1688, James II's wife gave birth to a son who was christened Catholic, and so James II was deposed and exiled. Parliament invited Mary and her husband, William, who was stadtholder of the Netherlands, to take the throne as William III and Mary II.

The son of James II, the Old Pretender, would attempt a revolution in 1715 in Scotland. The Old Pretender married and had two sons: Charles the Young Pretender or Bonnie Prince Charlie, and Henry, who became a priest and called himself Cardinal York.

7

Bonnie Prince Charlie attempted another Scottish revolution in 1745. By then, the British were satisfied with their German king and their evolving constitutional monarchy.

The House of Orleans

We need to take note of the House of Orleans because of their role in the French Revolution and because they did eventually win the throne in 1830. Louis XIV had a younger brother, Philippe I, who became Duke of Orleans upon the death of his uncle Gaston in 1660. He was also made Duke of Chartres, and the family tradition became for the son of the Duke of Orleans to be given the title Duke of Chartres. Philippe I was known to the French court as *monsieur*. He was effeminate and homosexual (his relationships are well-documented), which helped him in his relationship with Louis XIV, as it made him appear to be less of a threat. Nevertheless, he fathered five children with two wives, was an astute businessman, and even gained some military glory against the Dutch, after which Louis XIV never gave him another command. He owned the Palais-Royal and Saint Cloud, two of the most famous structures in Paris. His direct descendants in the male line claim the throne of France to this very day.

The son of Philippe I was Philippe II (1674–1723), who was known as the regent because he ruled France during the time that Louis XV was a minor. Louis XIV had lived until 1715, surviving his son and his grandson, and Louis XV was his great-grandson and succeeded to the throne at the age of five. Philippe II served as regent until February 1723, when Louis XV turned thirteen. He moved the royal court back to Paris, installing Louis XV in the Tuileries, while he himself lived in the Palais-Royal. Philippe II died in December 1723. The city of New Orleans was established in 1718 during his regency and was named for him. He also had a daughter, Elizabeth Charlotte, who married the Duke of Lorraine and was therefore the grandmother of Empress Maria Theresa's sixteen children.

The son of Philippe II was Louis I (1703–1752), who had an Army career until about 1740, when he became religious and semiretired.

THE GREAT GLOBE ITSELF

The son of Louis I was Louis Philippe I (1725–1785), known as Louis Philippe the Fat. He briefly served in the field during the First Silesian War (1742–1744) but spent most of his career in court intrigue or expanding his wealth, which was almost as great as the king's. He was the archetype of the greedy noble, raping the peasants of their meager possessions, the kind of man that disgusted and fascinated Thomas Jefferson when he got to Paris in 1785. His wife was suspected of various liaisons, and Louis I refused to acknowledge the children she bore to Louis Philippe I. When she died in 1759, Saint Cloud was shuttered. The duke remarried and lived in another palace. One of his final acts before his death was selling Saint Cloud to Marie Antoinette in 1785.

The son of Louis Philippe the Fat was Louis Philippe II (1747–1793). His sister was the mother of the Duke of Enghien, who would play a tragic role in the events leading to Napoleon Bonaparte becoming emperor. Louis Philippe II is the famous duke whose fingerprints can be found on so many of the early events of the French Revolution because he wanted to be king. His short period of military service took place in 1778, when he participated in the Battle of Ushant, left early, and when he got to Paris, he loudly announced, prematurely, a victory in a battle that was, at best, a draw. He made improvements to the Palais-Royal that made it *the* destination in Paris. When the Bourbons fell in August 1792, he started calling himself *Philippe Egalite*, and his sister was *Citoyenne Verite*. The political faction that supported his becoming king was the Gironde, but they were toppled by the Montagnards in June 1793, who then ordered the arrest of all the Bourbons, including the House of Orleans. When the Terror started in October 1793, Louis Philippe was tried and sentenced to death. All of this is discussed in great detail below.

The son of Louis Philippe II was Louis Philippe III (1773–1850), who was a man of considerable political and military ability, commanding a division at age nineteen. He managed to avoid getting arrested in 1792, as he was at the front, and defected to the Austrians. His two brothers were arrested, and they both contracted tuberculosis while in prison and died young. He was in exile from 1792 to 1815. He held important offices under the Bourbon Restoration and was able to claim the crown when the revolution of 1830 deposed Charles X. He was the last king of France, from 1830 to 1848, being deposed himself in the revolution of 1848.

Poland and Russia

The Dukes of Moscow had been consolidating their power since the late 1300s. By 1480, Ivan III was able to defeat the Golden Horde, one of the successor states to Genghis Khan's Mongol Empire, and exert the power of the Duchy of Moscow over Siberia. In 1472, Ivan III married Sophie Paleologue, niece of the last Byzantine emperor Constantine XI. Their son Vasili III adopted the title and the double-headed eagle of the Byzantine emperors in his correspondence but made no official claim to be emperor. He continued the Russian successes against the remnants of the Golden Horde as well as the Polish-Lithuanian commonwealth, capturing Smolensk and annexing it in 1514. His wife was barren, so he divorced her, with his new wife producing an heir, Ivan IV, who was three when Vasili III died in 1533 of a large abscess in his thigh.

Ivan IV grew up to be Ivan the Terrible (the Russian word *grozny* is more accurately translated as "formidable") and ruled from 1533 to 1584. In 1547, at the age of sixteen, he was crowned emperor, sending a message that he was a new Augustus, Moscow was a new Rome, and he had the right to plant his flag in Constantinople and Rome.

Standing in the way of Russia's march to Rome and Constantinople were Poland and Lithuania, who formed a commonwealth in 1569 to oppose Russian expansion. The commonwealth was unique in that the kingship was electoral and not hereditary, which proved to be a weakness when its rapacious neighbors began interfering in the election process. The commonwealth reached a peak under John III Sobieski, from 1674 to 1696.

After Ivan IV's death in 1584, Russia entered a period of instability that lasted until Michael Romanov was elected emperor in 1613. His great-aunt was the wife of Ivan IV. During the time of troubles, Russia lost ground to the Swedes and the Polish-Lithuanian

Commonwealth. Michael died in 1645 and was succeeded by his son Alexis I, whose reign was from 1645 to 1676. Alexis was able to come to an agreement with the Ukrainian Cossacks, who immediately rebelled against the Polish-Lithuanian Commonwealth, which fun-

damentally changed the balance of power in the region against the commonwealth. As we noted above, English-Scottish-Irish unity occurred at the same time as Russian-Ukrainian unity—about 1650—and made both entities powerful new factors in European affairs, which heretofore had been a three-way affair between Spain, France, and Austria.

The sons of Alexis I contended for the throne because the oldest was handicapped, and the second oldest was incapable. The third oldest eventually took the throne as Peter I the Great, and he ruled from 1682 to 1725. He was called "the great" because he made great strides against Sweden and the Ottomans, founding a new capital at Saint Petersburg on the Baltic Sea and a new naval base at Taganrog on the Black Sea. He also made efforts to make Russia look more like Western Europe. For example, he noted that the aristocrats in France and Austria were clean-shaven, so he established a beard tax where nobles who chose to keep their beards had to pay one hundred rubles a year. In 1717, he visited France and met the child King Louis XV, picking him up and giving him a kiss. He was two meters (6'8") tall and probably could have done the same with Louis XIV. Peter I failed to produce a son, so the next few rulers were weak, but in 1741, Peter's daughter Elizabeth took the throne, and she was there to oppose Frederick the Great of Prussia for the next twenty-one years.

PETER HARDY

Freemasonry and the Enlightenment

Freemasonry was a product of the Enlightenment. The term *the Enlightenment* refers to the process of dissemination of knowledge through publishing that had been occurring since the invention of the printing press in the 1400s.

Freemasonry provided a vehicle by which the ideas of the enlightenment could be spread among men who held no titles but were wealthy and educated. Commoners with talent were excelling at the law, trade, and manufacturing, while the titled nobility, with their feudal privileges and their monopoly on landownership fell behind financially but maintained their air of superiority. Things might have gone differently if France's nobility had done a better job of co-opting talented commoners into their ranks. It was through election to office that the noble Romans of old co-opted wealthy plebeian families into the ranks of the aristocracy, but in eighteenth-century France, the old nobility guarded its privileges fervently, and even when commoners obtained titles, there was still a strict dividing line between the old order, the nobles of the sword, and the new order, the nobles of the robe. Naturally, resentments built up among the wealthy commoners.

In Masonic initiation rituals, the blindfolded candidate is asked what he wants and is coached to respond "light" at the first degree, "more light" at the second degree, and "further light" at the third. Light and enlightenment. Paradoxically, the rituals require candidates to memorize all the questions and answers without the aid of written materials, while the Enlightenment would not have occurred with the invention of the printing press.

Whether or not Masonic lodges were founded as secret societies to divest power from those who held it by any means necessary, they provided a road map for revolutionary movements starting in 1789. The *Carbonari* in Italy, the Union of Salvation in Russia, and the *Filiki Eteria* (Society of Friends) in Greece were all secret societies that organized resistance movements to, respectively, the Austrian, Russian, and Ottoman rulers.

An important element of the Enlightenment was rediscovering the classics in Renaissance Italy: Plutarch with his tales of the noble Romans and Greeks; Tacitus with his portrait of imperial tyranny; and Livy with his tales of Roman virtue and the workings of a very aristocratic form of government. They revealed a civilization that had thrived without tyrants and suffered with them. Another important element was the Reformation, which showed the same thing on the religious side of the coin, that a righteous people did not need a pope in Rome, especially one presiding over a system corrupted by sexual misconduct and greed, to be a holy and righteous nation.

In 1717, the Grand Lodge of England was formed in London, the oldest verifiable organization of Freemasons. Four London lodges, which had existed for some time, came together at the Goose and Gridiron Tavern in Saint Paul's churchyard, declared themselves a Grand Lodge, and elected a man named Anthony Sayer as their grand master. Lodges in York, Scotland, and Ireland would be formed over the next twenty years. Lodges would also be formed in The Hague, Rotterdam, Paris, and Dresden over the same period.

In 1733, the Grand Orient of France, today the largest Masonic organization in France, was founded. Masonry gets much credit for conspiracies and fomenting of the Revolution. The most famous Paris lodge, the Nine Sisters (*Les Neuf Soeurs*), was not established until 1776 and had Ben Franklin as a member. By 1789, there were 1,250 lodges operating under the charter of the Grand Orient. 1733 was also the first year that Masonic lodges began operating in British North America.

Montesquieu and The Encyclopedia

In the years following the death of Louis XIV in 1715, Baron Charles de Montesquieu, not to be confused with the French revolutionary general Montesquoi, made important contributions to the Enlightenment by publishing numerous works containing observations on French society and the Catholic Church, comparing and contrasting it with British society and Protestantism. He wrote a book about the causes of the rise and fall of Rome because in those days the British and the French loved to compare themselves to the Romans. He was famous by 1721, but his greatest work was *The Spirit of Laws*, published in 1750. It consisted of over a thousand pages in thirty-one books. His three major themes are the classification of governments as either republics, monarchies, or despotisms; the separation of powers into legislative, executive, and judicial authority; and the political influence of climate. His work was renowned at the time, has been considered authoritative ever since and remains important today.

In 1751, *The Encyclopedia*, or a *Systematic Dictionary of the Sciences, Arts, and Crafts* began publication. The editor in chief was Denis Diderot (1713–1784). Today there are lots of collections of knowledge called encyclopedias, but this was *the Encyclopedia*. The work comprised thirty-five volumes, with 71,818 articles and 3,129 illustrations. The first seventeen volumes were published between 1751 and 1765; eleven volumes of plates were finished by 1772. In 1775, Charles Joseph Panckoucke obtained the rights to reissue the work. He issued five volumes of supplementary material and a two-volume index from 1776 to 1780. Some scholars include these seven "extra" volumes as part of the first full issue of the *Encyclopedia*, for a total of thirty-five volumes, although they were not written or edited by the original authors. The impact of this product of the Enlightenment was very great. It was a summary of thought in the Age of Enlightenment. In *The Encyclopédie and the Age of Revolution*, a work published in conjunction with a 1989 exhibition of the *Encyclopedia* at the University of California, Los Angeles, Clorinda Donato says:

> The encyclopedians successfully argued and marketed their belief in the potential of reason and unified knowledge to empower human will and thus helped to shape the social issues that the French Revolution would address. Although it is doubtful whether the many artisans, technicians, or laborers whose work and presence are interspersed throughout the Encyclopédie actually

read it, the recognition of their work as equal to that of intellectuals, clerics, and rulers prepared the terrain for demands for increased representation. Thus, the Encyclopédie served to recognize and galvanize a new power base, ultimately contributing to the destruction of old values and the creation of new ones.

The Encyclopédie denied that the teachings of the Catholic Church could be treated as authoritative in matters of science. The editors also refused to treat the decisions of political powers as definitive in intellectual or artistic questions. Given that Paris was the intellectual capital of Europe at the time and that many European leaders used French as their administrative language, these ideas had the capacity to spread.

Approximate size of the *Encyclopédie*:
17 volumes of articles, issued from 1751 to 1765
11 volumes of illustrations, issued from 1762 to 1772
7 volumes of supplements and indexes, 1775 to 1780
18,000 pages of text
75,000 entries
44,000 main articles
28,000 secondary articles
2,500 illustration indices
20,000,000 words in total
Print run: 4,250 copies (note: even single-volume works in the eighteenth century seldom had a print run of more than 1,500 copies)

It would not be rivaled as a publishing achievement until the publication, starting in 1809, of *The Description of Egypt*, publishing the findings of the 1798 French Expedition to Egypt.

PETER HARDY

Colonization in North America

New Spain

Hernan Cortes landed on the east coast of Mexico at the site of Vera Cruz with five hundred men in 1519. He made alliances with the people who hated the Aztec oppressors in Tenochtitlan, and by 1521, the conquest of the Aztec Empire was complete. Cortes named the place New Spain and established Mexico City on the ruins of Tenochtitlan. For the record, the name of tribe that ruled the Aztec Empire was called The Mexica. The name Aztec was coined by Alexander von Humboldt in the early 1800s as a portmanteau of Aztlan (place of the heron) and Tecatl (people of). New Spain was made the first viceroyalty of the Spanish Empire in 1535. From the beginning of New Spain, all power was concentrated in Mexico City. This had some advantages in the early years, but as time passed, it became inefficient to have every decision made there. Governors in remote regions had a great deal of independence but would run into difficulties when they needed something from the central government. Cortes brought horses with him in 1519, and they soon spread out through trade networks as well as by escaping to and thriving in the wild. The current science on horses is that they evolved in North America, spread out into Asia across the Bering land bridge, then went extinct in North America relatively recently (five to ten thousand years ago) until Cortes brought them back. The causes of the extinction are hotly debated between humans hunting them for food or climate change destroying their food supply.

Florida was explored in 1513 by Ponce de Leon, who was looking for the fountain of youth, which can still be visited today in Saint Augustine. There is a Leon County in Florida today. Horses were introduced into the present-day United States in Florida in 1538. De Soto landed in Florida in 1539 and explored the future USA for years. There is a de Soto County in Florida today, located in the vicinity of where he was thought to have landed, at the point where the Peace River debouches into Charlotte Harbor. Pensacola was founded in 1559 but was soon destroyed in a hurricane. The site was abandoned until 1698. Saint Augustine was founded in 1565 and endured. Spain controlled Florida until 1763, when they ceded it to Great Britain in exchange for the British ending the occupation of Havana, which they had seized the previous year. The Spanish recovered Florida in 1783 and controlled it after a fashion until Andrew Jackson conquered it in 1819. Jackson noted that it was four hundred miles from Pensacola to Saint Augustine and founded a new capital halfway between them, evicting the Indians who were living there under Chief Tallahassee.

The Spaniards encouraged commerce along the preexisting roads in New Spain radiating north, south, east, and west of Mexico City and made investments in road improvements. The route north, El Camino Real de Tierra Adentro (Royal Road of the interior) terminated sixteen hundred miles north in Santa Fe. North from El Paso, the road ran along the Rio Grande. Spain established missions and presidios in New Mexico starting in 1610. In 1680, the natives in Santa Fe evicted the Spaniards, who retreated to El Paso. In 1692, the governor Diego de Vargas reconquered Santa Fe permanently. Albuquerque was founded in 1706 and was named (with one less *r*) after the current viceroy of New Spain, the Duke of Alburquerque. After the Louisiana Purchase in 1803, the Santa Fe Trail from Kansas City (Franklin), Missouri, to Santa Fe was pioneered by Zebulon Pike and others and officially established in 1822 to promote trade between the United States and newly independent Mexico.

According to data from a paper published by Richard L. Nostrand in the *Annals of the Association of American Geographers* in September 1975, at the time that New Mexico was annexed into the United States in 1848, the Mexican citizen population was about 57,000, not counting untaxed Indians. That included the Mexican citizen population of El Paso, as well as the area of the 1853 Gadsden Purchase. I am not sure what made northern New Mexico thrive as compared to Texas and California. It must have had something to do with trading horses and other goods to the Comanche and Apache.

It wasn't until 1718 that New Spain took an interest in Texas, establishing the Mission San Antonio de Valero, the Alamo, the first permanent Spanish settlement in Texas. The Saint Anthony for whom the mission was named was not from Valero; he was from Padua and lived from 1195 to 1231. The Valero part came from the Duke of Valero, viceroy of New Spain from 1716 to 1722. The presidio at the Alamo was called San Antonio de Bexar, Bexar being another title held by the Duke of Valero, whose full name was Balthazar Manuel de Zuniga y Guzman Sotomayor y Sarmiento. At the time of Texas independence in 1836, the population of Mexican citizens in Texas was about 14,000, not counting untaxed Indians. That includes the population of Mexican citizens between the Nueces and Rio Grande Rivers, except for the El Paso District, which was included in the New Mexico count. The total taxed population of Texas in 1850 was 213,000.

California was settled even later than Texas. Mission San Diego was established in 1769. Mission San Francisco was established in 1776. Mission San Gabriel was founded in 1771, and ten years later, Los Angeles, formally named the Village of Our Lady the Queen of the Angels, was founded. Monterey was founded as a presidio in 1770 and was made the capital of the province in 1777, which it still was when the Americans took over on July 7, 1846. California became part of the United States in 1848, and there were about nine thousand Mexican citizens and a very low number of foreigners. That changed with the announcement of the gold finds, and the 1850 census shows a total population, not counting untaxed Indians, of ninety-three thousand, of which nine thousand were Mexican citizens.

According to the 1850 US census, there were about 80,000 Mexican citizens in the lands acquired by the United States from 1845 to 1848: 57,000 in New Mexico; 14,000 in Texas; and 9,000 in California. The 1848 Treaty of Guadalupe Hidalgo made them all full-American citizens. They all had the option to repatriate to Mexico, and about 20,000 did. Issues came up regarding landownership as they had in the Northwest, Mississippi, and Louisiana Territories. As far as the number of untaxed Indians, this is a subject of scholarly debate regarding the precontact population size and the effects of disease brought by Europeans. My own view is that from the time of Columbus, the number of Indians in North America was never very large, given that hunter-gatherer cultures require a lot

THE GREAT GLOBE ITSELF

more land per capita than cultivating cultures. There is a wide range of opinion because, of course, the Indians didn't leave any records.

The citizen (taxed) population of Mexico in 1850 was about 7.8 million, almost all of whom lived within three hundred miles of Mexico City. Therefore, the population of Mexican citizens living in what was ceded to the United States in 1848 was 1 percent of the population, living on what was then half of what constituted Mexico, about one million square miles of land. Half of the Mexican citizens of California and Texas were hostile to Mexico City. They called themselves *Texanos* or *Californios*, rather than *Mexicanos*, and called the troops and officials sent from Mexico City *Ciudados*. Half of them welcomed the gringos when they started coming in the 1820s. Santa Fe had cherished its splendid isolation for centuries and was hostile to everyone at first, but the Santa Fe Trail soon established an important link with the United States.

The point is that in 1848, the United States took a lot of vacant land from Mexico. The overwhelming majority of Americans of Mexican descent arrived in the United States after 1900. The ones who say "We didn't cross the border. The border crossed us" don't know what they're talking about.

Brazil

After Columbus made his voyage in 1492, Spain and Portugal were both interested in colonizing the western hemisphere. Pope Alexander VI was asked to identify the boundary between Spanish and Portuguese territories, which he did in a 1493 papal bull. Pedro Álvares Cabral sailed to what is now Porto Seguro in April 1500 and claimed the land for Portugal. The Portuguese noticed trees that could be used to produce red dye, which they called pau brasil trees, Portuguese for redwood. Harvesting the trees for dye became the first European enterprise in Brazil. There was no Inca or Aztec civilization there; it was a collection of primitive tribes living in a state of nature. The natives were variously enslaved or evangelized. Importation of African slaves began in the 1540s, with five million slaves brought into the country for agricultural and, later, mining purposes by 1860.

By comparison, the number of African slaves imported to the British American colonies between 1619 and 1807 was about two hundred thousand.

In 1549, Portugal organized Brazil as a crown colony, establishing the capital at Salvador. In 1555, France established a colony they named Fort Coligny, which is near what is now Rio de Janeiro, a thousand miles south of Salvador. The French did not recognize the validity of the 1493 papal bull. Portugal established São Paulo in 1560 and Rio de Janeiro in 1565. The Portuguese mappers were in a hurry and wrongly assumed that Guanabara Bay was the outlet of a hypothetical Rio de Janeiro that does not in fact exist. The geography of the maps was corrected but not before the city was founded and named. The Portuguese drove the French out in 1567. After that, they were secure in their domain, with the French going to Quebec and Louisiana and the Spanish being very busy in their huge American empire. The royal court of Portugal was based in Rio de Janeiro from 1808 to 1821. Brazil declared independence from Portugal in 1825.

New France

Samuel de Champlain founded Quebec in 1608 and explored the Great Lakes. Montreal was founded in 1642. In the 1680s, Rene Robert La Salle established a chain of forts along the Mississippi River, from the Gulf of Mexico to Lake Michigan. Mobile was established in 1703, and another chain of forts was established up the Alabama River to near the present site of Montgomery. New Orleans was established in 1718. Its potential as a port to receive all those goods floating down the Mississippi River was immediately recognized. The major occupation of the French was fur trapping. The French maintained good relations with the Indian tribes in New France. It was hard to get French women to come to America, so France endorsed intermarriage. Even so, by the time of the French and Indian War, there were one million British colonists to fifty thousand French in Quebec, with another fifty to one hundred thousand or so in the Mississippi Valley. France lost their North American

THE GREAT GLOBE ITSELF

possessions to Great Britain and Spain in 1763. They kept their West Indies possessions of Cayenne (French Guiana), Saint Dominique (Haiti), Martinique, Sainte Lucie, and Guadeloupe.

New England, Virginia, Maryland, and the Dutch colonies

Jamestown was founded in 1603. Plymouth was founded in 1620. Boston was founded in 1630. Baltimore was founded in 1632. Providence was founded in 1636. Hartford was founded in 1636 near a Dutch settlement. Charleston was founded in 1680. The leading reason for all these settlements was a desire for religious freedom. They all became proper English towns that depended on farming and trade.

In between the southern and northern British colonies, the Dutch established their own colonies in the Connecticut, Hudson, and Delaware Valleys. The Hudson Valley had New Amsterdam, Wiltwijck, and Fort Orange, while the Delaware Valley had Fort Wilhelmus. The Dutch established Fort Hope at the mouth of the Connecticut River, but the English were pouring in from Plymouth to establish Hartford, and the Dutch soon abandoned it. In 1664, the English seized all the Dutch colonies, and they became, respectively, New York City, Kingston, Albany, and Wilmington. The Dutch fought back but ultimately had to cede their colonies to the English. The English moved up the Delaware and established Philadelphia, Pennsylvania, in 1682. William Penn signed a treaty with Chief Tamanend, who good-naturedly consigned his people to oblivion, earning him the status of a secular saint in America and becoming the namesake of the Tammany Hall political organization. The rest of the land of Dutch colonies became New Jersey, which got its name because Charles II had been treated with hospitality on the island of Jersey, in the days when he had been on the run after the execution of his father in 1649.

The English colonies (which we can call British colonies after the Act of Union in 1707) were loyal to the crown as long as there were French and Spanish to worry about. But after 1763, they were

1700–1754: Europe and North America

The War of the Spanish Succession, 1701–1714

Charles II of Spain died at the age of thirty-nine in 1700. He had been married twice with no issue. He was sickly his entire life, which has been famously blamed on the inbreeding in his family, although the case for that is far from proven as he had two sisters who were perfectly healthy. His sister Maria Theresa was married to Louis XIV, and his sister Margaret Theresa was married to Leopold I, the Holy Roman emperor. Louis XIV's grandson Philip and Leopold I's son Charles were the two contenders to succeed Charles II. It should be noted that Margaret Theresa had died with no surviving children and so was not the mother of Leopold I's son Charles, but Charles was closely enough related to Charles II of Spain to make a claim anyway. Also, having the Bourbons on the throne of both France and Spain was intolerable to Great Britain and to Austria. The Habsburgs had been on the thrones of Spain and Austria for centuries, and having a Bourbon on the throne of Spain presented a big shift in the balance of power in Western Europe.

Charles II died on November 1, 1700, and the Spanish throne was offered to Philip. It took a while, but by May 1702, England, Austria, and the Netherlands—the so-called Grand Alliance—were at war against France and Spain. During this period, both James II and William III (Queen Mary had died in 1694) died, and Louis XIV recognized the Catholic son of James II as King James III. The English crowned Anne, the daughter of James II, instead.

Through the seventeenth century, England had refrained from involvement in wars on the European continent. The English Civil War kept them busy among themselves, and then they concentrated on building trade systems in India and North America. They had only been concerned with continental politics insofar as it affected their trade. They probably could have held to that policy if James II had agreed to raise his son as a Protestant. And here, for the first time, we see a phenomenon of British historical writing in which disputes over foreign and defense policy are disguised as fights between Catholics and Protestants. James II was a Catholic because he was convinced that France was invincible on the continent and wanted peace with them. His enemies were Protestants because they wanted to weaken France on the continent by supporting the Dutch and German Protestants who were in France's line of fire. William of Orange, the ruler of the Netherlands, especially wanted more British involvement on the continent, but James had refused. James II was deposed, William became king of England, and England allied itself with the Holy Roman Empire. England was now mired in continental politics and war and would be for decades. The Netherlands got more than they bargained for as Great Britain proceeded to dominate them for most of the eighteenth century until the French Revolutionary Armies kicked them out in 1795. Over the next twenty years after that, the British took over every single Dutch colony in the world, most importantly the Cape Colony in what is now South Africa. The Netherlands recovered Indonesia and some Caribbean possessions after 1815, but little else.

At the outset of the War of the Spanish Succession, France had the advantage but was forced on the defensive as time went on. During the course of the war, the English worried about the loyalty of the Scots, and in 1707, Scotland signed the Act of Union with England and Wales, forming an entity called Great Britain. Scots were now represented in the Parliament of Westminster. The Union Jack became the flag of Great Britain. It differed from today's Union Jack in that it had no Irish component to it. That was added in 1801 when Ireland and Great Britain united to became the United Kingdom.

The North American component to the War of the Spanish Succession was called Queen Anne's War. The population of the English colonies (British colonies after 1707) was about 250,000 during the war. There were plenty of skirmishes among the French, Spanish, and English colonists, but the map of North America did not change.

Joseph I was the older brother of Charles, the Austrian candidate for the Spanish throne. Joseph I died in 1711. This made Charles the new Holy Roman emperor as Charles VI, so now the Habsburgs had no candidate for the Spanish throne, and the war became pointless. A peace treaty was signed in Utrecht in 1715, leaving Philip on the throne of Spain as Philip V, and his descendants sit on the throne to this very day. The current king is Philip VI. Spain and France remained in almost continual alliance except for a brief period from 1793 to 1795, after Louis XVI was executed. I consider the alliance held after Joseph Bonaparte became king of Spain in 1807 and that the Spaniards who fought him were rebels. Spain had been a great power in the 1500s but had been in decline for many years and was definitely the junior partner in the relationship, similar to that of Great Britain and the Netherlands. The causes of their decline were the atrophying of their Army due to lack of any enemies to fight on land and the regular beatings administered to their Navy by the British Royal Navy.

The British were negotiating peace in 1714 when Queen Anne died at the age of forty-nine without any surviving children. The poor woman, married to the brother of the king of Denmark (he died in 1708), had been pregnant seventeen times between 1684 and 1700, resulting in seven miscarriages, five stillborn children, and five live births. The five live births were Mary, who died after twenty months; Anne, who died after nine months (they both died of smallpox in 1687); William, who lived eleven years; Mary, who lived for two hours; and George, who lived for a few minutes. After her last miscarriage in 1700, she was in constant pain and had to be carried around in a chair. She had given her all for her country, politically and personally.

An act of Parliament in 1701 decreed that only Protestants could become kings or queens of England. The act was modified after 1707 to extend the exclusion to Scotland. James III was therefore excluded, and in 1714, the British named a German, George the Elector of Hanover, as King George I. George I didn't speak a word of English, so court affairs were handled in French. The people considered the selection of a foreign prince as king over James III to

THE GREAT GLOBE ITSELF

be outrageous, and there were riots in England and Scotland. As far as they were concerned, the war with France was as good as over and didn't understand why Parliament remained hostile. Parliament was hostile because they saw that the struggle with France continued in North America, India, and the Caribbean.

In December 1715, James III landed in Peterhead, Scotland, and attempted to reestablish a separate crown for Scotland, but the British were ready for him and sent an Army after him. Within six weeks, he was heading back to France. This had a negative effect on his Scottish support. He was not allowed to stay in France because Louis XIV was dead, and the regent, the Duke of Orleans, held to the Treaty of Utrecht, which included a clause where France promised not to shelter James III. The pope offered him a palace in Rome. He got married and had two sons: Charles Stuart (1720–1788), a.k.a. Bonnie Prince Charlie; and Henry Stuart (1725–1807), a.k.a. Cardinal York.

An eastern adjunct to the War of the Spanish Succession was the Great Northern War of 1700–1721. Charles XII of Sweden led a coalition against Peter I of Russia. Charles XII invaded Russia in 1708. His Army was destroyed in 1710. Charles XII was killed in battle in 1718. Sweden lost its empire to Russia and was no longer a great power.

The War of the Austrian Succession, 1740–1748

The War of the Austrian Succession resulted from the House of Habsburg failing to produce a male heir. Austrian emperor Joseph I died in 1711 and was replaced by his brother Charles VI. One of the first things Charles did was to disinherit the daughters of Joseph I in favor of his own daughters. At the time, he was relatively young and thought he might have a son, but he never did, so he expended a lot of energy and political capital in an effort to ensure that his daughter Maria Theresa would inherit his hereditary domains. He also found a suitable husband for her, Francis of Lorraine, whom he thought had potential as a Holy Roman emperor. Charles VI negotiated an extremely complex realm exchange where Francis gave up Lorraine in exchange for Tuscany, while Lorraine went to the former king of Poland, who just happened to be the father of the queen of France.

Unfortunately for the Austrians, there were three German realms that had grown significantly since 1700 and were eager to challenge Austria. These were the electorates of Bavaria, Saxony, and Prussia, and they all had numerous and belligerent male princes running their states. An electorate was a German state, of which there were nine, where the ruler got a vote in who was elected Holy Roman emperor. They were the highest-ranking princes in the empire. In 1740, there were six secular and three ecclesiastic electors:

Ecclesiastic: Archbishops of Trier, Mainz, and Cologne

Secular: Prince electors of Bohemia (Austria), Brandenburg (Prussia), Saxony, Palatine, Bavaria, and Brunswick-Lüneburg (Hanover)

It didn't help Austria that the daughters of Joseph I, the disinherited nieces of Charles VI, were married to the rulers of Saxony and Bavaria. They all represented a threat to Austria, but on the bright side for Austria, they were all jealous of each other, and when it came down to it, they were not able to form a cohesive and lasting alliance, a fact that Austria was able to take advantage of.

In 1740, Charles VI died, and Maria Theresa inherited the Habsburg domains of Austria, Hungary, Bohemia, Silesia, and Belgium. In December, Frederick II of Prussia invaded Silesia, starting the War of the Austrian Succession. Frederick had an inheritance claim on Silesia that his ancestors had been litigating with the Habsburgs for generations. Frederick and Maria Theresa were both in their twenties at the time and were at the beginning of a lifelong rivalry. Prussian-Austrian dualism would be the defining theme of German history for 130 years. Prussia, France, Spain, Bavaria, Saxony, and Sweden lined up against Austria, Great Britain (and Hanover), the Netherlands, and Russia. Officially, France was only at war with Great Britain. Russian and Swedish operations were restricted mostly to fighting each other from 1741 to 1743. The sides were the same as those of the War of the Spanish Succession.

The year 1688 had been a battle for Great Britain's soul, and when James II had been expelled, that battle was won in favor of the nation being parliamentary, Protestant, and anti-France, characteristics that were unchanged for centuries. Great Britain's prime directive since then was to keep France in check in Europe by supporting the strongest continental enemy of France, which in 1740 was Austria. George II of Great Britain, who had succeeded his father in 1727, was also elector of Hanover. Hanover was in danger of being overrun by France, and George II asked the British Parliament to subsidize the Hanoverian Army. This was an unpopular idea among the British people, and William Pitt the Elder, who was thirty-two in 1740, took up the cause to defeat it. He succeeded in a way, as Hanover got the subsidies, but only indirectly, as the British sent the money to Austria, who passed it through to Hanover. Nevertheless, this was enough to put Pitt the Elder on George II's permanent enemies list.

Not long after Frederick II invaded Silesia, a combined French-Bavarian-Saxon Army under the command of French marshal Saxe began marching on Prague, the capital of Austrian Bohemia. Prague was captured on November 26, 1741, and Saxe became famous overnight. Saxe had a claim on the Duchy of Courland (in Latvia) and left the French Army to pursue that. The Bavarian elector Charles Albert was crowned king of Bohemia. He was married to one of Charles VI's disinherited nieces, Maria Amalia. In February 1742, he was crowned Holy Roman emperor Charles VII, the first non-Habsburg emperor in three hundred years. The vote was unanimous, with even George II voting for him, even though Hanover and Great Britain were at war with Bavaria. Frederick of Prussia attacked Moravia, and the Austrians decided to let the Prussians have Silesia for now while they went after Bavaria. The Austrians signed a truce with the Prussians and advanced against the French and their allies toward Munich and Linz. France, Bavaria, and Saxony now found out about the truce that Prussia had signed with Austria, and they were furious with Frederick.

Austria was able to get Saxony to change sides. The Saxon elector Frederick Augustus II, who was also king of Poland, was married to Maria Josepha, the other disinherited niece of Charles VI. They were dissatisfied with the results of their alliance with France,

Bavaria, and Prussia. Bavaria had obtained Bohemia, and Prussia had obtained Silesia, but Saxony was empty-handed.

Now the Austrians were able to concentrate on Charles Albert and his protector, France. They laid siege to Prague and kicked Charles Albert and the French Army out of Bohemia and Bavaria. Things might have been different if Saxe had still been in command. Charles Albert spent the next two years in Frankfurt. The British defeated the French at Dettingen in June 1743, with George II commanding the British Army, the last time a British monarch would command troops in the field. By the end of 1743, France had given up on operations in Germany. France's ally Spain was more successful on the southern flank of the Habsburg Empire, winning victories in Parma under Duke Philip of Spain, a younger son of Philip V.

One of the adjuncts to the War of the Austrian Succession was the so-called War of Jenkins' Ear, a naval conflict in the West Indies between Great Britain and Spain. Jenkins was the captain of a British brig who got one of his ears cut off by Spanish coast guardsmen who were searching his ship for contraband. No territories in the West Indies were exchanged as a result of the conflict, but it did lead to Spanish neutrality for the first few years of the Seven Years' War. George Washington's brother Lawrence was a Marine Corps officer in the War of Jenkins' Ear, serving under Admiral Edward Vernon. When Lawrence returned to civilian life, he built a new house on his plantation and named it Mount Vernon in honor of his old commander. When Lawrence died in 1752, George leased it from Lawrence's widow, Anne, and inherited it when Anne died in 1761.

Upon the death of the Duke of Orleans, who was regent during Louis XV's childhood, the office of chief minister fell to Cardinal Fleury, who had been Louis's tutor. Fleury died in 1743, and Louis, in emulation of his predecessor, Louis XIV, acted as his own chief minister for the next sixteen years. Louis XV and Philip V agreed that in 1744, they would take on the Royal Navy and also support a Stuart uprising in Scotland. There were Fleet engagements in Toulon and Dunkirk. The Toulon Fleet was kept from sailing to Dunkirk to support the uprising, and the French invasion Fleet sailing from Dunkirk was destroyed by storms in the English Channel. The inva-

THE GREAT GLOBE ITSELF

sion was canceled, and so was French support for the Stuart uprising. The decision to devote resources to an invasion Fleet had been controversial among Louis XV's ministers, and after the Fleet's destruction, there were a lot of recriminations and a rededication to the war on the continent. Charles Stuart, who was twenty-four this year, was encouraged to leave France, but he managed to stick around by begging, borrowing, and stealing and was convinced that he could pull off an uprising, French invasion or no.

In 1744, Austria invaded Alsace and France, with Marshal Saxe back in command, invaded the Netherlands. France's ally Prussia took advantage of this and invaded Bohemia. The Bavarians were able to reoccupy Munich. Saxony had been an Austrian ally since 1742, and now they helped the Austrians in pushing Frederick back into Silesia.

In January 1745, three months after returning to Munich, the Holy Roman emperor Charles Albert died, forty-eight years old. This was beneficial to British ally Austria, as it left the throne of the Holy Roman Empire vacant. As we shall see, there would be many princes who would die in circumstances and timing that were suspiciously beneficial to Great Britain, who must have operated an outstanding assassination organization. Charles Albert's son Maximilian III Joseph did not attempt to run for emperor but supported Francis of Lorraine/Tuscany, the husband of Maria Theresa of Austria, who was elected as Emperor Francis I. Bavaria gave up on their imperial pretensions and ended the war with Austria. This allowed France to focus on the Netherlands, winning a battle at Fontenoy under Marshal Saxe.

Encouraged by the French victory at Fontenoy, in July 1745, Charles Stuart landed in Eriskay, Scotland, to claim the Scottish throne. For the next nine months, he would raise an Army and defeat several forces sent against him. In April 1746, he was finally defeated at the Battle of Culloden by the Duke of Cumberland, a younger son of George II. The duke became very popular for his victory, even in the American colonies. It was just now that they were pioneering west of the Appalachians. Pioneers from Virginia explored the Cumberland River Valley and gave it its name. Later, the area would have the Cumberland Mountains and, in 1750, the Cumberland Gap, at the point where Kentucky, Tennessee, and Virginia meet. Technically, the area belonged to France as they had claimed the entirety of the land drained by the Mississippi River, to which the Cumberland was tributary. Daniel Boone widened the gap for wagon traffic in 1775 and became famous in 1784 when a book about his adventures was published.

Charles Stuart returned to France to find that his brother Henry had become a cardinal, meaning he would neither marry nor father any children. What was more irksome was that his father had encouraged it, and it had happened without him being consulted. He stayed in France, but only until the end of the war, as one of the provisions of the peace treaty of Aix-la-Chapelle was that he be ejected. He stayed in Avignon and Lorraine, two areas technically not yet part of France. In 1750, he made a secret visit to London, where he converted to Protestantism, but it was too late; George II and his eldest son, Frederick, both had large families, and there were numerous heirs. Charles Stuart began a decline that was very apparent by 1759, when the French brought him in as a potential leader for another invasion of Great Britain that they were planning. They concluded that Charles would be of no use.

Speaking of the American colonies, there was a North American component to the War of the Austrian Succession called King George's War that focused on Acadia, now known as Nova Scotia. The British succeeded in capturing the fortress of Louisbourg in Nova Scotia. This was a very strategic installation as it guarded the entrance to the Saint Lawrence River and the French colonies of Montreal and Quebec. In the treaty of Aix-la-Chapelle, Great Britain returned it to France in exchange for Madras (known today as Chennai) in India, which the French had captured. Pitt disagreed with this decision at the time and would expend a great deal of energy recapturing Louisbourg during the French and Indian War.

There were also operations in upstate New York, where the French in Montreal and the British in Albany attempted to gain alliances with the Indians in the Hudson Valley, Mohawk Valley, and Lake Champlain.

The Stuart uprising proved to be enough of a distraction to the British that France and Marshal Saxe were able to make significant gains in the Netherlands from 1746 to 1748, causing the Dutch and

THE GREAT GLOBE ITSELF

British to ask for peace. France evacuated the Austrian Netherlands (Belgium) in compensation for Austria losing Silesia. Maria Theresa was recognized as ruling empress. There was much dissatisfaction with the peace, and all sides looked at it as an opportunity to catch their breath and go at it again, which they did in 1754.

North America at the start of the French and Indian War

Population of the American colonies, 1750–1780:

Population of the American Colonies and Quebec before Independence								
Colony	1750		1760		1770		1780	
	White	Black	White	Black	White	Black	White	Black
Maine			20,000	300	31,257	475	49,133	458
New Hampshire	27,505	550	39,093	600	62,396	654	87,802	541
Vermont					10,000	25	47,620	50
Massachusetts	188,000	4,075	202,600	4,566	235,308	4,754	268,627	4,822
Rhode Island	33,226	3,347	45,471	3,468	58,196	3,761	52,946	2,671
Connecticut	111,280	3,010	142,470	3,783	183,881	5,698	206,701	5,885
New York	76,696	11,014	117,138	16,340	162,920	19,112	210,541	21,054
New Jersey	71,393	5,354	93,813	3,567	117,431	8,220	139,627	10,460
Pennsylvania	119,666	2,872	183,703	4,409	240,057	5,761	327,305	7,855
Delaware	28,704	1,496	33,250	1,733	35,496	1,836	45,385	2,996
Maryland	141,073	43,450	162,267	49,004	202,599	63,818	245,474	80,515
Virginia	231,033	101,452	339,726	140,570	447,016	187,605	538,004	220,582
North Carolina	72,984	19,800	110,442	33,554	197,200	69,600	270,133	91,000
South Carolina	64,000	39,000	94,074	57,334	124,244	75,178	180,000	97,000
Georgia	5,200	1,000	9,578	3,578	23,375	10,625	56,071	20,831
Kentucky					15,700	2,500	45,000	7,200
Tennessee					1,000	200	10,000	1,500
Total	1,170,760	236,420	1,573,625	322,506	2,116,819	459,347	2,731,236	574,962
Quebec	51,900	unknown	63,100	unknown	81,200	unknown	103,900	unknown
France	24,700,000	unknown	24,800,000	unknown	24,900,000	unknown	25,800,000	unknown
Great Britain/Ireland	10,300,000	unknown	11,000,000	unknown	11,700,000	unknown	12,500,000	unknown

With over a million white English settlers in North America and only fifty thousand French in Quebec in 1750, the outcome of the French and Indian War seems preordained. In Europe, France had a population over twice the size of Great Britain and Ireland combined, but their obligations in continental Europe limited the scope of what they could do elsewhere, and because France is such a pleasant place to live, French leaders tended to pursue policies that focused on Europe rather than overseas. Nevertheless, if France had ever decided to go on the defensive in Europe and concentrate on an overseas empire, Great Britain would have been in trouble.

Young George Washington

In 1749, seventeen-year-old George Washington was appointed surveyor of Culpeper County, thanks to the influence his brother Lawrence had with the Fairfax family. George had the advantage of being taller than most people. He also displayed adequate intellect and exceptional maturity. In 1752, Lawrence died of tuberculosis. He had other heirs, but eventually, George inherited most of the property of his father and older brothers. Washington also inherited Mount Vernon, which eventually became his primary residence.

In November 1752, George Washington entered into membership at the Masonic lodge in Fredericksburg. Washington was very serious about Masonry as an organization that guided men on how to behave as individuals and in groups. In 1753, he was commissioned as a major in the Virginia militia. He was sent to Western Pennsylvania, where the French were inciting the Indian tribes. In those days, Virginia claimed the Ohio River Valley as part of their territory, although it was later made part of Pennsylvania. That was where he was when he caused the international incident that sparked the Seven Years' War.

1754–1763: The Nine Years of the Seven Years' War

Fort Necessity, 1754

War started in North America two years before it did in Europe, where it is called the Seven Years' War. This makes for some confusion, and there is even a book with the title *The Seven Years War, 1754–1763*, which probably intrigued as many as it infuriated.

In 1844, William Makepeace Thackeray published his novel *The Luck of Barry Lyndon*, and this is what he had to say about the impending struggle:

> It would require a greater philosopher and historian than I am to explain the causes of the famous Seven Years' War in which Europe

was engaged; and, indeed, its origin has always appeared to me to be so complicated, and the books written about it so amazingly hard to understand, that I have seldom been much wiser at the end of a chapter than at the beginning, and so shall not trouble my reader with any personal disquisitions concerning the matter.

He makes a pretty good point; it takes a long time to sort out the events, as we shall see. One thing we should note about the war is that it is transitional, meaning that wars before this had been run by monarchs who had limited objectives and went to the negotiating table when they judged that they had used enough force to obtain those objectives. After this war, we see that revolutions occur, and the people rather than monarchs decided what the objectives of wars were going to be, and these wars turned out to be much bloodier. Monarchs considered soldiers as capital to be preserved, while the people considered them as income to be spent. But this war was in between those periods, as the career of William Pitt the Elder, the prototype of the demagogue, will illustrate.

Virginia militia major George Washington caused an international incident. His unit attacked the French at Jumonville Glen, in what is today Southwest Pennsylvania, in May 1754. Washington wrote a letter to his brother after the event in which he said, "I can with truth assure you, I heard bullets whistle and believe me, there was something charming in the sound." This quote made it into one of the newspapers in London. George II was told about this and said that Washington must not have heard many of them. Washington was soon forced to abandon Fort Necessity to the French in July 1754.

In June 1754, there was a conference of the American colonists in Albany with representatives from Connecticut, Maryland, Massachusetts, New

Hampshire, New York, Pennsylvania, and Rhode Island. The purpose was to form a common defense against the French, including alliances with the Indians. Benjamin Franklin published the famous *Join or Die* cartoon in support of the idea. This was the drawing showing a snake cut up into eight pieces, with New England as a single piece, Delaware included with Pennsylvania, and no Georgia. The colonial legislatures and the British government rejected the idea of local defense, instead setting up a British Army command in February 1755 under General Edward Braddock, consisting of two regular British regiments and a regimental-size agglomeration of American militia units, mostly Virginians.

The British prime minister Henry Pelham died and was replaced by his brother the Duke of Newcastle. The duke was a member of the House of Lords with two strong allies in the House of Commons—William Pitt and Henry Fox —but the duke chose a man named Thomas Robinson as the leader in the Commons because he could dominate him. Pitt wrote to Fox that "the duke might as well have sent us his jackboot to lead us."

Reversal of alliances, 1755

In June 1755, Braddock and two thousand troops set out from Alexandria, Virginia, to attack the French and Indians on the Ohio River but, in July, were ambushed by them near Fort Duquesne, present-day Pittsburgh. Braddock was killed. At the same time, the British invaded Acadia and began deporting the Acadians, who were descendants of French settlers and Micmac Indians. They spoke French and lived like Europeans. Many of the expelled Acadians settled in what is today Louisiana and are known as Cajuns. The British soon established a naval base and a town called Halifax. These actions made a diplomatic settlement between France and Britain impossible.

Later in 1755, the great powers of Europe initiated the reversal of alliances known as the Diplomatic Revolution of 1756. The War of the Austrian Succession in 1740–1748 had been France and Prussia fighting against Great Britain, Russia, and Austria. The upcoming struggle would be Russia, France, and Austria on one side, and Prussia and Great Britain on the other. The reversal of alliances caused turmoil in Russian politics for a while, as Foreign Minister Bestuzhev, who had served Empress Elizabeth from the beginning of her reign, had made his career on the principle that France was the mortal enemy of Russia, while the empress was of the mindset that it was Prussia who needed to be contained. Bestuzhev wanted to keep his job and dutifully launched attacks against Prussia, but he was soon in competition with another official, Vorontzov, who was authentically pro-French.

Britain and Prussia made the first diplomatic move with the Westminster Convention, which was driven by Britain's evaluation that Prussia would better protect Hanover than Austria would. During the debate leading up to the Westminster Convention, the issue of subsidies to Hanover and other countries came up as it had in 1740, and Pitt once again spoke at great length against them. The Duke of Newcastle dismissed Pitt from his job as paymaster of the forces. At the same time, Fox was named secretary of the Southern Department, which was responsible for affairs in southern and western Europe, as well as the colonies, so he had a lot of power and would be running the war against France. Pitt and Fox were allies but subsequently developed a rivalry, which their sons would inherit in the days of the American and French Revolutions.

Opening moves, 1756

Subsequent to the Westminster Convention, France and Austria signed an alliance in Versailles. Austrian foreign minister Wenzel von Kaunitz (1711–1794) led the negotiations. He would still be in office in 1792, the year that the Franco-Austrian Alliance collapsed. Russia and Austria continued their alliance. Except for some operations conducted in support of Bonaparte's 1812 invasion of Russia, they never fought each other until 1914, although Austria's hostile neutrality during the Crimean War in the 1850s started the strain. But until that time, they had the common interest of taking advantage of their weak neighbors Poland and the Ottoman Empire.

In January 1756, the Earl of Loudon arrived in Virginia as governor and commander of the Army to replace Braddock. About the same time, French general Montcalm arrived in Montreal. Austria and France sealed their alliance in May, and Great Britain declared war on France the same month. It took Loudon some time to organize his forces after the defeat of Braddock. In March, the French were attacking British strongholds in New York and inciting the Indians in the Ohio Valley to raid settlements.

Immediately upon the declaration of war, the Royal Navy sallied from Gibraltar to Minorca to attack the French Fleet that was operating there. The Royal Navy was defeated, the French captured Minorca, and the commanding admiral, John Byng, was court-martialed, sentenced to death, and executed in March 1757. Voltaire referenced the execution in his 1759 novel *Candide* with the line, "*Dans ce pays-ci, il est bon de tuer de temps en temps un admiral pour encourager les autres*" (In this country, it is thought wise to kill an admiral from time to time for the encouragement of the others).

In August, Prussia invaded Saxony, one of Austria's allies. Frederick II intended to preempt a Franco-Austrian invasion of Silesia, the province he had won in the War of the Austrian Succession. He held onto Saxony but failed to prevent the occupation of Silesia. Also, he was unable to carry the war into Bohemia as he had hoped. Frederick's ally Great Britain was not told of the attack on Saxony beforehand but began shipping him supplies as soon as possible. In Hanover, the Duke of Cumberland was put in charge of the defenses there.

Meanwhile in Calcutta, Siraj-ud-Daulah, the nabob of Bengal, had ordered the British and French to halt construction of forts that they were building to protect themselves from each other. The French complied, but the British did not, whereupon the nabob laid siege to the British fort. On June 20, the fort surrendered: 146 British and allied POWs were crowded into a small cell, and 123 died that night. Historians debate the numbers. In August, word got to British HQ in Madras that the fort had fallen, and Robert Clive was sent to retaliate. The Black Hole of Calcutta went down in infamy, and

THE GREAT GLOBE ITSELF

although these days most people have still heard of it, they would be hard-pressed to identify the date or circumstances.

The British were having a hard time of it, and Fox resigned in October, followed by Newcastle in November. Fox was replaced by Pitt, and Newcastle was replaced by the Duke of Devonshire. Pitt was also made leader of the Commons. Pitt had insisted that he would only join the government if Newcastle was replaced, and this proved to be a mistake because Newcastle still had a lot of influence in the Commons, and of course, George II was still hostile to Pitt. Pitt had said to Devonshire that, "My lord, I am sure I can save this country, and no one else can." He also was completely reliant on the Commons for his political support, the first time in British history that a man was called to power by the people instead of the crown or the nobles.

Pitt the Great Commoner, 1757

At the beginning of the year, there was an assassination attempt on Louis XV, the first such attempt since Henry IV was assassinated in 1610. Louis was devastated that there was someone out there who hated him that much and vowed to change his ways but was soon backsliding. The sentence on Admiral Byng was carried out, much to the distress of the general population. In March, Pitt directed Governor Loudon to attack the French fortress of Louisbourg and provided ships for that purpose. This seaborne assault was much to be preferred to an overland invasion through the upper Hudson Valley from Albany to Quebec, as the area in between would have been lethal to the British, being full of France's Indian allies.

Operations in North America were delayed when Pitt was dismissed from office in April for, once again, speaking against British policy on the continent as well as for objecting to the execution of Admiral Byng. The people shared Pitt's opinion that only he could save the country, and he was reelected to office by a large vote, reinstalled into office, and subsequently known as the Great Commoner. Fox and Newcastle were also returned to the government.

Pitt sounds like a demagogue to me, but he did eventually produce results. Not in 1757, though, as Louisbourg proved to be well defended by French ships and the weather; and as far as the Hudson Valley, the British Fort William Henry was besieged by the French, had to surrender, and the garrison was treacherously slain by the Indians afterward. Loudon was sacked and replaced by Jeffrey Amherst. The siege of Fort William Henry forms part of the backdrop for James Fenimore Cooper's *The Last of the Mohicans*. In the fall, the French ships returned to their ports in France, which Pitt ordered the Navy to blockade in order to keep them from returning to Louisbourg in the summer.

In India, Clive captured Calcutta in January. In June, he defeated the nabob of Bengal at the Battle of Plassey. The nabob got away but was soon captured and executed after a price was placed on his head. The French had been supporting the nabob, and this battle had a serious impact on French operations in India. After Plassey, they gave up many of their trading posts, and when the peace treaties were signed years later, they gave up the right to use military force in India, which proved fatal to French ambitions there.

In Europe, Frederick II invaded Bohemia, defeating the Austrians in the Battle of Prague in May. The Austrians retreated into the fortifications of Prague, and the Prussians commenced a siege. The Austrians sent a relief force, which lifted the siege. The Austrians inflicted two defeats on the Prussians at Kolin and Zittau, and the Prussians were forced back into Saxony. It was still only June, and the Austrians had linked up with a French force to pursue the Prussians, but the Prussians turned the tables by defeating the Franco-Austrian force at Rossbach in November and then Leuthen in December. This was not enough to bring Austria to the table because of the successes of France in Hanover and Russia in Prussia. However, the Battle of Rossbach was one that the French should have won, and Bonaparte would say that Rossbach was only avenged at Jena and Aürstadt.

The French Army invaded Hanover in two groups. The first group advanced to the city of Hanover, which was defended by the Duke of Cumberland. The two sides fought the Battle of Hastenback, which the French won. In September, the Duke of Cumberland signed

THE GREAT GLOBE ITSELF

the Convention of Klosterzeven, where Hanover withdrew from the war and was occupied by France. At the time, this was authorized by George II, but hearing that the Russians had returned to Russia, and after Frederick's victory at Rossbach in November, George II disavowed it. George II welcomed his son at court as the man who "has disgraced himself and ruined me." The man who had been a hero in 1746 and had all those terrain features in North America named after him resigned all his offices and retired. He made a comeback during the early years of George III 's reign but died of heart disease in 1765, fat, suffering from old war wounds, and only forty-four years old. In 2005, the BBC named him the worst Briton of the eighteenth century for his massacre of the Scots after Culloden.

In Russia, Bestuzhev promoted Stepan Apraksin to field marshal and commander of the Russian Army. In those days, Russia had a smaller population than France, about 23.3 million compared to 24.8 million for France. The days of the "Russian steamroller" belong to 1914. The Russians were able to move an Army from Riga across Poland and invaded East Prussia. Apraksin scored a victory against the Prussians in August at the Battle of Gross-Jaegersdorf, in what is today the Russian enclave of Kaliningrad. It seemed that the Russians were poised to advance on Königsberg, but word reached Apraksin that Elizabeth had suffered a fainting spell. Apraksin began a return to Saint Petersburg, intending to support the crown prince, Peter III, who, like Apraksin and Bestuzhev, believed France, not Prussia, to be the biggest adversary of Russia. Elizabeth was livid after she recovered. The Russian victory brought Sweden into the war against Prussia. Theoretically, that meant that Frederick II was fighting a four-front war against France, Sweden, Austria, and Russia, but Sweden's attacks from Swedish Pomerania were consistently ineffectual.

Poland did not participate in the Seven Years' War, even though King Augustus III of Saxony was also the king of Poland. Since Saxony and Russia were allies, it made sense that Poland would allow the Russians right of passage. There are many reasons for Poland sitting out the war, involving internal strife, symptomatic of why it got partitioned out of existence by 1795.

George Washington, having been the spark that lit the flame of a global conflict, was still in the British Army but spent the year in Virginia, as no decision was made to try to retake Fort Duquesne. He clashed with his peers and superiors over seniority issues and the nature of his commission. He was a twenty-five-year-old militia colonel, and the British command had no high opinion of him, especially after his conduct at Fort Duquesne and Fort Necessity.

Louisbourg, 1758

In Russia, Chancellor Bestuzhev was removed from office in February and replaced by Vorontzov, who was pro-French. General Apraksin was removed from command of the Army at the same time and replaced with General William Fermor. The Austrian and French ambassadors in Saint Petersburg added their voices to those denouncing Bestuzhev and Apraksin. Fermor advanced into Prussia. In August, the Russians and the Prussians fought the Battle of Zorndorf, a bloody struggle which resulted in the Russians retreating. Fermor was relieved of command and replaced with Peter Saltykov. Fermor served as Saltykov's subordinate in 1759.

The British became more active in Europe this year. Somebody had talked sense into Pitt, who, until now, had argued for as little European involvement as possible. The British conducted several amphibious assaults on the French Atlantic Coast that diverted French land forces. They passed a militia act that freed up regular Army troops, who were deployed to Hanover to serve under the Duke of Cumberland 's replacement, the Duke of Brunswick. He was the father of the famous Duke of Brunswick, who issued the Brunswick Manifesto in 1792 and was later killed in action at Jena in 1806. The current duke was more successful than his son, and in June, he defeated the French at the Battle of Krefeld. The Royal Navy bottled up the French Fleet in Brest and fought the Toulon Fleet at Cartagena. These were the ships that were supposed to protect Louisbourg from the Royal Navy, so these operations had the very important effect of leaving Louisbourg unprotected. The British also sent huge subsidies to Prussia. France decided to invade Great

THE GREAT GLOBE ITSELF

Britain, a good move seeing as how the British Army was on the continent. The Duke of Choiseul had advocated this and was named foreign minister, to carry it out in 1759. Louis XV was forty-nine this year and soon gave up being his own chief minister, turning that job over to Choiseul too. He had done the job since 1743.

In Germany, Prussia invaded Bohemia, but in June, the Austrians fought Prussia at the Battle of Domstadtl, forcing the Prussians to retreat into Silesia. The Prussians stayed on defense in Silesia while responding to the Russian invasion, defeating them at Zorndorf in August. The Austrians invaded Saxony, and Frederick fought them at the Battle of Hochkirk in November. The Austrians defeated Frederick, and it shook him pretty badly, as he was running low on men and money.

In North America, there was activity in the Hudson Valley, Nova Scotia, and the Ohio Valley. In the Hudson Valley, the French under Montcalm defeated the British, capturing Fort Ticonderoga in July. The victory did the French little good because a few weeks later, the British captured the now-defenseless fortress of Louisbourg, and all of a sudden, Quebec and Montreal were open to attack. Montcalm withdrew from the Hudson Valley into Quebec City to prepare for its defense.

In May, George Washington and Martha Dandridge Custis were engaged. There were other suitors for her hand, but he came out on top. George Washington married another man's wife, and they never had children, one of many things he would have in common with Napoleon Bonaparte and Andrew Jackson. In July, Washington was elected to the House of Burgesses, where he served for the next sixteen years, when he was elected to the Continental Congress. But in 1758, he was still in the Army and took part in the Forbes Expedition, back into the Ohio Valley.

The Forbes Expedition was a repeat of the 1755 British operation to march from Alexandria to capture Fort Duquesne. Much of the expedition involved improving the roads in the area and negotiating with the Indians. In August, the British under Bradstreet captured Fort Frontenac at the east end of Lake Ontario, cutting the Ohio country off from Quebec. Fort Frontenac is still there, inside the city of Kingston, Ontario. The French garrison at Fort Duquesne knew the place was doomed. They abandoned the fort, blowing it up as they left. The British built a new fort nearby that Forbes dubbed Fort Pitt, which came in useful later as the Indians under Chief Pontiac continued the struggle after the French departure. During the American Revolution, the British incited the Indians in the area against the Americans, and three thousand militia had to be sent to Fort Pitt. Virginia and Pennsylvania disputed sovereignty over the site until 1780, when the Mason-Dixon line was extended, and it became part of Pennsylvania. Over time, Fort Pitt evolved into Pittsburgh, sometimes with an aitch, sometimes without.

In November, Washington's regiment accidentally engaged Lieutenant Colonel George Mercer's unit around Fort Ligonier, Pennsylvania, in an unfortunate friendly fire incident. Thirty-eight British and American soldiers were killed or wounded. It cost Washington any chance he might have had at a career in the British Army. Washington himself complained about the prejudice against colonials and the preference that officers imported from Great Britain received. He complained now, but when he was commander in chief of the Continental Army, his disdain for militias would be as great as that of his superiors in the year 1758. If Washington had been educated in England, as many American aristocrats were, he might have had a military career. Even though his chances in the British Army were gone, he was still considered to be a war hero in Virginia. He settled down to the life of a Virginia planter and stood at the head of the class in his community. Like Bonaparte and Jackson, he had already, in his twenties, established himself in a position well ahead of what could be expected of someone his age. However, the British sneered that if this was the best the colonials had to offer, God help them.

In France, Francois Quesnay published *The Economic Table*, which provided the foundations of the ideas of the Physiocrats. The Physiocrats initially called themselves the Economists, inventing that word, but are now known as the Physiocrats to differentiate them from later economists and the generic term *economist*. This was the first work to attempt to describe the workings of the economy in an analytical way and was one of the first important contributions to economic thought. Among Quesnay's disciples were Victor Mirabeau, father of the 1789 revolutionary; Pierre Samuel Dupont DeNemours, the father of the founder of the American company Dupont; Jacques Turgot, future minister to the king of France; and Adam Smith, author of *The Wealth of Nations*. Among their topics over the years was the idea of overpopulation, an idea always preying in the back of the collective French mind in the eighteenth century.

White House plantation

On January 6, 1759, George Washington married Martha Dandridge Custis at her home in White House plantation, New Kent County, Virginia. Many believe that the house of the president of the United States is called the White House for this reason, not because it was whitewashed after getting burned by the British in 1814. White House plantation was the couple's first residence, although the seat of operations gradually shifted to Mount Vernon, another White House, as time went by. They must have looked back at those first years of marriage as an idyllic time.

White House plantation was five thousand acres in size. During the Civil War, White House was the residence of Mary Custis Lee, wife of Robert E. Lee. She was Martha Washington's great-granddaughter. Their son Rooney Lee was the owner. Early in the war, Mrs. Lee left Arlington and moved to White House. The plantation was convenient to rail and river transport, and so it became part of the combat zone in 1862, when Union troops under General George B. McClellan used it as a supply base during the Peninsula Campaign, a failed attempt to capture the Confederate capital of Richmond. Mrs. Lee left White

House for Richmond. After the war, she lived in Lexington with her husband.

During the Peninsula Campaign, Frederick Law Olmsted, designer of New York City's Central Park, among his many accomplishments, served as executive secretary of the US Sanitary Commission, a precursor to the Red Cross, in Washington, DC, which tended to the Union wounded during the Civil War. Olmsted headed the medical effort for the sick and wounded at White House until McClellan abandoned it as he retreated with his troops during the Seven Days' Battles. The manor house of White House plantation burned to the ground during the seven days.

Rooney Lee graduated from Harvard in 1857 and joined the US Army. He then fought for the Confederacy at Fredericksburg, Chancellorsville, and Gettysburg. He was taken prisoner at Brandy Station and was exchanged a year later. He then fought at the Wilderness and Spotsylvania Courthouse. He surrendered with his father at Appomattox. Rooney Lee married in 1859, but his wife and children died during the war while he was away. He returned to White House in 1865 and built a modest house there. He married again in 1867, having two children who lived long lives. In 1874, he moved from White House, leaving it unoccupied. In 1875, he was elected to the Virginia Senate. In 1887, he was elected to the US House of Representatives, where he served until his death in 1891. I suppose that he had to file some sort of appeal to clear himself from the effects of the Insurrection Clause, as did the many other Confederates who held office after the war. The house built by Rooney Lee in 1865 burned to the ground in 1880. White House plantation, inspiration of the most famous residence on earth, has fallen into oblivion.

Annus Mirabilis, 1759

In February, the Duchess of Orleans, Louise Henriette de Bourbon, died at the age of thirty-three. She was labeled as a beautiful but promiscuous woman who constantly cheated on her husband, the Duke of Orleans, whose level of attractiveness can be judged by the fact that he was known as Louis Philippe the Fat. The painting of her shows a very attractive woman. This may all have been slander and libel put out by the enemies of her son in the 1780s to question his legitimacy.

Louis Philippe the Fat was thirty-four at the time of his wife's death, and great-grandson of the original purchaser of the Chateau de Saint Cloud, but he abandoned Saint Cloud on his wife's death. He moved to the Chateau de Bagnolet with his mistress, Etienne le Marquis, a dancer and actress with whom he had three children. In 1769, he sold Bagnolet and moved to the Chateau de Raincy, and that same year, he took up with Madame de Montesson, whom he married in 1773. He gave the Palais-Royal to his son Louis Philippe II in 1780. Louis Philippe II had the same demagogic instincts as Pitt. He did marvelous things with the Palais-Royal and turned it into the beautiful public place that it remains today. The Chateau de Saint Cloud was shuttered for twenty-six years until 1785, when Marie Antoinette purchased it.

In North America, the British captured Fort Ticonderoga and Fort Niagara in July. Having already captured Fort Frontenac, they had now cleared both the east and west sides of Lake Ontario as well as Lake Champlain from French occupation. The Indians realized that without the French, their choice was to submit to the British or die. Some made one choice, some the other. The decisive battle between the British and the French was fought on September 13. The Battle of Quebec resulted in a British victory that would give Great Britain Canada, the Great Lakes, and the Mississippi Valley. The British had sailed up the Saint Lawrence from Louisbourg, landed troops near Quebec and had scaled the walls to get into the fortress. The French commander Montcalm and the British commander Wolfe were both killed in action. Montreal remained to be taken, but that was a matter of marching. Quebec was the decisive event. Another important event of the year in North America was the death of General Forbes, who appears to have been suffering from stomach cancer, and he was replaced by General Amherst.

In Europe, the Prussians and the British/Hanoverians faced attack from France, Austria, and Russia. In France, the Hanoverians defeated the French Army at the Battle of Minden in August. The French retreated and conducted no further operations in Europe that year, focusing once again on an invasion of England. One ray of hope came through for France this year, as Charles III became king of Spain and promised to have closer ties with France than his brother Ferdinand VI. Also in August, a combined Russian-Austrian Army defeated the Prussians at the Battle of Kunersdorf. It seemed that the luck of Frederick had at last run out as his Army disintegrated during the battle. His despair was complete but premature. His scattered troops recongealed, and four days after the battle, he had twenty-six thousand men under his command. The Austrians and the Russians crossed the Oder into Prussia but lost their nerve and failed to occupy Berlin, which they could have done. This was the first Miracle of the House of Brandenburg.

In France, preparations to invade Great Britain were well underway. Hundreds of barges were constructed in LeHavre, Brest, Saint-Malo, Nantes, Morlaix, and Lorient. Fifty thousand troops were staged in those ports and practiced embarkations, getting the time down to seven minutes. There was disagreement among the French as to how much protection the barges would need from the Royal Navy, with Choiseul saying that only a favorable wind was needed. They were also confident that twenty thousand Scottish Highlanders would rise in support of putting a Stuart King on the throne of Scotland. The French had no confidence in Bonnie Prince Charlie, so the thought of toppling the Hanoverian kings in England was not considered.

The British did not change their troop dispositions in Germany, trusting in the Royal Navy and in the militia troops that would be called up to counter any invasion. In June, they bombarded the barges in LeHavre, doing some damage but not enough to worry

THE GREAT GLOBE ITSELF

the French about their invasion plans. France decided to prioritize a landing in Scotland, but this required the Fleet. In August, the Toulon Fleet was engaged by the British when they emerged from Mediterranean off the coast of Lagos, Portugal, and made ineffective. Finally, in November, the British defeated the French in the naval Battle of Quiberon, putting an end to the threat of invasion. Quiberon is an island off the coast of France not too far from Nantes. Naval historian Alfred Thayer Mahan called Quiberon the Trafalgar of the Seven Years' War.

There was also some military activity in India, as the British were able to lift a French siege at Madras in February.

Because 1759 constituted a year of great British victories at Madras, Quebec, Quiberon, and Minden, it became known as the *Annus Mirabilis*, the "Miraculous Year," which has become a byword for whenever somebody has a good year. The credit for the success went to Pitt the Elder, who devised the strategy of focusing on the colonies and was wise enough to back off when everyone advised him against his judgment that Great Britain needed to provide more resources to Europe. This change in strategy kept the French forces away from Louisbourg and enabled victory in North America.

This year, Pitt's wife gave birth to the future prime minister Pitt the Younger, while his wife's brother George Grenville became father to future prime minister William Grenville. The older Grenville had been treasurer of the Navy since 1754. The younger Pitt and Grenville would work together for the years between 1789 and 1801, but politics and ambition would push them into separate camps after that.

Interesting sidenote: The French finance minister this year was Etienne de Silhouette, who attempted to reign in government spending, and the term *a la Silhouette* became a term meaning "on the cheap." At the same time, a new form of portraiture became popular, because it was inexpensive compared to painting or sculpture. This consisted of a profile of the subject cut from black paper and was named after the penny-pinching finance minister.

George III, 1760

In North America, the French sallied from Montreal in an attempt to retake Quebec. They were able to lay siege to it but were unable to stop the British Navy from cutting off their line of communication back to Montreal or from resupplying the British garrison at Quebec. In July, General Amherst led an assault on Montreal, the French capitulated in September, and the war in North America was mostly over.

In Europe, the Austrians invaded Silesia in May and surprised a Prussian corps, which surrendered after running out of ammunition. The Austrians continued their advance into Silesia and the Prussians fought them at the Battle of Liegnitz in August. The Prussians held their ground and the Austrians retreated. Prussia remained in possession of Silesia and continued to occupy Saxony.

It must have been painfully clear to the French that they were taking a thrashing from the British, and now all they could do to end the war favorably was to destroy Prussia. But the failed invasion of Britain in 1759, like the one in 1743, had been expensive, and the means were lacking. Nevertheless, the French went on the attack. In July, the Hanoverians and the French collided at the Battle of Korbach and the Hanoverians were defeated. We hear for the first time about Hessians (from Hesse-Kassel) fighting on the side of the British, and the history books I learned from in elementary school used the fact that the British hired German mercenaries in the American Revolution as proof that the British were evil. The Hanoverians retreated from Hesse-Kassel into Westphalia, and the French pursued. The Battle of Warburg occurred at the end of July, and the Hanoverians held their ground, although the French could say that they had succeeded, having kicked the Hanoverians out of Hesse. The Hanoverians then sent a corps across the Rhine, where the French met and defeated them at Kloster Kamp (Camp Abbey) near Essen in October. The Hanoverians retreated across the Rhine.

The Austrian-Russian force under Saltykov and General Maurice Lacy were inactive all summer, a sign of logistical deficiency, financial distress, and war weariness. Frederick simply refused to go

THE GREAT GLOBE ITSELF

down. In October, the Austrians and Russians decided to occupy Berlin. Frederick was in Silesia at the time. The Prussians had a force of eighteen thousand in Berlin that retreated into Spandau. The locals in Berlin paid a ransom of 1.5 million thalers and endured some pillaging over four days, and then the Austrians and Russians retreated, as they received reports that Frederick was marching their way. The Austrians halted their retreat and met the Prussians at the Battle of Torgau in November. Both Frederick and the Austrian commander Daun were wounded in action. The battle was very bloody, with both sides losing a third of their forces. The result has been described as a "Prussian Pyrrhic victory," as he was running out of men to fill the ranks. The Austrians were not faring much better. Obviously, the Russians were also losing their taste for the war, as their relative inactivity demonstrates.

The war was taking its toll on royalty too. In October, George II died after thirty-three years on the British throne. He was seventy-seven years old and vigorous until his last day, although hard of hearing and blind in one eye. The new king was his twenty-two-year-old grandson, George III, whose father, Frederick, Prince of Wales, had died in 1751 at the age of forty-four. Frederick left nine children behind, including George III. An epigram went around at the time:

> Here lies poor Fred who was alive and is dead,
> Had it been his father I had much rather,
> Had it been his sister nobody would have missed her,
> Had it been his brother, still better than another,
> Had it been the whole generation, so much better for the nation,
> But since it is Fred who was alive and is dead,
> There is no more to be said!

Until 1919, there was a position in the households of English/British kings and Princes of Wales called Gentleman of the Bedchamber. One of Frederick's Gentlemen was Francis North, Earl of Guilford, who served as such from 1730 to the prince's death in 1751. His son Frederick, Lord North, would serve as prime minister from 1770 to 1782. George III and Lord North looked alike, and some suggested that they were half-brothers, with George IV remarking, "Either my royal grandmother or North's mother must have played her husband false." It certainly seems possible to me.

King George III was proud to be an Englishman. He never traveled abroad during his entire reign, not even to visit his realm in Hanover. His first task as king was to end the current war successfully, and he authorized the beginning of peace negotiations with France. George III had no intention of negotiating a separate peace apart from Prussia, but he informed Frederick II that British subsidies to Prussia would end in June 1762 to pressure Frederick into joining him at the negotiating table. Based on the events of 1761, I doubt that any serious negotiations occurred until after the fighting season.

George III's first fifteen years on the throne were very good for Great Britain, until he ran up against George Washington, the former colonial militia officer who had been found so dreadfully wanting in the French and Indian War.

Bourbon family compact, 1761

In Westphalia, the French crossed the Rhine in March to reinforce a French force that was in Hesse-Kassel. The French and the Hanoverians clashed at the Battle of Grunberg. The French were victorious, and the Hanoverians retreated east. The French pursued.

THE GREAT GLOBE ITSELF

The Hanoverians turned and stood at the Battle of Vellinghausen in July and caused the French to retreat. There was great rejoicing in Great Britain at this victory. France had an ace up their sleeve and signed the Bourbon family compact with Spain in August. Spain was worried that British naval dominance was a threat to their empire. As it turned out, their worry was 100 percent justified, as the British would be behind every independence movement south of Mexico in Spanish America in the early nineteenth century. Now in 1761, Pitt recommended a preemptive attack on Spain, which George III and every member of the cabinet rejected, and Pitt resigned. No one in politics was sad to see him go, including his brother-in-law George Grenville, and there was bad blood between them for years.

Also in March, at the same time that the French were crossing the Rhine, the British were capturing Belle Isle off the coast of Brittany, declaring that they intended to put a naval station there to permanently guard the English Channel from French attack. The British were mostly bluffing about this, intending to trade Belle Isle for Minorca, although there was always a hardcore element in the Royal Navy that was serious about ideas like that. The Royal Navy had not entered the Mediterranean since Admiral Byng 's defeat in 1756.

The Austrians were unable to mount any military operations this year, but at the end of the year, the Russians captured a port and were now able to supply their troops by sea. They failed to make any significant advances. Even so, Frederick believed he was doomed at the end of the year, as he was out of men and was soon to be out of money.

There are other things in the year 1761 to talk about besides the war. In July, the Bridgewater Canal, built by and named for the Duke of Bridgewater, opened for business. According to Mark Twain, in the 1840s, one of the duke's descendants would be teaming up with Louis XVII, the Dauphin of France, swindling people along the Mississippi River. The canal was built to carry coal to Manchester, where it powered engines used in cotton mills. The canal reduced the time and cost of transporting cotton and coal by 50 percent. In September, George III married Queen Charlotte, a princess from Mecklenburg. They would have a huge family as she gave birth to fifteen children between 1762 and 1783, twelve of who grew to adult-

The last battles, 1762

As they had promised, the British ended subsidies to Prussia in June of 1762, which was the end of the British-Prussian alliance. Now, Britain's only allies in Europe were Portugal, Hanover, and Hesse. This isolation would cause Britain difficulty during the American Revolution. They would not have a major European power as an ally again until 1788, when they signed the Triple Alliance with Prussia and the Netherlands.

In the final year of campaigning in Europe, the Hanoverians were victorious over the French at Wilhelmsthal in June. The French were making one last attempt to capture Hanover before negotiations began but came up short. At the same time, the Prussians, despite the lack of British subsidies, were victorious over the Austrians at Burkersdorf in July. The Austrians were making one last attempt to capture Silesia before negotiations began but also came up short. Prior to opening negotiations with the British, France ceded their holdings in the Mississippi Valley to Spain in the Treaty of Fontainebleau. The following year, Spain ceded the portion east of the Mississippi River to Great Britain in the Treaty of Paris, keeping New Orleans. France made the cession in lieu of payment on a loan that Spain had given them earlier to finance the war.

Having disposed of Pitt, the British government took his idea and declared war on Spain on January 4. Spain, soon after, declared war on Great Britain and Portugal. I would imagine that most of the British government wanted peace in 1759, but because of Pitt's sway over the people, the war had continued, another demonstration of how democracies display all the compassion of a Roman crowd watching gladiators fight to the death. Pitt was not finished in politics, serving as prime minister from 1766 to 1768, but his physical and mental health showed a great deal of decline from this point forward until his death in 1778.

THE GREAT GLOBE ITSELF

George III exerted his power to get rid of Pitt and Newcastle. The two men had won the war for Great Britain, but George III did not trust them with the future direction of British affairs. He and his former tutor, Lord Bute, forced Newcastle's resignation, and Bute was appointed prime minister. The two of them had a vision of a British Empire based on trade between India, Europe, and America that would be free of continental entanglements. They thought they could appease France by leaving them their empire in America west of the Mississippi River and their possessions in the West Indies, but France thought of nothing but revenge.

In May, Spain invaded Northern Portugal with twenty-two thousand men, intending to occupy Oporto. What ensued was a preview of the French invasion of 1807–1814. The British landed seven thousand troops in Lisbon. The Spanish in the north were harassed by guerilla bands and eventually had to withdraw. They invaded again in August, with two larger forces that included some French forces, this time further south. The two sides got bogged down, and a stalemate ensued. Two British names, Burgoyne and Townsend, appear in these accounts, and we will hear from them in a few years when they are dealing with the colonies in America. The Spanish used their Navy to attack Portuguese possessions in Brazil, with mixed results. The British were more successful, using their Navy to capture Havana in August and Manila in October. The British also occupied Newfoundland in September. The British capture of Havana was significant, as Great Britain was able to obtain East and West Florida in exchange for evacuating it.

An armistice was signed in December, as France and Great Britain began negotiations in Paris, while Prussia began negotiations with Austria in Hubertusburg, a palace in Saxony, at the same time.

Russian empress Elizabeth died on January 5, 1762, at the age of fifty-two, another opportune death for the British. She had successfully led her people through the War of the Austrian Succession and the Seven Years' War, but I don't think that Prussia was as close to extinction as the history books claim. Frederick II called her "the Messalina of the North," which was by no means a compliment. One thing we haven't really noted about the era since 1740 is that Austria and Russia were both run by empresses and that Louis XV was under the control of Madame Pompadour. This feminine dominance of Europe lent an air of refinement and restraint to European wars and politics that would soon give way to the masculine excesses of the French Revolution. It was, after all, Madame Pompadour, not Louis XV, who said, "After us, the deluge," which she said this year, knowing that France had dug itself into a deep hole financially and strategically.

Elizabeth was succeeded by her nephew Peter III, who was the son of Elizabeth's sister Anna and her husband, the Duke of Holstein-Gottorp. Peter III had married Catherine II in 1745, and they had a son, Paul I, in 1754. Paul was taken from his parents and lived at court with Elizabeth until her death in 1762. As we recall, Peter III was pro-Prussian, and in March, he signed an armistice with them, soon followed by the Treaty of Saint Petersburg on May 5, 1762. This was the second miracle of the House of Brandenburg. Peter III then planned to attack Denmark for some slight to his father's relatives in Holstein, but he was deposed in July and replaced by Catherine II as regent for her son Paul I. Peter III soon died from mysterious circumstances. France and Austria had been completely outraged by Russia's separate peace with Prussia, and there was a large party at court that was still anti-Prussian, and they carried out this coup against Peter under the leadership of Gregory and Alexei Orlov. The Orlovs and Nikita Panin were Catherine's main advisers in the early years of her reign. Gregory Orlov fathered a child with Catherine II, who was born in April 1762, named Alexei Bobrinski. She had to conceal it from her husband, who knew any child that came out of her in 1762 was not his. Gregory was commander in chief of the Army. His brother Alexei had a similarly high-flying career. Paul I was Panin's ward, and Panin was responsible for foreign policy. It was Alexei Orlov who told Catherine in July that Peter was dead, and it was time for her to put away childish things and become a monarch.

Catherine II had been born in Germany and raised Lutheran. Four of the five monarchs of the great powers of Europe were now Germans, three of them were Protestants (although Catherine soon converted to Russian Orthodoxy), and two of them were women. France, which is to say the Paris mob, vaguely resented this German dominance. When Marie Antoinette, daughter of the Austrian empress, came to be queen of France, she would be subjected to vicious libels surrounding her German upbringing.

In France, Jean-Jacques Rousseau (1712–1778) published *The Social Contract* and *Emile: On Education* within months of each other. As a result, he was forced to flee France. His ideas included: man in a state of nature is good and is corrupted by society and landowner-ship. Very contrary to the Christian doctrine of the perfect creation of Adam falling through disobedience to God. Rousseau had a vision of a social contract where all men would be equal and responsible to the general will.

> Man was born free, and he is everywhere
> in chains. One man thinks himself the master of
> others but remains more of a slave than they.

The extent to which his ideas were formed by pondering Indians in America is an open question, as the notion of the noble savage was becoming popular in Europe in those days. It was a con-ception cherished by these European philosophers who never went to America, much less met a real Indian. Robespierre and the rest of the Terrorists of 1793–1794 would all have well thumbed through copies of Rousseau's works. His idea of a social contract was opposed by the Physiocrats' idea of natural order.

Virginia had long considered the war over. George Washington came back from the war to White House, but soon his thoughts turned to Mount Vernon. Washington rebuilt the house in 1774 on the existing foundations. He always seemed to embark on these home-improvement projects just before military service. Washington wanted an estate along the Potomac, convinced by his travels around Fort Pitt of the potential for connection by canal of the Potomac and Ohio Rivers. It was an idea he pursued all his life, even after the state lines in the west were drawn that would require it to be a multistate project rather than one that could be done just by the state of Virginia. He had the concept, but he didn't have the contour maps. Later, when Jefferson was president, his engineers told him that the elevations to be overcome would be too great. Instead, in 1805, Jefferson got Congress to authorize a road from Cumberland, Maryland, on the Potomac to Wheeling, Virginia, on the Ohio, and today you can still drive the route, long known as the National Pike but now just US 40. Canals were still feasible if the land wasn't too mountainous, and in 1817, New York began building the Erie Canal from Albany to Buffalo, using state resources only.

Chief Pontiac, 1763

Lord Bute negotiated the Treaty of Paris, which was signed on February 10. Great Britain and Spain supplanted France in North America. Great Britain got everything east of the Mississippi, including West and East Florida, which had been held by Spain since 1513. East Florida—present-day Florida, east of the Apalachicola River—and West Florida, the land between the Pearl and Apalachicola Rivers, south of the 31st parallel. The capital of East Florida was Saint Augustine, and the capital of the West Florida was Pensacola. Spain would regain the two Floridas in 1783 as a reward for helping France defeat Great Britain that year. The area south of the Ohio River and north of the 31st parallel was called the Indian Reserve. The area north of the Ohio River was called the Ohio and Illinois Country. It was annexed to Quebec in 1774 to punish the Americans for the Boston Tea Party.

The years from the days of Columbus until now had been a long period of rivalry among the nations of Western Europe for colonies and trade. Great Britain had spent the eighty-five years since 1688 deeply enmeshed in the politics of continental Europe for the purpose of inflicting harm on France. Now they found that their efforts had resulted in the exclusion of France from North America and India and the West Indies. I have read British historians who claim that Great Britain obtained their empire in an "absent-minded fashion," but it is apparent that they worked long, hard, and smart to obtain it. After 1763, no European power wanted to enter an alliance with them. Frederick II complained bitterly for the rest of his life about how the British had deserted him in 1762 after achieving their

THE GREAT GLOBE ITSELF

goals in North America and India. He signed an alliance with Russia. Austria and France maintained theirs.

Prussia, Austria, and Saxony signed the Treaty of Hubertusburg on February 15. The situation of 1756 prevailed, with Prussia confirmed in its possession of Silesia. In 1740, Prussia had been at the same level as Saxony and Bavaria, but now thanks to Frederick, Prussia was considered to be in the first tier of European powers. The securing of Silesia had done it all. France and Austria maintained their alliance until 1792. With the success of Prussia in 1763, we see for the first time the five-power dynamic of European politics in the interaction of Great Britain, France, Austria, Prussia, and Russia. The British had no allies in Europe but still had plenty of enemies. The British thought they were out, but their enemies wanted to pull them back in—to beat them up and regain their lost possessions.

Bute and George III wanted a lasting peace—the better to focus on the empire—and made some concessions that got Bute into trouble. We read that there was originally an agreement for Great Britain to concede fishing rights in Newfoundland to France in exchange for the island of Guadaloupe, but they softened their stance and let France keep Guadaloupe, after which Bute came under attack and had to resign after only ten months in office. George Grenville, whose sister was married to Pitt the Elder, was appointed, and he served until 1765. George III was very unhappy to lose Bute but went along because Bute took the spear for him. Grenville tried to accommodate king, Parliament, and public opinion, and it wasn't easy. One thing that he had to deal with was the war waged by the Indians of the Great Lakes under Chief Pontiac. Pontiac and his allies had had a good relationship with the French but distrusted the British, who considered the Indians to be a conquered people. The Indians didn't remember losing any battles and disagreed. Rumors of war, famine, pestilence, and death circulated among the Indians around the Great Lakes, literally, because the Indians had been evangelized by Christian preachers and foresaw the apocalypse that was headed their way. It's no wonder that the primary memory of Pontiac's War is the story of the smallpox-infected blankets given to the Indians in an early attempt at germ warfare. This occurred in Pittsburgh in August

1763. The Indian resistance in Ohio and Pennsylvania was crushed within a few months, but the anti-British sentiment remained west of there in the Illinois Country until 1766.

Grenville and George III issued the Proclamation of 1763 on October 7. It established the Appalachian Ridge line as the western boundary of British settlement. The idea was not that of a permanent boundary but rather one that could be extended west over time. The position of His Majesty's government was that they owned the land, and it would be sold by them in an orderly manner. Only the crown could establish land grants; colonial officials were not so authorized. Purchase of land by private individuals or companies from the Indians was outlawed, an issue that came before the US Supreme Court in the 1820s. There were already several settlements beyond the Proclamation Line, and the crown was prompt to negotiate treaties with the Indians and adjust the line. I presume that if the settlers had already paid somebody for the land, they weren't required to pay for it again. Although the Proclamation of 1763 ranks high in the history books on the list of American grievances against Great Britain, it should be noted that the first major piece of legislation passed after the 1783 Treaty of Paris by the Confederation Congress was a verbatim restatement of the Proclamation of 1763, only substituting "The United States" in place of "His Majesty."

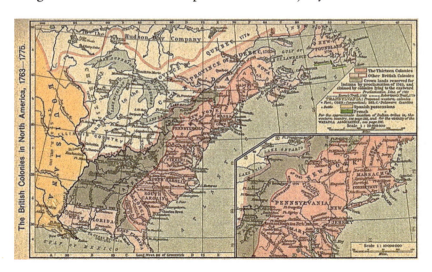

THE GREAT GLOBE ITSELF

The French threat having been removed from North America, the British colonists looked forward to an era of peace and reduced taxes, but Parliament had other ideas. Spain, an ally of France, was still a threat, and so were the Indians, and Parliament wasn't going to leave it to colonial militias to defend the place. Just look at how incompetent that fellow Washington was! Regular British troops would be required, and the colonists would have to pay their share. They weren't treating the Americans any differently than they treated Ireland. The colonists didn't concur. If the British Parliament could levy taxes, they could pass other laws onerous to the colonists, such as outlawing slavery or restricting manufacturing and trade. They were being treated just as badly as Ireland.

In France, Choiseul survived in his job as chief minister, vowing to rebuild the military and make good the losses of the Seven Years' War. He worked closely with Spain to make life as miserable as possible for the American colonists. He would remain in office until 1770, when he attempted to provoke a war with Great Britain by seizing the Falkland Islands. Louis XV wanted peace and replaced him with Rene Nicolas de Maupeou.

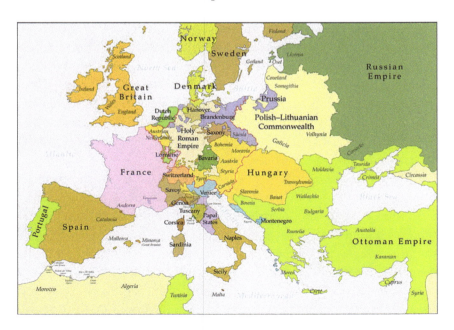

CHAPTER 2

Revolution in America, 1764–1783

1764–1774: Striking at Their Chains

Great Britain and North America, 1764–1774

Taxing the American colonies, 1764–1766: The city of Saint Louis was founded in 1764 on the west bank of the Mississippi River, south of the confluence with the Missouri, in Spanish America. Pierre Leclede ran a large fur-trading operation in New Orleans, and this year he sent his stepson August Chouteau to be founder of a colony. The place thrived under weak Spanish rule, mostly governing itself until the Louisiana Purchase in 1803. Names like Soulard and Gratiot came to Saint Louis to add to its luster. In 1804, Lewis and Clark began their expedition there, and in 1806, Zebulon Pike did too. The population was big enough by 1821 for Missouri to attain statehood in an important compromise.

In London, Grenville's government calculated that the expenses of a ten-thousand-man Army in the American colonies would be £200,000 per year and proposed that the Americans should contribute £80,000 of that through new taxes or, more accurately, enforcement of taxes that had been in the books since 1733, which was the year that Parliament passed the Molasses Act, placing a tariff on any molasses that was imported from a non-British colony. Molasses was used to make rum, a huge industry in New England. The British colonies didn't produce enough molasses to supply American demand, and the Americans protested. The British didn't need the money at the time, so to appease the Americans, they laxly enforced the law and turned a blind eye to smugglers. Now in 1764, the law was revised by cutting the tariff in half but with the intent to enforce it. There was anger about it in New England, but we don't hear about any riots or significant attempts at evasion. I couldn't find out how much money the tax raised.

In March 1765, Parliament passed the Stamp Act, which was a direct tax on the colonists, not a tariff that importers passed on to consumers. The Americans had been subject to direct taxes but only those passed by colonial assemblies. Reaction to the Stamp Act was strong in America. Grenville was dismissed in July 1765 and replaced by the Marquess of Rockingham, who was soon reducing the Molasses Tax from three pence per gallon to one and taking steps to repeal the Stamp Act.

American response: In May 1765, the Virginia House of Burgesses passed the Virginia Resolves, protesting the Stamp Act, and Patrick Henry gained fame saying, "Caesar and Tarquin each had his Brutus, Charles I his Cromwell, and George III —" (Henry was interrupted at this point by cries of "treason" from the opposition) "may profit by their example." He then added in response to the cries, "If this be treason, make the most of it." Twenty-two-year-old Thomas Jefferson said, "He appeared to me to speak as Homer wrote."

Americans were baffled that no British Army had been in America before 1754, when the French were strong, and wanted to know why one was needed now that the French were gone. Some in America asserted that the real reason an Army was being posted in America at their expense was to provide sinecures for British officers who were now unemployed, thanks to the end of the war, and this was widely believed. The phrase "Taxation without representation is tyranny" was popularized in the American colonies by a Boston pamphleteer named James Otis. The phrase had been used for a long time without effect in Ireland. Otis did not have the stomach or the mind for revolution. By 1770, he was bypassed by characters that had more fire and fortitude than he did. The cause of his death in 1783 was reportedly being struck by lightning. The response of the British government to the idea that the Americans were unrepresented was to push the idea of virtual representation, which was that Parliament represented the *interests* of all members of the empire. That dog didn't hunt, as the Americans would say.

In May, while Grenville was still prime minister, Parliament passed the Quartering Act of 1765. It did not require private individuals to open their homes to British soldiers (which is what I was taught in school), but it did require colonial governments to pay the cost of housing and feeding them. One thousand five hundred British troops arrived in New York Harbor, and the New York Assembly refused to supply billeting, so they remained aboard their ships.

In October 1765, twenty-seven delegates from nine colonies met in New York City. Virginia, North Carolina, and Georgia were prevented from attending because the governors there didn't call the assemblies into session. New Hampshire declined to send delegates. This congress was an unauthorized assembly and was recognized as such by many members, including its Tory president Timothy Ruggles. It produced a fourteen-point document, The Declaration of Rights and Grievances, to be submitted as an address to the king, a memorial to the lords, and a petition to the Commons, which, for the record, is the correct nomenclature. One of the points contained a veiled threat to boycott importation of luxury goods into America, which lent some urgency in Great Britain toward repeal. Crown, lords, and Commons all refused to hear any words produced by an unconstitutional assembly of colonists, but being practical men, they soon found other reasons to repeal the Stamp Act.

The parliamentary debate on repeal of the Stamp Act commenced in January 1766. Pitt stated that everything done by the Grenville Ministry with respect to the colonies "has been entirely wrong. It is my opinion that this kingdom has no right to lay a tax upon the colonies."

Grenville replied:

> Protection and obedience are reciprocal. Great Britain protects America; America is bound to yield obedience. If, not, tell me when the Americans were emancipated? When they want the protection of this Kingdom, they are always ready to ask for it. That protection has always been afforded them in the most full and ample manner. The nation [Great Britain] has run itself into an immense debt to give them their protection; and now when they are called upon to contribute a small share towards the public expense, an expense arising from themselves, they renounce your authority, insult your officers, and break out, I might also say, into open rebellion.

> Pitt's response to Grenville included, "I rejoice that America has resisted. Three millions of people, so dead to all the feelings of liberty as voluntarily to submit to be slaves, would have been fit instruments to make slaves of the rest."

Death of James Stuart, the Old Pretender, 1766: In the midst of all this, the Old Pretender, James III Stuart, died in Rome, aged seventy-eight. The pope had recognized James as the British king but did not extend that honor to his son Charles. The pope did allow Charles to move into the palace that James III had lived in. Charles wrote to Louis XV and Charles III of Spain, but they didn't recognize his claim either. He gained an interview with Choiseul in 1770, who suggested that the fifty-year-old bachelor stop drinking, get married, and produce an heir if he wanted to show he was serious about regaining his throne. France had given up on him, but the British didn't know that, and maybe if he straightened up, the British might still think he was a threat. Charles found a young princess whom he married in 1772, but they separated in 1780 without ever having any children. Charles died of a stroke in 1788, and his celibate brother, Cardinal York, became the heir.

The death of James Stuart in this year is symbolic in that the biggest source of divisions in Great Britain—between Protestants and Catholics, between English on one hand and Scots and Irishmen on the other—had been removed, and now all of the people of the British Isles became united in the idea that the American colonies were and of right ought to be part of the British Empire.

Parliament doubles down, 1766–1770: Rockingham was dismissed in July 1766 and replaced by Pitt as prime minister, with another man, the Duke of Grafton, appointed as first lord of the Treasury. This was unusual and is the only ministry in British history in which different men served as prime minister and first lord of the Treasury. Rockingham had gone too far in appeasing the Americans. Pitt had posed as a champion of the Americans, but he, or Grafton, allowed his chancellor of the Exchequer, Charles Townshend, to pass legislation to raise revenue in America by more tariffs on more products, including tea. The excuse offered by Pitt's biographers is that he was physically and mentally incapacitated during this time. Well, he shouldn't have accepted office then. More likely is the idea that the British were hoping that the Americans would accept tough love from the man who had removed the French menace from the Americans' midst. It was a bad idea, and the Americans didn't differentiate based on the name of the British politician that was bullying them.

Collection of the revenue from the tea tax was to be administered by a Customs Board based in Boston. They also passed an act to punish New York for not quartering those soldiers in 1766, although New York had relented by now. Townshend stated that the purpose of the revenue was to pay colonial judges and governors, not the Army. The Americans were still paying the tariff on molasses that had been passed years before, but they objected to these new tariffs, which was confusing to the British. Now the Americans were moving the goalposts and saying that there was no difference between a direct tax and a tariff. The revenue to be raised was £40,000 a year, but Townshend intended to gradually expand it until the Americans were paying their

THE GREAT GLOBE ITSELF

own way. The laws were passed in June and July of 1767. Townshend died suddenly soon after from a fever in September 1767, aged only forty-two. He was replaced as chancellor of the Exchequer by Lord North. In February 1768, Grafton created the new cabinet position of secretary of state for the colonies, to administer the Townshend Acts in North America. The secretary was the Earl of Hillsborough, who later had a county in Florida, among other places, named after him.

General Thomas Gage had been in North America since 1755 and had been commander in chief of British forces since October 1763, with his headquarters in and around New York City (possibly including West Point), although he had responsibility for all of North America, including Canada. We can assume that the force he commanded had reached the ten-thousand-man level and was deployed in areas along the Spanish frontier as well as where settlers along the Proclamation Line might come into contact with Indians.

In 1768, Boston became the center of unrest because that Customs Board was headquartered there. At the board's request, HMS *Romney* was dispatched and arrived in Boston in May. In June, John Hancock was prosecuted for smuggling, in a sensational trial. John Adams defended him. The case was eventually dropped. The governor of Massachusetts, Francis Bernard, recommended to Hillsborough that troops be brought to Boston, and in September, Gage ordered four regiments (later reduced to two) of British troops there, and they established a camp on Boston Common. This show of strength was duly effective in stifling dissent in Boston. Pitt resigned in October 1768, citing his poor health. Maybe he just now was finding out what was happening in America. He was replaced by Grafton, who was already running the government for the impaired Pitt. The Massachusetts Assembly formally requested Bernard's recall, and he left Boston on August 1, 1769, to much celebration. His successor, Thomas Hutchinson, would be just as hard-line. Throughout the American colonies, resistance through boycotts of British goods was organized, although results were mixed, and the boycotts had petered out by the end of 1770.

The Duke of Grafton resigned as prime minister in 1770. France had invaded Corsica the year before, and his response had been weak, as described below. George III had run through six prime ministers in ten years, and now his seventh was Lord Frederick North, his rumored half-brother. The king finally found a man he could work with, and North lasted until 1782. North was tested early on by Choiseul, who incited Spain to seize the Falkland Islands, and North responded by mobilizing the Fleet. Louis XV told Spain to stand down and replaced Choiseul with Rene Maupeou, a career legal expert with the title of chancellor of France, who spent his time attempting to reduce the power of the parlements, as they were the chief obstacle to financial reform.

The presence of two thousand British troops in Boston was a constant source of friction that erupted in the Boston Massacre on March 5, 1770, resulting in the death of several colonists. Samuel Adams and others used the incident for their propaganda machine, and it was effective in raising colonial sentiment against the British all up and down the coast. Massacre Day was solemnly commemorated in Massachusetts from 1771 to 1783. Parliament soon repealed all the Townshend Acts except for the tariff on tea. I don't know if the tariff on molasses was repealed at this time or not. I suspect that the Customs Board remained on duty in Boston to collect the tariff on tea at least, since the British troops remained. People were shocked by the violence in Boston, and nothing much happened in 1771.

Somerset's case, 1772: Now in America and Great Britain, we play the race card by changing the subject from tariffs to slavery. This makes it a preview of what later happened in the United States during the Nullification Crisis in the 1820s. The shift in focus was accomplished in London by Lord Chief Justice William Murray, Earl Mansfield, presiding over Somerset's case in 1772. James Somerset was a slave owned by an American named Charles Stewart (an interesting coincidence that he had the same name as the Stuart pretender to the throne), who brought Somerset with him to Great Britain when he went there on business. Somerset attempted to escape. He was recovered and detained on board a ship. The ship was headed to Jamaica, where Stewart intended to sell Somerset. The people that Somerset had sought refuge with claimed to be his godparents and filed a writ of habeas corpus, and so a trial ensued as to whether Somerset's imprisonment was legal. The case gathered a lot of public

THE GREAT GLOBE ITSELF

interest. If the American public was being brainwashed over taxes and the Boston Massacre, then the British public was being brainwashed about the evils of American slavery.

In June 1772, Mansfield judged that a master could not carry his slave out of England or Wales by force and ordered Somerset freed. Some say that ten thousand slaves were freed in England and Wales (where Mansfield had jurisdiction) because of his decision. Others say there were not near that many slaves in England and Wales at the time. Whatever the actual consequences of Mansfield's decision were, the perception that came to George Washington and all the other American slaveholders was that George III was coming for their slaves. The ruling had a positive effect on unifying British attitudes toward Americans, but it also had the unintended effect of giving Southern slaveholders and New England merchants a common cause. Technically, slavery was still legal all over the world, as it had been since the dawn of time, but here we have the birth of the immorality of slavery, concocted by the British to garner public support against their rebellious colonists in America.

I first found out about this case when reading about the life of Julius Caesar and his heir, Octavian. The story goes that after Caesar's assassination, his father-in-law, Piso, who was executor of Caesar's estate, rejected the advice of Mark Antony to stall giving Octavian his inheritance. He said, "Let justice be done, though the heavens fall!" Mansfield used this quote when he handed down his verdict in Somerset's case.

The idea of freeing slaves was horrifying to white Americans of all regions, not just the South. Here is a typical opinion of a pre-Civil War American politician Peter Hardeman Burnett (I didn't pick him because of the similarity of his name to mine), the first governor of California, 1849–1851:

> For some years past I have given [slavery] my most serious and candid attention; and I most cheerfully lay before you the result of my own reflections. There is, in my opinion, but one of two consistent courses to take in reference to

this class of population; either to admit [Blacks] to the full and free enjoyment of all the privileges guaranteed by the Constitution to others or exclude them from the State. If we permit them to settle in our State, under existing circumstances, we consign them, by our own institutions, and the usages of our own society, to a subordinate and degraded position, which is in itself but a species of slavery. They would be placed in a situation where they would have no efficient motives for moral or intellectual improvement, but must remain in our midst, sensible of their degradation, unhappy themselves, enemies to the institutions and the society whose usages have placed them there, and forever fit teachers in all the schools of ignorance, vice, and idleness.

The Boston Tea Party and other aggravations, 1773–1774: Conditions in India now had an impact on British-American relations. There had been intermittent drought and famine in Bengal from 1769 to 1773 that had cut into the revenues of the East India Company. A huge surplus of tea had built up in London. Lord North came up with what he thought was an ingenious scheme to sell the tea to the Americans at a discount but with a tariff on it. The tea

would still be cheap even with the tariff, and Parliament would still assert the right to assess tariffs on the Americans. The East India Company would make a lot of money. This scheme was embodied in the Tea Act of 1773. In theory, everybody won. Ships filled with tea were dispatched to Boston, New York, Philadelphia, and Charleston. The agents in every city but Boston were not allowed to take possession of the tea, and it was either held at Customs or returned to London. Governor Hutchison held the line and the tea ships pulled into Boston Harbor. On December 16, a company-sized group of men, disguised as a Mohawk War Party boarded the ships and threw the tea into the water.

After the Tea Party, Parliament passed what they called the Coercive Acts and what the Americans called the Intolerable Acts. Lord North said:

> The Americans have tarred and feathered your subjects, plundered your merchants, burnt your ships, denied all obedience to your laws and authority; yet so clement and so long forbearing has our conduct been that it is incumbent on us now to take a different course. Whatever may be the consequences, we must risk something; if we do not, all is over.

The Coercive Acts were:

- The Boston Port Act closed the port of Boston until the tea was paid for and order restored.
- The Massachusetts Government Act made almost all government positions subject to appointment by the royal governor and limited town meetings to one per year, unless the governor called one.
- The Administration of Justice Act allowed for trials of royal officials to be held in Great Britain. This was in response to the trials of the soldiers involved with the Boston Massacre, who had been tried in America.
- A new Quartering Act was passed, and it applied to all the colonies. It appeared to be the same as the previous act.
- The Quebec Act annexed the land between the Great Lakes and the Ohio River to Quebec.

- Massachusetts governor Thomas Hutchinson was replaced by General Thomas Gage, who kept his job as commander in chief in British North America
- Land grants to veterans of the French and Indian Wars were restricted to British regulars only, depriving American veterans of their due.

All of these coercive measures had the effect of unifying the colonists. Positions on both sides had hardened to the point where the Coercive Acts were as popular in Great Britain as they were loathed in America. In America, committees of correspondence had been active in several colonies since 1764 to oppose this or that measure. By May 1774, all thirteen colonies had them. It was a vast network of about eight thousand people who coordinated activities and were led by the best men in each state. The committees were instrumental in organizing the First Continental Congress.

George Washington was one of the seven Virginia delegates elected to the First Continental Congress. At the same time, the House of Burgesses convened in Williamsburg in defiance of the governor's order, calling itself the Virginia Convention.

On September 5, the First Continental Congress convened in Philadelphia. Georgia, considered a convict colony, did not send representatives. Fifty-six delegates from twelve colonies met at Carpenter Hall, which is not to be confused with Tun Tavern, birthplace of the US Marine Corps, although the Carpenter family built both. Peyton Randolph of Virginia presided. His son Edmund would be Washington's first attorney general. Organizing an Army was on the agenda, and Washington was sized up as a potential commander-in-chief. He was, after all, the most prominent *American-born* veteran of the French and Indian War. His status as a native-born American won him the loyalty that evaded British-born generals like Horatio Gates and Charles Lee, who might have been better soldiers, but they could always flee the country if the situation deteriorated. Washington was born and raised in America. His home and his life were there. His only option was to serve America, and that is what

THE GREAT GLOBE ITSELF

secured the loyalty of his Army no matter how bad his record on the battlefield was, and it was pretty bad.

While the First Continental Congress convened, the rebels in the state of Massachusetts set up a rival government styled the Massachusetts Provincial Congress, which, among other things, began organizing an Army under the command of militia major general Artemas Ward. Militia brigadier general Israel Putnam was the field commander. They controlled the entire state except for the city of Boston and began stockpiling munitions and other supplies. General Gage concentrated all of his naval and land forces in Boston. In February 1775, Parliament declared the colony to be in open rebellion, setting the stage for Lexington and Concord two months later. The Massachusetts Provincial Congress lasted until 1780.

The First Continental Congress ended on October 26, 1774, having drafted an address to the king, which was ignored. They may also have sent it to the lords as a memorial and to the Commons as a petition. They agreed to boycott British goods starting December 1, 1774, which duly went into effect on that date. It was relatively successful, although it had only been in effect for five months by the time the war began. They further agreed to reconvene in May 1775 to react to whatever the British response was. By that time, the war had started.

The Industrial Revolution in Great Britain

In 1712, Thomas Newcomen built the first engine that used steam to drive a piston inside a cylinder, thereby converting heat energy to mechanical energy. His work was the result of combining the ideas of predecessors who had experimented with using steam to drive pumps. Newcomen lived in Dartmouth, Devonshire, where there were deep mines that needed to have the water removed, and Newcomen's engines drove the pumps that did so. In 1769, James Watt, thirty-three that year, was granted a patent for a steam engine that was a great improvement over the Newcomen engine. The improvement was related to conserving the heat in the piston so that the piston didn't have to be reheated on every stroke. That saved a lot of fuel. He was also able to borrow the technology used in making cannon to increase the pressure inside the piston so that more work could be done with the engine. Watt's business was based in a town in Scotland called Borrowstounness, which is about seventeen miles north of Edinburgh.

In Birmingham in 1766, Matthew Boulton built a manufactory that produced a wide range of products such as buttons, buckles, and boxes as well as luxury items made from silver. Boulton needed more power than was provided by the millstream and was soon in contact with Watt to install an engine at the manufactory in Birmingham. Boulton and Watt then went into business manufacturing the engines, building 450 engines between 1775 and 1800, when their patent expired. The firm of Boulton and Watt continued to prosper under their descendants, including the sale of a steam engine to Robert Fulton in 1807 that he used to construct the first working steamboat on the Hudson River. The Boulton and Watt engine had a million and one uses, including pumping water out of mines, running flywheels at textile plants, and turning grindstones at flourmills. Any work that was done by waterwheels and horses or slaves could now be done by a steam engine, so it's not a coincidence that slavery came to be seen as immoral at the same time that the machines were being developed.

In order to measure the increase in efficiency, Watt developed the concept of horsepower. After some experiments, he determined that a horse could lift 550 pounds one foot per second, so 1 horsepower is 33,000-foot-pounds per minute. The efficiency was measured by calculating how much coal was burned to produce horsepower. Boulton and Watt made their money by claiming a portion of the savings achieved by switching to their engines. With the development of the metric system, the watt was developed, and 1 horsepower equals 746 watts.

In 1771, Richard Arkwright developed a cotton mill in Cromford, Derby, which is between Birmingham and Manchester. The mill combined water frames, pumps, and unskilled labor in one building in a system to produce cotton thread on a scale never before seen. Arkwright's system used steam engines to pump water into elevated storage tanks as the power source for the water frames. One of the innovations of the mill was regular working hours. The ordering of people's lives by the clock rather than the sun was a major shift in human existence, living to a mechanical rather than a celestial rhythm.

Watt's partner in Scotland before he moved to Birmingham to join forces with Boulton was a man named John Roebuck, who developed a process for manufacturing sulfuric acid, which, like the steam engine, had a million and one uses, including maintenance of the machines and dying clothing. Roebuck made some bad business decisions which prevented him from backing Watt financially, but his contributions to the Industrial Revolution were as vital as those of Watt, Boulton, and Arkwright.

The Industrial Revolution was confined to Western England for a long time before it gradually spread out across the British Isles and then Western Europe. An Englishman named William Cockerill moved to Liege, Belgium, in 1802 and established a factory that manufactured machines that made cloth out of wool. He became a French citizen and was awarded the Legion of Honor. He retired in 1813, probably because he had supported Napoleon, and turned the business over to his sons. The Cockerills were instrumental in the spread of industrialization in Europe during the first half of the nineteenth century.

France, 1764 to 1774

The last years of Louis XV: In 1764, Louis XV was fifty-four. He and his queen, Marie Leszczynska, had ten children between 1727 and 1737 but grew apart after that. He also fathered numerous children with his many mistresses. He had met Jeanne Antoinette Poisson, a.k.a. Madame Pompadour, in 1745. Their romantic relationship ended in 1750, but she was an influential adviser until her death at the age of forty-two in 1764. She had picked Choiseul in 1758, supported the Physiocrats, was a great friend to Voltaire, encouraged the publication of the *Encyclopedia*, and was a general patron of the arts.

After Madame Pompadour's death, further tragedy ensued in 1765 when Louis XV's son Louis the Dauphin died of tuberculosis in December 1765. His wife, Maria Josepha the Dauphine, died in March 1767. Louis' father-in-law, former king of Poland Stanislas Leszczynski, died in February 1766, and Louis's Queen Marie died in June 1768. The Dauphin and Dauphine had left five children behind, three boys and two girls. The sons all served as kings of France between 1774 and 1830, taking a break from 1793 to 1815. It was a rough five years for Louis.

In 1769, Louis roused himself from his *ennui* and took up with twenty-six-year-old Madame Jeanne du Barry. The next year, Marie Antoinette arrived from Vienna and married the Dauphin Louis, the future Louis XVI. The marriage had been negotiated by Choiseul. Marie Antoinette and Choiseul both disliked du Barry, but he was dismissed in 1770 because of the Falklands crisis, as described below. Marie Antoinette refused to speak to du Barry until 1772, and then only grudgingly. Du Barry had nowhere near the influence that Pompadour did, but she provided comfort and diversion for him. Louis said that she was the only woman in France who could make him forget that he was in his sixties. Du Barry was ejected from Versailles two days after the death of Louis. She lived quietly until she was arrested in 1793, at the start of the Terror, and was guillotined seven weeks after Marie Antoinette. Louis died at Versailles of smallpox in May 1774, having been king for fifty-nine years. It was Madame Pompadour, not him, who said, "After us, the deluge" in 1757.

Corsica and Lorraine: Corsica had been part of the Republic of Genoa since 1284, but in 1755, Pasquale Paoli proclaimed Corsica to be independent and a republic. Paoli was supported by the British, who hoped to extend their naval footprint east from Gibraltar and Minorca to Corsica. Genoa contested the independence of Corsica until 1767, when France negotiated a secret treaty with Genoa to purchase it. Choiseul knew the British were backing Paoli and had no intention of letting the Royal Navy set up shop in Corsica. Besides, it was an important element in France regaining some confidence after losing their possessions in America and India. In 1768, France made

THE GREAT GLOBE ITSELF

the treaty with Genoa public and sent an expedition to conquer Corsica. The French invasion caused a crisis in British politics, with Grafton losing his job as prime minister to Lord North. Paoli's forces were defeated in 1769, and he fled to Great Britain. where he became one of George III's poodles. He was welcomed into the literary circle that had the unimaginative name of "The Club" of Edmund Burke, Samuel Johnson, James Boswell, and other luminaries of the day. Paoli had a pretty good life in London but returned to Corsica in 1790 to work to tear it away from France, but as we shall see, the British would betray him, attempting to claim Corsica as a crown land of George III with the same status as Ireland. The Bonapartes opposed Paoli, and he ejected them in 1793. Paoli declared himself against the regicides, and he aligned himself firmly with the British until France finally established control in 1795. He died in London in 1807.

France also acquired Lorraine in 1766. The story of how that came to be is a great illustration of the complexities of eighteenth-century diplomacy. In 1704, Charles XII of Sweden invaded Poland and placed Stanislas Leszczynski on the Polish throne. Augustus II, the previous king, got some help from Russian emperor Peter I the Great, who, in 1709, defeated Charles XII and deposed Stanislas. Stanislas moved to Wissembourg in Alsace after the death of Charles XII in 1719. In 1725, Stanislas's daughter Marie married King Louis XV, and she became queen of France. In 1733, Augustus II died, and Stanislas was once again elected king of Poland with the support of France and Sweden. The Russians and Austrians protested, and the War of the Polish Succession ensued. The Russians and Austrians prevailed in the struggle, putting Augustus III, son of Augustus II, on the Polish throne, and Stanislas was forced to abdicate again in January 1736, returning to Alsace.

Meanwhile, the daughter of the Holy Roman emperor Charles VI, Maria Theresa, needed a husband. Charles VI had no sons, and he had spent his career arranging for Maria Theresa to succeed him. Her husband needed to be an extraordinary person, and Francis, the Duke of Lorraine, was the preferred candidate. France and Louis XV could not abide the husband of the future empress to be the Duke of Lorraine, as its adjacency to France represented a clear and present danger. The solution was that Francis exchanged Lorraine for Tuscany. Tuscany was ruled at the time by Gian Gaston de Medici, who was childless. He had an heir (a nephew) but was forced by the Habsburgs to agree to this arrangement. Lorraine was given to Stanislas, and he was to rule it until his death, after which Lorraine would revert to France. Stanislas died in 1766. This was all agreed to in the 1738 Treaty of Vienna, which, for the record, was the last treaty written in Latin, because the official language used between Austria and their most important ally, Hungary, was Latin.

The Falklands crisis, 1770: As mentioned above, Choiseul was dismissed in 1770 because of a crisis in the Falklands. Spain and Great Britain both claimed that their explorers had discovered the Falkland Islands first, and it was a long-standing but low-priority bone of contention between them. Choiseul sent an expedition there in 1764 to plant a colony of Acadians, claiming he had nothing to do with it, as it was the act of a private individual (that he had put up to it). In 1765, the British founded their own colony on the islands. When Spain found out about the French colony, they made France turn it over to them, which occurred in 1767. Spain then found out about the British colony and, in June 1770, sent a flotilla to the Falklands and kicked them out. Great Britain was enraged, and Lord North and George III, perceiving this to be a test of North's resolve, mobilized the Fleet. Choiseul was ready to back Spain all the way, but Louis was not. He told his cousin Charles III of Spain that, "My minister wishes for war, but I do not." Charles III then allowed the British colony to be restored, although it was abandoned in 1774 anyway, as the British were preparing to fight the Americans. The islands had no permanent population until 1845 when the British established Port Stanley.

Struggle with the parlements: Choiseul's successor was René Nicolas de Maupeou. He spent his time as first minister challenging the power of the parlements, judicial organizations that were the courts of final appeal of the judicial system, and typically wielded power over a wide range of subjects, particularly taxation. Laws and edicts issued by the crown were not official in their respective jurisdictions until the parlements gave their assent by publishing them. The parlements were the stronghold of the nobles of the robe, the bourgeoisie who got rich practicing the law and then bought their judgeships, which came with titles of nobility and also robes. They had been thwarting the efforts of the king and his ministers to balance the budget in the name of fighting despotism. De Maupeou was successful in reducing their powers and was reforming the parlements to be more malleable to the royal will when Louis XV died in 1774. Louis XVI didn't want to be called a despot, so he reinstated the powers of the parlements, an error of which can be said was his first step on the road to the guillotine. He dismissed de Maupeou and brought in the Physiocrat Jacques Turgot as finance minister and the Comte de Vergennes as foreign minister. One of de Maupeou's protégés was Charles Francis Lebrun, who, in 1799, became third consul of France, in charge of all things monetary and fiscal for all the days of the consulate and the empire.

Central Europe, 1764–1774

Austria and Maria Theresa, 1764–1774: Empress Maria Theresa had spent the years from 1737 to 1763 pregnant and at war. She had failed to recover Silesia from Prussia, but she did manage to bring ten of her sixteen children to adulthood, and her son Leopold managed to match her in the offspring department, fathering sixteen children himself, from 1767 to 1788. In the 1760s, she faced a wave of deaths in the family like Louis XV had. Smallpox killed her son Charles and her daughter Johanna in 1762. Her oldest son, Joseph II, lost both his wives to the disease in 1763 and 1767. Her husband,

Francis I, died suddenly in August 1765, fifty-six-years-old, and was succeeded by Joseph, though Maria Theresa continued to rule. She herself got smallpox in 1767, coming close enough to death that she was given the last rites, but she recovered. Her daughter Josepha died of it in 1767, a few months after Maria Theresa's recovery. In 1768, her daughter Elizabeth got smallpox, and although she recovered, her face was disfigured to the point where she was unmarriageable, which was a shame because she was all set to marry Louis XV at the same time that her sister Marie Antoinette was to marry Louis XVI.

Austria and France were still allies, but it was more of a default than a true alliance. Neither country wanted anything to do with Great Britain after the Seven Years' War, and Prussia and Russia had formed their own alliance. Austria and France blamed each other for the failure to snuff out Prussia in the Seven Years' War. France had lost most of America and India, and Austria had lost Silesia and their position as the leading German state. As we recall, the Austrian chancellor Wenzel von Kaunitz, having engineered the reversal of alliances in 1756, based his whole career and reputation on the French-Austrian alliance, and he advised staying with it. Von Kaunitz also advised Joseph to reconcile with Frederick, and the two rulers met in 1769 and 1770, laying the groundwork for the First Partition of Poland in 1772. Maria Theresa supposedly objected to the partition as she considered it a betrayal of the king of Poland but went along with it for reasons of state, causing Frederick to remark, "She cries, but she takes."

Prussia and Frederick II, 1764–1774: Prussia was in an extremely weakened state at the end of the Seven Years' War. Frederick II, who was always at war but whose wife was never pregnant, would never forget or forgive that George III had pulled the plug on subsidies to Prussia in 1762, at a time when it was convenient for Great Britain but very inconvenient for Prussia to end the war. It was only by the miraculous death of Russian empress Elizabeth that he and Prussia still existed. He vowed he would never again have Great Britain as an ally, and he kept that vow the rest of his life. Catherine II and her ministers were soon in touch, and they had some ideas about an alliance to shore up their borders with Poland. The Russian-Prussian

THE GREAT GLOBE ITSELF

alliance was called the Northern System, and it would last until 1788, although it was more of a formality after 1780, when Maria Theresa died, and Catherine saw an opportunity to team up with Joseph II against the Ottomans.

Frederick was fifty-two years old in 1764. He had no children, and his heir was his nephew Frederick William II, who was twenty in 1764, so a bride was found for him. In 1765, Frederick William was married to Elizabeth Christine, not to be confused with the Elizabeth Christine that was Frederick's queen. They had a daughter in 1767, who was, one day, to marry the second son of George III, Frederick Duke of York. Frederick William was what would be called today a sex addict and was of the opinion that as long as he kept impregnating his wife, he was free to engage in one-night revelries with dancers and actresses. Elizabeth Christine disagreed and was enraged by his behavior, as he did little to hide it. She began acting, out of spite, like a sex addict herself, engaging in sexual encounters with various guards and court musicians. This all became known to Frederick, and he, of course, was concerned that the legitimacy of his heirs might be questioned. When Elizabeth Christine was impregnated by and attempted to flee with one of her lovers, a court musician named Pietro, Frederick had to act. The baby was aborted, Pietro was beheaded, the marriage between Frederick William and Elizabeth Christine was annulled, and Elizabeth Christine was imprisoned. She was later released from prison and sent to a nunnery, then given more freedom as time went on and memories faded. She died in 1840 at the age of ninety-three.

Frederick William then married another princess, Frederica Louise of Hesse-Darmstadt, and they had four sons and three daughters. His second marriage did not settle him down any more than the first one did, and although he did his job in the legitimate offspring department, he often failed to do his job as crown prince, and he spent all of his spare time drinking and carousing with a series of mistresses. Frederick was aggravated by this debauchery and sloth and would often say that he wished he could give the throne to his other nephew, the Duke of Brunswick, who was the son of his sister

Philippa. Frederick gave the crown prince no important duties during his reign.

Catherine II and Russia, 1764–1774: In 1764, Russia and Prussia signed the alliance which they called the Northern System, as described above. Russia proposed including Great Britain, but Frederick II was having none of that. One of the first projects of

the Northern System was to engineer the election of Stanislas Poniatowski as king of Poland in 1764. His pro-Russian policies led to the formation of the anti-Russian Bar Confederation, an alliance of Polish nobles which struggled against King Stanislas and the Russians starting in 1768. A young Charles Dumouriez, who became a famous commander in 1792, was sent from France to organize and lead the forces of the Bar Confederation, but the rebellion was crushed by 1772. France and Austria were sympathetic to the Polish rebels but could do nothing unless they wanted to start another round of the Seven Years' War.

The Ottomans were drawn into the conflict on Poland's side when Polish rebels fled into Moldavia, Taurica, and Crimea. This led to the Russo-Ottoman War of 1768–1774. Russia had been preparing for this war since 1764 when they established the *Novorossiya* or New Russia governate in the sparsely settled land between southern Russia and Crimea. Russia had crushed the Ottomans by 1772 as well, but peace talks broke down when Russia demanded Crimea. The Ottomans broke off the peace talks, so Russia conducted one more successful offensive under Suvorov in 1774, after which the Ottomans had to agree to Crimean independence. The whole process seems very similar to the way Mexico had to agree to Texas independence in 1836. Russia annexed Crimea in 1783. The Ottomans also agreed to grant Russia the position of protector of all Orthodox Christians in the Ottoman Empire, which theoretically meant they could land troops anywhere the Christians of the Ottoman Empire

THE GREAT GLOBE ITSELF

made a complaint. This started coming up in the 1820s during the Greek Revolution.

Since 1762, Catherine II had acted more like a reigning monarch than a regent for her son, which was allowed because in Russia, there was no law on the subject of who should be emperor other than what was in the will of the current Russian sovereign and because Catherine was successful. Her official position was unclear—regent or regnant—but none of that would matter until 1772, when Paul I turned eighteen. Since people love a winner, they were already calling her Catherine the Great. Paul suggested corule, the same as the situation in Austria between Maria Theresa and Joseph II. Panin and Gregor Orlov put Paul off by arranging his marriage to Wilhelmina Louise of Hesse-Darmstadt, the sister-in-law of Crown Prince Frederick William II. Paul may have thought, or even been told, that he would certainly reign once he had established a family. The marriage took place in 1773.

In 1774, Gregor Orlov began losing influence to Gregor Potemkin, a hero of the Russian-Ottoman War. Orlov went to live abroad for the next ten years. He may have been given an ambassadorship, or he may have just been told to make himself scarce. Russia had a breathing spell from shooting wars between 1774 and 1787 and used the time to do some assimilating, in Poland and in the Crimea, and probably in some parts of Finland, as they were still tangling with the Swedes in those days. They started developing the fur trade in the east and improving relations with Japan. Russia reorganized the Polish and (nominally independent) Crimean areas into several districts.

One other interesting event in Russia during this period was Pugachev's Rebellion. Pugachev was a Cossack soldier who, in 1773, claimed to be Catherine II's husband, Peter III. He attracted a large following in the Volga River region (near Stalingrad) and had success for about a year before he was defeated in battle, taken to Moscow, and beheaded. His support was the same people who considered Catherine to be a usurper.

First Partition of Poland, 1772: As soon as it was apparent that the Russians had crushed the Bar Confederation, an agreement was made between Russia, Prussia, and Austria that the best thing to do in the interests of peace was for them to annex the pieces of Poland that were on their borders and bring order to them. What remained of Poland would be more manageable for the Polish Kingdom, or so they reasoned. The forces of the Bar Confederation were located in the areas that were now, in 1772, annexed by Austria, Prussia, and Russia. France was Austria's ally, so they couldn't do anything to help Poland, and Great Britain was dealing with their own rebels in America. Poland was forced to sign a treaty agreeing to the cession of their territories in September 1773. Peace reigned in Central Europe.

The Jews of Central Europe, 1764–1774: Because of the First Partition of Poland, the great powers of Austria, Prussia, and Russia, for the first time, incorporated large numbers of Jews into their countries. Jews had lived in Poland since before the Crusades. Jews that were expelled from Spain, Portugal, and other parts of Europe found refuge in Poland, and by 1550, 80 percent of the world's Jews lived there. Most of the rest lived in the Ottoman Empire. There were some in the Rhineland.

Judaism was practically nonexistent in Russia until 1772. When Catherine agreed to the First Partition of Poland, Jews were, at first, treated as a separate people, defined by their religion (including their dietary laws) and their language (Yiddish). In keeping with their treatment by the Polish government, Catherine allowed the Jews to separate themselves from Christian society, for a cost. She levied twice as much tax on them but exempted them from military service. If a family converted to the Orthodox faith, the tax burden was decreased, but liability for service was added. I suppose that if a Jew wanted to volunteer for the Army, most recruiters would overlook his religion, as was happening at the same period in Great Britain whenever a Catholic joined up. Since Russia had plenty of men to serve, the Jews could stay in their shtetlach and farm the land. Someone needed to grow food. In addition, converted Jews could gain permission to enter the merchant class and farm as free peasants under Russian rule. Polish and Ukrainian Catholics suffered no disabilities compared to the Orthodox regarding taxes or military service.

THE GREAT GLOBE ITSELF

In an attempt to assimilate Jews into Russia's economy, Catherine II included them under the rights and laws of the Charter of the Towns of 1782. This was in keeping with the spirit of the times, where Frederick II of Prussia, Joseph II of Austria, and Charles III of Spain were also operating as enlightened despots. The experiment failed in Russia because the Jews had as little interest in assimilating into Russia as the Orthodox Russians had in including Jews into their country. In 1785, only three years after the Charter of Towns, Catherine II declared that Jews were officially foreigners, with foreigners' rights. If they spoke a different language and worshipped another God, then they were certainly strangers in the land. As Russia expanded, restrictions on where Jews could live were increased. The Pale of Settlement was established in 1791, with the boundaries and rules changing over the years as circumstances dictated, although the laws related to the Pale of Settlement did not start referencing Jews until 1835.

Austria's portion of the First Partition of Poland was called Galicia, and it became a Habsburg crown land. Maria Theresa had opposed the partition, and one of the reasons was that she didn't like non-Catholics in her realms, regarding them as dangerous. Her policy was to attempt to convert the Protestants, but she considered the Jews to be beyond redemption. After her death, Joseph II issued Edicts of Tolerance for Protestants in 1781 and Jews in 1782. The one for the Jews read, "This policy paper aims at making the Jewish population useful to the state." This was part of his general campaign of assimilation of all non-German-speaking and non-Catholic subjects that drew a lot of negative reaction across the realm, because his subjects, including the Jews, were attached to their local ways and didn't want to be assimilated. Joseph and his successor, Leopold, soon had to rescind most of these reforms.

Prussia's acquisition at the First Partition was called West Prussia and was good for them because it connected the Prussian territories of Eastern Pomerania and East Prussia. A major deficiency from the Prussian point of view was that they did not acquire the port city of Danzig. Frederick II considered West Prussia to be a barren land of sand, pine forests, and Jews, although the number of the latter was small compared to Austria. He considered the inhabitants to be as backward as

American Indians and looked forward to colonizing it in the same manner the Americans were colonizing the Ohio Country. Prussia already had strict regulations regarding the status of Jews in effect, and this policy did not change. The policy was that there was a small number of families that had privileged or protected status, presumably because they were useful to the state as doctors, merchants, or financiers. The rest needed to keep their heads down and hope to join the ranks of the privileged somehow or immigrate into what was left of Poland.

1775–1777: Potemkin and the Greek Project

The American Revolution, 1775–1777

Massachusetts: In March 1775, Patrick Henry delivered his "give me liberty or give me death" speech (not to be confused with his "if this be treason, make the most of it" speech ten years before) at the Second Virginia Convention in Richmond. The convention also elected delegates to the Second Continental Congress and authorized the raising of volunteer militias. The liberty-or-death line came from Joseph Addison's 1713 play *Cato, a Tragedy*, which was frequently quoted by Americans during the war. Washington would stage productions of it in Continental Army camps. Patrick Henry was governor of Virginia from 1776 to 1779, and again from 1784 to 1786, but he faded from the spotlight because he was a true states' rights

THE GREAT GLOBE ITSELF

advocate, interested only in Virginia and opposing the Constitution. He died in 1799, about six months before George Washington, sixty-three years old.

In April, British troops sallied from Boston to find and destroy military stores that the militias, under the leadership of General Artemis Ward and the direction of the rebel Massachusetts Provincial Congress, were accumulating in Concord. They were met by American militia at Lexington and Concord. The war was on. In 1836, Ralph Waldo Emerson wrote *Concord Hymn*, which begins:

> By the rude bridge that arched the flood
> Their flags to April's breeze unfurled
> Here the beleaguered farmers stood
> And fired the shot heard round the world.

In 1861, Henry Wadsworth Longfellow wrote *Paul Revere's Ride*, which begins:

> Listen, my children, and you shall hear
> Of the midnight ride of Paul Revere,
> On the eighteenth of April, in Seventy-five,
> Hardly a man is now alive
> Who remembers that famous day and year.

Revere was a silversmith, good at metalworking but bad at soldiering, and went back to his business after the war. He died in 1818 at the age of eighty-four.

Having accomplished their mission, the British returned to Boston. On May 25, 1775, HMS *Cerberus* arrived in Boston with Generals William Howe, Henry Clinton, and John Burgoyne aboard. The American press made much of the three-headed-dog imagery. The Americans pursued the British to Boston and started a siege. When the Continental Congress came into session on May 10, General Ward called on it to take charge of the war. On June 14, 1775, the Continental Congress appointed George Washington as commander in chief, along with four major generals and eight brigadier generals. The Massachusetts militias had, by now, been joined by their comrades from Connecticut, New Hampshire, and Rhode Island. There were also militias in New York under the command of Philip Schuyler (he was one of the newly appointed major generals). These forces constituted the new Continental Army. Washington departed Philadelphia to take charge of the siege of Boston and authorized Schuyler to send an expedition up the Hudson Valley to acquire the cannon at Fort Ticonderoga and bring them back to Boston. Schuyler sent Ethan Allen and Benedict Arnold up the Hudson in May. As we recall, this fort had been very strategic in defending the Hudson Valley from French and Indian attacks from Quebec.

John Hancock was elected president of Congress, which office he held until October 1777. He had previously been president of the Massachusetts Provincial Congress. After he famously signed the Declaration of Independence, his name became a byword for "signature." Hancock was a wealthy aristocrat who went into politics, but he wanted to be president and needed some military laurels. He left Congress and tried his hand at military operations, resulting in a fiasco in Rhode Island in 1778. He was then in elected office continually, mostly the governorship, even as his health started declining in 1785, and he died in 1793, aged fifty-six. He just happened to be in Congress rather than serving as governor in 1786, the year of Shays' Rebellion, and I am not sure whether that was just luck or if he knew something was going to happen and got out of town. His detractors said he was only prominent because of his inherited wealth, and I can't find anything wrong with that assessment.

On June 17, while Washington was en route to Boston, American general Israel Putnam ordered the occupation of Breed's Hill. The British decided not to give them that advantage, so Gage sent Clinton to attack it. The Americans then withdrew to Bunker Hill, and so the battle came to be inaccurately known as the Battle of Bunker Hill. The British took hundreds of casualties, which to them was shocking. Clinton had read his Plutarch and described it as a Pyrrhic victory. General Putnam may or may not have told his troops not to fire "until you see the white of their eyes," a phrase made famous by Frederick II during the Seven Years' War. Both sides refrained from any further actions, and a phony war ensued. Neither side had any problem getting resupplied, but the militias, unused to the quotidian life of the soldier, were getting bored, winter was coming, and their enlistments were expiring. The British reorganized by sacking Gage and replacing him with Howe in the American colonies and with General Guy Carleton in Montreal, American propagandists accused Howe of spending his time in Boston gambling and committing adultery with loyalist wives, which, in general, is not part of the quotidian life of the soldier.

Washington arrived in Boston on July 2. He wanted to attack but was advised, possibly by Charles Lee, that it would be suicidal, as the soldiers were not adequately trained or supplied. Lee was a former British officer who had owned a Virginia plantation but only since 1773. If the term *carpetbagger* had been around in 1776, Lee would have been called one. Some say he was truly sympathetic to America, while others say he was an ambitious mercenary. He was soon a rival to Washington. He had moved to Virginia at the suggestion of Horatio Gates, who was another 1773 carpetbagging British Virginia plantation owner and rival of Washington's. As we recall, one of the Coercive Acts of 1773 was to deprive American veterans of the French and Indian War of land grants in preference to British regulars, and it may be that Gates and Lee took advantage of this, which would have contributed to resentment against them from American colonists. Lee, Gates, and Washington had served together in the Braddock Expedition of 1755.

Washington considered attacking the British in Boston because he was concerned that the Army would disintegrate, and here he found his gift, which was keeping the Army together. No doubt he began staging productions of Addison's *Cato*. In January 1776, the cannon from Ticonderoga started arriving, and it began firing at British targets in the city. In March, General Howe ordered Boston evacuated, and the British Army relocated to Halifax, Nova Scotia. A lot of the loyalists who would plague the farmers of Shays' Rebellion in 1786 departed with him. There in Halifax, Howe plotted with his brother Richard, who was an admiral, to occupy New York in the summer of 1776. British and Hessian troops began arriving in Halifax, and soon there were twenty-six thousand of them. Washington had another gift: spy craft. He found out about their plans and sent General Lee to New York to organize the defenses.

The Continental Navy: While waiting for the guns from Ticonderoga, the Americans attempted to cut off British resupply by sea by creating a Navy. That is not something you can improvise on the fly, but they gave it a shot. On October 13, 1775, the Continental Congress established the Continental Navy and authorized the purchase and outfitting of two ships. Of course, if you have a Navy, you need a Marine Corps. On November 10, 1775, the Continental Marine Corps was born at Tun Tavern in Philadelphia, as two battalions of Continental Marines were recruited. The story goes that first Marine received a free beer for signing up. The second Marine was a harder sell and received two beers. The first Marine said, "Two beers? Let me tell you about the *old* Corps."

On December 2, 1775, John Paul Jones took command of the CNS *Alfred* and hoisted the Continental Colors, which happened to be identical to the flag of the British East India Company, for the first time. Jones was from Scotland and immigrated to America in 1772. He had been sailing since he was thirteen. He had killed a sailor in a dispute over wages, allegedly in self-defense, and fled to his brother's home in Fredericksburg, Virginia. But good captains were hard to find, and he was one of the best, so he found employment in the Continental Navy. The Marines would conduct their first amphibious assault in March 1776, when two hundred of them hit the beach at Nassau in the Bahamas, seizing gunpowder, which had been stored there by the royal governor of Virginia.

As far as the flag that was flown on American ships, Washington soon adopted it for use at his camp in Boston. The Continental Colors were identical to the flag of the British East India Company, a fact that has no known explanation but has fostered one or two conspiracy theories. The thirteen stripes were there, but there was a Union Jack in the corner instead of a blue field with stars. It was probably selected simply because it was a flag that was already designed and available and could be distinguished from the British flag. The use of a flag with the Union Jack on it is evidence that the Americans were still just after more rights, not independence.

Canada: After the capture of Fort Ticonderoga, Congress ordered General Philip Schuyler to invade Canada. A force under General Richard Montgomery moved north from Fort Ticonderoga, while another under Colonel Benedict Arnold moved north from Boston. After battles and hardship along the way, the two forces linked up in front of Quebec City on December 2. The city refused to surrender, and Montgomery was killed in action while assaulting the city on December 31, 1775. Arnold was wounded in action. Aaron Burr was also on the scene, attempting to drag Montgomery's body back to friendly lines. Montgomery had been well-known in Great Britain, but George III shed no tears and called him a "brave, able, humane and generous rebel." Arnold continued to serve in upstate New York until the British arrived in force in 1776.

The New York City campaign, 1776: After the British left Boston, the Continental Congress took steps toward declaring independence. They didn't think the British had given up; in fact, they thought the opposite—that the British were *reculer pour frapper un plus grand coup* (backing up to strike a bigger blow). They expected the British would implement a policy of crushing the rebels without mercy, which, after all, is really the only way to handle rebels. Louis XVI should have learned something from this. Abraham Lincoln sure did. The only way for America to win was to get France as an ally, and the only way to get France as an ally was to declare independence. The British onslaught began just as the ink was drying on the Declaration of Independence.

General Lee had been reassigned from the defense of New York City to command the Southern Department in March 1776. He was in command on June 28 when a British force, under General Clinton, attempted to capture Charleston in the Battle of Sullivan Island. Clinton's force was only one thousand men, and it was either a reconnaissance to see what they were facing or a feint to distract the Americans from the real objective: New York City. It could have been both, as the British would later occupy Charleston. Clinton failed to capture Charleston and returned north to participate in the New

York campaign with Howe, after which Lee also departed Charleston to assist Washington in New York and was appalled at the beating that the Army was taking there. He was convinced that Washington had to go and that he was the man to replace him.

According to the Betsy Ross legend, in June 1776, George Washington, Robert Morris, and another Pennsylvania congressional delegate named George Ross visited the wife of Ross's nephew, Betsy Ross, in Philadelphia and had her sew a flag that they had sketched up. The Continental Colors were modified by replacing the Union Jack with thirteen stars in a circle. The story has its defenders, although it only dates to 1870 when the grandson of Betsy Ross submitted a paper to a local historical society, reporting an oral history he had heard from Betsy's sister. It would make more sense that Washington was spending as much time as possible in New York, getting the Army ready for a British assault, but it is documented that he made visits to Philadelphia during this time. Betsy Ross became famous during the 1876 centennial. When I was taught it in school, it was presented as fact. It makes sense that if the Americans were going to assert their independence, the flag shouldn't include the Union Jack. Because of the disasters that were about to overtake the Americans, it wasn't until June of 1777 that they recovered enough nerve to pass a flag resolution.

The Howe brothers set sail from Halifax and began landing troops on July 2 on Staten Island. Twenty-six thousand British troops faced off against nineteen thousand Americans. American history books tend to focus on what was happening in Philadelphia in early July 1776, where Thomas Jefferson was winning lasting fame as the author of the Declaration of Independence, taking the first step on the road to the White House. In New York, things on the battlefield were about to get bad for the Americans.

In August, the British crossed the Narrows into Brooklyn, attacking the Americans near today's Prospect Park and Grand Army Plaza. The Americans retreated across the East River to Manhattan but to Harlem, not Washington Square. The land that became Washington Square in 1826 was, in 1776, known as Little Africa because its residents were black. In 1776, Harlem was occupied by Dutch farmers. It strikes me that there is a lot going on here that raises echoes of future racial issues. Howe attacked Harlem in October, and the Americans retreated north to White Plains. Howe detached Clinton with six thousand troops to occupy Newport Rhode Island for the Royal Navy, detached Cornwallis, who had been in America since January 1776, to pursue Washington, and he himself stayed in Harlem to reduce the American camps known as Fort Washington and Lee. Washington crossed the Hudson and retreated into New Jersey, all the way to Trenton on the Delaware River, which was close enough to Philadelphia that Congress left town and reassembled in Baltimore until March 1777. The British occupied New York City as their major stronghold for the rest of the war.

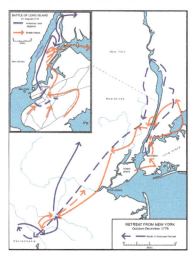

Alexander Hamilton was serving in the artillery of a New York militia unit, and his conspicuous service came to Washington's attention during this campaign. Hamilton had all of the spirit, ambition, and intellect of a Napoleon. In another reality, he might have been an emperor. Like Napoleon, he was foreign-born. Like Napoleon, he was trained in the artillery. For the next twenty-three years, he and George Washington made a very effective, if sometimes contentious, team. Hamilton soon became the most trusted aide of Washington. As such, he wrote orders, developed plans, and generally provided vital assistance to General

Washington in the administration of the Army and determination of strategy. He came to know Washington's mind so well that he was able to issue orders without consulting him. That may be the same thing as saying that Hamilton ran the Army. He never had any conflicts with Washington's other surrogate son Lafayette. I think it is very interesting to note that Washington survived as commander in chief of the Continental Army because he was the only senior officer who was a native-born American, while his aide Hamilton had been born in the West Indies, and his other aide Lafayette was a foreigner. Even in 1776 Washington was more a symbol of America than a fighting general.

During the retreat, Charles Lee started writing letters to Congress detailing Washington's shortcomings. In his dealings with Washington personally, he supposedly became insubordinate (such claims come from Washington's defenders). Lee was captured by the British in December 1776, and upon his release in April 1778, he was suspected of getting captured on purpose, the better to collaborate with the enemy. Howe set up a chain of forts from Staten Island to Trenton and went into winter quarters. The Continental Army had been whipped for six months but gained some face by crossing the Delaware River to attack a Hessian camp on December 31, 1776, the subject of a famous painting. Later, they captured Princeton.

Supposedly, Hamilton, a Columbia grad, fired a cannon through one of the buildings as vengeance for the college not accepting him years before, traces of which are still joyfully shown to visitors by students to this day.

The Philadelphia campaign, Brandywine, and Germantown, 1777: At the beginning of 1777, the British controlled New York and much of New Jersey and were in a good position to resume operations in the spring, with Philadelphia in striking distance. As stated above, Howe detached General Clinton with six thousand men to occupy Newport, Rhode Island, as a base for future operations against Boston and Connecticut (Clinton occupied Newport in December 1776 without opposition). The British thought that Newport would serve as a fine naval station, an opinion shared by the Americans because it serves in that capacity to this very day.

The British perceived that New England was beyond redemption but that the middle colonies could be coaxed back into loyalty, so a force could come down from Montreal, occupy Albany, and isolate New England. Another force could depart from New York City and occupy Philadelphia. Howe then sketched a campaign for the following year in a letter to London: ten thousand men at Newport; ten thousand for an expedition to Albany (to meet Burgoyne's Army descending from Quebec); eight thousand to cross New Jersey and threaten Philadelphia; and five thousand to defend New York. If additional Hessian troops were made available from London, operations could also be considered against the Southern states. Later, Howe decided to increase the number of troops in New Jersey, and so he didn't have anyone to support Burgoyne. Neither Burgoyne nor the boss in London, St. Germain, were made aware of this change in time to save Burgoyne.

In June 1777, the Marquis de Lafayette, age twenty, landed in South Carolina. He was made a major general after agreeing to serve for free. The rank was honorary and carried no eligibility for command, although this may not have been clear to Lafayette. He made his way to Philadelphia and met Washington, who appointed him as an aide.

On June 14, the Marine Committee of the Continental Congress passed the Flag Resolution, which stated, "Resolved, that the flag of the United States be thirteen stripes, alternate red and white; that the union be thirteen stars, white in a blue field, representing a new Constellation." The date may have been deliberately selected as the anniversary of the establishment of the Continental Army.

In July 1777, Howe loaded his troops onto transports in New York and sailed them to Chesapeake Bay. Word came to Washington of the embarkation, but no one knew their destination. In August, the British began landing near Elkton, Maryland, at the very north end of Chesapeake Bay and fifty-five miles south of Philadelphia. Howe thought he would get more loyalist support than he did, and he wrote to his boss in London that he would need all the troops he could get and would not be sending any reinforcements up the Hudson Valley to help Burgoyne as stated above.

The British advanced toward Philadelphia and defeated the Americans at Brandywine Creek on September 11. Congress fled to Lancaster, Pennsylvania. They convened in Lancaster for two weeks and then, for some reason, reconvened across the Susquehanna River in York until June 27, 1778. Lancaster and York were the two families that contended for the English throne in the Wars of the Roses, from 1455 to 1485. Now in 1777, we have another English civil war in which two namesake towns alternate as hosts for the Continental Congress. I suppose those who were up on their Shakespeare commented on it.

Philadelphia was undefended, and Howe entered on September 26. Howe left three thousand troops in Philadelphia and moved the bulk of his force to Germantown, a few miles north of Philadelphia. Washington rallied his forces and then advanced on the British in Germantown, hoping to repeat the success of Trenton, but Howe was ready for him. Washington's plan required precise timing and coordination between the advancing columns, which they were unable to execute. The Americans were defeated and retreated to Valley Forge, which is twenty miles from Germantown. Washington hired a Prussian mercenary, von Steuben, to give the Army some training over the winter in the hopes it would improve their performance.

Horatio Gates and Saratoga, 1777: In Quebec, by the spring of 1777, the British had assembled a force of ten thousand men. Burgoyne was given command and told to occupy Albany. On July 4, he arrived at Fort Ticonderoga, the "Gibraltar of the North" (a moniker that would also be applied to Luxembourg in 1795), to find that the Americans had abandoned it as described below. At this point, he learned that Howe would not be sending reinforcements up from New York. He had to decide whether to continue to Albany or return

THE GREAT GLOBE ITSELF

to Quebec. Maintaining a chain of depots between Quebec and Fort Ticonderoga was not an option. He decided to cut his line of retreat and stake everything on being able to reach Albany.

At the same time that the British took Ticonderoga, Vermont declared itself to be an independent republic. Its position was shaky since it was being settled and organized by both New York and New Hampshire, so there was some confusion over land titles and county boundaries. It seems pretty clear from the original land grants in the 1600s that the border between New Hampshire and New York was the Connecticut River, so Vermont was, in effect, seceding from New York, where slavery was still legal in 1777. While declaring itself independent, it applied to the Continental Congress for recognition, which was not forthcoming because the Constitution Vermont produced outlawed slavery, stating that no person could be bound as servant, slave, or apprentice against their will beyond the age of twenty-one for men and eighteen for women. Now was not the time for the Americans to have a debate about slavery. The stunt with slavery-free Vermont was a British ploy intended by Burgoyne to divide the Americans and distract them from his advance. The Continental Congress ignored Vermont's application as they knew that it had been inspired by Burgoyne's agents.

Since April 1776, the American command in upstate New York and Vermont had been called the Northern Department and was commanded by General Philip Schuyler. Schuyler's second-in-command was Horatio Gates, and the two men had a rivalry going. Gates had command of Fort Ticonderoga but resigned his post three weeks before the British arrived. His replacement, General Saint Clair, had command of 2,500 militia. He and Schuyler decided to abandon Fort Ticonderoga. The Americans were appalled, and the British were thrilled at this decision. Washington had not considered the possibility that the place could be lost. John Adams started talking about shooting generals for the encouragement of the others. Lord North was elated and sent a demand to France and Spain for them to close their ports to American trade, which was rejected.

Schuyler and Saint Clair were both removed from command and court-martialed, being suspected of treason. They were later cleared of all charges and had significant lengthy careers in the service

of the United States after the war. Gates was delighted at Schuyler's fall and was now given command of the Northern Department to fight Burgoyne.

Benedict Arnold, American hero, 1777: Washington sent Benedict Arnold, Benjamin Lincoln, and Daniel Morgan to assist. There was previous bad blood between Gates and Arnold over Arnold's rank and seniority. I suspect that Washington sent Arnold up there on purpose to stir up dissent. He may have made that explicit to Arnold under the pretext of telling Arnold that he suspected Gates of treason, purposely weakening Ticonderoga, although I have no evidence of that. I just know that Washington had a nose for rivals and a knack for neutralizing them. Regardless, during the campaign, Gates and Arnold quarreled to the point where Gates fired him. Nevertheless, the Americans managed to keep the British out of Albany, and British manpower and supplies started to run low. Arnold ignored Gates' firing of him, or maybe the paperwork was still in process, or maybe he hadn't fired Arnold at all

when, on October 7, Arnold led an assault on the British line and breached it. Arnold was seriously injured in the attack (his leg was crushed), but he gained great fame and glory as a result. Actually, it's not clear when his leg was crushed, as the story was also told that it happened in Quebec in 1775. It might have happened on both occa-

THE GREAT GLOBE ITSELF

sions, although one would think that two serious injuries to the same limb would be permanently incapacitating.

Arnold spent the next six months healing and then returned to the Army at Valley Forge in May 1778. Burgoyne surrendered on October 17, 1777, and people argue to this day as to whether Gates or Arnold should get more credit for this event that altered the course of the war and the history of the world. One person who got no credit was Washington, and at the end of 1777, he was at the lowest point in his life and spent the next few months fighting to keep his job. Congress was so happy about the victory that in November 1777, they sent the Articles of Confederation to the states for ratification.

When Howe got the word that Burgoyne had surrendered, he wrote a letter of resignation, which was accepted, and Clinton was appointed in his place in May 1778, by which time France had entered the war, and a change in strategy was required because of the threat to the West Indies. Howe's brother, the admiral, stayed on for a while, although there would be a lot of turnover in the North American naval command, with five men succeeding Admiral Howe over the next three years. Generals Howe and Burgoyne were suspected of treason and later cleared, but they were in the doghouse until 1782, when Lord North and his government resigned. Appointed as Clinton's second-in-command was Charles Cornwallis, who had been in America since January 1776 and had fought in all the major campaigns against Washington.

Great Britain, 1775–1777

English literature, 1775–1777: In 1776, Great Britain was producing classical works of literature while they were fighting the Americans. Adam Smith, one of the Physiocrats, published *An Inquiry into the Nature and Causes of the Wealth of Nations.* This was a groundbreaking work that defined and analyzed economic terms like *labor, money* and *wages, rent* and *land, income* and *capital, profit* and *interest.* He had a mostly academic career in Scotland and died in 1790. One term Smith used that I didn't understand was *stock,* which he defined as any resource created or owned by an individual or business. It can be raw materials, provisions, finished goods, or money. I don't know if he considered stock to be the same thing as equity, which is defined as the difference between a company's assets and liabilities. The value of a company's stock is equal to the equity and is shared among the partners. I will show this paragraph to a real economist for corrections.

Edward Gibbon published volume 1 of *The History of the Decline and Fall of the Roman Empire*. It would be completed with volume 6 in 1789 and covered the period from 98 to 1590. Gibbon wrote, "The various modes of worship, which prevailed in the Roman world [in the second century AD], were all considered by the people, as equally true; by the philosopher, as equally false; and by the magistrate, as equally useful." A true man of the Enlightenment, he was projecting the ideas of his days to those of ancient Rome. The purpose of that was to assert that Europe was facing a similar decline and fall, which he attributed in large part to the victory of Christian superstitions. When he finished writing the last volume in 1787, he said:

> It was on the day, or rather the night, of 27 June 1787, between the hours of eleven and twelve, that I wrote the last lines of the last page in a summerhouse in my garden...I will not dissemble the first emotions of joy on the recovery of my freedom, and perhaps the establishment of my fame. But my pride was soon humbled, and a sober melancholy was spread over my mind by the idea that I had taken my everlasting leave of an old and agreeable companion, and that, whatsoever might be the future fate of my history, the life of the historian must be short and precarious.

Sober words and true!

In January 1776, Thomas Paine published *Common Sense*, selling five hundred thousand copies within one year in the American colonies. Paine made several specious arguments against British rule in America: It was absurd for an island to rule a continent; America

THE GREAT GLOBE ITSELF

was not a "British nation." It was composed of influences and peoples from all of Europe. Even if Britain were the "mother country" of America, that made her actions all the more horrendous, for no mother would harm her children so brutally. Being a part of Britain would drag America into unnecessary European wars and keep it from the international commerce at which America excelled. The distance between the two nations made governing the colonies from England unwieldy. If some wrong were to be petitioned to Parliament, it would take a year before the colonies received a response. The New World was discovered shortly before the Reformation. The Puritans believed that God wanted to give them a safe haven from the persecution of British rule. Britain ruled the colonies for its own benefit and did not consider the best interests of the colonists in governing them. There are some ridiculous points, some practical points, and some good points in his arguments.

France, 1775–1777

New king, new ministers: When Louis XV died, Madame du Barry was not the only one exiled from Versailles. Louis XVI replaced all the ministers. The Comte de Vergennes was named foreign minister. His view was that European politics ought to be dominated by France, Spain, and Austria and that the power of Great Britain, Russia, and Prussia in Europe ought to be diminished. This desire to return to the seventeenth century was unrealistic, but Louis hired him for his overall grasp of international affairs. The fact that he had lived outside France since 1739 was a point in his favor. He advocated for supporting the Americans in their rebellion against Great Britain. By the end of 1777, he had convinced Louis to support America and declare war on Great Britain, pointing to the victory at Saratoga as evidence that the American colonies could succeed. Although in principle, Vergennes wanted to marginalize Russia as much as Great Britain, he found few opportunities to do so.

At the same time that Vergennes was appointed foreign minister, Jacques Turgot was appointed as first minister and controller general of finances. He had spent the previous ten years in Limoges as a tax collector but got attention as a thinker when he published *Reflections on the Formation and Distribution of Wealth*, which got him the big job when Louis XVI took over as king. His efforts to balance the budget of France conflicted with Vergennes's idea to build up the Army and the Navy to strike Great Britain. One thing Turgot realized was that food shortages in France were the result of internal trade barriers, and his attempts to drop them met with opposition from the people who made money by erecting these trade barriers. Turgot was forced to retire in May 1776. He was replaced as first minister by the Comte de Maurepas, who was seventy-five, and as finance minister by Jacques Necker, who got the job by telling Louis it would be no problem to finance a war against Great Britain. Accommodations in the actual title of the job had to be made because it was illegal for the Protestant Necker to hold the position. It was Maurepas who advised Louis to reinstate the parlements, which would lead to the downfall of the monarchy.

Louis XVI struggles: Louis XVI's coronation was in June 1775 at Reims Cathedral, the first such event since October 1722. Louis XVIII did not undergo the process, but Charles X did in 1825, and it hasn't happened since. Louis XVI and Marie Antoinette had been married since 1770, and she had not conceived a child. And now the printing press, the technology that had facilitated the spread of the Bible, Newton's laws of motion, and the *Encyclopedia*, was now used to explain why Marie Antoinette was not pregnant. Joseph II was reported as saying that, "Louis had confided in him the course of action he had been undertaking in their marital bed; saying Louis 'introduces the member,' but then 'stays there without moving for about two minutes,' withdraws without having completed the act and 'bids goodnight.'" Joseph apparently then told Louis about the birds and the bees. The idea that the mechanics of lovemaking had to be explained to the king and queen of France must have been hilarious to the readers of the vulgar pamphlets that contained this story. Other stories say that Louis had some sort of deformity that made erections painful. Since men that age get a lot of erections, he must have been in pain a lot. The deformity was supposedly corrected by surgery. Anyway, Marie Antoinette 's first pregnancy was announced in May 1778, and daughter Marie Therese was born in December 1778.

THE GREAT GLOBE ITSELF

The nobles and the bourgeoisie used the power of the parlements to prevent the enacting of laws they didn't like. Laws passed by the king were not technically enacted until they were registered in the parlements. The nobles were not monolithic. The nobles of the sword looked down upon the nobles of the robe. Many nobles of the sword traced descent from Frankish invaders of the fifth century, and their prestige was based on landownership and military service. After 1789, the revolutionists attempted to use their pedigrees against them, calling them invaders. The nobles of the robe were holders of hereditary titles sold to them by the king in honor of their judicial or administrative service. However, all the nobles and the bourgeoisie would close ranks against any attempts to raise taxes on their class.

Necker took office as finance minister in October 1776, temporarily solving the government's problems by borrowing heavily. His daughter was the famous author Germaine De Staël. Necker, a Swiss Protestant who would be the first hero of the revolution, served as finance minister until May 1781 and then again in early days of the French Revolution. He became a celebrity in France, because of his reforming ways, his wife's salon, and the impression of the Protestant ethic that he projected. Today, the stereotype is that all Jews are financial wizards, but in 1776, that applied to the Swiss. His reforms included economies and efficiencies within the royal household. The cuts in the royal household were more symbolic than anything else, similar to calls today to cut the salaries of congressmen.

Russia, 1775–1777

Gregor Potemkin: With the First Partition of Poland accomplished, Russia and Prussia considered that their alliance had served its purpose, although it remained in effect for as long as Frederick II lived. In Russia, Potemkin began to let his presence be felt. Potemkin had seen extensive cavalry service against the Turks in the 1768–1774 war. Somehow he got into the inner circle in Saint Petersburg and impressed Catherine as "one of the greatest, the most comical and amusing characters of this iron century," in her words. He seems to have been a latter-day Mark Antony, a mixture of coarse humor and fearlessness in battle, and

Catherine was his Cleopatra. In 1774, he was appointed governor general of the newly established (in 1764) governate of New Russia and as commander in chief of the Cossacks, who were the primary military force in the area. By 1776, Catherine had thrown Potemkin over for a new favorite but still relied on him as her man in New Russia. Panin and Potemkin would spend the next five years scheming against each other. Panin continued to favor the Northern System, while Potemkin thought that an Austrian alliance would be more useful to his Greek Project. By the end of 1777, Catherine was still thinking about it. She probably would have liked to have been in alliance with both Prussia and Austria, but the only thing they could all three agree on was the partitioning of Poland, and further partitions were not in the cards, as promises had been made to King Stanislas Poniatowski.

The Greek Project was a plan to kick the Ottomans out of the Balkans. The kingdom of Byzantium was to be formed from Macedonia, Bulgaria (Rumelia), and Constantinople and ruled by an as yet unborn grandson of Catherine II. Austria was to receive Bosnia and Serbia. The Republic of Venice was to receive the Peloponnese (Morea), Crete (Candia), and Cyprus. Potemkin himself was to be made king of a new land called Dacia, formed from Romania (Wallachia) and Moldavia. The Ottomans would be reduced to their possessions in Asia and Africa.

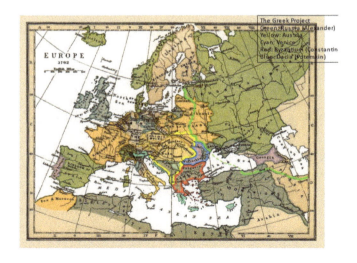

THE GREAT GLOBE ITSELF

Paul I: Paul I turned twenty-one in 1775. He had probably been told that he would start to rule once he had fathered a son, so he spent all his time focusing on that. In fact, after his marriage, he was invited to start attending meetings of the council of state. His wife, Wilhelmina, was soon pregnant, but she and the child died in May 1776. A new bride was quickly found—Sophia Dorothea of Wurttemberg, who was rechristened Maria Feodorvna. They were wed in October 1776, and their first son, Alexander, the future conqueror of Napoleon, was born in December 1777, followed by Constantine in April 1779. The overjoyed Catherine gave Paul and Maria Feodorvna a Saint Petersburg estate called Pavlovsk to call home, but the title of emperor was not forthcoming.

Altogether Paul and Marie Feodorvna would have four sons and five daughters who made it to adulthood. After Paul I's death in 1801, Marie Feodorvna would continue to exert influence over the course of affairs in Russia until her death in 1828, most significantly when she refused to allow any of her daughters to marry Napoleon Bonaparte. This was a major bone of contention between Russia and France in the lead-up to the French invasion of Russia in 1812, and the invasion probably would not have happened if she had relented. The hand that rocks the cradle rules the world.

We should recall all the deaths that occurred to the families of Louis XV and Maria Theresa in the 1760s due to smallpox. The death rate for people who caught it was 20 percent. There was folklore that milkmaids didn't get smallpox and that somehow doing their job provided immunity. Doctors theorized that they got a mild version of smallpox through the blisters on their hands from the cows they milked. That, along with other information, was gathered by doctors and scientists and turned into, first, inoculations that helped the survivability of smallpox victims starting about now, and then vaccinations starting in 1796. *Inoculation* is implanting a pathogen to provide immunity. *Vaccination* is implanting a vaccine to do the same thing. Only one of Paul and Marie's children died before adulthood, and that was from a tooth abscess. Women continued to have a large number of pregnancies, but more children survived, with staggering demographic implications for Europe and North America.

PETER HARDY

1778–1779: Great Britain against the World

The American Revolution, 1778–1779

The Conway Cabal, 1778: On October 17, 1777, the same day that Burgoyne surrendered at Saratoga, Congress reorganized the agency that administered the Continental Army, the five-member Board of War. General Gates, bedecked with the laurels of victory, was appointed to the board, and at the suggestion of quartermaster general Thomas Mifflin, another member of the board, was made its president, technically making him George Washington 's boss, even though Washington outranked Gates and all other officers in the Army. Well, that's what we call checks and balances. General Mifflin had been quartermaster general since August 1775, with field commands between stints. It was a thankless job: money was always short, and contractors charged exorbitant prices. Mifflin was accused of corruption on occasion, and when that would happen, he would offer to resign, but they always brought him back because no one else wanted to do the job. Another member of the board was Commissary General Joseph Trumbull, who had traveled the same road as Mifflin while trying to feed the Army. Mifflin, Trumbull, and Gates were in a position to remove and replace Washington and thought they had the backing of a majority of Congress to do so. There was a significant element in Congress that despised Washington, having twice been forced to flee Philadelphia because of his lost battles. The Pennsylvania congressmen were especially annoyed at him.

Between November 1777 and the spring of 1778, there was an effort among some generals and some members of Congress to replace Washington with Gates. The effort is now referred to as the Conway Cabal, named for General Thomas Conway, who was named inspector general of the Army in December 1777. I don't know what relationship the IG had with the Board of War, but I imagine there was one. The hagiography on Washington is still so strong that the facts on what the IG and the Board of War were ready to do is still buried. Conway was an Irishman who had served in the French Army. Almost all of the officers that were in favor

104

of replacing Washington were either Pennsylvanians, foreigners, or recent British transplants like Lee and Gates. Washington retained the loyalty of the vast majority of the Continental Army officers, because they were colonial Americans like Washington and preferred a colonial American to command the Army, and there was no one else. Washington may have been incompetent at handling an Army in battle (and he never improved), but the Army would stick with him. When they made it loud and clear that Washington retained their loyalty, congressional talk of replacing him died.

Mifflin left the Board in 1778, then got elected to Congress in 1782. He was president of Congress when he accepted Washington's resignation from the Army in December 1783, which must have given him some satisfaction.

Gates left the Board in 1778. He managed to keep a straight face when his rival, Benedict Arnold, betrayed Washington in 1780. He was given command of the Southern Department after Charleston fell in 1780, lost his military reputation at the battle of Camden, and left the Army in 1784.

Trumbull left the board in 1778, citing ill health, which must have been true because he died three months after leaving, only forty-one.

Conway left the IG office and the Army in April 1778 (replaced by von Steuben), was challenged to a duel and injured by one of

Washington's friends in July, and returned to France after recovering. He opposed the French Revolution and fought in the royalist forces in southern France. He fled France and disappeared from history.

Washington was now firmly in charge. There was rejoicing when news of the French alliance came in the spring of 1778. The Carlisle Commission, a British peace delegation, came and went in April with Congress turning down the offer of dominion status. Charles Lee returned to the Army after being swapped in a prisoner exchange. Washington pretended to welcome him back with open arms, but somehow a whispering campaign began in the Army over what arrangements Lee may have made with the enemy during his captivity. It was no coincidence that Congress now ordered that the military take an oath of allegiance to the United States of America, which Washington carried out in Valley Forge in May 1778.

The Battle of Monmouth, June 1778: In the spring of 1778, the Continental Army remained in Valley Forge until it became clear what the British intentions were. Howe and Burgoyne were gone. Clinton was given command, and Cornwallis was made his second-in-command. Clinton was ordered to deploy eight thousand troops to the Floridas and the West Indies. The remaining troops would consolidate in New York and adopt a defensive posture. That meant the evacuation of Philadelphia, which was the first order of business. The British troops were to march across New Jersey from Philadelphia to New York.

In June, the Continental Army moved to Monmouth, New Jersey, in order to waylay what they presumed was a vulnerable British rear and baggage train. Charles Lee was placed in command. Lee had, at first, refused command of the operation but then asked for and received it when it appeared that Lafayette's force was too small and that he was mishandling it. On June 28, Washington sent Lee forward with two

THE GREAT GLOBE ITSELF

brigades and orders to take charge of Lafayette's force. Cornwallis was in command of the British rear guard. He realized that Lee's force was too far from Washington's main body and attacked it. Lee ordered a retreat. Washington met Lee as he retreated and strongly berated him, curse words and all. Lee was relieved on the spot and his command given to Lafayette. Washington and Lafayette were able to establish a defensive line. Cornwallis then withdrew, as his objective was to get to New York, not fight a battle. The story of Molly Pitcher springs from this battle, the woman who swabbed cannon and got water for the American artillerymen. The British made their way to Sandy Hook and were able to cross into New York City a few weeks later. The battle was spun by Washington's friends as a victory that would have been complete had it not been for Lee's treasonous conduct. Lee protested and demanded a court-martial. Washington obliged him, and on August 12, he was convicted and sentenced to twelve months' suspension.

In December, Lee published a vindication of his conduct at Monmouth. After a rancorous debate, Congress upheld his court-martial conviction and sentence. Later that month, John Laurens, one of Washington's aides and the son of the current president of the Continental Congress, challenged Lee to a duel, with Hamilton as his second. Laurens was aroused to action by the language used by Lee in his publication. Lee was wounded in the duel, which surely had Washington's blessing. Lee recovered and retired but died in October 1782. He outlived John Laurens by five weeks, as Laurens was killed in action in August 1782 in his home state of South Carolina, in the course of a minor British plundering raid.

There had been a debate going on as to whether military power should be focused on Washington's Army versus state militias. Lee had been the last man to speak in favor of a militia-centric organization. It was the first reduction of state rights. Washington had dispatched the last of his rivals. In the words of Washington loyalist Elias Boudinot, "None dare to acknowledge themselves his enemies." Washington began to be called the father of his country, in imitation of Caesar Augustus. He was called the "indispensable man." All hopes for independence now rested on him and the Army.

It seems odd that the British, who seem to be so good at assassinating the leaders of countries who gain military advantages over them, never got around to sending some against Washington. I suppose the British never got around to it because they never had any reason to have any respect for him, seeing him as the same bungling militia officer from the French and Indian War. If the British were having difficulties, they thought it was because of a fault in strategy or communications in the senior command. They had beaten Washington every time he showed his face on the battlefield; why have him assassinated?

American attack on Newport, 1778: The French Fleet under D'Estaing arrived in Wilmington and Philadelphia in July. The British were gone, back to New York. The French followed, but the draft of their ships was too deep to cross the Narrows into New York Harbor. A plan was then developed to use D'Estaing and his Fleet (which also had four thousand troops embarked) to attack the British in Newport. I don't know how often these ships needed to resupply, especially with all those embarked soldiers, but it must have been often. Also, Lafayette was the primary liaison between D'Estaing and Washington.

If you read about John Hancock, he had left Congress and was exercising his rank as a major general of the Massachusetts militia to lead this operation, but if you read about the operation, Hancock was invisible, and the execution of it was by D'Estaing and American generals John Sullivan and Nathanael Greene. As the operation was getting underway, there was a major storm that scattered the French Fleet. They turned in to Boston for repairs, then headed to Sainte Lucie in the West Indies. With no French Fleet in support, the American militia evaporated. John Hancock thought that he would be able to come in at the end and take the credit, but instead, his desire for military credibility was thwarted along with his ambitions to be president of the United States. Washington was well aware of Hancock's ambitions and had set him up for failure, giving him enough rope to hang himself.

The British stayed in Newport for another year, but in October 1779, they abandoned the place for New York City as part of the

THE GREAT GLOBE ITSELF

British defensive consolidation and to free up more men for the move to Florida, which evolved into the Southern campaign.

Washington returns to New York, 1778: After the Battle of Monmouth Courthouse Washington moved the Army back through the same path that he had retreated along in 1776, the New Jersey countryside west of Newark, then Rockland County, New York, then crossing the Hudson at Tarrytown into Westchester and encamping the Army at White Plains, where it remained until the British evacuated New York in 1783. His plan was to gather enough intel and strength to launch an assault on the New York City, but he never did get enough of either. The Continental Army also had a base at West Point, where it guarded the entrance to the Hudson River, having constructed a large chain in the water that could be raised to block ships attempting to enter it. The man who constructed the chain was Timothy Pickering, future secretary of state, who was adjutant general of the Continental Army at the time. To this day, plebes at West Point have to know how many links were in it (the answer is "approximately 1,200").

The major operation of Washington's New York Army in 1779 was the Battle of Stony Point, an action involving about a thousand men on each side with no strategic value. Stony Point is on the same side of the river as West Point, about halfway from West Point to White Plains.

British attack on Savannah, 1779: While the British were consolidating in New York City, Clinton was ordering the capture of Savannah, Georgia, which was assaulted and occupied by 3,500 men under Lieutenant Colonel Archibald Campbell, who quickly secured the city in December 1778. A British force under General Augustin Prevost marched up from Saint Augustine to reinforce the British force in Savannah. In June 1779, Clinton issued the Philipsburg Decree, encouraging slaves to run away and join the British Army. The decree was valid only in the rebelling colonies, as the British had no intention of freeing any slaves in loyal East Florida. Abraham Lincoln employed the same idea in 1862 with the Emancipation Proclamation. So many slaves came to Savannah to report for duty that the British were forced to tell them to return home. Some of them were sold back into slavery by both Patriots and Loyalists. But about three thousand ex-slaves eventually served in the British forces. After the war, they were relocated to Nova Scotia, and many of them eventually settled in Sierra Leone.

Benjamin Lincoln was commander of the Southern Department, with his headquarters in Charleston, South Carolina. By June 1779, he gathered a force of about six thousand men and secured the assistance of the French Fleet under D'Estaing, which had been operating in the West Indies. The mission was to retake Savannah. One of the battles leading up to the action at Savannah was the Battle of Stono Ferry, where Andrew Jackson's brother Hugh died of heat exhaustion. In September 1779, the French and Americans arrived at Savannah. D'Estaing had no intention of staying there long, and so on October 16, Lincoln attempted to take the place by storm. This was unsuccessful, and Lincoln and D'Estaing had to retreat. Bells were rung in London upon hearing the news. D'Estaing returned to Toulon after a two-year deployment, and Lincoln returned to Charleston, where he was in 1780, when Clinton and Cornwallis turned the tables on him.

Spanish attack on West Florida, 1779: As noted above, Spain had entered the war in 1779 on France's side. They had been running the Louisiana territory since 1763 from New Orleans, and now the governor, General Bernardo de Galves, sallied from there to attack West Florida, capturing Baton Rouge, Natchez, and Mobile by 1780 and then the West Florida capital of Pensacola in 1781. They never got to Saint Augustine, but in the peace settlement, Great Britain ceded all of East and West Florida to Spain in exchange for the Bahamas. Galveston, Texas, is named for General Galves.

Bonhomme Richard versus Serapis, September 1779: In September 1779, John Paul Jones, commanding the *Bonhomme Richard*, engaged HMS *Serapis* in the Battle of Flamborough Head, off the coast of Yorkshire, on the east coast of England. *Bonhomme Richard* sank two days after the battle, but he captured the *Serapis*. Jones said his famous phrase "I have not yet begun to fight!" during the battle. The joke there is about the sailor below decks hearing this statement coming from the bridge and saying to his shipmate, "Some bastards never get the word!" Ben Franklin's *Poor Richard's Almanack* had been

THE GREAT GLOBE ITSELF

published in France as *Les Maximes du Bonhomme Richard*. Jones served in the American Navy until 1788 and then took a job in the Russian Navy, where his performance against the Turks failed to meet Potemkin 's expectations. Knowing France was inclining to war, he moved to Paris, where he died in 1792, waiting for a command. His grave was forgotten but was located in 1905, and his remains were interred in a crypt at the United States Naval Academy in 1906, with President Theodore Roosevelt presiding at the event.

Benedict Arnold in Philadelphia, West Point, and with the British Army

Philadelphia, 1778–1780: With the British gone from Philadelphia, Congress reconvened there on July 2, 1778, making it the best Fourth of July ever. Benedict Arnold was installed as military commander. He made his headquarters at the Masters-Penn House, built in 1767 at 524 Market Street. It had been the home of loyalist Richard Penn, grandson of William Penn and Pennsylvania governor, until he departed for England in July 1775. General Howe had used it as a headquarters when he occupied Philadelphia from September 1777 to June 1778. Arnold was there from June 1778 to August 1780, when he left to take command of West Point. He began corresponding with the British in May 1779. After Arnold left, there was no further need for a military commander in Philadelphia, and the house was lived in by a man who was a purchasing agent for the French Army, who departed after the battle of Yorktown. Robert Morris then purchased the house from Richard Penn and lived in it while superintendent of finance in the days of the Articles of Confederation. He let Washington live there in 1787 during the Constitutional Convention. Washington and Adams used it as their home during their presidencies, from 1790 to 1800, and I wouldn't be surprised if George and Martha called it White House after that home they had shared in the 1750s. After the capital moved to Washington in 1800, the building was converted into a hotel until 1832. It was then gutted and converted into three stories. The structures were demolished in segments by 1951. Today there is a mon-

111

ument to the slaves that the Washingtons owned while living there, which was built in 2010. I don't approve of punishing historical people for the crime of being people of their times, and I hope somebody modifies this display soon.

In order to ensure that stockpiles that might be useful to the Army weren't transported away, and that tranquility prevailed, Arnold declared martial law. The Pennsylvania state government and their allies in the Continental Congress viewed Arnold as Washington's man. Washington was the man who had lost the battles of Brandywine and Germantown, resulting in the nine-month British occupation of Philadelphia. Now Washington was the symbol of an Army that represented the slippery slope of central power over states' rights, which might have been acceptable if Washington had at least shown some competence in command. Arnold was therefore the face of incompetent tyranny in Philadelphia, and he came under attack from the states' rights patriots.

The leader of this opposition to Washington and his surrogate Benedict Arnold was Joseph Reed, a former aide of Washington's who had been fired when a letter he wrote after the 1776 New York campaign describing Washington as weak was discovered. Reed served in the Continental Congress for most of 1778 and then, in December 1778, was elected governor of Pennsylvania, although his title was president of Pennsylvania. Reed led prosecutions of suspected loyalists. Arnold's attempts to be evenhanded were thwarted by claims that he was pro-British and corrupt. In February 1779, Reed laid charges against Arnold that were referred to Congress, who referred them to the Army. In April 1779, Arnold got married to a young woman named Peggy Shippen, whose family was not loyalist but neutral, despite what has been written by Washington's hagiographers. The happy occasion was ruined as Reed made the charges public at the time of the marriage. It was at this time that Arnold began corresponding with Major Andre, a friend of his wife's, who he thought could help him inflict some damage on Reed, who, after all, was opposing the policies of Washington.

In June 1779, a court-martial was convened to try Arnold on the charges that had been brought by Reed, but the trial was delayed

THE GREAT GLOBE ITSELF

because of military action in the Hudson Valley. Operations had wrapped up around Stony Point by August, but Arnold's trial didn't start until January 1780, because Reed requested delays to gather evidence. Arnold was cleared of all charges except for two minor charges: one for allowing a ship to sail when the port was closed and another for using government wagons to move goods he owned, which Arnold admitted to but pointed out that he had paid for their use at the time. The court required that Arnold be publicly reprimanded, which Washington did in April 1780. To add insult to injury, right after that Congress completed another investigation, concluding that Arnold owed the government £1,000 from the Quebec campaign in 1775, never mind that he had been wounded, there had been a long winter retreat, and the records had been lost along the way. That was the last straw, and Arnold submitted his resignation, convinced that America wasn't going to make it.

It's not a coincidence that Pennsylvania passed An Act for the Gradual Abolition of Slavery in March 1780. It was Joseph Reed sticking a finger in the eye of George Washington. The act prohibited further importation of slaves into the state, required Pennsylvania slaveholders to annually register their slaves (with forfeiture for noncompliance and manumission for the enslaved), and established that all children born in Pennsylvania were free persons regardless of the condition or race of their parents. Those enslaved in Pennsylvania before the 1780 law went into effect remained enslaved. Another act of the Pennsylvania legislature freed them in 1847. Pennsylvania thus became the first of the thirteen colonies to deal with slavery, but like Vermont's Constitution, it had a hidden agenda behind it.

West Point, 1780: Maybe by now, Arnold had already decided he would offer his sword to the British no matter what, but Washington felt the need to explain to Arnold that Reed had him over a barrel and was threatening to delay or halt Pennsylvania's support to the Continental Army. To make it up to Arnold, he offered him a command in the Army in New York. Arnold said he was disabled and unfit for the field, but he did accept command of West Point, reporting on August 3, 1780. He made an agreement with General Clinton to surrender West Point for £20,000, which agreement was

113

discovered on September 24, when Major Andre was captured with incriminating documents in his possession. Arnold fled down the Hudson River to New York and found refuge with the British Army.

Benedict Arnold in Virginia and Connecticut, 1781: Clinton gave Arnold a commission as a brigadier general and, in January 1781, sent him to Virginia to raid Richmond, where he made Governor Jefferson flee. Jefferson was never much of a fighter. Arnold returned to New York in June after turning his command over to Cornwallis in Portsmouth. Cornwallis had come up from Wilmington after campaigning in North Carolina against Nathanael Greene. Arnold was sent on another raid to New London, Connecticut. After Cornwallis surrendered at Yorktown, Clinton ended military operations. Arnold and his family departed for England in December 1781, on the same ship with Cornwallis. He spent the rest of his life involved with trade and died in 1801.

As it was now practically illegal to criticize Washington, criticism was heaped upon Arnold's head for the next two hundred years. His every act was interpreted as motivated by cruelty or greed. Every single author of a biography of Arnold is an amateur psychiatrist, examining his relationship with his parents and the effects of his personal pains and anguishes on his actions and decisions. Great pains have been taken to make Washington come out as well as possible, while the role of Reed and the other players were minimized. I think that the hagiography of Washington over the last 230 years is just as misplaced as that ridiculous attempt with the president's house in Philadelphia to vilify him as a slave owner.

The Coalition War against Great Britain, 1778– 1779

Benjamin Franklin in France, 1778: Benjamin Franklin had been in Paris since October 1776, head of a diplomatic commission, sent there by the Continental Congress. He was born in 1706 and had been famous in America and Europe since the publication of *Poor Richard's Almanack* in the 1730s, celebrated for his rustic New World genius. In the wake of Saratoga, British offers of peace and French offers of alliance started coming his way. In January, Louis XVI sent a diplomat with the authority to make a deal, so Franklin turned the British down and started negotiating. France entered into a trade and military alliance with the Americans and recognized them as the United States of America, the first country to do so. Franklin and the other two commissioners signed the treaty on February 6, 1778. John Adams, a future commissioner, arrived in France soon afterwards. France informed Great Britain of the treaty on March 13, and Great Britain declared war on France on March 17. They sent the Carlisle Peace Commission to negotiate with the Continental Congress in 1778, offering them dominion status of the kind enjoyed in Canada today, but Congress demanded either recognition of independence or immediate withdrawal of all British forces, and the commission went home empty.

Franklin was not impressed by his colleague John Adams and sent letters to Congress complaining about his inability to hide his distaste for the French. Because Ben Franklin was Ben Franklin, he was promoted to minister plenipotentiary (full powers), another commissioner was sent to be minister to Spain, and Adams received no instructions at all, so he went home. Adams learned his lesson, though, and remained useful.

French and Spanish military operations, 1778–1779: In April 1778, a French Fleet under Admiral D'Estaing sailed from Toulon to conduct operations in Wilmington, Philadelphia, New York, and then Newport before sailing to Sainte Lucie in the West Indies. In 1779, the Fleet was doubled in size and sailed to Saint Vincent, then Barbados, and then Grenada. They then sailed to Savannah in a failed attempt to retake the city from the British, as described above. The results of all these engagements were mixed, and D'Estaing was replaced at the end of 1779. D'Estaing's 1778 operations were meant to divert British strength from the English Channel, so he was successful in that respect. The French Fleet at Brest under Admiral D'Orvilliers sailed from Brest on July 8, 1778. The Royal Navy under Admiral Keppel caught up with them on July 27, near the island of Ushant, the westernmost point of metropolitan France. The battle was indecisive, and no ships were sunk. I can't find out why the French left port to begin with or what their destination was, but after the battle, they returned to Brest for repairs. I have to assume that they sallied from port in order to attack the Royal Navy, as I haven't read anywhere that they had troops or transports or were ready to invade.

There were serious political implications in France of the Battle of Ushant. Louis Philippe II, the Duke of Chartres and the son of the Duke of Orleans, participated in the battle, commanding a squadron. Chartres gained permission from D'Orvilliers to travel to Paris to announce a victory, which was granted. He made the announcement and received the applause of the city. This was annoying to Louis XVI and Marie Antoinette, as they had not been informed prior to the duke's announcement to the city of Paris. When later reports made it clear that the battle had been a draw, questions and then rumors about Chartres's conduct during the battle circulated. Chartres was forced to resign from the Navy. Chartres blamed the king and queen for poisoning the environment and blackening his reputation, and his future activities aimed at replacing them on the throne stem from this incident. On the other hand, he should have known better.

In 1779, Spain joined the war against Great Britain. In July, the Spanish and French Fleets rendezvoused off the northwest Spanish coast. They now had sixty-six ships of the line compared to thirty-eight British. Meanwhile, forty thousand men were waiting at Le Havre and St. Malo to board transports and assault Plymouth and Portsmouth. The Franco-Spanish Fleet sailed into the English Channel to find that the coast was clear, so to speak, with the Royal Navy under Admiral Charles Hardy (no relation to Lord Nelson's shipmate Thomas M. Hardy) out of position west of the Channel at the Isles of Scilly. The Franco-Spanish Fleet was in sight of Plymouth when orders came to change the objective to Falmouth in Cornwall. D'Orvilliers knew that Falmouth could not support his Fleet over the winter and asked them to reconsider. While they waited, the Royal Navy sailed past them and made it to Portsmouth, now able to refit for battle. It was late in the year, and the French gave up. I don't think their heart was in it. Anyway, we read that both the war and

THE GREAT GLOBE ITSELF

Navy ministers in France lost their jobs soon after, as did Admiral D'Orvilliers.

Alfred T. Mahan, author of *The Influence of Sea Power Upon History, 1660–1783*, chalked it up to "the flabbiness of coalitions" and seems just as perplexed about it as I am, saying in a footnote:

> The details of the mismanagement of this huge mob of ships are so numerous as to confuse a narrative and are therefore thrown into a footnote. The French Fleet was hurried to sea four thousand men short. The Spaniards were seven weeks in joining. When they met, no common system of signals had been arranged; five fair summer days were spent in remedying this defect. Not till a week after the junction could the Fleet sail for England. No steps were taken to supply the provisions consumed by the French during the seven weeks. The original orders to D'Orvilliers contemplated a landing at Portsmouth, or the seizure of the Isle of Wight, for which a large Army was assembled on the coast of Normandy. Upon reaching the Channel, these orders were suddenly changed, and Falmouth indicated as the point of landing. By this time, August 16, summer was nearly over; and Falmouth, if taken, would offer no shelter to a great Fleet. Then an easterly gale drove the Fleet out of the Channel. By this time the sickness which raged had so reduced the crews that many ships could be neither handled nor fought. Ships companies of eight hundred or a thousand men could muster only from three to five hundred. Thus, bad administration crippled the fighting powers of the Fleet, while the unaccountable military blunder of changing the objective from a safe and accessible roadstead to a fourth rate and exposed harbor completed

the disaster by taking away the only hope of a secure base of operations during the fall and winter months. France then had no first-class port on the Channel; hence the violent westerly gales which prevail in the autumn and winter would have driven the allies into the North Sea.

Spain provided a lot of resources for the invasion of England, but the primary reason they entered the war was to kick the British out of Gibraltar, the point of land in Spain that controlled access into and out of the Mediterranean Sea. It had been a British possession since the end of the War of the Spanish Succession in 1713. The Spanish laid siege to it by land and blockaded it by sea, but the place was so defensible that the British were able to hold on to it. At the end of 1779, food was being rationed, and scurvy broke out among the garrison, but resupply was on the way. The siege lasted four years. Gibraltar had come under siege many times, but this was the Great Siege.

Meanwhile, in India, the British began seizing all the French colonies that were left, starting with Pondicherry in August 1778. By the end of the year, all the French colonies were occupied. France would send a Fleet to India in 1782 under Admiral Pierre Andre Suffren, and he would be quite successful, but not enough to where the British had to give up any possessions in India.

Central and Eastern Europe, 1778–1779

The Potato War, Bohemia, 1778: Whenever the British are losing a war, you can count on some monarch dying suddenly. Now after the surrender of Burgoyne at Saratoga, the elector of Bavaria, Maximilian III Joseph, died of smallpox at the age of fifty in December 1777. We can't pin the blame directly on a British assassin, but the fact is that any incitement of France's continental enemies against France or its allies would have been a welcome relief to Great Britain. Along came the War of the Bavarian Succession.

THE GREAT GLOBE ITSELF

Maximilian Joseph had no son, but he had an heir that everyone agreed was the new elector: Charles Theodor, the elector of the Palatinate. Emperor Joseph II had a claim to large portions of Bavaria, which were based, like Frederick II's claim on Silesia, on some long-ago inheritance issues. Charles Theodor agreed to relinquish these claims to Joseph II because he had no legitimate children but did have some bastards that Joseph II promised to elevate to the status of princes of the empire. In addition, Charles Theodor didn't really care about Bavaria. Unfortunately, Charles Theodor had a legitimate heir, Duke Charles of Zweibruecken, who objected to Bavaria being sliced up. When Joseph II occupied his portion of Bavaria, Duke Charles appealed to Frederick II, who mobilized his Army on the Bohemian border, viewing the addition of Bavaria as a new Habsburg crown land as too upsetting to the balance of power within the Holy Roman Empire. Prussia's ally Saxony was ready to supply twenty thousand troops. It was 1740 all over again, with the change that Russia was on Prussia's side this time, and Catherine appeared ready to honor her alliance with them. France, on the other hand, was at war with Great Britain and had them where they wanted them: isolated in a one-on-one war overseas, where France had a chance to recover their colonial empire. They intended to sidestep their obligations to their ally Austria.

In July 1778, Prussia and Saxony invaded Bohemia with eighty thousand troops. The Austrians were entrenched on the south bank of the Elbe, and the Prussians stayed on the north bank, while the diplomats shuttled between Berlin and Vienna. Operations consisted of raids to steal supplies from the other side, thus giving the conflict the name of the Potato War. There was nothing stopping Frederick from attacking the Austrians, but he was now sixty-six years old. He was not the brash young man that had seized Silesia in 1740, and he was not willing to risk what he had gained. He also realized that a war in Europe would only benefit Great Britain, a country he had despised since 1762.

Maria Theresa, along with Foreign Minister von Kaunitz, took matters into their hands and conducted diplomacy behind Joseph's back. They spoke to Catherine, who spoke to Frederick. An offer was made for Austria to keep a sliver of land in Bavaria. Joseph II was furious with his mother and threatened to abdicate, but she assuaged him, or maybe she called his bluff and told him to quit and let his brother Leopold take over. Most of the Prussians withdrew from Bohemia in October 1778. Small-scale raids and skirmishes continued over the winter. In May 1779, the Treaty of Teschen ended the Potato War and kept the status quo, with Austria getting that sliver of Bavaria. Joseph II kept his dream of acquiring Bavaria, though, and this would come up again in 1785. The British must have been seriously disappointed that a war hadn't flared up in Europe.

Russia interferes in the Crimea, 1779: Catherine had said she was ready to stand by her Prussian ally, but she was actually more interested in what was happening in Poland, in the Balkans, in the Crimea, and at home in Saint Petersburg. She was wrestling with assimilation issues in her new Polish territories. Crimea was nominally independent, but in 1779, the Crimean Khan Devlet IV attempted to renew their dependence on the Ottoman Empire, which would have been like Texas attempting to rejoin Mexico after gaining independence. Catherine forced Devlet to abdicate. She was listening to Potemkin, who was advocating his Greek Plan that would require close cooperation and alliance with Austria and paying less attention to Panin and her son Paul, who advocated the Northern System of alliance with Prussia. Supporting Prussia against Austria would have wrecked the Greek Plan.

The Ottomans pointed out that Russian intervention in Crimea was contrary to the 1774 treaty that Russia and the Ottomans signed to end their 1768–1774 war. The Russians then negotiated a new treaty with the Ottomans, the Treaty of Aynalikavak, which was and is a palace in Constantinople, where both sides promised not to interfere in Crimean politics. The treaty was signed in March 1779. At home in Saint Petersburg, Catherine was still fending off the demands of her son for the crown he considered rightfully his, and he wasn't wrong about that.

THE GREAT GLOBE ITSELF

1780–1783: Solid as the Rock of Gibraltar

The American Revolution, 1780–1781

The British capture of Charleston: In January 1780, Generals Clinton and Cornwallis departed New York City with 8,500 men, leaving the Hessian general Wilhelm von Knyphausen in command in New York. The objective was Charleston, South Carolina, defended by Benjamin Lincoln and five thousand troops. Clinton landed in Savannah, already under British control, and moved his force north. By early April, he had cut Charleston off by land and sea. General Lincoln attempted to surrender under "honors of war" conditions and was denied. In May, he surrendered unconditionally, the largest surrender of American forces until the Confederates captured Harper's Ferry in the 1862 Antietam campaign. Clinton left Cornwallis in Charleston with eight thousand men and returned to New York. Lincoln and Washington would remember the terms of surrender when Cornwallis's turn came in 1781. Because Lincoln was a native born American, he retained the confidence of Washington and was given a command in Washington's New York Army after he was exchanged in November 1780. At the same time that he was serving as Washington's subordinate in the Army, on March 1, 1781, the Confederation Congress, on the first day of its existence, made Lincoln Washington's nominal boss as secretary at war, which, for the record, was the correct title until 1789, when Washington changed it to secretary *of* war. Lincoln served in both roles until after Cornwallis surrendered, and then he resigned his position in the Army. He went back to Massachusetts and led a force that suppressed Shays' Rebellion in 1786.

The French Fleet in Newport and the West Indies, 1780: Meanwhile, in July 1780, a French Fleet under Admiral De Barras, along with six thousand French troops under General Rochambeau, landed in Newport, Rhode Island, which, as we recall, the British had evacuated in October 1779. This was the *Expédition Particulière*, or "Special Expedition," that would eventually bottle up Cornwallis at Yorktown and end the war. Most of the Royal Navy was on the other side of the Atlantic, in the midst of organizing a Fleet to resupply Gibraltar, so they were unable to oppose the French Fleet's movements. There was another French Fleet under Admiral De Grasse based in the West Indies. Both of these Fleets would be used in 1781 against the British at Yorktown.

Young Andrew Jackson: After capturing Charleston, Cornwallis conducted some mopping-up operations that thirteen-year-old Andrew Jackson and his brother Robert participated in. They were captured in 1781, and this was when Jackson was ordered to clean the boots of a British officer. He refused and was whacked with a sword for his impertinence. One thing we notice about pictures of Andrew Jackson is that most of them feature someone brandishing a weapon. Robert and Andrew were sent to a prisoner of war camp where they got smallpox. Robert died in April 1781, but Andrew survived and was returned to his mother. She got cholera and died in November 1781 while caring for other sick ex-prisoners of war. Andrew Jackson's entire family was dead, and henceforward, he carried a lifelong personal dislike of all things British. Perhaps it was big news in the South at the time that the Spanish were overrunning West Florida, and if so, Jackson would remember this when he conquered it in 1819 to international outrage.

His mother's relatives took in the angry fourteen-year-old orphan. They taught him the saddling trade, but in 1785, he traveled the seventy miles from Waxhaw to Salisbury, probably on a saddle he made, and began the study of the law with a local attorney. He worked hard, and he played hard. The activities of young men in that time and place included cockfighting, horse racing, brewing and drinking bourbon whiskey, and lots of carousing with prostitutes. By 1788, he was practicing as an attorney in the western district of North Carolina, a.k.a. Tennessee. The town where he lived and worked had been founded on the Cumberland River in December 1778 as Fort Nashborough. It was named for Francis Nash, a North Carolina militia brigadier general who had been was killed in action at the Battle of Germantown in October 1777. It became the city of Nashville in 1784 and the capital of the new state of Tennessee in 1798. There are those who assert that the name Tennessee was selected by Jackson and that Nashville became the capital of Tennessee also because of Jackson, but others say that Jackson is getting too much credit.

Cornwallis in the South, 1780–1781: Washington detached Continental Army units from Southern states down to Greensboro, North Carolina, and appointed General Horatio Gates to command of the Southern Department. Gates arrived in Greensboro on July 25 and immediately marched his force, which was mostly militia, into South Carolina. He set up a defensive position near a British outpost at Camden. On August 16, Cornwallis moved out from Charleston and scattered Gates' Army at the Battle of Camden. The remnants rallied in Hillsborough, North Carolina. Gates was replaced with General Nathanael Greene. *Sic transit gloria mundi.* Gates was assigned to Washington's staff for the rest of the war and retired after the Treaty of Paris in 1783. It should be pointed out that Greensboro was called Capefair at the time and was renamed Greensboro in honor of General Greene.

As far as Cornwallis was concerned, he had returned Georgia and South Carolina to the old loyalty and now intended to do the same in North Carolina. He raised loyalist militias in South Carolina and then planned to pursue Greene's Army in North Carolina. In October 1780, loyalist militia faced off against patriot militia in the Battle of King's Mountain, and the loyalists were defeated by the patriots. John Sevier was one of the patriot commanders; he would be the first governor of Tennessee and a bitter political rival of Andrew Jackson. Of course, *all* of Andrew Jackson's rivalries were bitter ones. The American victory at King's Mountain forced Cornwallis to retreat back into South Carolina. One of Greene's subordinates, Dan Morgan, encountered and defeated Cornwallis's subordinate Banastre Tarleton at the Battle of Cowpens in January 1781.

Cornwallis now pursued Greene's Army across North Carolina. Greene retreated to his base in Greensboro, North Carolina, where he received reinforcements from the Virginia militia. He then turned and faced the British at the Battle of Guilford Courthouse. The British won the battle, but attrition began to factor into Cornwallis's plans. He marched to Wilmington, where he made contact with the Fleet, and learned that Benedict Arnold was in Virginia. Cornwallis arranged to meet up with Arnold's force in Portsmouth in May 1781. Cornwallis took command of the combined force, while Arnold returned to New York, where he took another command that launched an assault on Connecticut, as described above. Washington sent Lafayette to Virginia to counter Arnold and then Cornwallis, but Lafayette was instructed not to directly engage the enemy.

General Greene now saw an opportunity to reestablish patriot control over South Carolina and Georgia, even though most of his militia had disbanded after Cornwallis retreated. He headed back to Camden to face the British there and was defeated on April 25, 1781, but the British abandoned Camden soon after and returned to Charleston. Greene continued to fight and lose, and the British continued to win and retreat, and by October 1781, British control of the South was limited to the coastal strip between Savannah and Charleston. General Greene had won a great name for himself, and the "indispensable" George Washington, who knew that cemeteries are filled with indispensable men, let it be known that Greene would be the best person to fill his shoes if anything happened to him.

American victory at Yorktown, 1781: Cornwallis spent the month of June operating between Portsmouth and Charlottesville, destroying thousands of pounds of tobacco. He attempted to capture Thomas Jefferson, who was governor at the time, but he was unsuccessful as Jefferson once again fled. After the British left Virginia, there was an inquiry into Jefferson's conduct, which ultimately decided it had been honorable.

Rochambeau's Army marched from Newport and linked up with the Continental Army on July 7, 1781, at Dobbs Ferry, west of White Plains. Clinton braced for an assault on New York, which was what Washington, but not Rochambeau, wanted. Clinton sent a letter to Cornwallis, telling him to find a good spot for the Navy to come pick him up and bring him and his Army back to New York. Cornwallis brought the Army to Yorktown, set up a defensive position next to some good anchorage (there is still a naval station at Yorktown today), and waited for Admiral Graves, the current flavor of the month commanding the Royal Navy's North American station, to come down from New York. Graves had been in command of the North American station since March 1781.

Rochambeau and Washington began moving south to Virginia on August 19. At the same time, the West Indies French Fleet under De Grasse came up to rendezvous with the Newport Fleet under De Barras. On September 5, 1781, the combined Fleets engaged Admiral Graves' Fleet. They got the best of the engagement, and Graves returned to New York Harbor.

Cornwallis faced only the small force of Lafayette until Washington and Rochambeau arrived in late September. The siege lasted three weeks, and Cornwallis surrendered on October 19. As had happened at Saratoga, a large British force had been defeated by venturing too far from its base. In New York, repairs were made to the ships, but it was October 25 by the time Clinton was able to send relief. They were on the way to Yorktown when they learned of Cornwallis's surrender, and they returned to New York. Washington stated that the terms of surrender would be the same as when Lincoln surrendered Charleston, which is to say, unconditionally. Cornwallis pled sickness and sent his second-in-command, so Washington sent *his* second-in-command, Benjamin Lincoln.

The victory at Yorktown was dampened somewhat by the death of John Parke Custis, Washington's stepson, on November 5. The cause of death was camp fever (either dysentery or typhus) at the age of twenty-six. He had not been with the Army long, only joining when it came to Yorktown. You have to wonder if maybe the sudden appearance of Washington's stepson just at the moment of Washington's triumph raised any alarms at the prospect of a Washington dynasty in America's future rather than a republic. If so, that alarm was silenced by the suspiciously premature death of John Parke Custis.

Despite his early death, he left seven children behind, born between 1775 and 1781. His remarkably fertile widow, Eleanor Calvert, who was descended from Lord Baltimore, the founder of Maryland, remarried and had sixteen more children. Jack Custis had been a charming man who made some land purchases, including tracts that are now Washington National Airport and Arlington Cemetery, under unfavorable terms. His son George Washington Parke Custis was the father of Mary Anna Randolph Custis, who married Robert E. Lee in 1831. If Washington had made himself a king, Robert E. Lee would have been the consort of a queen!

After the victory at Yorktown, French Admirals De Grasse and De Barras sailed back to the West Indies and Newport, respectively. De Grasse was later defeated in April 1782 by Admiral George Rodney at the Battle of the Saintes, thwarting a planned French-Spanish invasion of Jamaica for the purpose of regaining it for Spain. This was the last major engagement of the Anglo-French War of 1778–1783. After Yorktown, Clinton submitted his resignation. He was replaced in May 1782 by General Guy Carleton, who would be responsible for evacuating New York after the peace treaty was signed. Clinton continued to have a military and political career until his death in 1794, aged sixty-four.

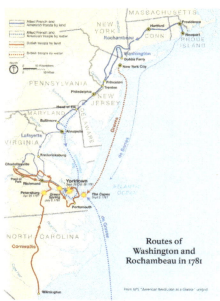

Routes of Washington and Rochambeau in 1781

THE GREAT GLOBE ITSELF

Great Britain lost the war because France and Spain declared war on them, and Russia and Prussia formed a naval armed league of neutrality against them. The British had no allies because of their bad behavior to their ally Prussia in 1762, so George III only had to look in a mirror to know who to blame. If they could have fought America alone, they would have been able to complete that Hudson River move, isolating New England. Then they could have completed that operation where Georgia, South Carolina, and North Carolina would be successfully returned to their loyalty. Then they might have offered independence to Pennsylvania, New Jersey, Delaware, Maryland, and Virginia and let the sectional differences tear the Union apart.

Other theaters of war, 1780–1783

Gibraltar, Minorca, and India, 1780–1783: The British garrison in Gibraltar had been under siege since June 1779. Supplies became scarce, but a relief convoy under Admiral George Rodney made it through on January 25, 1780. A second relief convoy under Admiral George Darby made it through on April 12, 1781. Great Britain could resupply Gibraltar at will. A proverb, solid as the Rock of Gibraltar, entered the English language on both sides of the Atlantic, and I doubt many Americans know that it derives from a battle won by the British in the midst of our War for Independence.

In August 1781, a French-Spanish force invaded Minorca, and the British there surrendered in February 1782. The losing commander, General James Murray, avoided the fate of Admiral Byng and, instead of a firing squad, received only a reprimand. Lord North had been on thin ice after Yorktown, but it was only now after Minorca that Parliament passed a vote of no confidence against him, and he resigned, replaced by the Marquess of Rockingham. Spain kept Minorca after the war, although the British captured it once again in 1798 but returned it to Spain in 1802, and it is part of Spain to this day.

The victorious French general at Minorca, the Duke of Crillon, now vowed to repeat his success in Gibraltar. He ordered the construction of floating batteries to strike the British, but the British guns destroyed them when they approached Gibraltar in September 1782. In October 1782, a third convoy under Admiral Howe relieved Gibraltar, and the Spanish told their ally France that they wanted an end to the war.

France sent a Fleet to Pondicherry under Admiral Pierre Andre Suffren. Between February 1782 and June 1783, he fought the British five times. His service was viewed as credible, and he was lauded by Louis XVI, but France gained no possessions in India as a result.

The United States, 1781–1783

The Continental Army, 1781–1783: In October 1781, Cornwallis 's disarmed Army was led off to winter quarters in Maryland and Virginia. The Continental Army wintered in the vicinity of Yorktown. Washington spent the winter at Mount Vernon, and he and the Army departed Virginia in March 1782, establishing his headquarters at Newburgh, New York. This was fifty miles north of White Plains and fifteen miles north of West Point. Clinton and his Army were still in New York City in large numbers. The Confederation Congress was unable to pay the Army as the states were not providing them any financial support, as the states were also facing financial problems. The Army blamed the lack of pay on the inability of republican forms of government to collect taxes, and pointed out that the dictator Oliver Cromwell never had any difficulty obtaining funds. These thoughts came to Washington's attention in a letter written in May 1782 by Colonel Lewis Nicola, an Irishman descended from Huguenot refugees who had lived in Pennsylvania since 1766. Washington may or may not have put Nicola up to it, with Nicola writing the letter just to give Washington the opportunity to loudly and publicly denounce any idea that he would use the Army to make himself another Cromwell.

In August 1782, Washington established the Purple Heart Order of Merit. He called it the Badge of Military Merit. It was awarded to soldiers until such time as the Continental Army was disbanded. I suppose it was some sort of compensation in lieu of pay. It was inspired by the French award the Cross of Saint Louis,

THE GREAT GLOBE ITSELF

awarded for wartime valor—"*Bellicae Virtutis Praemium*," as it said on the medal. The Purple Heart was revived in 1932 by Douglas MacArthur, who used it to replace the Army Wound Ribbon, given to soldiers in World War I who were wounded or killed in action.

Also in August 1782, General Carleton, Clinton's replacement in New York, advised Washington that peace talks had been opened in Paris, which Washington already knew because his superiors were telling him the same thing, but as there was no official truce, Carleton was making it clear that he had no intention of conducting any offensives.

In December 1782, the British evacuated Charleston. General Nathanael Greene marched in a few hours later. Greene was a native Rhode Islander, but when he returned there after the war, he found that his finances were in disarray, and he was heavily in debt. The government of Georgia had awarded him a plantation near Savannah in gratitude for his service, so he left Rhode Island and went back to Georgia to work on it. Greene had only been there a year when he died of sunstroke at his plantation in June 1786, at the age of forty-three. I guess there wasn't anyone around reminding him that he wasn't in Rhode Island anymore. I think it's suspicious that the man who was identified as the replacement for the indispensable man died so suddenly at such a young age. He left a young wife, Catherine, and seven children. Catherine kept the plantation going, which was the same one where Eli Whitney invented the cotton gin, short for engine, in 1794, as will be described below.

In March 1783, Washington addressed a group of officers who were agitating for guarantees of rewards for their military service. Washington pleaded with them to resist any man who "wickedly attempts to open the floodgates of civil discord and deluge our rising empire in blood." The most effective part of the speech was when he pulled out a pair of glasses (they had just been prescribed) and said, "Gentlemen, you must pardon me. I have grown gray in your service and now find myself growing blind."

In November 1783, the British evacuated New York, and Washington entered the city. It must have been with mixed feelings, given the way he had been chased out in 1776. A few weeks later, he bade farewell to the Continental Army at Fraunces Tavern, New

York. Washington said, "With a heart filled with love and gratitude, I now take leave of you. I most devoutly wish that your latter days may be as prosperous and happy as your former ones have been glorious and honorable." All the equipment used by the Continental Army was hauled to West Point for storage and training purposes. The Army also kept a few border outposts on the western frontier. Training of cadets as artillery and engineer officers (a single branch in those days) at West Point predated the official establishment of the United States Military Academy by nineteen years.

Slavery and other sectional differences: The Treaty of Paris between the United States and Paris was finally signed on September 3, 1783. Great Britain signed a separate treaty with France, Spain, and the Netherlands. The British conceded all land east of the Mississippi River to the United States of America, as they were so "stiled" by the Articles of Confederation. Spain continued to own the Louisiana Territory and received East and West Florida. They also received Minorca. It now only remained for the treaty to be ratified.

Great Britain, having run North America for 180 years, was well aware of the challenges facing the United States: the Spaniards to the west and south, the Indians to the north, and the internal contradictions between trade-dependent New England, the slave-dependent south, and the central states full of farmers. If the British were smart, they would exploit all of these weaknesses. They were smart, but Washington would be smarter in every case.

Great Britain also made peace with France. War continued with the Netherlands for a few more months. France did not get a good return on its investment in its Navy, as it failed to obtain the colonies to generate the trade that Britain used to pay for their Navy. The seeds were sown for the financial crisis that would lead to the French

Revolution. For seventy years since the death of Louis XIV, France had been losing to Great Britain the way that Austria would be losing to France in a few years: continually, expensively, and in humiliating fashion. This hardly made up for it.

The war being over, America turned its thoughts to sectional differences, with slavery at the top of the agenda. In April 1783, the Commonwealth of Massachusetts effectively ended slavery as a result of a ruling by Chief Justice William Cushing in the case of *Commonwealth v. Jennison*, in which a fine of forty shillings was upheld on Jennison for beating his slave Kwaku "Quock" Walker for running away. Quock had long since been freed, but the decision upheld the idea that the Massachusetts Constitution as written was incompatible with slavery. The 1790 census showed a population of zero slaves in the state. Slavery was not officially abolished in the state until 1865. Cushing later presided over the trials of members of Shays' Rebellion and then was an associate justice of the United States Supreme Court from 1789 to 1810.

As described above, Pennsylvania had passed a law of gradual emancipation in 1780, and other states now followed suit in the following sequence: New Hampshire, 1783; Connecticut and Rhode Island, 1784; New York, 1799; and New Jersey, 1804. Slavery remained legal in Delaware, Maryland, Virginia, North Carolina, South Carolina, and Georgia. Of the thirteen colonies, plus Vermont, there were eight free states and six slave states. The Northwest Ordinance of 1787 prohibited slavery in the Northwest Territory.

The Articles of Confederation, 1781 to 1783: On March 1, 1781, the Continental Congress implemented the Articles of Confederation, all thirteen states having ratified them. They declared the Continental Congress adjourned. The next day, the same congressmen went to the same building with the same powers and the same organization and leadership and declared the United States Congress convened.

As far as an executive authority, the Articles of Confederation said:

> The united *[sic]* States, in congress assembled, shall have authority to appoint a commit-

tee, to sit in the recess of congress, to be denominated, "A Committee of the States," and to consist of one delegate from each State; and to appoint such other committees and civil officers as may be necessary for managing the general affairs of the united states under their direction—to appoint one of their number to preside; provided that no person be allowed to serve in the office of President more than one year in any term of three years...

The Board of War, which had been used in the days of the Conway Cabal in an attempt to oust Washington, was dissolved in February 1781, and the first appointment made under the Articles of Confederation was Benjamin Lincoln as secretary at war on March 1, 1781. As stated above, Lincoln kept both his position in the Army and his cabinet position until Cornwallis surrendered, and his primary task seems to have been to perform any duty that Washington felt not to his liking. Lincoln resigned in November 1783, and the office was vacant until Henry Knox took the job in March 1785. Lincoln went home to Massachusetts, played a part in suppressing Shays' Rebellion in 1786, stayed active in Massachusetts government until 1809, and died in 1810 at the age of seventy-seven.

Congress also established the office of superintendent of finance and nominated Robert Morris for the position. He negotiated with Congress as to the powers of his office and eventually convinced them that his powers should be similar to what Jacques Necker held in France, which is to say he was equivalent to a prime minister. Morris also took on the role of agent of Marine, a precursor to the job of secretary of the Navy, as it was the tool for the government to stop smuggling by issuing letters of marque to mercenary warships. Morris had a thankless job ahead of him as the war had damaged the economy through spending and destruction. He did what he could, establishing the Bank of North America as a Pennsylvania state bank, acquiring, with help from John Adams, a loan from the Dutch to capitalize the government, and issuing paper currency backed by the

THE GREAT GLOBE ITSELF

capital of the bank to replace the Continental currency. Although legally a private bank, it was the first central bank of the American government and lasted ten years until the Bank of the United States replaced it in 1791. Morris also established a mint, the decimal currency, and the use of the term *dollar* as well as the symbol $. He didn't invent the term *dollar*; he borrowed it from Spain. Spanish silver dollars portrayed two columns draped in an *s*-shaped scroll.

Morris had a hard time acquiring revenue as all the states were in financial difficulties. The United States stopped payments of interest on the war loans it had received from France, furthering the financial instability that led to the French Revolution. Morris resigned from his offices in November 1784, and his duties were taken over by boards. He was a senator from 1789 to 1795, lost all of his money in 1797 after a financial panic, spent time in debtors' prison from 1798 to 1801, and spent his last years quietly and modestly, dying in 1806 at the age of seventy-two.

To handle foreign affairs, Congress established the office of secretary of foreign affairs. They appointed Robert R. Livingston as the first secretary, and he took office in 1781. His duties seem to have been restricted to reporting to Congress on the status of the negotiations of the 1783 Treaty of Paris. He took office after Yorktown and resigned in June 1783. The cause of his resignation was that the American delegates (Benjamin Franklin, John Jay, John Adams, and Henry Laurens) had disregarded his instructions and sought a peace with Great Britain separate from Spain and France, which was a good move because the United States was able to get the land between the Appalachians and the Mississippi River out of it. The office remained vacant until John Jay took it in December 1784, just at the time that Morris was resigning.

In June 1782, Congress adopted the Great Seal of the United States, which can be seen today on the back of the $1 bill. The act established the bald eagle as the national bird, along with three Latin slogans: *Annuit Coeptis* (He has approved our undertakings); *Novus Ordo Seclorum* (New order of the ages); and *E Pluribus Unum* (Out of many, one). The eagle holds an olive branch with thirteen leaves in its right claw and thirteen arrows in its left. The Founding Fathers were fond of comparing the American Republic to the Roman Republic and its legionary eagles, and Napoleon Bonaparte would lift a leaf from their book on that line.

In December 1782, Alexander Hamilton got himself elected to Congress from New York, where he served for about a year. It was the only time he held elective office. He served at the same time as James Madison. They both figured out soon enough that Congress was not the place to be. Madison was soon back in Virginia serving in the House of Delegates, while Hamilton was back in New York founding the Bank of New York a few doors down from Federal Hall.

Thomas Jefferson was supposed to be in Paris, but he was tending to his wife, Martha, who was very ill after giving birth to a child. She died on September 6, 1782, and the child died in 1785. Jefferson worked on his book *Notes on the State of Virginia* during this time. Jefferson wrote that:

> It will probably be asked, "Why not retain and incorporate the blacks into the state, and thus save the expense of supplying, by importation of white settlers, the vacancies they will leave?" Deep rooted prejudices entertained by the whites; ten thousand recollections, by the blacks, of the injuries they have sustained; new provocations; the real distinctions which nature has made; and many other circumstances, will divide us into parties, and produce convulsions which will probably never end but in the extermination of the one or the other race.

In June 1783, the Continental Army soldiers in Pennsylvania responsible for the security of the US Congress demanded their pay. Congress sent a request to the Pennsylvania state government asking for state militia to protect Congress. The state government declined, saying that they had talked to their generals, who could not assure them of the militia's reliability. That may have been true, or it may have been that the state of Pennsylvania refused to submit to the demands of a few hysterical congressmen. Congress then adjourned to Princeton, New Jersey, and stayed there for the next four months. The building used by Congress, Nassau Hall, on the campus of Princeton, is still there today. Congress stayed away from Philadelphia until 1790, when a law was passed, establishing the District of Columbia and Washington City, with Philadelphia to serve as the capital until 1800.

The first important act of Congress after the Treaty of Paris was the Confederation Congress Proclamation of September 1783. It prohibited "all persons from making settlements on lands inhabited or claimed by Indians, without the limits or jurisdiction of any particular State, and from purchasing or receiving any gift or cession of such lands or claims without the express authority and directions of the United States in Congress assembled." It was an almost verbatim restatement of the Proclamation of 1763, the policy of the orderly settlement of the western territory. It asserted that the US government, like His Majesty's government before them, was owner of all the land west of the Appalachians, and they were going to get paid for it before anyone settled on it. The policy was affirmed in the 1820s, when the Supreme Court heard cases invalidating title to land purchased from Indians directly by private individuals or corporations.

Congress adjourned from Princeton on November 3, 1783, and convened in Annapolis on November 26. On December 20, Washington resigned his commission there and departed for Mount Vernon. This act of self-denial, unprecedented since the days of Cincinnatus, had tremendous impacts on the history of America. Benjamin Franklin wrote to one of his British friends, "An American planter was chosen by us to command our troops and continued during the whole war. This man sent home to you, one after another, five of your best generals, baffled, their heads bare of laurels, disgraced even in the opinion of their employers." There was Gage, Howe, Clinton, Cornwallis, and Burgoyne, so we will give Franklin some credit for being able to count.

Washington's self-denial was noble but was also a well-calculated political move. He had read the Articles of Confederation and saw that he would be unable to do anything unless nine states agreed he could, and that he would be a creature of Congress. So he went home.

Great Britain, 1780–1783

The League of Armed Neutrality, 1780–1783: Since the start of the war between France and Great Britain in 1778, Great Britain had been executing a policy of unlimited searches of neutral shipping for French contraband. This had affected Danish, Swedish, and Dutch ships. In March 1780, Russia declared that neutral countries had the right to trade with countries that were at war (that is, France) except for contraband, which was strictly defined as weapons and ammunition, and that Russia would view countries who interfered with such trade (that is, Great Britain) as hostile. Denmark and Sweden signed on to the declaration, and the League of Armed Neutrality was formed. The Netherlands tried to sign on as well, but Britain declared war on them in 1781, so they were no longer neutrals. Prussia, Austria, the Ottomans, Sicily/Naples, and even Portugal had joined by 1783. Much of the shipbuilding material used by the Royal Navy came from the Baltic, so Great Britain backed down on their ship-searching policy. The league disbanded in 1783, when the war between France and Great Britain ended. It was considered such a success that Paul I tried it again in 1800, forming the Second League of Armed Neutrality, but that ended when Paul I was assassinated by the British.

The Gordon Riots, 1780: In June 1780, Lord George Gordon, a member of Parliament and a younger brother of the fourth Duke of Gordon, led a demonstration of fifty thousand people that marched on Parliament to present a petition for the repeal of the Catholic Emancipation Act of 1778. A similar action by him in 1779 had been successful in Scotland in stopping the law from being passed by the Scottish Parliament. Parliament should have called out the Army, but since Gordon was an MP, they took a different approach. They did not take any votes that day but promised to consider it the following Monday. The demonstrators were well organized, waving blue flags and wearing blue cockades in their hats. For the next few days, there were riots, destruction of Catholic churches and homes, and a mass release of all prisoners at Newgate Prison, with a large graffito on the wall saying, "Released by order of King Mob!" The phrase "King Mob" later became associated with Andrew Jackson and his followers. The home of the chief justice, the Earl of Mansfield, he who had outlawed slavery in England in 1772 by his ruling in

Somerset's case, was destroyed. I think this was because the subtext behind the rioting was opposition to the war in America, and Mansfield had incited anti-American feeling by his ruling in Somerset's case. We've seen the British play the slavery card against the Americans before.

Three hundred people died in the rioting. There was no such thing as riot police in those days, and the Army had to be called in after all. Gordon was arrested and confined to the Tower of London. He was tried for high treason in 1781 but acquitted. In 1786, he was excommunicated from the Anglican Church for refusing to take an oath, and in 1787, he converted to Orthodox Judaism, looking Hasidic in an eighteenth-century kind of way. Also in 1787, he was convicted of defaming Marie Antoinette, the French ambassador, and the administration of justice in England. He escaped to the Netherlands. The government of France requested that the Netherlands deport him, which they did in 1788. He was apprehended by the authorities in Great Britain and sent to prison for five years. He died in November 1793 of typhus, not long after his release from prison, aged forty-two. Charles Dickens wrote a novel about the Gordon riots called *Barnaby Rudge* in 1841.

Instability in the prime minister's office, 1782–1783: George III's policies had lost Great Britain the United States and Florida. George had paid a price for it when his man Lord North had been forced to resign as prime minister. As stated above, North was able to survive the surrender at Yorktown, but the February 1782 loss of Minorca, which brought up echoes of Admiral Byng from back in 1756, was the last straw, Parliament passed a vote of no confidence, and North resigned in March 1782, the first time a prime minister was forced from office by such a vote. The Marquess of Rockingham, long in opposition to George III, was named prime minister. As we recall, Rockingham had previously served as prime minister in 1765 and had attempted to appease the Americans on taxes. Rockingham was again in full appeasement mode, but he died of the flu in July 1782 after only four months in office. He was replaced by his deputy, Shelburne, who was not ready for prime time and soon found himself vulnerable to a coalition between Lord North and Charles James Fox. Shelburne was forced out of office in April 1783 after negotiating the Paris Peace Treaties, ending all of Great Britain's wars.

Charles James Fox had been an outspoken opponent of the war in America since the beginning, expressing great amusement at every British setback and often showing up at Parliament wearing a buff and blue suit that resembled a Continental Army uniform. There was no politician that George III loathed more. Fox had served under Rockingham but refused to serve under Shelburne and had made common cause with North to bring down Shelburne's government. North was settling some old scores with Shelburne by teaming up with Fox, but George III never forgave him. From April to December 1783, Fox and North led a coalition government, but neither had the title of prime minister, which went to the Duke of Portland. North

THE GREAT GLOBE ITSELF

remained in Parliament but began to go blind in 1786. He died in 1792 at the age of sixty.

The maneuvering against Shelburne had been all parliamentary in nature, with George III as nothing more than a spectator, and he felt he had lost all his power. Things were just as bad in his private life, where two-year-old Prince Alfred died after being inoculated for smallpox in 1782, and then the next year, the same thing happened to four-year-old Prince Octavius. George III was at a low point and would have considered abdicating had it not been for his unwillingness to turn the crown over to his twenty-one-year-old son, George, the Prince of Wales, who was closely tied to Fox and whose only ability, the king thought, was that he could swear in three languages. Leslie Mitchell, author of a biography of Fox, says, "George III let it be widely broadcast that he held Fox principally responsible for the Prince's many failings, not least a tendency to vomit in public."

Fox and Portland had been imposed on George III against his will, but he carried on, convincing the lords to defeat a bill Fox submitted regarding India in December 1783 and then recruiting William Pitt the Younger to take the job of prime minister. The only condition that he placed on Pitt was that he could not appoint Lord North, whom he considered to have betrayed him, to any position. Pitt was only twenty-four. A verse went around, "A sight to make all nations stand and stare/a Kingdom entrusted to a schoolboy's care." Parliament refused to accept Pitt and passed a vote of no confidence. Pitt stayed in office while an election was conducted in March 1784, with Pitt obtaining a majority. The king had asserted his right to appoint the ministers he wanted, and Pitt had started an eighteen-year-long term of office.

The Irish Constitution of 1782: In 1778, the Catholic Relief Act had gone into effect in Great Britain. It eliminated many legal burdens on Catholics that had been around since the days of Queen Elizabeth I, providing that the Catholic person took an oath that, among other things, denounced the Stuart family and its right to the British throne. The law was passed, in part, to allow (or legalize something to which a blind eye had long been turned) the enlistment of English and Irish Catholics into the British Army for service in

America. Legalizing Catholic military service was a sign that it was getting harder for the Army to recruit, and that people were tiring of the war. It was also thought that the act would appease the Irish, who were getting ideas about rebellion from what was happening in America.

One thing that Rockingham managed to accomplish during his brief watch was to pass the Constitution of 1782, a series of acts that increased the legislative and judicial independence of the kingdom of Ireland. For years, there had been a lot of talk among the Irish about repeating the success of the American Revolution to create a free and independent Republic of Ireland, and this put an end to it for now. The chief executive of Ireland was still the lord lieutenant sent from London, but the Irish government was given a great deal of control over its own legislation, judicial system, and military matters. The system worked well, and the 1798 Irish Rebellion was brought under control completely by the Irish government with no involvement of British troops. Nevertheless, for various reasons, the Parliament in London would decide to formally unify Great Britain and Ireland into the United Kingdom by the 1801 Act of Union.

France, 1780–1783

French financial problems, 1780–1783: France was spending a lot of money on supporting the American Revolution and their other operations against the British. Necker was doing a lot of borrowing and no raising of taxes. After the failures of 1779, he began warning Vergennes that money was growing short. Vergennes and others, including Marie Antoinette, began accusing Necker of corruption and incompetence. Necker complained about not being on the royal counsel due to his Protestantism. Anti-Necker pamphlets began to circulate, and in February 1781, Necker retaliated by publishing a pamphlet titled *Compte Rendu au Roi* (Account Rendered to the King), which claimed that revenues exceeded expenses by ten million livres. Release of government financial data was unprecedented in France and made Necker 's critics very angry just for that reason. They were even angrier when it became apparent that Necker was leaving out fifty-six million livres in interest payments. In response, Necker claimed that he was demonstrating that it was the war that was ruining France. Whatever his intent, the pamphlet was misleading. Necker had become popular, but he was fired and replaced by Jean Francois Joly de Fleury in May 1781. This Fleury may have been related to the Cardinal Fleury who had been Louis XV's tutor and minister until 1743, but I have been unable to locate the family tree. To pay for the war, Fleury raised taxes on the nobles and cut Louis XVI's court budget, but the war was over in May 1783, and Fleury was soon out. His replacement, Henri d'Ormesson, cut the taxes. D'Ormesson was replaced by Charles Alexandre de Calonne in November 1783, two months after the Paris peace treaties were concluded. Vergennes and Louis XVI vowed to stand by any plan Calonne had to balance the budget.

The Duke of Orleans and the Palais-Royal: It was in 1780 that the

Duke of Orleans, Louis the Fat (1725–1785), gave his son and heir, the Duke of Chartres, Louis Philippe II, the title to the Palais-Royal in Paris. Chartres had lived there since his marriage in 1769. His son, the future King Louis Philippe, was born there in 1773. As we recall, Chartres had been humiliated in 1778 by Louis XVI and Marie Antoinette after prematurely announcing a victory at Ushant when it had been, at best, a draw. He began developing the Palais-Royal with theaters, shops, and salons, and in 1784, it debuted as the place for all levels of society to hang out. Aristocrats shopped and promenaded there, and the debauched solicited prostitutes. Sometimes the aristocrats solicited higher-class prostitutes. It made Chartres very popular in Paris. The saying went around, *"Le Palais-Royal est à Paris ce que Paris est à la France"* (The Palais-Royal is to Paris as Paris is to France).

Louis was always busy operating the executive machinery in Versailles, so he never visited Paris unless it was for a séance or a lit de justice, two processes used to force the royal will over the parlements. Sometimes the parlement came to Versailles to undergo one process or the other. People in Paris compared the always-present Chartres favorably to the always-absent Louis. Chartres gained a good feeling for the attitude of the people of Paris and understood their potential power. He was also a believer in the Enlightenment and was well-read on Rousseau, Voltaire, and the contents of the Diderot's *Encyclopedia*. He was also grand master of the *Grand Orient de France*, the country's central Masonic organization. He used this position to operate a Paris-based network of bourgeoisie lawyers, businessmen, and politicians that spread throughout France and Europe and even to America. No one can know for sure when Chartres decided that he was going to overthrow Louis and supplant him as king. He certainly gained inspiration from the American Revolution. Some people say that he was innocent of attempting revolution, but those people are wrong. His adherents were called Girondists during the Revolution and Orleanists after. The fact that his son Louis Philippe spent his career angling for and attaining the French crown as a pro-British bourgeoisie monarch provides strong evidence that Chartres sought the same thing during his lifetime.

The Segur Ordinance, 1781: The war against Great Britain required more men for the military, and members of the bourgeoisie bought titles so they or their sons could serve as officers. They would have said they were acting out of love of king and country, but the hereditary nobility accused them of mercenary motives and that only the hereditary nobility acted out of duty. In France, before 1789, there was no such thing as militia, only regular professionals. Military service provided social prestige, financial security, and exemption from taxes. Louis and his ministers feared that in some future contest, the new bourgeoisie officers might be more inclined toward Chartres than Louis, so in May 1781, they enacted the Segur Ordinance (Segur was the minister for war from 1780 to 1787), which required officer candidates to show four generations of nobility in the male line. The only exception was for the sons and grandsons of men who had been awarded the Cross of Saint Louis, which was the *ancient regime* version of the Legion of Honor. This caused an outcry among the bourgeoisie, who, after all, ran in the same social circles as the nobles and were sending their kids to the same colleges. The law was never repealed, but it became moot in 1789, when the National Assembly organized militias in the forms of the National Guards and Federes.

Central and Eastern Europe, 1780–1783

The reforms of Joseph II: In November 1780, Maria Theresa caught the flu and died at the age of sixty-three. She was widely mourned, even by her archnemesis Frederick II. Her son Joseph II now had a free hand to rule as he saw fit. In February 1781, he issued a decree reducing state censorship of the press to blasphemy of the church, subversion of the state, and immorality. The power to censor and ban was taken from local authorities and centralized. The number of banned tracts in the Austrian crown lands decreased from four thousand to nine hundred.

In October 1781, Joseph issued a decree of toleration for non-Catholic Christians. They were allowed to buy or build and use meeting houses to hold services, as long as they didn't look like churches. Mixed marriages were regulated. If the father was Catholic, all children had to be Catholic. If the mother was Catholic, only the daughters had to be Catholic. In 1782, a similar decree was issued for tolerating the Jews, which it was supposed could only be done by making them more German. Jewish schools had to use the German language primarily. Jewish communities had to dismantle their courts, had to take family names, and Jews became subject to conscription. There has always been a tension between Jews who want to assimilate and those who want to be a people apart. Joseph had been listening to the assimilators, who, as it turned out, were in the minority of the Jewish population, and the nonassimilating Jews resisted.

In November 1781, Joseph issued a decree modifying the conditions of serfdom in his realms. Serfs could now marry who they wanted, work for the landlord they wanted, and pursue the career they wanted. The nobles who were responsible for carrying out the decree did so in proportion to how much it benefited themselves and how much they perceived that their serfs benefited. Many serf communities were opposed to the decree, seeing enemy invasion and the destruction of the old ways if it were carried out.

Joseph engaged in a round of anticlericalism, closing monasteries and using the assets for new parishes and charitable institutions. He nationalized the Catholic seminaries and forbade bishops from communicating directly with Rome. He issued a decree changing marriage from a religious institution to a civil contract. He began appointing bishops without obtaining the pope's approval. The pope Pius VI made a visit to Vienna and spent eight weeks there, from February to April 1782, but he was only able to get Joseph to promise not to revise any dogma or attack the dignity of the pope. There is usually a connection between enlightened rulership and Freemasonry, but in the case of Joseph, we find no evidence that he ever joined a lodge, which the pope would have disapproved of. My guess is that he was a Mason but kept it a secret. By the end of 1783, Joseph looked forward to reaping the fruits of his enlightened policies. He was about to find out that it is possible to change the world, but you probably shouldn't try.

Russian-Austrian Alliance, 1781: On the diplomatic front, Joseph and his foreign minister von Kaunitz concluded an alliance with Russia in June 1781. Potemkin must have shown them that map of the Greek Project with the Ottomans getting ejected from Europe and Austria gaining Bosnia and Serbia. Forming this alliance was a great achievement for Potemkin and raised his standing above that of the pro-Prussian party at the Russian court, although Russia maintained its alliance with Prussia, the Northern System, on paper until 1788. This often seems to be the case with alliances in these days, where the parties to a treaty have both gotten what they sought from it and only stick to the letter of it until the clock runs out. Nikita Panin was dismissed in May 1781 and died in April 1783. His replacement in the foreign office was Ivan Osterman, although the real power was wielded by a man named Alexander Bezborodko. From 1780 to 1783, Austria, Prussia, and Russia were all signed on to the League of Armed Neutrality in opposition to Great Britain, but the Peace of Paris in 1783 ended that arrangement. After that,

THE GREAT GLOBE ITSELF

Paul I was the only person left in Saint Petersburg advocating for the continuation of the Northern System, but even he was persuaded to support the Austrian alliance by the idea that one of its goals was to put his aptly named second son, Constantine, on the throne of a Christian Greek Kingdom, with its capital in Constantinople. When Constantine was born in 1779, that had been more of wish, but now Catherine was taking steps to make it a reality. Paul's sons, Alexander and Constantine, needed to learn about court life and were taken in by Catherine in 1783, where they were educated by Frederic-Cesar de la Harpe, taught about government by Nikolai Saltykov, and received religious instruction from Andrei Samborsky, who also taught them English.

Russia annexes Crimea, 1783: After the signing of the Treaty of Aynalikavak between Russia and the Ottomans in March 1779, there was a brief period of peace in Crimea. In 1781, a new rebellion against the pro-Russian-Crimean government began. By May 1782, the rebels had gained the upper hand. Catherine sent Potemkin to restore the situation, which he did by October 1782. The Russians lost confidence in the Crimean government and soon came up with an excuse to topple it. At the same time, they laid the foundation for a naval station in Crimea in a new city called Sevastopol, which is Russian for city of Augustus. It is an important Russian naval station to this day and the cause of much of the current turmoil in Eastern Europe, not to mention the US, since 2014. Odessa would be founded in 1794. Both of these Greek names signified a Russian desire to reestablish the eastern Roman Empire. In April 1783, Catherine proclaimed the annexation of Crimea. A treaty was signed with the grumbling Ottomans in December 1783 recognizing this.

CHAPTER 3

Assemblies, Congresses, and Conventions, 1784–1791

1784–1786: The Blood of Patriots and Tyrants

The United States, 1784–1786

The US Congress, 1784–1786: After Washington resigned his Army command, Congress remained in session in Annapolis until June 1784, waiting for a sign from Washington that he intended to participate in the government. Washington wasn't interested in a system where the executive served at the pleasure of the Congress and stayed at Mount Vernon, but he offered advice on who they should appoint. John Jay had been chief justice of the New York Supreme Court and then was president of the Continental Congress from December 1778 to September 1779, where he had been 100 percent behind Washington. After that, he was minister to Spain from September 1779 to May 1782, when Spain joined the war against Great Britain. He was not officially received at court in Madrid, as Spain hesitated to recognize the United States because of concerns it might encourage their colonies to rebel too. Jay was, however, able to secure unofficial assistance in the form of loans. Jay left Spain for Paris, where he was one of the American peace commissioners to negotiate the peace treaty with Great Britain.

146

THE GREAT GLOBE ITSELF

Jay was a devout Christian who owned slaves when it was still legal to do so in New York, purchasing them, training them in a trade, and then freeing them when he thought they could contribute to society. Later, when he was governor of New York, he signed the law that gradually eliminated slavery in New York. Washington was running a plantation and didn't have the luxury of engaging in Jay's kind of benevolence. He needed labor and wasn't in a position to free his slaves, and it was the same across the South for all the plantation owners. But he did agree with Jay's intentions. Jay and Washington held similar views on just about everything, and that was why Jay was appointed secretary of Foreign Affairs. In September 1784, Congress added some domestic duties to the office and renamed it secretary of state.

At the same time that Jay was appointed, Robert Morris ' position as superintendent of finance was disbanded and replaced with a three-man Treasury Board. Morris went back to Philadelphia, where he struggled against the states' rights faction to advocate for a stronger central government. He was successful in reinstating the charter of the Bank of North America, but the Confederation government did not use it for their deposits, as Jay and Congress performed their duties in New York City.

Henry Knox resigned from the Army on June 20, but before he left, he was tasked to reorganize it. Congress issued a resolution on June 2, 1784, that ordered:

> That the commanding officer be directed to discharge the several officers and soldiers now in the service of the United States, except 25 privates to guard the stores at Fort Pitt, and 55 to guard the stores at West Point and other magazines, with a proportionate number of officers; no officer to remain in service above the rank of a captain; those privates to be retained who are enlisted on the best terms; provided Congress, before its recess, shall not take other measures respecting the disposition of those troops.

The next day, Congress authorized the organization of the First US Army Regiment, which began its existence in August 1784, with the recruitment of troops in New York, New Jersey, Pennsylvania, and Connecticut, which states were also responsible for their training, support, and pay. Today's Third Infantry Regiment, the Old Guard, which carries out all the ceremonies at Arlington Cemetery, traces its lineage to this unit. The June 3, 1784, Congressional resolution reads:

> Resolved, That the Secretary at War take order for forming the said troops when assembled, into one regiment, to consist of eight companies of infantry, and two of artillery, arming and equipping them in a soldier-like manner: and that he be authorized to direct their destination and operations, subject to the order of Congress, and of the Committee of the states in the recess of Congress.

Knox returned to Massachusetts, where he spent his time purchasing the extensive landholdings of his wife's loyalist family through various unscrupulous means.

The state of Pennsylvania provided the largest contingent for the First US Regiment, and so they picked the commander, a man named Josiah Harmar, who took command in August 1784. He would command the regiment for six years until he was defeated in battle in 1790 and replaced by General Saint Clair. The regiment was ordered to Fort Pitt to secure the western frontier. They arrived at the end of 1784. Knox returned to the government in March 1785 as secretary at war. It was now that the states north of the Mason-Dixon line (which had been surveyed by Mason and Dixon between 1763 and 1767) attained their final western boundaries. Many of them claimed lands in the Ohio Country based on the wording of the original land grants from Great Britain. Congress passed land ordinance acts in 1784 and 1785, declaring that new states would be formed in the Ohio Country and that the United States would own the land

and sell it. This was meant to fund the Confederation government in lieu of taxes and tariffs. There were problems with these two acts that led to the Northwest Ordinance Act of 1787. Meanwhile in the south, Virginia, North Carolina, and Georgia kept their claims to the Mississippi River.

Alexander Hamilton took his cue from Washington and left Congress. In June 1784, he, along with two other prominent men who were anxious to be associated with Washington's right-hand man, established the Bank of New York. One of them was Franklin Roosevelt's great-great-grandfather. This became the bank where the Confederation government deposited their funds after it relocated to New York. The current building at the site, Forty-Eight Wall Street, was built in 1928 and was originally called the BONY building. The current BONY building is at One Wall Street and, since 2007, has been known as the BNY Mellon building. About the same time, John Hancock and a few other famous names founded the Massachusetts Bank in Boston. Baltimore and Charleston established state banks in 1792.

The French Arms Tavern and New York City Hall, 1784–1785: Congress adjourned the day after authorizing the First Regiment, agreeing to meet on November 1, 1784, in Trenton, New Jersey, at a building called the French and Indian Arms or, more informally, the French Arms Tavern. The name French Arms gave rise to many jokes of both a military and a sexual nature. They were in session until December 24, 1784. The main business of the session was to send appeals to the states to send their congressional delegations. The national government was at a low ebb, with all of the important people running away from the Confederation government as fast as their legs would carry them. Washington remained on his plantation. Adams left Congress and was on his way to Great Britain. Jefferson left Congress and was on his way to Paris. Madison left Congress and returned to Virginia politics. Hamilton left Congress and helped found and run the Bank of New York. Robert Morris left Congress and returned to Pennsylvania politics. Only John Jay remained.

Congress convened at New York's City Hall at Twenty-Six Wall Street on January 11, 1785, where it would continue to sit as the

Confederation Congress and then for one session as the US Congress until August 12, 1790, at which time it moved to Philadelphia in accordance with the compromise of 1790.

Adams and Jefferson in London and Paris, 1785–1788: John Adams had been involved in diplomacy in Europe since 1778. Assigned that year to work with Ben Franklin in Paris, he found out that he didn't like the French, who he thought were fighting the war solely in their own interest. He told Vergennes so in March 1780, and Vergennes responded that he would only talk to Franklin thenceforward. Franklin sent a letter to Congress critical of Adams, whose performance so far could definitely be said to be lacking in diplomacy. Adams then went to the Netherlands, as Russia had just announced the League of Armed Neutrality, and the Netherlands had been the biggest target of Great Britain as far as searching and seizing vessels. The Dutch government refused to meet with him even after Great Britain declared war on the Netherlands in December 1780. He was finally recognized as United States ambassador in April 1782. He then went to Paris as part of the team negotiating the peace treaty. He and John Jay represented the part of the American delegation that disliked France, and they made the move to negotiate with Great Britain separately from France and Spain.

Adams was now appointed American minister to Great Britain and was received by George III on June 1, 1785. George III had been informed that Adams disliked the French and joked, "There is an opinion among some people that you are not the most attached of all your countrymen to the manners of France."

Adams replied, "I must avow to Your Majesty, I have no attachment but to my own country."

King George replied, "An honest man will never have any other." During the meeting, George III said, "I was the last to consent to the separation; but the separation having been made and having become inevitable, I have always said, as I say now, that I would be the first to meet the friendship of the United States as an independent power."

George III was in the minority. Neither side was able to live up to important obligations of the peace treaty. American states failed to pay debts owed to British merchants, and British occupation of forts

THE GREAT GLOBE ITSELF

in the Ohio Country continued, mostly because no American troops ever showed up to man them. In 1788, upon his election as vice president, Adams closed the embassy down based on the cool hostility he faced. It reopened in 1792 under Thomas Pinckney as Washington, officially proclaiming neutrality, began tilting toward Great Britain and against the French Revolution.

At the same time that Adams was setting up in London, Thomas Jefferson was setting up as American minister to France, succeeding Benjamin Franklin. This was the only time in Jefferson's life that he spent outside the country, and when he was he rarely left Virginia, except when duty called. He loved France, and France loved him, the author of the Declaration of Independence. Lafayette was his unswerving ally in Versailles. Like Adams, he faced monetary headwinds as there were trade barriers to American exports, tobacco and whale oil in particular. The *Ferme générale*, the same folks who were building that wall in Paris to make tax collection more efficient, resisted his efforts to lengthen the list of American merchants that could export to France, as they liked the cozy deals they had already made with their favorite merchants. As far as the war loans that France had made to the United States, the Americans struggled to pay them, suspending interest payments and then later defaulting completely.

Half of the literature concerning Jefferson's years in France is consumed with his immersion in French art, science, food, and wine and their profound effect on his thinking, then and in the future. Most of the other half is concerned with his relationship with the slave Sally Heming. Sally was brought to Paris to accompany Jefferson's daughter Polly when she moved to Paris to be with her father in 1787. She became Jefferson's "woolly headed concubine," in the words of vitriolic pamphleteer James Callender. Callender was editor of a Richmond Federalist newspaper and, in September 1802, published a series of articles saying:

> It is well known that the man, whom it delighteth the people to honor, keeps and for many years has kept, as his concubine, one of

151

his slaves. Her name is Sally. The name of her eldest son is Tom. His features are said to bear a striking though sable resemblance to those of the President himself. The boy is ten or twelve years of age.

There was a flurry of activity in 1998, when DNA testing supposedly proved that Jefferson was the father of her children, starting in 1789, when sixteen-year-old Sally gave birth to a child that died in infancy (presumably the Tom mentioned by Callender). This view is commonly accepted today except by a vocal minority of critics. I include myself with that vocal minority, as the accusations against Jefferson only started in the 1790s, when he was maneuvering for the presidency. I think that the Sally Heming's story is believed because since 1998, that's what people have wanted to believe.

The Annapolis Convention, 1786: George Washington was not completely inactive during these years. In March 1785, he hosted the Mount Vernon Conference, which produced an interstate compact between Virginia and Maryland, regulating commerce and navigation between the two states. In January 1786, the Virginia Assembly called for an interstate convention to address trade barriers between the various states. In September 1786, the Annapolis Convention was held with delegates from Delaware, New Jersey, New York, Pennsylvania, and Virginia. George Washington himself was not in attendance, but he kept informed of the proceedings, as one of the items on the agenda was his long-cherished plan to construct a canal connecting the Potomac and Ohio Rivers. Maybe he was just now getting the maps that were showing the three-thousand-feet elevation difference that would have to be overcome between Alexandria and Pittsburgh compared to the six hundred feet of difference between Albany and Buffalo in New York. Since he had spent the years 1779–1783 in New York, he probably had time to look into it.

As far as the Annapolis Convention, Massachusetts, North Carolina, New Hampshire, and Rhode Island appointed delegates who arrived too late or not at all. Connecticut, Georgia, Maryland, and South Carolina did not appoint any delegates. The convention met for three days and issued a report to Congress and the thirteen-state assemblies, requesting that another convention be held in Philadelphia in May 1787 for "the sole and express purpose of amending the Articles of Confederation," in the words of the edict of the Confederation Congress. All the states would send delegates to Philadelphia except for Rhode Island.

Shays' Rebellion, 1786

Central and Western Massachusetts in the eighteenth century was agricultural, heavy in assets and poor in cash. Goods were often traded through barter. In 1777, the arsenal at Springfield was established. It was the major manufactory and depository of infantry weapons during the American Revolution and for the next century. Even in World War I, the standard weapon issued was the Springfield rifle, 1903 edition. The arsenal is not far from where Shays' Rebellion started.

The war had cost a lot of money, and the government stepped up its collection of taxes. Rumblings of dissatisfaction began among the Massachusetts farmers even before the Treaty of Paris was signed. In February 1783, in Uxbridge, a mob seized property that had been confiscated by a constable and returned it to its owner. In 1784, various petitions were submitted to the legislature for debt relief and issuance of paper currency. The eastern merchants who dominated the legislature rejected these. More currency would have reduced the value of the debt. In March 1784, the Massachusetts legislature passed a law authorizing loyalists to make application to return to the state. As loyalists returned, they filed suits in local courts for payment of debts not collected while they were exiled in Canada.

In January 1785, John Hancock resigned as governor, citing illness but probably because he saw trouble coming with the farmers. He was profarmer and had collected taxes half-heartedly. In May 1785, James Bowdoin of Bowdoin College fame entered office as governor. He raised taxes and stepped up collection. In places like Springfield, these actions wreaked havoc on the cash-strapped farmers. In addition to existing debt, additional tax was levied to help repay loans taken by the Continental Congress during the war.

In August 1786, the Massachusetts legislature adjourned, having failed to hear any of the petitions that the farmers had presented. The petitions generally targeted local courthouses, the agencies that were in direct contact with the people, and therefore the target of the people's ire. Later that month, a mob of farmers in Northampton prevented the county court from going into session. These men called themselves the Regulators, a reference to something called the Regulator Movement of North Carolina, which sought to reform corrupt practices in the late 1760s, also probably related to tax collection. The idea was that a regulator balanced the power of the eastern merchants with the unheard voice of the people.

Luke Day was the initial leader of the Regulators. He was from one of the area's most prominent families. He was at Lexington and Concord in 1775 and then took part in the invasion of Canada, rising to captain. In 1783, he was made a member of the Society of the Cincinnati. It still exists today, but it doesn't seem to be a very influential organization. Maybe they just keep a low profile. In 1785, Day had spent time in debtor's prison. Day believed God spoke directly to him through the Bible, and he read Ecclesiastes 4:1, "Behold the tears of such were oppressed, and they had no comforter; and on the side of the oppressor there was power."

In August 1786, Day led a mob to the courthouse in Northampton, Massachusetts, twenty miles north of Springfield, and demanded that the court suspend the proceedings that were robbing the people of their meager possessions. Among the mob, wearing his Continental Army uniform, was Captain Daniel Shays. Shays was a minuteman from Brookfield who fought at Lexington and Concord, Bunker Hill, and Saratoga. By 1775, he had a son and two daughters and a 250-acre farm. By 1777, he was a captain in the Fifth Massachusetts Infantry. He was wounded in 1779, and in 1780, he was sent home, his pay in arrears. He was given an ornamental sword by Lafayette as a memento of his service. In 1780, Shays was summoned to court for debts incurred. He had not been paid, so he sold

THE GREAT GLOBE ITSELF

the sword, an act that his contemporaries frowned on. By 1786, he had lost half of his land.

While Day's men surrounded the approach to the courthouse, Day stood on the steps with a petition in his hand for the judges. The petition stated that it was inconvenient to the people of the state for the courts to sit that day, and entreated the judges to adjourn until the General Court might grant the petition. By the time the judges retreated to the tavern to consider the petition, the crowd of men had grown to over a thousand. The judges decided to "continue all matters pending" until November and adjourned.

The farmers were elated with their success, and they got organized. Day and Shays drilled the men and, over the course of the next several weeks, liberated Worcester, Concord, Taunton, and Great Barrington, in the same manner as they had Northampton. Day tended to quote the Bible in his harangues to the troops, which, as might be expected, was unpopular, and Shays was soon the leader. On September 2, Governor Bowdoin issued a proclamation condemning the treasonable and unlawful actions of the Regulators. When the Regulators shut down the court in Worcester on September 5, the militia failed to act against them, to the horror of Governor Bowdoin.

At the same time that Day and Shays were shutting down courthouses, the Annapolis Convention was meeting to discuss amendments to the Articles of Confederation, with Madison and Hamilton in attendance. The convention had been planned since January 1786, so there was no cause and effect between the rebellion and the convention. The rebellion was the most serious but not the only symptom of trouble for the United States. The British were inciting raids on the frontier, states were negotiating with foreign powers, loyalists in New York and South Carolina were being prosecuted out of spite rather than justice, and Congress could do nothing but watch.

On September 26, 1786, the Regulators advanced on Springfield, where the state Supreme Court was going to sit in session. This time they were met by a force under General William Shepard, the commander of the Massachusetts state militia. There was a standoff for two days, and then the court adjourned without hearing a case. There were about 1,200 Regulators versus about 800 militia. The Regulators returned to their bases, and the militia departed for Springfield arsenal. In October, the Massachusetts Assembly passed a Riot Act, making it unlawful for more than twelve men to assemble. They also suspended habeas corpus. False tales of British involvement in the uprising went around in Boston. The state government was broke, so former general Benjamin Lincoln asked for money from Boston merchants and raised a force of three thousand troops.

In late November, a three-hundred-man posse rode to Groton and arrested one of the Regulator leaders named Job Shattuck. Shattuck was wounded in the process. The Regulators vowed to overthrow the tyrannical government of Massachusetts. In January, General Lincoln advanced to Worcester, about halfway from Boston to Springfield. Shays advanced on Springfield armory, unsupported by Day, who was not ready to attack. He had sent a note to Shays that never reached him. Shepard was there with 1,200 men and cannon, which he loaded with grapeshot and fired at the Regulators, killing 4 and wounding 20.

Hearing of these events in January, Jefferson wrote a letter to Madison:

> I hold it that a little rebellion now and then is a good thing, and as necessary in the political world as storms in the physical. Unsuccessful rebellions indeed generally establish [limits on] the encroachments on the rights of the people that have produced them. An observation of this truth should render honest republican governors so mild in their punishment of rebellions, as not to discourage them too much. It is a medicine necessary for the sound health of government.

After Springfield, the Regulators retreated to Petersham. Over the winter, the passions of the Regulators ebbed. On February 3, Lincoln attacked the Regulators' camp in the middle of a snowstorm. The Regulators were caught completely unawares and scattered. Shays made it to Vermont, where he spent the rest of the year until

THE GREAT GLOBE ITSELF

Massachusetts issued an amnesty. Most made it over the state border, where sympathetic people sheltered them. Some made it to Quebec and requested British assistance in the form of a Mohawk War Party. This request was considered, but in the end, London vetoed it. The same day, February 3, the state government declared martial law. A price was placed on the heads of Shays, Day, and two others. Clemency was offered to all who surrendered their arms and took an oath of loyalty. That month, Massachusetts passed a law disqualifying rebels from holding office. On February 22, Day was captured in Vermont and imprisoned in Boston until March 22, 1788. He was ejected from the Society of the Cincinnati in July 1787. He died in 1801.

In April, Governor Bowdoin was defeated for reelection by John Hancock, along with many of his supporters. Hancock and the new legislature were conciliatory and passed laws reducing taxes and putting a moratorium on debts.

In November 1788, Jefferson wrote to William Stephens Smith:

> The tree of liberty must be refreshed from time to time with the blood of patriots and tyrants. It is its natural manure. Our [Constitutional] Convention has been too much impressed by the insurrection of Massachusetts: and in the spur of the moment, they are setting up a kite to keep the hen yard in order.

I think he meant that Washington was the kite who would have no limits on how long he could serve.

The second British Empire

Unrest in the Netherlands: Great Britain ended their war with the Netherlands in 1784 on terms favorable to them, including losses of the Dutch trade monopoly in Indonesia. The Dutch people were not pleased and blamed the incompetence, or possibly the treason, of the stadtholder William V. Starting in 1781, a party calling itself the Patriots formed in opposition to him. They had the full and secret backing of the French government. There were large demonstrations in Utrecht in 1786 and Amsterdam in 1787, when the situation came to a climax at the same time that Louis was struggling against the parlements to register his tax reforms.

Settlement in Australia: Captain James Cook had made three voyages of discovery in the Pacific Ocean between 1768 and 1779. He met his death in Hawaii in 1779 while trying to kidnap the king of Hawaii. The reasoning behind the kidnapping attempt was that he and his crew needed some bargaining chips to get them out of a dangerous situation, which didn't work, obviously. Cook had mapped and claimed for Great Britain the east coast of Australia in 1770. The area was called New Holland at the time, since the Dutch had visited the area a hundred years earlier. Plans were now made to transport convicts there, as they had formerly been sent to Georgia. After four years of discussing and planning it, Royal Navy captain Arthur Philip sailed into Botany Bay in February 1788, in what is now called New South Wales, with over a thousand settlers, eight hundred of whom were convicts. They established the town of Sydney, named after the British home secretary Thomas Townshend, Viscount Sydney. Sydney was probably related to Charles Townshend, author of the Townshend Acts in the 1760s, but I couldn't find out how except to determine they were not father and son. Sydney would be the only settlement until 1803, when a second one was founded on the island of Tasmania.

Reorganization in India: George III had said in 1783 that he would consider any lord who supported Fox's India Bill his enemy, but he supported Pitt's India Bill, which was not too different, and it became the India Act of 1784. It was this act which now distinguished between the commercial and political functions of the British East India Company. It laid the foundations of central administration in India. It designated the governor of Bengal as the governor general of Bengal and created an executive council of four members to assist him. It provided for the establishment of a Supreme Court at Calcutta, comprising one chief justice and three other judges. It prohibited the employees of the company from engaging in any private trade or accepting presents or bribes from the natives. It strengthened the control of the British government over the company by requiring the company's directors to report on its revenue, civil affairs, and military affairs in India. It made the governors of the Bombay and Madras presidencies subordinate to the governor general of Bengal, unlike earlier, when the three presidencies were independent of one another.

North America: As far as North America, the British considered that they had suffered a setback, but felt there would be opportunities to recover their position. They took notice of Washington's retirement, seeing in it resistance among the states to central authority. The "United" States were not living up to their new name. Many in Great Britain, including George, thought that some or maybe all of the American colonies might return to the old loyalty. We have already seen how, during the war, Burgoyne had used slavery as a wedge issue in Vermont in an attempt to divide the Americans, and now there were Canadians, loyalist refugees from the United States, who thought they could use the Indians against them. The Ohio Country, the land between the Great Lakes and the Ohio River, had been ceded to the United States. The Indians who lived there, led by an Iroquois chief named Joseph Brant, formed the Northwest Confederacy and vowed to resist American settlement in the Ohio Country. Supporting Joseph Brant and other chiefs was not British policy, at least not officially, but the United States was in the midst of reorganizing their Army and was slow to send troops to take over the British forts, so the British continued to occupy them. The idea of the Ohio Country as an Indian preserve would continue until the Jay Treaty was signed in 1794 and was revived after 1805 in the run-up to the War of 1812.

Göttingen: George III had a very large family and, in 1786, sent three of his younger sons—Ernest Augustus, Augustus Frederick, and Adolphus—to the University of Göttingen in Hanover, where they were tutored by Gerhard von Scharnhorst, future commander of the Prussian Army in the days of Prussia's tribulations, from 1807 to 1812. These three sons of George III all had careers, and Ernest even served as king of Hanover from 1837 to 1851. We can't really say this is an important piece of history, but I think it could be turned into an interesting story, with all of kinds of points that could be made about German-British relations.

PETER HARDY

France, 1784–1786

Economic crisis in France: After the end of the American Revolution and its associated operations in the West Indies, the Mediterranean, and India, France now entered a period of crisis that, in five years, led to the French Revolution. The rapidity of the French monarchy's collapse calls to mind Georges Cuvier 's paleontological observations of the rapid appearance, enduring stasis, and sudden disappearance of forms in the fossil record, with the years 1784–1789 being the period of sudden disappearance. The symptoms of the crisis included:

- Arguments over who was to blame for the inability to balance the budget: the excessive cost of a Navy; the extravagance of the court; the unwillingness of the nobles of the sword to pay taxes on their land because of their military service; the reluctance of the church to pay any tax at all; the resentment of the commons at shouldering most of the tax burden
- The schizophrenia in France as it related to the alliance with Austria, with Marie Antoinette coming under violent attack in the press for pushing closer relations between the two kingdoms
- The conflict between the crown and the bourgeoisie in the form of the struggle between the king and the parlements to enact financial reform legislation, with the parlements viewing themselves as the only thing stopping total despotism
- The presence of the Duke of Chartres, known as the Duke of Orleans after 1785, in the heart of Paris at the Palais-Royal, forever the subject of discussion about replacing the current dynasty as a constitutional monarch

Marie Antoinette and Saint Cloud: Marie Antoinette gave birth to children in 1778, 1781, and 1785, cementing her position at court. Louis XIV and Louis XV had taken mistresses after producing

THE GREAT GLOBE ITSELF

heirs, and these mistresses became powerful. Louis XVI was not the mistress-taking type, so it was his queen who became powerful. The primary focus of her intrigues was to ensure that France didn't forget that Austria was her primary ally in Europe. Only in pre-revolutionary France could working to maintain official government policy be considered an intrigue. Having been at Versailles since 1770, she knew her way around the place and made her presence known. In 1774, she was given the Petit Trianon, a small palace on the grounds, to use as a getaway. She and her ladies in waiting converted it into a hamlet, where they played at performing farming chores. Soon she wanted the palace of Saint Cloud, which was owned by the Duke of Orleans. Louis attempted to swap two of his other palaces for it so that there wouldn't be a cost involved.

As we recall, Saint Cloud had been shuttered since 1759, when the Duke of Orleans' wife, that is, the mother of the current Duke of Orleans, had died. Eventually, in 1785, Louis bought Saint Cloud for six million livres, and he turned the title over to Marie Antoinette. The stated reason for the queen wanting Saint Cloud for herself was that the air was fresher in Saint Cloud than Versailles and thus better for her children. She always couched her actions in terms of being a good mother, a way to counter all the filth that was spewing from the pamphlets regarding her sex life. As the regime was highly skilled at censorship, the pamphlets were printed in England and smuggled into Paris.

She was attacked for diverting resources from paying the deficit, for having the staff at Saint Cloud dress in her livery rather than the king's, and for insisting that palace regulations be signed "by order of the queen." New finance minister Calonne had not been informed of this transaction and was critical of it. For reasons not altogether clear, Marie Antoinette never liked Calonne, and she had wanted another minister named Etienne Charles de Brienne for the job, probably because he was more pro-Austrian.

In August of 1785 came the affair of the diamond necklace, a ridiculous farce in which Marie Antoinette was not even involved but which was used to blacken her reputation. Unfortunately, it worked. The necklace was worth two million livres, and word went around that the queen was frivolously spending millions on palaces and jewelry while the government struggled to pay interest on the debt. The Duke of Orleans was funding much of this vitriol in press. The resources he had inherited after his father's death in 1785 were substantial. The duke was very fond of Great Britain and was good friends with the Prince of Wales. As king, he would have pursued constitutional monarchy and an alliance with Great Britain, which was what his son did when he became king of France in 1830.

Calonne's tax reform proposals: By the time that Calonne took office as finance minister in November 1783, the 56-million-livre annual interest payment had doubled to a 110 million. These appear to be very large sums for interest payments. It may be that the source mistook the principal sum for the interest amount. The king and Vergennes promised Calonne their unwavering support for a financial reform program. By 1786, Calonne had developed one that probably would have worked if enacted. It included a single land tax (including on churches and nobles), elimination of internal trade barriers, taxes on salt and tobacco, and creation of provincial assemblies to replace the judicial parlements.

The parlements blocked the new tax proposals, saying they didn't have the authority to enact them. Calonne pressed for the convocation of an Assembly of Notables, an institution that had last met in 1626. Most legal authorities in France thought that only an estates general had the authority to approve new taxes but that an Assembly of Notables might be able to put pressure on the parlements. I don't know why the legal experts thought that, since the French government had been taxing the people for 180 years without the sanction of an estates general. Hidden agenda, I suppose. Calonne put forth a significant effort to organize the calling of an Assembly of Notables, but unfortunately for him, Vergennes' health collapsed (the symptoms indicate kidney fail-

ure) in 1786, and the assembly was delayed for months. During this time, Calonne was attacked as a corrupt spendthrift by friends of both Marie Antoinette and the Duke of Orleans, and he had a past that made those accusations stick. The assembly was finally scheduled for February 1787, even though Vergennes remained ill.

The Wall of the Ferme générale, 1784: One thing that Calonne did help make happen was the construction, starting in 1784, of a wall around the city of Paris to regulate and tax the commerce entering and exiting the city. It is referred to as the Wall of the *Ferme générale* because the tax collectors, or tax farmers as they were called, wanted it. The builders of the wall built it with no thought of any military function, although it probably could have served that purpose if needed. Its purpose was to collect revenue.

The circumference of the wall was twenty-four kilometers or fifteen miles. The wall was completed in 1791, but because the revolution had started by then, no taxes were collected until 1798. The *Ferme générale* wall came down starting in the 1840s, when the Thiers wall was approved. The Thiers wall was named after the French prime minister who passed the law authorizing it and which alignment defines the city limits of Paris today. Unlike the *Ferme générale* wall, the Thiers wall was built to defend the city, but it could also be used to collect taxes and, for many years, did both. The Thiers wall proved to be defensible during the 1870–1871 siege and Commune of Paris until it was breached by an Army under the control of none other than Thiers.

When Paris began building subways in the 1890s, the old *Ferme générale* wall alignment became the routes for the number 2 and number 6 metro lines. The Thiers walls started coming down after World War I, and now that alignment is occupied by the *Boulevard Peripherique*. The intersections of this boulevard and the radial roads heading into Paris are still known by their gate names, such as the *Porte Maillot* by the *Arc de Triomphe*. The *Ferme générale* wall contributed to the events of 1789, and the Thiers wall, completed in 1845, contributed to the events of 1848. The saying went around that "*Le mur murant Paris rend Paris murmurant*" (The walls around Paris make Paris murmur).

Central and Eastern Europe, 1784–1786

The negative effects of Joseph's reforms: In Austria, Joseph II continued to issue edicts designed to create a homogenous centralized state, with himself as supreme autocrat. In Austria's case, the nobility and bourgeoisie weren't strong enough to form a cohesive resistance, unlike France. For example, he made German the official language throughout his realm, including Hungary. Previously, all government correspondence between Austria and Hungary had been in Latin. To prevent any resistance to this German language edict in Hungary, Joseph simply kept the Hungarian Assembly out of session. It would be the Hungarians who would eventually muster the resistance to Joseph that led him to sacrifice his reform projects.

His finance minister, a man named Karl von Zinzendorf, served from 1781 to 1792 and was able to establish a credible financial system that balanced the budget and achieved good credit ratings. Of course, all that went out the window when the wars began in 1792.

In early 1784, there was a rebellion of Orthodox serfs in Transylvania, led by a man named Horea, who took advantage of the fact that the local nobility was ignoring the decrees coming out of Vienna regarding religious tolerance and increased liberty for the serfs. Horea organized about ten thousand serfs who engaged in some violent demonstrations that were targeted against Hungarian Catholic communities. By the end of 1784, there were about four thousand casualties. The Transylvanian nobles organized their forces and acted against Horea's forces. Joseph sent in the imperial troops in December 1784 on the side of the nobles, and Horea surrendered. Horea and two of his chief assistants were tried and then executed in February 1785, using the method of breaking them on the wheel.

THE GREAT GLOBE ITSELF

This rebellion made it evident to Joseph that his ideas of tolerance and liberty were having the effect of inciting civil war.

The Fürstenbund (League of German Princes), 1785: As we recall, the Potato War had broken out in 1778, when Frederick II objected to Joseph claiming large chunks of Bavaria. That had been smoothed over in 1779, but Joseph II still wanted to acquire Bavaria as it was Catholic, German-speaking, and adjacent to Austria. Since then, Joseph had been negotiating with the elector Karl Theodor to exchange Bavaria for the Austrian Netherlands (Belgium). Karl Theodor was also the ruler of the Palatinate, the area roughly bounded by Frankfurt, Luxembourg, Cologne, and Strasbourg, and he really didn't care about Bavaria. Belgium was a lot closer to the Palatinate than Bavaria and would have been a win-win for Joseph and Karl Theodor. Joseph even dangled the prospect of making him a king over the combined realm.

The electors in Saxony, Prussia, and Hanover opposed the exchange, and many of the smaller German states eventually sided with them. They formed the *Fürstenbund*, or League of Princes, to oppose Joseph. The archbishop of Mainz, who was also an elector, joined in with the league. The archbishop also held the title of arch-chancellor of the empire, which gave him some extra clout, and Joseph gave up on this sensible adjustment of the map of Europe. The alliance with Russia had been signed in 1781, but it was now that he decided to throw in with Russia and the Greek Plan and embark on military operations against the Ottomans to augment his domains by the acquisition of Bosnia and Serbia.

For Frederick, this was his last significant act on the European stage, and he died in August 1786 at the age of seventy-four. Queen Elizabeth Christine, to whom he had been married to for fifty-three years, lived until 1799. The only time he is ever recorded to have addressed her was when he returned to Berlin after the six years' absence in 1763, saying, "Madame has become more stout." They never produced any offspring. Most historians agree that he was a homosexual, but that seems incompatible with his military deeds, and maybe like J. Edgar Hoover, he just preferred the company of men.

Frederick William II, who, as we recall, loved women too much, now became king of Prussia at the age of forty-two. Frederick had not relied on him much nor had he given him great responsibilities. At the time of Frederick William's second marriage, he took an official mistress named Wilhelmine von Lichtenau, with whom he had five children. It's no wonder that he and Frederick had such a distant relationship. Upon becoming king, Frederick William appointed Johann Christoph von Wöllner as his chief minister. Wöllner had ideas on religion, justice, and finance that he put into action. The king was a lover, not a fighter, and he gave command of the Prussian Army to his cousin the Duke of Brunswick, who led it for the next twenty years. The mother of the Duke of Brunswick was Frederick II's sister and, back in 1749, had been married to the duke's father at the same time that Frederick II was married to Queen Elizabeth Christine, who was the Duke of Brunswick's sister. These close family ties ensured that Brunswick and Prussia always operated as a single entity when it came to military operations.

Potemkin in New Russia: Potemkin was doing great things in New Russia as far as building a Black Sea Fleet at Sevastopol in Crimea and bringing colonists into the area, especially in Crimea and in the Dnieper River Valley. He brought in settlers from Greece, Germany—anywhere he could find them. As for the Fleet, he recruited, among others, John Paul Jones. He was planning on taking Constantinople from the Ottomans and needed ships and fighting captains to do so.

1787–1788: If the King Does It, It's Not Illegal

The United States, 1787–1788

Constitutional Convention, May to September 1787: In 1787 and 1788, France demonstrated a complete inability to use its existing institutions to resolve its political problems, as described below. In the US, Washington and Franklin were leading the effort to create new institutions that would solve the problems that the Confederation government had experienced since 1781. In May 1787, the

THE GREAT GLOBE ITSELF

Constitutional Convention obtained a quorum in Philadelphia. From May to September 1787, George Washington presided over the convention. James Madison did a lot of the heavy lifting in drafting and obtaining majorities on votes on the final document. When they had finished their deliberations, a citizen asked Benjamin Franklin what kind of government they had crafted, with Franklin replying, "A republic, if you can keep it."

One provision of the Constitution states that only native-born Americans were eligible to be president. This was a legacy of the days of the Conway Cabal, when foreign-born officers had been the leading candidates to replace Washington from his post as commander in chief of the Continental Army. The American-born officers who had supported Washington through thick and thin felt strongly that the country's best hope lay in trusting those who had been born there. There was a loophole in the native-born clause because it also said the anyone who was a US citizen at the time of the adoption of the Constitution was eligible to be president. Future secretary of the Treasury Albert Gallatin, for example, was eligible to run for president, even though he had been born in Switzerland, because he was a US citizen when the Constitution was adopted.

Another interesting provision of the Constitution had to do with the state militias, giving Congress the power to "provide for calling forth the Militia to execute the Laws of the Union, suppress Insurrections and repel Invasions..." When the War of 1812 came along, militias were called up for federal service but were strictly forbidden by some states from obeying any orders to invade Canada, since the Constitution mentioned only suppressing insurrection and repelling invasion. I suppose there must have been some case law after 1812 that got around this restriction because the Army had no problem shipping my Louisiana National Guard grandfather off to France in 1918.

The last constitutional provision I'll comment on is the clause that slaves counted as three-fifths of a person. The wording reads:

> Representatives and direct Taxes shall be apportioned among the several States which may be included within this Union, according to their respective Numbers, which shall be determined by adding to the whole Number of free Persons, including those bound to Service for a Term of Years, and excluding Indians not taxed, three fifths of all other Persons.

The Southern states wanted slaves counted 100 percent, and the northern states didn't want them counted at all, because the more people a state had, the more congressmen they got. The Three-Fifths Compromise allowed the process to go forward, but it is widely misunderstood today as making slaves less than human.

Ratification of the Constitution: After four months of effort in Philadelphia, the United States Constitution was delivered to Congress, which then submitted the document to the states for ratification. Delaware, Pennsylvania, and New Jersey ratified the Constitution in December 1787. Georgia and Connecticut ratified in January 1788. Following that: Massachusetts, February 6; Maryland, April 26; South Carolina, May 23; New Hampshire, June 21; Virginia, June 25. Virginia was the largest state in terms of both white and black people, so getting Virginia's ratification was important. The vote there was close: 89–79. New York, still smaller than Pennsylvania but growing rapidly, ratified on July 26 in another close vote: 30–27. This was the tipping point because antifederalist activity was centered in New York, which is what happens when a city is occupied by the enemy for seven years. Madison, Hamilton, and Jay, the authors of *The Federalist Papers*, knew it was important to persuade New Yorkers, which was the reason why they were published there.

THE GREAT GLOBE ITSELF

North Carolina actually voted against ratification on August 2, 1788, and had to reconvene to pass it on November 21, 1789. The reason that North Carolina had voted down ratification had to do with their rebellious western counties, which had broken away to form the unrecognized state of Franklin (the name Tennessee lay in the future). The westerners were fed up with the inability of the state government to protect them from Indians and their refusal to allow navigation on the Cumberland River, which would have directed trade west to the Mississippi rather than east to the Atlantic. When the First US Congress convened in 1789, they threatened North Carolina with embargo, and the state ratified the Constitution.

In the case of Rhode Island, the coercion from Congress was even more blatant. That state had boycotted the Constitutional Convention, but after the federal government was constituted, Congress actually passed a law that "Rogue Island" would be embargoed by land and sea if they didn't get busy and ratify the Constitution. Rhode Island ratified the Constitution eleven days after this law passed, on May 29, 1790. Vermont ratified the Constitution in March 1791 and joined the Union in the same manner as the original thirteen colonies, whereas all future states had to have acts of Congress passed before they could enter the Union.

After New York ratified the Constitution in July 1788, Congress deemed it to be in effect and established dates for election and inauguration of officials. Starting in November 1788, the eleven United States held elections for federal officials. Sixty-five congressmen, twenty-two senators, one vice president, and one president were elected. Officials from the north generally favored Washington's policies, while Southerners generally opposed them.

Andrew Jackson, attorney at law: Andrew Jackson, who was twenty in 1787, began the practice of law on the frontier. North Carolina still claimed the land that would become Tennessee, calling it the Western District, while the more rebellious citizens of the area called it Franklin. In this bare-knuckle world of merit, he soon emerged as a man to be reckoned with. Most court cases on the frontier had to do with land claims or assault, two things that soon characterized Jackson's life and political career. Jackson soon had a reputation as a rake who enjoyed fast horses, old whiskey, young women, and more money. He made a few enemies with his temper but a lot of friends.

Jackson soon engaged in his first duel. The story is worth quoting at length, Jackson's misspellings and all, from an *American History* magazine article by Christopher Marquis:

> One day in court, Jackson found himself opposed to Colonel Waightstill Avery. Avery was an experienced and respected lawyer, of whom Jackson once had sought legal mentoring. In the course of an address to the court, Avery made a sarcastic quip regarding Jackson's constant reliance on a journeyman's law book, Matthew Bacon's Abridgement of the Law. Jackson, sensing his competence had been questioned, openly accused Avery of taking illegal fees. Avery denied this. Eyes ablaze, Jackson jotted down a message on a page of Bacon's law book, tore it out and placed it before Avery. The older man, wanting to avoid a duel, made no response. A day later, Jackson issued a public challenge. It is telling that this is Jackson's earliest known letter:

> Agust 12th 1788
> Sir: When a man's feelings and character are injured, he ought to seek a speedy redress; you recd. a few lines from me yesterday and undoubtedly you understand me. My charector you have injured; and further you have Insulted me in the presence of a court and larg audianc. I therefore call upon you as a gentleman to give me satisfaction for the Same; and I further call upon you to give Me an answer immediately without Equivocation and I hope you can do without dinner untill the business done; for it is consis-

THE GREAT GLOBE ITSELF

tent with the character of a gentleman when he
Injures a man to make a spedy reparation; therefore I hope you will not fail in meeting me this
day, from yr obt st.

Andw. Jackson
Collo. Avery
P.S. This Evening after court adjourned.

Unable to avoid an encounter, Colonel
Avery agreed to meet Jackson on a hill south of
Jonesborough. Fortunately, conciliators prevailed
on Jackson, and both men fired into the air. In
good humor, Avery presented Jackson with a slab
of bacon—a play on the law book at the center
of the dispute. Jackson didn't get the joke, and
an icy silence prevailed. No one thought that the
young man would be the George Washington of
his generation.

In August, Andrew Jackson married Rachel Robards. She was
still legally married to Captain Robards, but on the frontier, things
were seldom a matter of technical law but what the community recognized. Robards had applied for a divorce but had never followed
through, which the Jacksons may or may not have known. When
Jackson entered politics, any attempt to stain Rachel's honor would
be met with Andrew Jackson's fury. By all accounts, they were a great
couple, a perfect match and deeply in love, but like George and
Martha Washington and Napoleon and Josephine Bonaparte, they
remained childless.

Great Britain, 1787–1788

In March 1787, deliberations of the British Parliament were
opened up for the first time to press reporting, and fifty years later,
Carlyle attributed to Edmund Burke the first use of the term *fourth
estate*. Carlyle wrote in *On Heroes and Hero Worship,* "Burke said

there were three estates in parliament [lords spiritual, lords temporal, and commons], but in the reporters' galley yonder, there sat a fourth estate more important far than them all." In *The French Revolution*, he wrote, "A Fourth Estate, of Able Editors, springs up; increases and multiplies, irrepressible, incalculable."

Since 1783, the British had been delighted to see the United States erect trade barriers against each other and conduct their own separate foreign policies. It was what they had fully expected. They continued to occupy forts west of the Appalachians because the Army at Fort Pitt wasn't big enough to take possession of them. New York, Vermont, and Rhode Island were in communication with British officials in Quebec. The Congress had been unable to help the state of Massachusetts suppress Shays' Rebellion, and the state had to borrow money from Boston merchants to raise a private Army. Thus, it came as a big disappointment when the Americans produced their new Constitution in a convention presided over by Ben Franklin and George Washington. Were they finally getting their act together?

Three things that the British did to occupy themselves in 1787 were to continue to prepare Sydney, Australia, appease India by impeaching former governor Warren Hastings, and start an investigation of the international slave trade in May. The last one was aimed at George Washington and may have influenced the clause in the Constitution that outlawed the slave trade by 1807.

In 1788, the year after the Prussian Army rescued the Dutch royal family as described below, Prussia and Great Britain formed an alliance. The Netherlands was under Prussian occupation, but Dutch stadtholder William V was one of the curliest of George III's poodles, and he signed on to the alliance willingly, which became known as the Triple Alliance, not as catchy as Northern System in my opinion. Prussia was also soon allied with the Ottomans (in 1790), a countermeasure to the Austrian attacks in the Balkans. Great Britain did not sign an alliance with the Ottomans but did want to prevent Russian control of Constantinople, and there was a plan that if Russia was too successful against the Ottomans, that the Prussian Army would seize Riga while the Royal Navy neutralized the Baltic Fleet. If you're going to invade Russia, keep the objectives manageable and achievable. The

French Revolution was about to put all the British, Prussian, and Austrian schemes on hold, with associated unrest in Poland gaining Russia's attention at the expense of the Greek Project.

In the summer of 1788, George III began showing signs of insanity, just at the time that ratification of the US Constitution was completed, and Louis was agreeing to call the estates general into session. It's obvious that these events contributed to his condition. This was a problem for William Pitt, because if the Prince of Wales became regent, he would dismiss Pitt and replace him with Fox. Pitt used parliamentary stalling tactics to delay passage of a regency bill, and by February 1789, the king was feeling better and almost his old self again. In America, Washington had been called back to power, and it looked like he would stave off, for a few years at least, the inevitable sectional conflicts in America. France, after announcing the convocation of the estates general, had suspended loan payments until the estates general met in May 1789.

France, Great Britain, and the Netherlands, 1787–1788

Assembly of notables in France, 1787: In December 1786, Louis XVI announced the first meeting of an Assembly of Notables since 1626 to meet in January 1787. The assembly was unable to meet until February because of Vergennes' death on February 13. Louis and Calonne went ahead with the meeting, although the absence of Vergennes doomed the proceedings. There was no one to replace Vergennes, who could have defended Calonne from the attacks of his critics, led by the Duke of Orleans and Marie Antoinette, two people who despised each other but agreed that Calonne had to be stopped.

The Assembly of Notables finally met in Versailles on February 22, 1787. Although the Notables were prestigious men, they had been selected by the king and had no claim to any popular support or mandate of the people. The Notables consisted of 144 men, including seven princes of the blood, numerous dukes and marshals, and presidents of the parlements. Leaders included the Duke of Orleans, the Marquis de Lafayette, and Cardinal Brienne, who was Marie Antoinette 's financial adviser.

The king had promised to back Calonne to the hilt but did nothing when the Notables pushed back against his proposals. The Duke of Orleans and Marie Antoinette led the charge, with their main line of attack being that Calonne, a known spendthrift, was the wrong person to deliver the message of financial restraint. In private, Marie Antoinette told Louis that the same proposals could be put forward more credibly by her man Brienne. Louis eventually succumbed to Marie Antoinette 's henpecking and replaced Calonne with Brienne on April 8. Brienne came to the Notables a month later, with the same proposals that Calonne had. He was similarly shouted down (with the Duke of Orleans leading the shouts) amid calls for an estates general, an assembly that would have the sanction of the people. Well, at least the bourgeoisie had removed the mask about legality and admitted that it was about politics and not law. Marie Antoinette could get rid of Calonne, but she couldn't get Brienne accepted by the Notables, so Brienne dissolved it on May 25, 1787.

Brienne brought the reform program to the Paris Parlement in July. They rejected it, pointing out that the Notables had failed to endorse it and saying again that only an estates general who had the sanction of the people could authorize tax edicts, even though the parlements had been doing so since 1614. In response, on August 6, Louis conducted a lit de justice at Versailles to ratify the reforms. A lit de justice was a formal session between the king and the Parlement of Paris that was conducted in order to implement a registration of an edict, even against the will of the parlement. The next day, in a document called a Grand Remonstrance, the parlement declared the registration null and void. Louis issued letters of cachet exiling the parlement to the city of Troyes. Large protests broke out in Paris against the king. Brienne offered a compromise, rescinding all taxes not necessary to avoiding bankruptcy, payment of all other taxes for five years, and calling of the estates general in five years, that is, in 1792.

After the death of Vergennes in February 1787, the office of foreign minister was filled by Armand de Montmorin, who was supposed to be keeping an eye on what was happening in Europe. Unfortunately, France was fixated on their internal problems, and

Montmorin was unable to get Louis to pay much attention to what was happening either in the Netherlands, the Balkans, or the Crimea. Montmorin was able to interfere in the Netherlands, supporting the pro-French Patriot faction, who staged a large-scale protest in Amsterdam as described below.

The Batavian Revolt, 1787: In the midst of the drama in France, the struggle between the pro-French Patriots and the pro-British/Prussian Orangists came to a climax in the Netherlands. As we recall, the Patriots had been agitating against Stadtholder William V since 1784, when he ended the Fourth Anglo-Dutch War on terms unfavorable to the Netherlands. In June 1787, his wife, Wilhelmina, was detained by the Patriots from traveling to Amsterdam. After being held for a while, she was made to return to Nijmegen. Her brother had just taken the throne of Prussia as Frederick William II, and all this may have been a test of how warlike he was. He was warlike enough, as he sent the Prussian Army into the Netherlands in September 1787 to scatter the Patriots. Leading the Prussian invasion was the Duke of Brunswick. Forty thousand Patriots were ejected from the Netherlands and exiled to France. Many of them would be in French Army in 1795, when they conquered the Netherlands. It took only a month for the Prussians to restore order. The house of Orange was buttressed. Louis had been unable to mount any kind of military response to Prussia due to the financial crisis and the geographic reality that Austrian Belgium lay between France and the Netherlands and was criticized in Paris as weak and unable to support pro-French allies in the Netherlands. Marie Antoinette came in for her share of criticism for not lobbying Austria to allow the French Army passage through Belgium.

The British were starting to see the outlines of the Greek Project and were concerned about Austrian and Russian—mostly Russian—expansion in the Balkans and the Mediterranean. The worst-case scenario was the fall of Constantinople, the Austrian and Russian Fleets joining hands with the French Fleet, and the complete ejection of Great Britain from the Mediterranean. The basis of the British concern was the new Russian naval station at Sevastopol, which the Russians could use to expand out into the Mediterranean. The

Ottomans were at war with the Russians and the Austrians by 1788, August 1787, as described below. The Russians and the Austrians were generally successful in battle but, thanks to British and Austrian intrigues, faced other headwinds to obtaining their objectives.

Calling of the estates general, 1788: Meanwhile, back in France, Brienne's compromise was found acceptable to the parlements and a *séance royale* was called in Paris on November 19 to ratify it. This was a different procedure than a *lit de justice*. Things seemed to be going okay until Louis stood up and said he had heard enough and insisted that his edicts, that is, the package submitted to the *lit de justice* in August, be registered, using language appropriate to the lit de justice, not the *séance royale*. The Duke of Orleans told the king that what he was doing was illegal, which he probably could have phrased better, but I think he intended the words to come out as provocatively as they did. The mask of law disguising politics was once again in place. The king said that if the king does it, it's not illegal; it's an innovation. The duke carried his point about the difference between a *lit de justice* and a *séance royale* but earned himself an exile from Paris as the king issued a letter of cachet against him. The *séance royale* adjourned without ratifying Brienne's compromise, and pressure built for an estates general now, not in 1792.

The Duke of Orleans was acclaimed as the hero of the hour, and his Paris propaganda machine went into overdrive. Since becoming Duke of Orleans in 1785, he had hired a large staff, which included journalists such as Jacques Brissot, future leader of the Girondists, and Pierre de Laclos, author of the novel *Dangerous Liaisons*, a story of two nobles who spend their time corrupting and ruining others and, finally, each other. Brissot's passion was to eliminate Negro slavery from France, and then the world, and the duke had convinced Brissot that as king, he would work to do just that.

At the beginning of 1788 in France, the Parlement of Paris issued a series of pronouncements declaring that letters of cachet (such as the one used on the Duke of Orleans) were illegal (there's that word again) and that the king had to call the estates general if he wanted to raise taxes. The king issued letters of cachet against two members of the Paris Parlement and, in May 1788, issued an edict dissolving the parlements and replacing them with plenary courts. These displays of royal authority were resisted, and Louis became more unpopular.

The Day of the Tiles occurred in June 1788, in Grenoble, a lovely town in southeastern France, located at the foot of the Alps. Attempts to call a local estates general were met by the use of royal troops, who were pelted with roof tiles as they entered the town. The local assembly was allowed to convene a month later. It passed a few grievances that were delivered to the king's wastebasket.

As the nobles continued to resist royal authority, in August 1788, the king agreed to call the estates general into session. Later that month, Brienne resigned as finance minister, and Jacques Necker was reappointed, seven years after being fired. His first task upon returning to office was to organize the upcoming estates general. The bourgeoisie of the Third Estate had greatly increased in size and wealth since 1614, and Louis and Necker agreed to the idea that the size of the Third Estate should be twice that of the other two, so the First and Second Estates would have about three hundred delegates each, while the Third Estate would have six hundred. The question of whether all three estates would vote as a single body or as separate bodies was contentious and left for later decision.

Central and Eastern Europe, 1787–1788

Catherine tours New Russia, 1787: In January 1787, fifty-eight-year-old Catherine II celebrated twenty-five years of rule by conducting a six-month inspection trip of New Russia and Crimea, with Potemkin as her guide, along the Dnieper River. Joseph II was along for a part of the trip with one of his marshals. Also in attendance was French war minister Philippe de Segur of Segur Ordinance fame. All three later wrote glowing accounts of the region's prosperity. Catherine and Potemkin encouraged the foreign ambassadors to come along so they, too, could report what they saw to their governments.

By January 29, Catherine was in Kiev, where Potemkin, who was based in Sevastopol, met her and the imperial entourage. They remained in Kiev for six weeks, then loaded galleys for the trip down the Dnieper River. The galleys had been specially constructed by Potemkin's order and were very luxurious. Another similarity of Potemkin and Catherine to Antony and Cleopatra, who often used galleys to get around Alexandria and other towns. Part of the Dnieper formed the border between Poland and Russia, and King Stanislaus Poniatowski met the empress when the galleys went through that area. They made it down to Sevastopol in the Crimea, where they saw the new Black Sea Fleet growing in size and strength, to Great Britain's consternation, as mentioned above. Catherine was introduced to John Paul Jones, now a Russian admiral, and was convinced that Jones was the man to beat the Ottoman Fleet and make it to Constantinople. In July 1787, Catherine returned to Saint Petersburg dazzled.

Potemkin had his enemies in Saint Petersburg, not the least of whom was Paul I, and they refused to believe that New Russia and Crimea were as splendid as the reports made them seem. To this day, we use the term *Potemkin Village* to describe a hollow facade of a town with Hollywood-style tilt-up building fronts, and no people, a metaphor for any phony enterprise. A Swedish diplomat named Georg von Hilberg, who had spent much of his career in Russia and had developed a tremendous dislike of Potemkin, wrote a biography of him that contained the original Potemkin Village story. Potemkin was one of those men you either loathed or worshiped. In this case, we have to come down on the side of Potemkin and those who were impressed at what had been achieved by him along the Dnieper River and in the Crimea.

Ottoman-Russian, Ottoman-Austrian, and Russian-Swedish Wars, 1787–1788: The Ottomans considered Catherine's trip to be a provocation, and in August 1787, they declared war on Russia. The Ottomans attacked Kinburn and Ochakov, two towns in Crimea in the estuary, at the mouth of the Dnieper and Southern Bug Rivers. Kinburn was a Russian settlement that was defended by Suvorov. The Turkish attack was repelled. Suvorov was awarded the Order of Saint Andrew, the highest order in Russia. The Ottomans were unaware that Russia had a defensive treaty with Austria, and so they

THE GREAT GLOBE ITSELF

were surprised when Austria declared war on them in February 1788. Achievement of the Greek Plan now appeared to be within reach.

In April 1788, the Austrian Army, with Joseph II present, planned to capture Belgrade, which was occupied by the Ottoman Army, but the Austrians were thwarted in their efforts. Even though the Austrians had a huge Army (three hundred thousand men), they had a long border to protect and mostly performed siege operations that were, for the most part, successful. However, the Army did suffer from epidemics, and Joseph was not immune to these. He returned to Vienna in November 1788 but did not return to the front the following spring, being sick. He would spend most of 1789 slowly dying from whatever it was he had caught there. Prince Coburg, the Austrian commander after Joseph left, was able to link up with Suvorov, and they planned a land campaign in the Balkans for 1789.

In June 1788, Sweden entered into an alliance with the Ottomans and declared war on Russia. The war lasted until 1790. Britain and Prussia were delighted as they had encouraged Swedish king Gustav III in his course. Gustav was already being attacked by his domestic enemies, who were well funded by the Russians, so he didn't need to be egged on by the British or the Prussians. He sent an invasion force with the lofty ambition of capturing Saint Petersburg and over-throwing Catherine, but it was stymied by the Russian Navy, which was not under the command of John Paul Jones but under Admiral Vasily Chichagov, whose son would gain infamy as the man who let Napoleon escape from the Berezina River in November 1812. The war proved to be annoying to Russia and expensive for Sweden, and in 1790, both sides were ready to end it. They signed a peace treaty in August 1790.

In the Russian-Turkish War, several naval actions took place over a period of three weeks, starting in June 1788. Ochakov is adjacent to the fortress of Kinburn in the Dnieper/Southern Bug River Estuary. John Paul Jones commanded the Russian Fleet. The result of the naval actions that occurred was an Ottoman victory, and they successfully occupied the area. Catherine had reposed great confidence in Jones, but now he was now on Potemkin's list of losers and was sent to Saint Petersburg, being told that he was going to be given a command in the Baltic Fleet. When he got to Saint Petersburg, there was no command for him, and he spent several months in idleness, spending his time writing an account of the campaign. Jones finally realized he was being left to twist slowly in the wind and left for Paris in May 1790, hoping to gain a command with the French Navy. He died there on July 18, 1792. In April 1906, his body was interred at the US Naval Academy, in a ceremony presided over by President Theodore Roosevelt. In 1913, Jones's remains were moved to the USNA chapel, where they remain to this day.

Beginning in July 1788, Potemkin and Suvorov engaged the Turks in a six-month-long siege of Ochakov. Suvorov was all for storming the place, but Potemkin decided on a siege, which spared the troops for a while, but eventually they were worn down by the usual factors that make sieges horrible things for both sides, and the death toll was probably about the same, as if the place had been taken by storm. After Ochakov surrendered, Gavrila Derzhavin, the foremost Russian poet of the day, wrote an ode celebrating the victory.

In October, the Great Sejm (pronounced same) convened in Warsaw at the request of King Stanislaus Poniatowski, with about two hundred delegates. It would remain in session in various forms for the next four years. Catherine had approved of the Sejm, as she already had shooting wars underway in Sweden and the Crimea. One of the first things the Great Sejm did was to disband the Permanent Council, an organization that had been dominated by the Russian ambassador since 1775. The Russians led them on until they could wrap things up on the other fronts. For the first two years, the Great Sejm proceeded slowly, and few reforms were passed into law.

1789: A Tocsin for the Saint Bartholomew of the Patriots

The United States, 1789

The election of 1788: In the United States, the votes were counted in February 1789, and George Washington was unanimously elected the first president of the United States. John Adams was elected vice president, but not unanimously. In a scheme that originated with

THE GREAT GLOBE ITSELF

Alexander Hamilton and that was executed through a letter-writing campaign to various electors and state officials, several electors cast their second votes for other candidates. Out of 69 electoral votes, Adams got 34 and 10 other candidates split the remaining 35. North Carolina and Rhode Island had not yet ratified the Constitution, and so they cast no ballots, while in New York, a deadlock in the state legislature resulted in a failure to appoint any electors. The method of choosing electors varied from state to state, but only 6 of the 10 voting states used any form of popular vote, with the others relying on the state assemblies to appoint electors. The 10 voting states had a population of 2.7 million white and 0.6 million black (about 95 percent of black people was enslaved at this time, but this percentage would steadily decrease over the years), and the total number of popular votes in the election was 38,818, of which Washington got 35,866.

The convening of the First US Congress: On March 4, 1789, the First United States Congress convened at Federal Hall, New York City. It sat in session until September 29 and adjourned until January 4, 1790. Federal Hall, located at Twenty-Six Wall Street, had been built in 1700 to serve as city hall and resumed this function when the federal government moved to Philadelphia. The building was demolished in 1812. In 1842, a United States Customs House was built on the site. In 1882, a statue of Washington was placed in front of the building, the famous one with his hand stretched out, as if resting on a Bible. It was erected near the spot where he took the oath of office. The month of March was spent getting organized and electing leaders. In April, Congress officially counted the electoral votes and sent word to Washington and Adams of their election. John Adams took office on April 21. Having read through the Constitution, he began presiding over the Senate. Adams soon discovered that his only role was to cast a tie-breaking vote and that he was ineligible to control debate or rule on questions. He said, "My country has in its wisdom contrived for me the most insignificant office that ever the invention of man contrived, or his imagination conceived."

George Washington took office on April 30. Everything he did set a precedent. He requested to be addressed as Mr. President rather than Your Excellency, while his wife was referred to as Lady Washington. The term *First Lady* first appeared in print in 1860, in  reference to bachelor president Buchanan's niece Harriet Lane, who served as White House hostess during his term. If a married straight woman ever becomes president, her husband will be called *First Gentleman.*

On July 4, 1789, Congress passed the Tariff Act of 1789. The House version of the legislation called for discriminatory tonnage fees: 30¢ per ton for countries that had a commercial treaty with the US and 60¢ per ton for all others. France was the only country in the first category. The Senate version had 60¢ for everyone, and that's what went to Washington for signature. Later laws would be more complex, stipulating different tariff levels for different products to provide protection to this or that favored industry. Because high tariffs helped the north, and low tariffs helped the south, sectional differences over the tariff were the first of the internal contradictions the US had to deal with and tinkering with the tariff became Congress's chief occupation over the next several decades, just as tinkering with the tax code is today.

Congress passed laws establishing the State, Treasury, War, and Post Office Departments. Jefferson, Hamilton, Knox, and Samuel Osgood comprised the first cabinet. John Jay was acting secretary of state, as he had been since 1784, and then was appointed chief justice of the United States after Jefferson finally arrived in New York in March 1790. The same cabinet organizations had all been in operation under the Articles of Confederation.

Washington lived in Osgood's New York City residence from April 1789 to February 1790. The house was located at One Cherry Street near Fraunces Tavern. In February, he moved to the Alexander Macomb house at Thirty-Nine Broadway but moved out in August 1790, when the capital moved to Philadelphia. The Osgood house was demolished in 1856, and the Brooklyn Bridge is now on top of

THE GREAT GLOBE ITSELF

the site. The Macomb house became a hotel and was demolished in 1940.

In August, Washington's mother, Mary Ball Washington, died. Amid all the hagiography of George Washington sits the question of why it was that she and her son never quite clicked. She had, on occasion, during the revolution, written to Congress to complain about the indolence of her son.

In September, Congress passed the Judiciary Act, establishing the organization of the federal court system and the office of attorney general. Attorney general was considered a part-time job at first, and for years, the person holding the office could take other clients. The first attorney general was Peyton Randolph. The legal bureaucracy grew over time, and the Department of Justice was established in 1870 for the purpose of enforcing civil rights and suppressing the Ku Klux Klan in the former Confederate states. The first Supreme Court consisted of a chief justice and five associate justices. John Jay of New York was chief justice, and the five associate justices were John Rutledge of South Carolina, William Cushing of Massachusetts (who, as we recall, in 1783 had outlawed slavery in his state via judicial decision), James Wilson of Pennsylvania, John Blair of Virginia, and James Iredell of North Carolina. It was a good geographical balance. The Supreme Court did not hear its first case until 1791 and heard only thirteen cases in its first six years. The number of justices fluctuated until 1869, when it was set at nine and hasn't been changed since.

Later in September, the first ten amendments to the United States Constitution, a.k.a. the Bill of Rights, were passed and sent to the states for ratification, which was accomplished in 1791.

Tammany Hall: In New York, the Society of Saint Tammany, named after a Philadelphia-area Lenni Lanape (called the Delaware by the whites) Indian chief of the seventeenth century who was not really a saint, was incorporated in May 1789. It was the New York branch of the Tammany Society, established in Philadelphia in 1772. The society celebrated Native Americanism, by which they meant people of British stock, not Indians, although they used Indian terms; for example calling their place of meeting a wigwam. Celebrating

183

nativism implied opposing immigrants, and no place had more immigrants than New York City, so that branch of Tammany became influential.

Up and coming New York City politician Aaron Burr joined Tammany, having realized its potential to win votes. On October 12, 1792, the society, under Burr's inspiration and leadership, created and celebrated Columbus Day to mark the three-hundredth anniversary of his voyage. Lots of things would be named after Columbus in 1792. Tammany Hall would have a long and colorful history, with Martin Van Buren (who was rumored to be Aaron Burr's biological son) using it in 1828 to again transform American politics, reversing its purpose to support rather than oppose immigrants. As long as American politics revolved around New York City, which is to say until the 1940s, Tammany was a force to be reckoned with. The logo of Tammany was the red Phrygian cap of liberty, made famous in June 1792, when Louis XVI was asked to wear one, as described below.

France, 1789

The estates general becomes the National Assembly, May to June, 1789: In France, Necker had asked for input from the incoming deputies what they thought the estates general should be. In January, in response, Abbe Sieyes published *Qu'est ce-que le Tiers Etat?* "What is the Third Estate?" He asserted that everything but the Third Estate was a growth on the Third Estate, a foreign body attaching itself to the nation, a parasite. He also demanded that the estates general vote by head count, and not one vote per estate. He concluded, "What is the Third Estate? Everything. What has it been until now? Nothing. What does it desire to be? Something." Sieyes had a point. The crown nobles and clergy had once been the bulwark of peace and tranquility, but now they existed only to squeeze the people for everything they could.

In March, Necker and the king asked for lists of grievances, from each of the estates to help them set an agenda for addressing the concerns of the nation. All three estates had their own inter-

THE GREAT GLOBE ITSELF

nal divisions and conflicts based on wealth and position. There were rich worldly archbishops and poor devout parish priests; there were nobles of sword with ancient lineages and parvenu nobles of the robe who had bought their titles; and for the rest of the population, there were bourgeoisie, petite bourgeoisie, artisans, tradesmen, and peasants, all of whom had their grievances.

The First Estate, the clergy, shouldn't have had any grievances, but they did. They were divided along hierarchal lines. Rich bishops could live lives of luxury. They were not prepared to give up the dominant position that the church held over the nation. They did not intend to allow Protestants, much less the Jews, to practice their religions, and, under the authority of the revocation of the Edict of Nantes by King Louis XIV back in 1682, wanted to keep Roman Catholicism the only official religion in France.

The Second Estate, the nobility was divided between military and civic nobles. The military nobles tended to be of ancient lineage and conservative while the civic ones, judicial or administrative, were of recent vintage and were generally liberal. Many of them were bourgeoisie or the children of bourgeoisie who had bought their titles. The Duke of Orleans, of ancient lineage himself, lined up with the liberals. The common people of France were of two minds about hereditary nobility: repelled and fascinated. Everyone hated the nobles but wouldn't have minded being one.

The Third Estate, everyone who wasn't a noble or in the clergy, latched onto what Sieyes had written, viewing the church and the nobility as completely unnecessary parasitic attachments to the nation. To prove their point, they would say, observe the United States: they have no state church, they have no titled nobility, and they are getting along fine. The Third Estate was the nation, but it had no status in the nation except as a goose expected to give up its eggs and feathers to the other two. What the Third Estate expected was freedom of religion that would reduce the power of the church and an end to exclusions to career paths based on a title. There were about two hundred thousand clergy and four hundred thousand nobles who were going to resist the other twenty-five million.

The estates general convened in Versailles on May 5, 1789. Among the first leaders of the new National Assembly were:

- The Marquis de Lafayette: He was already famous from his service in the American Revolution
- Astronomer Jean Sylvain Bailly: He was already famous for his astronomy and was one of the first men elected to the rotating presidency of the National Assembly. Bailly had published papers calculating the orbit and next appearance of Halley's Comet and a description of the moons of Jupiter.
- Aristocrat Honoré Riqueti Comte de Mirabeau : His biography before 1789 tells a tale of a man governed by his passions. He had earned a living writing incendiary pamphlets, pornography, and unflattering portraits of other European courts. His personal life was as untidy as his career path.
- Clergyman Abbe Sieyes: He was mentioned above as the author of *What Is the Third Estate?*
- The Duke of Orleans, who viewed himself as the puppet master and stayed in the background
- Charles Talleyrand, bishop of Autun, a church administrator who had all the facts and figures regarding the extent of church assets in France

At the opening ceremony, Louis XVI made a speech that included reference to the "costly but honorable war" just concluded with Great Britain. Almost immediately after the convening, the deputies began to form clubs. The Breton Club, for example, was initially formed from deputies from Breton, but it was soon dominated by a particular political viewpoint, and that, rather than geography, determined who became a member. These clubs would form the foundation of political activity for the next ten years. At first, it was not cheap to join these clubs, limiting membership to the rich of all three estates. Later, it would be more democratic, with the Jacobin Club, for example, growing to half a million members across France by 1794. In May 1789, the Third Estate, in emulation of the British

Parliament, began to refer to itself as the Commons. In June, the estates general debated the relative power of each estate. If each estate had one vote on any issue, this would produce the undemocratic result of stifling the will of the people. The Commons proposed to combine all three estates into a unicameral chamber, but Louis and Necker resisted the idea. On June 17, by a vote of 490–90, the Commons unilaterally declared itself to be the National Assembly and invited the other two estates to join them. Two days later, the First Estate voted 149–137, along hierarchical lines, to do just that. The Duke of Orleans, emerging from the shadows, was polling the more liberal members of the Second Estate to follow.

As this debate was going on, Prince Louis Joseph, Dauphin of France, died of tuberculosis on June 4. He was eight. His four-year-old brother, Louis Charles, Duke of Normandy, got the title of Dauphin until he died in 1795. The king vowed to carry on.

The day after the vote from the clergy, June 20, the chambers of the National Assembly were locked by order of Louis. The members convened at the indoor tennis court and took an oath not to disband until a constitution was passed. This was a very emotional scene that the painter J. L. David later immortalized. It was now that orders went out from Louis for sixteen regiments, twenty-five thousand men, to converge on Paris and Versailles. A number of these regiments were foreign regiments, though not mercenary. These units from Switzerland, Flanders, and other places had long histories in the service of the French monarchy.

Mirabeau, 1789: On June 23, Louis XVI, still mourning the loss of his son, attempted to regain control of the National Assembly, offering some concessions about taxation and reasserting his authority to organize the proceedings. The National Assembly rejected these assertions, and the king backed down. Honoré Mirabeau became famous when he replied to the king's messenger that only bayonets would cause the representatives of the people to depart.

Mirabeau was the son of one of the Physiocrats. His family was noble, and he was Comte de Mirabeau. He joined the Army and saw cavalry service in 1767–1770. He participated in the subjugation of Corsica in 1769. He was married against his will in 1772 and engaged in numerous affairs and excessive spending. His father had him jailed in 1773, 1774, and 1775 by use of letters of cachet. He published *Essay on Despotism* in 1775. In 1776, Mirabeau ran off to Amsterdam with another man's wife. There he earned income writing vitriolic pamphlets against Louis XVI. He was arrested and sent to prison in Vincennes in 1777, where he met the Marquis de Sade. He was released in 1780 and published *Essay on Letters of Cachet* in 1782. He was probably against them. He divorced his wife in 1783 and soon moved in with another high-class woman. He lived in London in 1784 and 1785. He returned to Paris in 1786 and wrote anti-Necker pamphlets. He was sent on a diplomatic mission to Berlin in 1786. His published report of his time there, *The Secret History of the Court of Berlin*, denounced the Prussian court as scandalous and corrupt, describing Frederick William II as weak and overly emotional and labeling his uncle Prince Henry of Prussia as narrow-minded and incompetent. It created an international incident but was accurate in every respect and gained him a great deal of fame. In 1789, he was elected as a Third Estate representative from Aix in Provence.

The Bastille: On June 25, the Duke of Orleans and forty-seven other members of the Second Estate joined the National Assembly. France now had a unicameral legislature The clergy and nobles who had opposed this, now out in the cold, either went home or joined their regiments. Some emigrated. The same day in Paris, the local electoral college selected a city council, and the royal council, with no military support, abdicated. The Paris mob celebrated, realizing their power for the first time. The National Assembly renamed itself the Constituent Assembly, signifying its new mission to write a constitution. Louis XVI blamed Necker for letting the proceedings get out of hand and dismissed him and the other ministers on July 11. Necker was replaced by Joseph Foullon, a very conservative politician who was rumored to have said during a previous food shortage, "Let them eat hay." By now, the sixteen regiments were converging on the Paris area, and there were troops in place at Versailles, Sevres (between Paris and Versailles), the Champ de Mars, and Saint-Denis. About half the units were French royal regiments of Swiss or German volunteers. It was a good plan intended to nip the revolution in the bud. Two things going against the plan were the doubtful loyalty to the king of the French Guard in Paris and the desire of Louis to not commit violence against his people.

The next day, news of Necker's dismissal reached Paris. Busts of Necker and the Duke of Orleans were paraded in demonstrations. Camille Desmoulins, a well-known journalist and Freemason from the lodge of the Nine Sisters (which meant he was in the pay of the Duke of Orleans), leapt on a table outside a café near the Palais-Royal (owned and operated by the Duke of Orleans), and made a speech saying, "This dismissal is the tocsin for the Saint Bartholomew of the patriots!" He drew two pistols from his coat for effect. The reference to Saint Bart was to a government-sanctioned massacre of Protestants that occurred in 1572. He meant that the foreign troops, that is the German and Swiss regiments of the French Army, were coming to get them. He then fastened a green cockade to his hat, which became, for a little while, the symbol of revolt, until Lafayette's red, white, and blue tricolor gained greater acceptance.

The next day, July 13, the mob in Paris started to plunder any places that were thought to hold military stores. As feared, they had the help of the French Guard, a unit of the regular Army that had close ties, wives, and so forth with the people of Paris. They routed a unit, ordered to keep them in their barracks, and left the mob alone. The French Guard became the nucleus of the National Guard.

The next day was July 14, known today as Bastille Day. Crowds gathered at the Invalides, where weapons but not ammunition were acquired by the mob. For ammunition, they needed to go to the Bastille, a huge medieval fortress. About 130 soldiers manned the Bastille. It also served as a prison, although at the time, there were only ten prisoners inside. The Marquis de Sade had been imprisoned there recently, but he had, just ten days before, been removed from the Bastille and transferred to an insane asylum.

At about 10:00 a.m., a crowd of about a thousand gathered outside the Bastille to demand that the garrison give up the stores of weapons and ammunition therein. Things were tense, and shooting began from one side or the other. The crowd, led by members of the French Guard, stormed the fortress at about 3:00 p.m. The commander of the fortress, de Launay, surrendered at 5:00 p.m. One hundred members of the mob had been killed during the action. In revenge, de Launay was killed by the mob, his head sawed off and attached to a pike. Three officers and two soldiers were also killed. The royal troops on the Champs de Mars did nothing because their commanders felt the troops would disobey. The mayor of Paris (*prevot des marchands* or provost of the merchants), Jacques de Flesselles, was assassinated the same day. His head joined de Launay's on a pike. It had only been two months since the estates general had come to order. Necker 's replacement, Foullon, fled Paris but was tracked down a week later, brought back to Paris, and strung up on the lantern, along with his son-in-law, a man named Louis de Savigny. The two were then beheaded and their heads piked with Foullon's mouth stuffed with hay.

For the next few years, the anniversary of this event was called *La Fete de la Federation* and was celebrated in Paris with great ceremony. Observance of the event fell into disuse as war, Napoleon, restoration, and then another Napoleon came along. In 1878, it was revived under the Third Republic. Bastille Day is still celebrated as French Independence Day.

Bailly and Lafayette, 1789: On the next day, July 15, Jean Bailly left the Constituent Assembly and was made mayor of the newly established Commune of Paris. Bailly replaced the late Flesselles as mayor, no longer with the title of provost of the merchants but as mayor of Paris. The Commune of Paris was reorganized into forty-eight sections. The primary purpose was for military registration and organization of the National Guard but also for representative democracy. Each section was composed of a civil committee, a military section, and, later, a revolutionary committee. The same organization was used when the nation was reorganized into the system of departments. The Commune of Paris, which eventually gave its name to communism, began its political existence at this time.

On the same day, the Constituent Assembly proclaimed the establishment of the Bourgeois Guard, a militia organization that would provide security in the city of Paris. The Marquis de Lafayette was named commander, and he soon renamed it the National Guard. There was enthusiasm to join the ranks across France, and Lafayette wanted the name to reflect that. He immediately put his stamp on the organization by establishing the red, white, and blue cockade for military caps instead of the green cockades that had been suggested by Camille Desmoulins. Green was discarded when it was realized that it was also the color used by the Comte d'Artois, who, one day in the distant future, would be King Charles X, the last of the Bourbons. We read an explanation of the tricolor: red and blue as the colors of the city of Paris, with the white of the House of Bourbon put in the center. More likely is that red, white, and blue have associations with Freemasonry, with red representing the blood of man, white representing the light of God, and blue representing the sky, the path between man and God.

The National Guard took its oath to the Constituent Assembly rather than the king. In August 1789, the French Guard, so helpful to the mob on Bastille Day, was disbanded and the soldiers transferred into the National Guard, where they were used as cadres to train the new recruits. There were other militia organizations in France called *fédérés*, but the record is inconsistent in the use of the terms National Guards and fédérés.

More French nobles began to emigrate at this time, with hopes of forming plots or Armies that would overthrow the enemies of the crown and the insolent merchants and lawyers who dared to think that competent commanders could emerge from their degenerate ranks. They didn't know it, but their time was passing. Louis XVI's brother Charles, the Comte d'Artois was among the first out the door. He and his family departed for Turin in the Kingdom of Piedmont-Sardinia, as his wife was the daughter of the king there.

After the Bastille: Jacques Necker became the first hero of the revolution, but his triumph was short-lived, as the revolution would soon move past him. He failed to develop political alliances, and Talleyrand soon overshadowed him on the financial front. The Bastille was turned over to a contractor for demolition, and it was chipped away and sold in Berlin Wall fashion. Some of the stones were used to build a bridge across the Seine, today's *Pont de la Concorde.* The *Place de Bastille* is still there in Paris, a traffic circle on the east side of Paris that mirrors the *Place de l'Etoile* on the west.

On July 16, Louis attempted to conciliate the assembly. He dismissed the regiments around Versailles and Paris, keeping only the Swiss Guards, who served as his bodyguard. Even now, he was being advised to relocate to the provinces or even to flee outside the country. He decided he needed to stay in Versailles. On July 17, Louis recalled Necker and then visited the Hotel de Ville in Paris. He even donned a hat with a tricolor cockade, a gift of Bailly, and acknowledged shouts of long live the nation, mixed in with long live the king. All had now accepted the fact that the Constituent Assembly was authorized to pass laws as a single body, and this was exactly what they proceeded to do.

Journalism had a golden age in Paris now. Newspapers were founded and libelles (little books), a.k.a. pamphlets, were all over the place in Paris. According to Will Durant, we get the English word *libel* from the general nature of the contents of these pamphlets. Jean Paul Marat soon led the pack. Marat was formerly a physician for the bodyguard of the Comte d'Artois. I guess he didn't want to leave Paris. He left behind a life of science, medicine, and privilege to start an eight-page journal called *The Friend of the People.* It was a delight to the rabble of Paris for its attacks on the elite of all kinds. It was frequently shut down, and Marat was often jailed. It popularized the expression "to the lantern!" which were the streetlights that Parisians

THE GREAT GLOBE ITSELF

would hang victims from. One of his pamphlets may have been the "let them eat cake" attack on Marie Antoinette.

The Great Fear, 1789: From July 20 to August 6, a strange phenomenon occurred across large swaths of France called the Great Fear. Starting in rural Franche-Comte on the Swiss border, peasant uprisings occurred where they struck at their supposedly unpatriotic feudal lords to abrogate their feudal duties. It seemed to be echoes or ripples of the violence in Paris. On August 4, the Constituent Assembly passed a law abolishing feudalism and the tithe, Mirabeau described its passage as an orgy. To him, it was foolish to pass laws with such a lack of deliberation. Louis favored this law as it removed ancient privileges from the First and Second Estates. He was still fighting the tax-reform war from 1787 and 1788. When he signed the act into law, he was proclaimed the Restorer of French Liberty, a rare instance of good publicity for him. Two days later, the Great Fear evaporated, which makes it seem to have just been a Paris media campaign to force the abolition of feudalism. But no, the event left a long trail of burnt manors, proclamations, and court cases throughout France that can be followed in detail to this day. The Great Fear served to spur further changes.

On August 26, the Constituent Assembly passed the Declaration of the Rights of Man and of the Citizen. This was a document that was drafted by Thomas Jefferson (he remained in Paris until September 1789) and passed under the leadership of Lafayette. Its principles included popular sovereignty, equal opportunity, "liberty, property, safety, and resistance against oppression." The king was resistant to this declaration, implying as it did that these things were owed to the people and weren't the gift of the king's grace, the result of his wise and benevolent rule that ensured the tranquility of the realm. Some interpreted it as outlawing slavery, which France did until 1802, when Bonaparte gave his commanders in the West Indies leeway to reinstate it if it made sense to do so in a particular location. Louis did not sign the declaration, but it did become the preamble for the Constitution of 1791.

In September, the Constituent Assembly turned to work on the form of the new French Constitution. Ideas for an upper house were considered. Necker, influenced by the United States Constitution, argued for a bicameral legislature with a Senate. A house of lords elected by the nobility was rejected, and so was a Senate. The senators were supposed to be nominated by the people and selected by the king. A unicameral assembly was decided on. The power of the executive would be limited to a suspensive veto, which could delay but not strike down legislation. Aware that much of a sovereign's power stems from his control of military and foreign affairs, they discussed various ways to limit that control. The assembly would be in continuous session and perform, or at least heavily oversee, executive functions.

Provincial reorganization away from the traditional provinces was also contemplated. The reorganization into eighty-three departments (the original number was supposed to be three to the fourth power or eighty-one) of between three hundred thousand and four hundred thousand people was a blow at the provincial basis of the parlements and therefore struck at the rights of the nobility. The provincial reorganization would be implemented in 1790.

Throughout the summer of 1789, there was a real shortage of food in Paris, possibly caused by the Great Fear. The result was that journals called for demonstrations and marches on Versailles. Many in Paris believed the king and the Constituent Assembly would hear the voice of the people better if they were based in Paris rather than Versailles. That is to say, they were convinced that any constitution that was produced in Versailles would leave the king with too much power.

March of the Women: In late September, Louis became aware that the Paris Commune was agitating for the forcible removal of him, his family, and the government from Versailles to Paris. This was something that Louis XIV had defeated as a teenager in the days of the Fronde in the 1650s. To forestall any such coercive activity, he reinforced the Swiss Guards with the Flanders Regiment. Rumors in Paris went around that the king intended to dissolve the Constituent Assembly and that the troops were counterrevolutionary, removing the tricolor cockades from their covers. Bailly as mayor and Lafayette as commander in chief of the National Guard should have been squashing these rumors, but they weren't. The story came to Paris that in the course of a *soiree* at Versailles, the troops of the Swiss Guard and the Flanders Regiment had drawn their swords, removed their tricolor cockades, trampled them underfoot, and replaced them with Austrian-themed cockades. This story got a big reaction in Paris, where journalists now demanded that the court and the Constituent Assembly move their deliberations from Versailles to Paris. The stage was set for the next big set piece in the drama.

On October 5, a mob of seven thousand women rioting in the Paris marketplace for bread decided to march to Versailles. In July, Foullon had been hanged because he was rumored to have said of the people, "Let them eat hay," and maybe now the "Let them eat cake" story about Marie Antoinette was just now getting around town. The women marched the ten miles to Versailles. The leader of this escapade was the same fellow who led the assault on the Bastille: a twenty-six-year-old energetic but probably not too bright fellow by the name of Stanislas Maillard, who died in obscurity in 1794. They were joined along the way by thousands in what became something of a festive volksmarch. By some means, they procured cannon from the National Guard (I suppose some of them had husbands who were serving in the not-highly disciplined militia) and hauled it along with them.

Lafayette was ordered to follow the procession of women to make sure that order was kept. He did not have control of the situation. Many of the troops were the same men who had helped assault the Bastille. Nevertheless, he took command and was about four hours behind the women on the way to Versailles.

When the women got to Versailles, they were greeted by members of the Constituent Assembly, the same ones who had spread the tales about the Flanders Regiment. There were speeches and even an audience with Louis, and it was thought that most of the women would return to Paris. Some left with Maillard, but most were able to stay thanks to the presence of the National Guard. Late that night or early the next morning, some of the women (and National Guards) found an unlocked door and thought they might surprise Marie Antoinette in her sleep. When they encountered Swiss Guards, a struggle ensued, and shots were fired. Things got ugly and only gradually did Lafayette get things under control. He would not have been able to do so had Louis and Marie Antoinette not agreed to return to Paris. Incredibly, they left that very day. A convoy was assembled with the royal household staff and as much food and equipment as they could load into whatever wagons they had, and they started heading to the Tuileries Palace, which could not possibly have been ready to receive them. The mob sang as they accompanied the king that they were "bringing back the baker and the baker's wife and the baker's boy."

We presume that Louis thought he would be in Paris for a couple of weeks at most or until the constitution was written, but that process would drag out, and he and his family were, for all intents and purposes, prisoners. They never returned to Versailles, and Versailles has never since been used as a residence or court for any French king, emperor, or president. Lafayette had been tasked with protecting the royal family, and his failure to do so at this time earned him the undying enmity of Marie Antoinette. The Swiss Guards now reported to him along with the National Guards. The Flanders Regiment was no longer heard from, so they must have been sent back home.

Years later, when Louis XVIII was king, he would, on occasion, make day trips to Versailles and wander around the empty rooms. In 1837, Louis Philippe turned Versailles into a permanent museum, which it still is today. It was important in 1870–1871, during the siege and Commune of Paris as the headquarters of the German Army, Bismarck, and William I. After the siege, Thiers directed military operations against the communists from there. In 1919, it hosted Woodrow Wilson and the post-World War I peace conference.

The Duke of Orleans in London: The Duke of Orleans was widely suspected of orchestrating the march of the women, with Lafayette serving as his dupe. Louis and Marie Antoinette were convinced of it. An investigation was conducted, and hundreds of witnesses were called over the next several months. A week after the march, the duke was prevailed upon by Louis to accept a diplomatic mission to travel to London to discuss the response to the Brabant Revolution, discussed below, which he accepted. Mirabeau considered this as good as an admission of guilt and an act of political cowardice. Mirabeau had, at first, been supportive in principle of an Orleans monarchy, but having evaluated the character of the duke, he gave up that idea and offered his support to Marie Antoinette. As soon as the duke was out of the country, Mirabeau and Lafayette began denouncing him as desiring to replace Louis. By leaving the country, the duke made a mistake that proved to be fatal to whatever ambitions he had in France.

In London, the duke's instructions were to negotiate to join the British-Prussian-Dutch Triple Alliance that would force Austria to cede independence for Belgium. The leader of the new country would be the Duke of Orleans. This was not self-aggrandizement; those were his instructions. As we recall, the Austrians had been trying to exchange Belgium for Bavaria since 1778, but this deal no longer seems to have been on the table. The lack of any incentive on the part of the Austrians to accept such a proposal effectively doomed it. The duke had lots of friends in London, but the rumors of his involvement in causing the troubles in France preceded him, and many of his British friends avoided him. Pitt, George III, and the foreign minister—a man named the Duke of Leeds, who served in the office from 1783 to 1791—received him, not because they were serious about Belgian independence but because talking about it might get the Austrians to end their war in the Balkans. Shopping the duke around made them look like they were so serious about it that they even had a candidate.

Constituent Assembly, 1789: Two weeks after the march of the women, the Constituent Assembly reconvened in Paris and met in the Manege, a stable riding school that was then located between the Tuileries and the Place de Vendome. The Manege would be used for the assembly and its successor organizations until 1798, when the assembly, now styled the Council of Five Hundred, moved to the Palais Bourbon, where the lower house of the French Assembly still sits today. It was demolished in 1804 to make way for the Rue de Rivoli. The liberals sat on the president's left; the conservatives sat on the right, providing a useful addition to the lexicon of politics to the present day. There are other sources that say this left-right naming distinction didn't happen until October 1791, when the new constitution went into effect, but it is certain that it comes from the French Revolution. The nobles had emigrated in three successive waves, as many as 150,000 people, including many Army officers. The gaps in the ranks were filled with the sons of the bourgeoisie.

Now that the king and the assembly were in Paris, the political clubs took up new residences, which would give them their names. At first, they rented regular buildings for their meetings, but when the government took over church property, as described below, they started renting the monasteries in Paris for their meetings, giving us political names such as Jacobin, Cordelier, and Feuillant. Cordelier was a Franciscan monastery, Feuillant was Cistercian, and Jacobin was Dominican. In Great Britain, the name Jacobin dredged up memories of the Jacobites, those who advocated the overthrow of the Hanoverian Dynasty in favor of the Stuarts, so they tended to call the most radical French revolutionaries Jacobins.

Mainstream political opinion in late 1789 did not envisage anyone but Louis and his heirs on the throne, and the center of the debate between the two largest factions debated the extent to which Louis should share power. Regardless, the clubs all debated the full range of political possibilities, from radical republic to absolute monarchy and whether the monarch, if any, should be Bourbon, Orleans, or maybe a military leader like Lafayette. The policy of the clubs would vary as the revolution progressed, or if a club was too closely tied to a policy that became unfashionable, it was purged and disappeared. As an example, the Feuillants became associated with the goal of a liberal monarchy with the Bourbons on the throne, and when Louis was deposed in August 1792, all the Feuillants, notably Talleyrand, had to flee France. The Feuillants who failed to get away were killed in the September 1792 massacres. Another example is the Girondins, who wanted the Duke of Orleans as a liberal monarch who would serve the bourgeoisie, but if they couldn't get the duke to ring the bell, then their second choice was a conservative bourgeoisie republic. They were all purged in June 1793. A further factor in French politics was the position a club took on Great Britain, whether to oppose them or consider an alliance with them. Religion played a role as well, although very few members of the political class had genuine religious impulses, especially after all those conservative nobles who were genuinely religious emigrated.

Late in October, the Constituent Assembly, dominated by the bourgeoisie, passed a law distinguishing between passive citizens, active citizens, and electors. Males over the age of eighteen whose families paid, taxes equivalent to three days wages were active citizens. Active citizens were liable for military service and had the right to vote for electors. In 1789, there were about four million active citizens. Three million males over the age of eighteen were considered passive citizens. I suppose a passive citizen could always volunteer. Electors had an even higher economic level than active citizens and were eligible to cast votes for assemblymen and other elected officials. The active-passive-elector concept would be swept aside when the war came, when they needed everybody who could shoulder a musket to do so.

On November 7, the Constituent Assembly passed a law prohibiting members of the assembly from serving as government ministers. This was a bad move, as the most effective voices in the assembly ought to have been allowed to run the departments. The assembly was aiming this law at Mirabeau, as there was a feeling that combining crown and assembly would make the assembly subject to the influence of the crown and because they suspected Mirabeau was too close to the king and queen. Mirabeau had proposed a cabinet of Necker as prime minister, Lafayette as commander in chief of the Army, Talleyrand as minister of finance, Bailly as mayor of Paris, and himself as minister without portfolio, meaning he was to be the king's right-hand man. Mirabeau then suggested to the king that he leave Paris, set up shop in Rouen in Normandy, and summon the assembly there. The king rejected this idea, as he thought the assembly might simply depose and replace him.

In December 1789, Dr. Joseph-Ignace Guillotine, a member of the assembly, proposed a reform in capital punishment whereby all executions would be performed with a machine of his own invention, which he considered to be a humane improvement over hanging and axing. The idea was shelved for now.

Talleyrand, 1789: The carts of wheat brought from Versailles didn't do much to allay the hunger in Paris that had allegedly caused the march of the women. Maybe there was a decent harvest in the fall of 1789. Anyway, we don't hear any more about hunger, a sign that the whole thing was either a panic or a staged event, not a real shortage. Up until now, most of the political activity revolved around hunger and government-budget deficits. But now, as the politicians thought about how to solve their financial problems, they thought more and more about the wealth and property owned by the Catholic Church. Attacks begin on the institution, as one being parasitic and equally as oppressive and useless as the crown and the nobles of the sword.

The Catholic Church in France was an adjunct of royal policy as stated in the 1682 Declaration of the Clergy of France. In terms of priests keeping watch over their flocks, that mission was performed in adequate fashion, and outside of Paris and other large towns, religious observance was taken seriously. Hostility to the church was prevalent in all the large cities. Paris in 1789 was all in favor of sticking it to what they viewed as the finger-wagging religious bigots, busybodies, hypocrites, and self-righteous holy joes that constituted the church.

Right after the royal family moved to the Tuileries, on October 11, Talleyrand proposed to nationalize the Catholic Church, use the wealth of the church to balance the budget, and make the government responsible to "provide in a fitting manner for the expenses of public worship, the maintenance of the ministers, and the relief of the poor. The clergy are not proprietors but simple depositaries of the wealth that the piety of Kings and the faithful had devoted to religion." There was precedent for this. Henry VIII had dissolved the monasteries in 1536–1540 in England, and Joseph II had appropriated church properties in parts of the Habsburg lands. Those two had used the proceeds to help pay for their wars.

Talleyrand was an aristocrat, and since he had a lame foot, he became a priest instead of a soldier, despite the fact that he was never much of a believer. He was a church bureaucrat with the job of maintaining an inventory of church property, so he had information on the value of church property. Thus he was in a unique position to direct the process of turning church property into ready money for both funding the government and executing the revolutionary agenda. Talleyrand made himself famous by proposing this law and overshadowed Necker, who opposed the idea of the church taking on the full burden. Talleyrand was in his midthirties and was just now embarking on an extraordinary career serving the republic, the consulate, the empire, the restoration, and the July monarchy for the next half century. Although he showed a great deal of flexibility when it came to who he served, at heart, he always cherished the idea of a liberal legitimate monarchy under the Bourbon Dynasty as the one that was best for France. His ability to serve any regime is a credit to him, for beneath the silky, smirky, conniving surface lay the heart of a true patriot.

In early November, the Constituent Assembly passed Talleyrand's law to nationalize church property, 508–346. The value of the property was 3 billion livres. The amount of the budgetary deficits over the last few years had been on the order of 100 million livres per year. The amount of debt incurred by France in the American Revolution was about 1,300 million livres. In December, the government began issuing assignats, currency backed by the value of the churches. The assignats made it clear that the church lands were to be sold, not mortgaged. The church deemed assignats to be sacrilegious. Good Catholics were discouraged from using them as currency, but it solved the financial crisis for a while, enabling the assembly to continue writing a constitution. The government issued a lot of paper backed by the church property, and it had an inflationary effect. Four hundred million francs were issued at first. There is no question that this saved the revolution and bought the government several years.

Austria, Russia, and the Ottomans, 1789

The Brabant Revolution, 1789: Joseph II had tried unsuccessfully for years to trade Belgium for another realm, but in 1789, it remained an Austrian possession. From 1780 to 1792, it was governed by Maria Christina, sister of Joseph, and her husband, Albert, a younger son of the king of Saxony. They couldn't have children and adopted her brother Leopold's son Charles, who became one of the better Austrian Army commanders between 1796 and 1809. Belgium was one of the many Austrian crown lands that were on the receiving end of Joseph's reforming and centralizing edicts. As with the other Austrian regions, the edicts interfered with local customs and were resented. Great Britain, Prussia, and the Netherlands, a.k.a. the Triple Alliance, had, in 1788, defeated the French-supported Batavian Revolt, chasing the pro-French Patriot faction away to France. Now it was time for the Triple Alliance to go on the offensive and use Belgian dissatisfaction with Vienna to strike a blow against Austria and distract them from their operations in the Balkans. The British had good reasons for opposing Austrian and Russian attacks against the Ottomans, as explained above.

The Belgian rebels, aided by some of the French émigrés, defeated the local Austrian force on October 27, at the Battle of Turnhout. The Austrians retreated into Luxembourg and Antwerp, two well-provisioned and formidable fortresses, and called on Vienna for reinforcements. On December 20, the Belgians declared themselves the United States of Belgium. The Triple Alliance was supporting this revolt, and it strikes me as the British being a little too on the nose, practically taunting France with the term *United States.*

Since it was the Prussians who were occupying the Netherlands, the British and the Dutch claimed to disapprove of the Brabant Revolution and said they would never support it. They encouraged the Austrians to move in and suppress it, with the hidden agenda of impelling the Austrians to terminate their operations in the

THE GREAT GLOBE ITSELF

Balkans. Further impetus for Austria to act to suppress the Brabant Revolution was provided when the Duke of Orleans came to London in October with instructions from Paris to offer himself as the ruler of an independent Belgium, as described above. I don't know if the British foresaw that the people of France would feel threatened by a large Austrian Army in Belgium. I doubt it, because as far as they could determine, Austrian-French alliance was still in effect. The only objective at this point was to get the Austrians out of the Balkans. At the end of 1789, the Austrians were paralyzed with indecision, being committed to fighting a campaign in the Balkans in 1789, and with Emperor Joseph on the verge of death and unable to make decisions on strategy or troop dispositions.

Austria and Russia in the Balkans, 1789: There wasn't much activity in the Crimea or on the Black Sea in 1789, but in the Balkans, the Austrian and Russian Armies, under Coburg and Suvorov respectively, linked up and defeated an Ottoman Army at the Battle of Focsani, located in what is now Eastern Romania, in July. In September, the Austrian Army, under Marshal Laudon, began the siege of Belgrade. The siege would conclude successfully only three weeks later. This would be the only time the Austrians would ever occupy Belgrade; they gave it back during the peace negotiations in 1790. In September, Suvorov and Coburg cooperated again to defeat the Ottomans at the Battle of Rymnik, and Catherine gave Suvorov the victory title of Count Rymnikski. The battle resulted in the retreat of the Ottomans from the Danubian principalities, which is to say, the Ottoman territories north of the Danube: Wallachia and Moldovia. At this point, the British were worried that Russia might make it to Constantinople after all, and engaged in the actions described above to distract and disrupt the Austrians. They were also encouraging Sweden to keep up the fight against the Russians.

Austria did begin to get distracted. The emperor was dying, and his successor, Leopold II, remained in Florence. The foreign minister von Kaunitz had been in office for over forty years and was past eighty. The Prussians, who had an alliance with the Ottomans, were making threats in their rear. The Austrian Netherlands (Belgium) had declared independence. The Holy Roman Empire was in tur-

203

moil because of the many unpopular edicts from the emperor, who was way too far out in front of his people. Nevertheless, the Austrians were confident in their alliances with Russia and France and stayed the course for now.

1790: "Ca Ira" (It'll Be Fine)

The United States, 1790

The Compromise of 1790: The second session of the First US Congress convened at Federal Hall in New York City, from January 4 to August 12, 1790. During the course of the session, they passed a law that the capitol would be built in a new federal district close to Mount Vernon and would move there by 1800. In the meantime, the national capitol would be in Philadelphia. In return, the federal government assumed all state debt, meaning they would now have the power to impose taxes. The taxes would be either excise taxes or tariffs, the same sort that the colonies had so fiercely resisted when Parliament attempted to impose them in the '60s. This was the Compromise of 1790, a bargain between Hamilton on the one hand and Jefferson and Madison on the other.

In the future, the Union would be preserved by sectional bargains in 1820, 1850, and 1877, as it would seem that the country needed them every thirty years or so. After 1877, the dominance of the northeastern quadrant of the country was firmly established, which is what happens when you win a civil war. I remember growing up in Texas and being informed that the Pilgrims of Plymouth Colony were the first Englishmen to settle in America, as we would cut pilgrim hats out of black construction paper and reenact the first Thanksgiving. I don't think I found out about Jamestown and Pocahontas until I was in high school.

Robert Morris, who was a senator at the time, agreed with the financial part of the compromise but still hoped for the capital to stay in Philadelphia. The vote to establish the capital on the Potomac had been close, so he thought he could change some minds. He purchased land and constructed buildings intended to house the federal government, which later became the campus of the University of Pennsylvania. He also managed to carve out a Great Lakes frontage for Pennsylvania in Erie as part of the deal.

Alexander Hamilton, 1790: In January, Hamilton issued the First Report on Public Credit, outlining the plan to assume all public debt from the states. It borrowed heavily from Robert Morris ' work done in 1784, when he was superintendent of Finance. The finances of the federal government were placed on a firm footing as a result.

The Report on a National Bank, December 1790, titled Second Report on Public Credit, recommended the establishment of a national bank, which would be enacted into law in February 1791. It was part of the compromise, but Jefferson and Madison opposed it anyway and vowed to kill it when they gained power. It was a hot-button political issue in the days of Andrew Jackson, who killed it in 1832.

The Report on the Establishment of a Mint, January 1791, was enacted into law in April 1792. As we have seen, a mint had already been established by Robert Morris in 1781, and this law involved some tweaks.

The Report on Manufactures, December 1791: The idea behind this report called for subsidizing American industry and using federal funds to pay for interstate roads and canals. This was opposed by Jefferson and Madison, as they thought that it would result in too-cozy relationships between rich businessmen and government officials. It never became law, but when Jefferson was president, he could not resist the urge to use federal funds to build roads. The ideas of the Report on Manufactures were later championed by Henry Clay under the name the American system.

Funding of the federal government now came from tariffs or from smugglers caught by the Revenue Marine, later known as the US Coast Guard. It was the only naval service until the reestablishment of the United States Navy in 1794. Ten vessels were authorized for the Revenue Marine, supported by the local custom houses, to intercept smugglers.

The first US census was published in August and reported that there were.7 million slaves, 3.1 million whites, and 60,000 other free persons, that is, free blacks and taxed Indians. New York City was the largest city, but Pennsylvania still had more people than New York. Virginia still had the highest free population, along with the highest slave population, which was 39 percent of the free population. It's estimated that the white population grew from an immigrant population of about 1 million people from Europe that migrated between 1603 and 1790, and about 200,000 black "immigrants" during the same period.

The first ever midterm elections took place. Congress was divided between pro-Washington and anti-Washington factions. The pro-Washington faction gained one Senate seat and three House seats and maintained control of both chambers.

Great Britain, 1790

Great Britain remained focused in Australia, India, and Canada. They continued to aggravate the US as much as they could by supporting the Indians in the Ohio Country and moralizing about the international slave trade. In June, there was a general election in Great Britain, the first in six years, with William Pitt gaining a third term, defeating Charles James Fox.

The British kept the Duke of Orleans around in London until June, by which time the Austrians had ended their war in the Balkans, and the British no longer needed to parade him around as a potential king of Belgium. By that time, Austria and Prussia were in accord with the Treaty of Reichenbach, and they also had no further business with the duke, so he went home. Pitt had achieved his objective of thwarting Russian and Austrian aggression against the Ottomans. Austria was focused on the French, and the Russians were focused on the Poles. The Prussians were helping Austria and Russia. The Triple Alliance was still technically in effect, but Great Britain turned their attention to the things that were interesting to them: India, Australia, and tormenting the United States.

In November, Edmund Burke, who had opposed the war in America against the colonies, published *Reflections on the Revolution in France*. His opposition to the revolution caused a sensation because

THE GREAT GLOBE ITSELF

he had favored the American cause. It was the March of the Women incident that turned him against the revolution. Burke wrote:

> It is now sixteen or seventeen years since I saw the Queen of France, then the Dauphiness, at Versailles; and surely never lighted on this orb, which she hardly seemed to touch, a more delightful vision. I saw her just above the horizon, decorating and cheering the elevated sphere she just began to move in—glittering like the morning star, full of life, and splendor, and joy. Oh, what a Revolution! And what a heart must I have to contemplate without emotion that elevation and that fall! Little did I dream when she added titles of veneration to those of enthusiastic, distant, respectful love, that she should ever be obliged to carry the sharp antidote against disgrace concealed in that bosom; little did I dream that I should have lived to see such disasters fallen upon her in a nation of gallant men, in a nation of men of honor, and of cavaliers. I thought ten thousand swords must have leaped from their scabbards to avenge even a look that threatened her with insult. But the age of chivalry is gone. That of sophisters, economists, and calculators has succeeded; and the glory of Europe is extinguished forever.

Burke correctly predicted the revolution would end in a military dictatorship, but given the example of Cromwell, that wasn't hard to figure. He probably thought that Lafayette would be that dictator.

France, 1790

The Constituent Assembly, Paris, 1790: On New Year's Day, in France, the new departmental organization of France began a phasing in period, with the new organization to become effective on

March 4, 1790. Eighty-three departments were formed, each with a population of between three and four hundred thousand people. Departments could now appoint judges and bishops, organize military units, and collect taxes. During the Terror, the convention would be able to send representatives on mission to the departments, and their orders would be carried out, thanks to this apparatus. The mechanism was National Guards (sometimes called *fédérés*) organized at the department level and paid with assignats. It replaced the provincial control once exercised by the nobility and the clergy through the system of tithes and parlements. Tithes had been eliminated in the feudal decrees of August 1789.

In February, the Constituent Assembly passed a law abolishing monastic vows. The technical term used to describe this piece of legislation is *anticlericalism*, which can mean either anti-Catholic or antireligious. The problem was that too many Frenchmen confused the two. I remember the pastor at the Methodist Church I used to attend recounted a conversation he had with a French atheist who said that he was an atheist because he didn't believe that statues could come to life or that Jesus's mother would appear in various incarnations. My pastor told him that that he didn't believe that either. That's the difference between anti-Catholic and antireligious. Anyway, this was when all those fine buildings where the monks lived now emptied out for the use of the political clubs.

In May, the assembly abolished all titles of nobility. Soon it would be fashionable for the French to call each other citizen. In June, the Constituent Assembly declared France to be a constitutional monarchy, although a new constitution remained as yet a work in progress. The assembly called for all eighty-three departments to send National Guard units to a holiday celebrating the anniversary of the Bastille on July 14.

In July, the assembly passed the Civil Constitution of the Clergy. Priests were now officially state employees. The rules were as follows: Catholicism is the official state religion. Protestants and Jews have freedom of worship but must pay their own way, worship-wise. Bishops would be elected, one per department, which meant that the number of bishops was reduced from 134 to 83. Protestants, Jews,

THE GREAT GLOBE ITSELF

and nonbelievers who were "active citizens" could vote for bishops. The pope would be informed of the results but had no say. All priests were required to take an oath to the state in order to receive their pay. Those who refused to take the oath were called nonjuring priests. One hundred thirty of 134 bishops and 46,000 of 70,000 priests refused to take the oath. The Constituent Assembly, predominantly agnostic and supported by the bourgeoisie, was in growing conflict with the conservative church and its millions of adherents. Louis was in long correspondence with Pope Pius VI, and he said he could not sign the law until their conferencing was done. This law divided the believers in the nation against the agnostics. It would be a long-term schism. Many felt that the law called on them to choose between God and the revolution.

May 1790: The song "Ca Ira," which means "It'll Be Fine," became a popular revolutionary tune. Songs and rumors were the ways that the illiterate working class got their information in 1790.

Ah! ça ira, ça ira, ça ira	Ah! It'll be fine, it'll be fine, it'll be fine
Le peuple en ce jour sans cesse répète,	The people on this day repeat over and over,
Ah! ça ira, ça ira, ça ira	Ah! It'll be fine, it'll be fine, it'll be fine
Malgré les mutins tout réussira.	In spite of the mutineers everything shall succeed.
Nos ennemis confus en restent là	Our enemies, confounded, stay petrified
Et nous allons chanter « Alléluia! »	And we shall sing "Alleluia!"

Early in May, Louis XVI began paying Mirabeau large sums of money to defend the monarchy to the Constituent Assembly. Mirabeau worked all day, drank all evening, and slept with opera dancers all night. His rationalization was that he was getting paid to do what he believed anyway. "Paid but not bought" was his description. Mirabeau was now the prime counselor to the crown. He gave advice to the king and queen and made proposals in the assembly for compromise and reconciliation between the crown and the assembly. Mirabeau's last days would be spent as the darling of the people with his eloquence, but he never earned the trust of the bourgeoisie.

In July, the Duke of Orleans returned from Great Britain and took his seat in the assembly, having been in Great Britain since October 1789. Mirabeau's and Lafayette's constant criticism of him while he was absent had had their effect, and the duke found his ability to control public opinion in France was greatly diminished. The revolution was getting ready to pass him by, too, but unlike Necker and Mirabeau, he had the ability to grab hold of the reins again and seize control of events. Mirabeau didn't think the duke would and told Louis that the duke was but a phantom of his previous self and presented no danger to the throne. Publicly denying his ambition, the duke was waiting for Louis to make a foolish mistake, such as him or his relatives trying to escape from Paris.

Bastille Day celebrations: The duke was back in Paris in time to participate in the first Bastille Day, on July 14, a huge celebration, including Mirabeau making a speech, Lafayette on a white horse leading a parade, Talleyrand saying a Mass at a huge altar on the *Champs du Mars*, and Louis and Marie Antoinette swearing loyalty to the people of France. The evening was filled with fireworks and ballroom dancing. Three hundred thousand Parisians and fifty thousand National Guards from every corner of France held a gigantic festival. It was the best Bastille Day ever. The royal family was given some leeway and freedom of movement as a result of their oath of loyalty. Soon after Bastille Day, Marie Antoinette was able to start meeting regularly with Mirabeau at Saint Cloud.

The Nancy affair, 1790: In August, another convulsion occurred. In what was called the Nancy affair, three regiments (including a Swiss one) mutinied, accusing their officers of theft and confining them to their quarters, actions that mirrored exactly what the assembly had done to Louis in October 1789. The assembly, led by Lafayette on this issue, ordered the regional commander in Metz, General Francois Marquis de Bouille, to suppress the mutiny. The mutineers resisted, and hundreds were killed or wounded in the

THE GREAT GLOBE ITSELF

battle that ensued. Afterward, the ringleaders were tried, with the French units obtaining a degree of clemency while those in the Swiss unit, operating under Swiss law, faced severe punishment.

Metz and Nancy are not far from the Austrian fortress at Luxembourg, which, as discussed below, had just been reinforced with the Austrian troops from the Balkans. We can imagine that the cause of the mutiny was the worry of the soldiers over the adjacency of the Austrian troops in Belgium and Luxembourg, followed by the officers truthfully telling the troops that Austria was France's ally and presented no danger to France. The troops would have been hearing the rumors from their friends and relatives in Paris that the Austrians were going to betray France and invade in order to secure the release of Marie Antoinette. They would have then started mistrusting their officers, who were mostly inclined to be against what was happening to Louis and Marie Antoinette, and would see, or imagined they saw, signs of their officers in Metz and Nancy being in cahoots with the Austrians across the border in Luxembourg, and voilà, you have a mutiny.

Bouille's harshness, though fully authorized in advance and enthusiastically approved afterward by Lafayette and everyone else in the government, earned him the disapproval of the people and a negative mention in *The Marseillaise*. Bouille's command would also be the destination of Louis and his family during their flight from Paris in June 1791. In early September 1790, a large mob, forty-thousand strong, gathered outside the Tuileries denouncing Lafayette and blaming Louis for the so-called massacre. In this instance, nobody lost their job.

Necker's departure, 1790: In September, Necker, once the hero of the mob, resigned from his position of finance minister and minister of state and went home to Switzerland. It was his inability to stop the Austrian suppression of Belgium that did him in. Now there were thirty thousand Austrian troops on the French border who could enforce any demand for the release of Louis and Marie Antoinette. Necker was replaced as first minister by the foreign minister, the Comte de Montmorin, who, as we recall, had replaced Vergennes as foreign minister in 1787. Montmorin was dominated by Mirabeau,

211

who, after all, had the trust of the queen and the people. He stayed in office until Louis appointed a Feuillant war cabinet in November 1791. Necker died in 1804, but his daughter Germaine de Staël became a literary light and leading opponent of Napoleon.

At the end of the year, Louis and Marie Antoinette could look back with some satisfaction at how they were faring. They were able to come and go from the Tuileries to Saint Cloud, they had gotten rid of Necker, had neutralized the Duke of Orleans, had taken the despised Lafayette down a peg, and had made important alliances with Mirabeau and Talleyrand. The only thing that was wrong was the length of time it was taking to write the new constitution, the thing that was delaying their liberty.

Central and Eastern Europe, 1790

Austria, 1790: Joseph II of Austria died in February at the age of forty-eight. Joseph's health had been ruined in 1788, during his time fighting against the Turks in the Balkans. Joseph had lost two wives to smallpox in 1763 and 1767 and never had any children. His mother, Maria Theresa, dominated him personally and politically until her death in 1780. He had issued a civil code in 1786, anticipating the Napoleonic Code by sixteen years. He had abolished serfdom and made all religions equal before the law. He had granted freedom of the press. He had taken control of the Catholic Church and dissolved all monastic orders not involved in medicine or education. His program to create a German-speaking centralized state with no feudalism had been a failure because for the most part, his subjects loved their local ways.

Joseph's brother Leopold II was elected emperor. In order to suppress the Brabant Revolution and the United States of Belgium, Leopold II asked for an armistice in Austria's war with the Ottomans and sent thirty thousand troops to Belgium. In July, Leopold II signed the Treaty of Reichenbach with Prussia, which gave the Austrians a free hand in Belgium in return for ending the war with the Ottomans in the Balkans. Not coincidentally, it was at this time that the British decided they had no more business to discuss with the Duke of Orleans. The Greek Plan was postponed, temporarily, it was thought. Russia and Austria would again try to team up against the Ottomans to drive them out of the Balkans in 1804, but that was derailed when the Grand Army marched into Ulm in 1805. Prussia and Austria, normally adversaries, were glancing warily at the revolutionaries in France when they made their peace. Leopold was also looking at the need to rescue his sister Marie Antoinette, although he was thinking in terms of negotiation, not invasion. Having an Army camped in Belgium would be an asset if it came to negotiating for her safety. As described above, his troops in Belgium caused consternation in France, inducing the fall of Necker.

In September, the Austrians fought the Belgian revolutionaries at the Battle of Falmagne and were victorious. The Austrians then occupied Brussels. The Brabant Revolution was at an end. It was viewed as a triumph of reaction by the revolutionaries in France.

Prussia, Russia, and Poland, 1790: In March, Prussia signed a treaty with Poland. They were maintaining their aggressive stance against Russia and still had an Army ready to seize Riga, although the British started losing interest in that project once the Austrians had withdrawn from the Balkans. Prussia's primary objective was to annex Danzig one way or the other, and that was why they signed an alliance with Poland, but the Polish Sejm subsequently decreed that no subtractions from the territory of Poland would ever be considered. Since Danzig was a Polish enclave surrounded by Prussian territory, this declaration was annoying to the Prussians, and they soon began looking for loopholes in the Polish alliance and began negotiating with Russia. The foundations of the Second Partition of Poland were being laid.

Poland also began negotiating with Russia, attempting to become part of the Russian-Austrian alliance but had been rebuffed. Russia was telling the Poles to their face that they would love to have them on board but then would have "internal problems" processing the request. There was definitely a factional split in the Russian government between those who favored and those who opposed further annexations of Polish territory, but Catherine II was always there to make timely decisions.

In July, Sweden won a sea battle over the Russians, the Second Battle of Svenskund. The Russians decided it was time for peace and, in August, signed the treaty of Varala, ending the war. Russia guaranteed Sweden they would not interfere in internal Swedish affairs, which, believe it or not, was quite a concession on the part of Russia. The two countries would sign an alliance in October 1791.

1791: A Sham of Royalty

The United States, 1791

The US Congress, 1791: The federal government established the first Bank of the United States on February 25 in Philadelphia. It had a twenty-year charter. The building is still there today at 120 South Third Street. Although establishment of the bank was part of the Compromise of 1790, it became one of the major dividing lines in American politics for the next forty years. It was considered by its opponents to be a power grab by the federal government, while its adherents found a national bank to be a very convenient tool of efficient governing. It led to the establishment by Madison and Jefferson of the Republican Party in opposition to Hamilton and the Federalists. Washington and Adams were Federalists at heart, but they never engaged in the work of organizing a faction into an opposition dedicated to the defeat of political opponents. Washington didn't have to, having vanquished all of his rivals during the revolution, and Adams, because he and Hamilton loathed each other.

The First US Congress then went out of session on March 3, 1791. The next day, the Second US Congress convened for one day and adjourned until October 24. The one action that they took on March 4 was to admit Vermont to the Union as the fourteenth state. It was only ten months since Rhode Island had joined as the thirteenth. As we recall, Vermont had been incited to declare independence from New York and outlaw slavery by General Burgoyne when he invaded New York in 1777. There were now eight free states and six slave states. Well, slavery was legal in New York until 1799 and New Jersey until 1804, so technically it was eight slave and six free.

THE GREAT GLOBE ITSELF

In September, the commission overseeing the construction of the new national capital officially named it Washington City and, at the same time, named the land ceded by Maryland and Virginia for the capital as the District of Columbia. Because of the upcoming tricentennial of Columbus's voyage, Columbia was a popular name to give things around this time. The Columbia River in the Pacific Northwest; Columbia, South Carolina; British Columbia; Columbia University; Columbus, Ohio; and the song "Hail Columbia" were named, along with several cities and counties in the United States. Alexandria, Virginia, and Georgetown, Maryland, were incorporated into the new District of Columbia. The federal government would neglect the Virginia portion of the district, establishing no important offices there. It wasn't until World War II that the Pentagon would be built there on a former airfield. So the Virginia portion of the district was returned to the state of Virginia in 1846, and the land outside of Alexandria was renamed Arlington County.

At the end of the year, the Bill of Rights was ratified into the Constitution. The lack of a Bill of Rights had led to a lot of nay votes during the ratification process, and the document gained more favor as a result of this action.

The western frontier, 1791: In November 1790, the United States Army, under General Arthur Saint Clair, was defeated in the Battle of the Wabash by a coalition of Miami, Shawnee, and Lenni Lenape (Delaware) Indians. The leader of this coalition was a chief named Little Turtle. General Harmar, who had commanded the Army since 1784, had resigned the year before after a defeat, and it was plain to see that America's best and brightest were not lining up to join the Army. The Wabash River runs almost entirely in the state of Indiana, but the battle was fought in the most upstream reaches of it, in western Ohio, within two miles of the present Indiana-Ohio border.

The Indians had been supplied by the British and were fighting to establish Ohio as an Indian land. American settlers had been in the area since 1783, when the Treaty of Paris had ceded the land to the United States. Since the Indians had not been a party to the treaty, they viewed American settlement as encroachment. Many violent clashes had occurred between settlers and natives, most of which were instigated by the settlers. At the Battle of the Wabash, over six hundred Americans were killed or captured, with only fifty Indian deaths. As a result of the battle, Congress passed a law directing Washington and Secretary Knox to establish the Legion of the United States to remove the Indian threat. Congress also passed the Militia Acts, two laws that regulated and standardized the organization, equipment, and training of state militias and authorized the president to call them into national service. This was a good idea because it wouldn't do the federal government any good to have militia on hand if they all came with different weapons and doctrines.

General Saint Clair was forced to resign by a furious President Washington and was refused a court-martial. Congress began an investigation into the defeat, setting a precedent for the congressional investigation power, and subpoenaed executive department documents. Washington also set a precedent by claiming executive privilege, although he later turned over all the requested documents. The investigation largely sided with Saint Clair, stating that Washington and Knox had provided insufficient training and resources to the Army. Saint Clair lost his military command but kept his job as governor of the Northwest Territory, until Jefferson removed him in 1802 as a Federalist partisan.

Great Britain, 1791

In January, the British passed the Constitutional Act of 1791, which divided mainland Canada into Upper Canada, later Ontario, and Lower Canada, later Quebec. This was the second constitution after the United States Constitution. They issued it ahead of France, who had been working on theirs since the Tennis Court Oath in June 1789. Poland was close to completing theirs. The Duke of Kent, fourth son of George III and, in 1819, the father of Queen Victoria, was sent to Canada in May as a figurehead of royal authority. He was there for ten years, based in Halifax, Nova Scotia, which was a province separate from Upper and Lower Canada.

In March, Thomas Paine replied to Edmund Burke's *Reflections on the Revolution in France* by publishing *The Rights of Man* in Great

Britain. As the book advocated that the people had the right to overthrow their government, a warrant for his arrest was issued, and Paine had to flee to France. He was tried in absentia and found guilty. He was given a seat in the French Convention in September 1792 (one of the privileged few who was awarded honorary French citizenship), but his Girondist (most Girondists were Orleanists) views caused him to be arrested and imprisoned in December 1793. He survived, narrowly, and was released thanks to the intervention of James Monroe, US minister to France, in November 1794. He stayed in France until 1802, calling Napoleon "the completest charlatan that ever existed." He moved to New York in 1802 and died in June 1809.

The Duke of Leeds had been British foreign minister since December 1783, pursuing a policy of hostility to France, the United States, and Russia. The unrest in France and Poland starting in 1789 necessitated a review of this policy. Leeds lost his job in April 1791 and was replaced by Pitt's cousin William Grenville. Pitt's mother and Grenville's father were brother and sister. This occurred just at the time that in France, Mirabeau had died, and then Louis XVI and Marie Antoinette had been kept from traveling to Saint Cloud. In Poland, the Sejm was about to adopt the new constitution, and this was Leeds' failing because the British-Prussian-Dutch Triple Alliance failed at this point on his watch. Prussia and Russia were set to cooperate on suppressing Polish aspirations and then partitioning it. Pitt and George III must have been very displeased with Leeds at the time of his dismissal as he never had any further involvement in the government.

When the escape to Varennes, described below, became known, doubt and confusion prevailed in Great Britain over what was going to happen to the Bourbons. For a while, it looked like France might turn to the Duke of Orleans after all. Great Britain maintained its aloofness from continental affairs. If the Duke of Orleans was made king of France, a British-French alliance, something unthinkable since 1688 might lie in the future. But the duke was the kind of man who would walk up to the bell but wouldn't ring it, and Louis stayed on the throne. At the end of the year, Grenville had his hands full, as it was apparent that there was going to be war in both France and Poland in 1792.

PETER HARDY

Eastern Europe, 1791

In the Balkans, the Austrians were negotiating an end to their war with the Ottomans, but the Russians continued operations. In July, the Russian Army defeated the Turks at the Battle of Macin, in present-day Romania. Kutuzov, the future Russian commander against Bonaparte in the War of 1812, was one of the wing commanders in the battle and played a decisive role in the victory. Russia asked for a truce immediately afterward, and negotiations ensued. The Treaty of Jassy was signed on January 9, 1792. The Ottomans recognized the annexation of Crimea into Russia and also gave up a swath of land between the Southern Bug and Dniester Rivers, where the city of Odessa was founded.

During the negotiations in Jassy, Potemkin died at the age of fifty-two on October 16, probably of pneumonia; although some said he was poisoned. The Balkans had killed Joseph II, and now they killed Potemkin. Or, as always, we can suspect British assassins, as it was another opportune death for the British. Alexander Bezborodko was dispatched from Saint Petersburg to complete the treaty negotiations. Empress Catherine II was distraught, and Derzhavin wrote an ode called "Waterfall" to his memory. One of the things that later got Paul I in so much trouble was that when he became emperor, he went out of his way to desecrate Potemkin's memory, turning his palace into a barracks and ordering the destruction of his grave, which order was, fortunately, slow-rolled by Paul's subordinates until his death.

One evening, at the height of his power, Potemkin declared to his dinner guests:

> Everything I have ever wanted, I have. I wanted high rank, I have it; I wanted medals, I have them; I loved gambling, I have lost vast sums; I liked giving parties, I've given magnificent ones; I enjoy building houses, I've raised palaces; I liked buying estates, I have many; I adore diamonds and beautiful things—no individual in Europe owns rarer or more exquisite stones.

THE GREAT GLOBE ITSELF

> In a word, all my passions have been sated. I am
> entirely happy!

Potemkin was a mass of contradictions. Criticisms include "laziness, corruption, debauchery, indecision, extravagance, falsification, military incompetence and disinformation on a vast scale," but supporters hold that only devotion to luxury and extravagance are truly justified, stressing Potemkin's intelligence, force of personality, spectacular vision, courage, generosity, and great achievements. Though not a military genius, he was able in military matters. French war minister Ségur had met him in 1787 and wrote that "nobody thought out a plan more swiftly, carried it out more slowly and abandoned it more easily." Political opponents such as Semyon Vorontzov agreed; the prince had "lots of intelligence, intrigue and credit" but lacked "knowledge, application and virtue." He had a battleship named after him, and the battleship had a classic movie named after it.

The Russians ended the war in the Balkans because they couldn't carry on without the Austrians and because of the situation in Poland. On May 3, the Great Sejm adopted a written constitution, a liberal monarchy under King Stanislaus Poniatowski. The Russians had gone from approving the actions of the Sejm to being alarmed by them. They were listening to the Prussians who were talking about another partition of Poland. The new constitution was rammed through the Sejm on a party line vote consisting of the king and the leading bourgeoisie. The Polish nobility opposed it to a man, and they appealed to the Russians, who answered the call.

In October, the Prussians declared their alliance with Poland to be void, in that they had had no say in the passing of the Polish Constitution. The real reason, of course, was their hopes of acquiring Danzig being dashed. The Russians and the Prussians got ready to intervene in Poland. The Prussians were now committing themselves to send troops to both France in the west and Poland in the east, but they thought that would be okay because they would be in a supporting role in both cases.

PETER HARDY

France and Austria, 1791

Conflicts in Paris, January to March 1791: Louis started the year 1791 in a good position, but it soon deteriorated. On January 21, he finally signed the Civil Constitution of the Clergy. All bishops who refused to take the oath were deposed and replaced. Pope Pius VI issued a statement that the law was against the beliefs of the church and chastised Louis. Louis responded in repentant fashion by getting himself a new confessor who was a nonjuring priest, which put him in violation of the law he had just signed. The reaction in Paris toward Pius's statement was extremely negative toward the Catholic Church. The theaters began producing plays highlighting the horrors of the Inquisition, the hypocrisies of the people in monasteries and convents, and greedy priests. There was a whole class of theater hacks who could churn out scripts in days in response to current events.

Soon after the Civil Constitution of the Clergy was signed, Louis's two aunts *Mesdames* Adelaide and Victoria decided that they would make a pilgrimage to Rome as a protest and a penitence. This was an opportunity for the Duke of Orleans to regain his position in the revolution. The Paris mob was alerted, and another march of women was organized at the Palais-Royal. On February 20, *les Mesdames* were able to depart before the mob arrived. The two of them were accused of the same crime as the émigrés, leaving the country to organize a counterrevolution. They did make it to Rome, where they lived until France invaded Italy in 1796. They fled to Naples until France invaded there in 1799. They fled to Trieste, where Victoria died in 1799, and Adelaide died in 1800. Their bodies were brought back to France in 1815 and interred in Saint-Denis.

As a result of the affair with *les Mesdames*, the Assembly passed a law restricting the travel of émigrés in and out of France. Mirabeau called the law barbaric and antiliberty, for which he was vilified. Simon Schama and Alistair Horne, two historians who would know, called this the turning point in the revolution, the point at which the assembly began to turn France into a police state.

On February 24, a mob showed up at the Tuileries, asking Louis to recall his aunts, as they feared he would follow their lead. Lafayette dispersed the crowd. February 28 was the Day of the Daggers. A rumor had started that there was a tunnel from the Tuileries to Vincennes, which would have been a very long tunnel indeed as it is six miles from the Tuileries to Vincennes. A mob appeared at Vincennes that was attempting to destroy the fortress in Bastille fashion, fearful that Louis was going to escape through the tunnel. Lafayette took a unit of Swiss Guards with him to Vincennes to disperse the mob. With the Tuileries undefended, four hundred nobles armed with daggers arrived at the Tuileries, volunteering as a makeshift bodyguard for Louis. They suspected Lafayette of purposely weakening the guard at the Tuileries to allow assassins in. After dispersing the mob at Vincennes, Lafayette returned to the Tuileries and attempted to arrest the nobles, accusing them of wanting to help Louis escape to Rome. Louis calmed everyone down and arranged an agreement where the nobles could leave after turning over their weapons.

Once again, the Duke of Orleans, taking advantage this time of the crisis brought about by the *Mesdames*, went up to the bell but failed to ring it. He must have thought that the bell was supposed to ring itself and that the throne had to really be unsought by him, not just seem to be. If the duke himself weren't orchestrating this, he certainly had his followers who would orchestrate it for him, with him having plausible deniability of their actions so he could play the part of the reluctant prince stepping forward to serve only because he heard the cry of the people. The duke's enemies frequently made this charge, which he always denied. There seems to have been some confusion among his followers, who made the mistake of believing him when he denied interest in the throne. Maybe he really didn't want the job at this time, fearing that he would become just as much a prisoner as Louis.

The assembly, January to May 1791: In March, the assembly passed the Le Chapelier Law, suppressing trades guilds, which were associated with royal monopolies granted to control the price of commodities. It also outlawed strikes. It remained in force until 1864. The master-apprentice system was retired in favor of one where the government issued licenses to individuals to practice a trade. The law enraged the artisan class of France, the *Sans Culottes*, named for the fact that they wore straight legged pants rather than knee breeches. This law demonstrated that the bourgeoisie and not the working class dominated the assembly.

Also in March, the assembly passed a regency law in the event of the death of the king. The first choice was the Comte de Provence, later Louis XVIII, and then the Duke of Orleans. The Comte d'Artois, later Charles X, was excluded, having left France in 1789. I would imagine that the Comte de Provence received his share of death threats at the time. This law was an indication of the revolutionaries taking a different approach, making the Duke of Orleans first regent and then king.

March was a busy month as the assembly accepted the proposal of the French Academy of Science that the distance from the equator to the North Pole through Paris, at sea level, was exactly 10 million meters, and the meter was fixed at its current length, equal to 39.37 English inches. The circumference of the earth is therefore 40 million meters, and the distance from the North Pole to the South Pole through the center of the earth is 40 million/π or 12.73 million meters or 12,730 kilometers or about 7,600 miles. The numbers were later modified, as it was discovered that the circumference of the earth at the equator is 40.074 million meters, while the pole-to-pole circumference is 40.008 million meters, making the earth an oblate spheroid, not a true sphere.

In May, members of the Cordeliers Club started to make their mark with the first documented use of the phrase "Liberty, Equality, Fraternity." Many in France believed that this phrase was blasphemous and was meant to replace the Father, Son, and Holy Ghost. The Cordeliers were republican in sentiment. They were prominent in the Paris Communes but not the assembly and so were still awaiting their opportunity. Camille Desmoulins, who, as we recall, had started the riot that led to the attack on the Bastille, was a Cordelier.

The death of Mirabeau, April 1791: On April 2, Mirabeau died at the age of forty-two, after a short illness related to heart disease. Historians make much of the fact that his final disease came hard upon a night spent with two dancers from the opera. His death was a blow to Louis, Marie Antoinette, and Lafayette but was good for the

THE GREAT GLOBE ITSELF

Duke of Orleans and the British. It also strengthened the hand of the small but growing number of republicans in the assembly. Barnave called Mirabeau the William Shakespeare of oratory. Mirabeau was the first to be buried in the Pantheon. His funeral was extensive and ornate, with three hundred thousand people following the cortege.

Once again, a death that is good for British policy occurs at just the right time, so we must suspect assassins. In 1794, after the king's complicity with Mirabeau was discovered among the king's papers in the *armoire de fer*, Mirabeau's corpse was removed from the Pantheon. Brissot objected to the use of the word *virtue* on Mirabeau's headstone, saying, "His tomb is not honored by a lie." Brissot was one of the Duke of Orleans' followers, the bourgeoisie faction which had just passed the Chapelier Law.

Escape to Varennes, April to June 1791: On April 18, Monday of Holy Week, Louis and Marie Antoinette got in their carriage at the Tuileries to travel to Saint Cloud, which, as we recall, was Marie Antoinette's private property, in order to receive the sacraments from their nonjuring priest. The new priest's name was Pere Hebert, presumably no relation to the foul-mouthed editor of Pere Duchesne. The National Guard troops guarding the Tuileries stopped them. The guard had not previously attempted to prevent royal travel to Saint Cloud. There was no doubt a lawyer in the unit who asserted that it was illegal for anyone to receive communion or any other sacrament from a nonjuring priest. It was especially egregious that it was the king and queen themselves breaking the law the king had signed. Letting them travel might expose them to a charge of aiding and abetting. Lafayette must have taken the day off because he didn't fix this problem.

As we recall, restricting the movements of the royal family had previously happened in the Netherlands in 1787, which had provoked a Prussian invasion. Louis and Marie Antoinette did not travel to Saint Cloud that day and were furious. It was clear that Lafayette had no control over the National Guard, and he resigned or, at least, threatened to. This was a frequent technique of his. Lafayette kept resigning, and they kept asking him back. For now, he exuded a residual aura of George Washington and was considered just as indispensable. As a result of this episode, Pope Pius recalled his nuncio in France, and France did likewise. Subsequently the assembly clarified the situation and declared that nonjuring priests could say Mass if they respected the law, which presumably set Louis and Marie Antoinette at liberty to travel to Saint Cloud. But they had had it and spent the next two months planning their escape, the mistake that the Duke of Orleans had been waiting for.

On June 20, two months after being detained at the Tuileries, the royal family attempted to escape from Paris for the fortress in Montmedy, where General Bouille had command of loyal forces and had been in contact with the Austrians in Belgium, as well as the émigrés. Montmedy was sixty miles northwest of Bouille's headquarters at Metz, within walking distance of the Belgian frontier. On the morning of the twenty-first, the disappearance was discovered, and an angry crowd gathered at the Tuileries. Lafayette issued an order for the arrest and return of the king. It was later amended to delete the word *arrest*, saying that the king had not fled but had been kidnapped. At the same time, the Comte de Provence fled to Belgium by a different route. Provence was successful, but the king was recognized and detained at Varennes-en-Argonne, only thirty miles from Montmedy. Varennes was completely destroyed in World War I, being part of no-man's-land in the Verdun sector of the Western Front, but it has been rebuilt.

Count Axel von Fersen, a Swedish diplomat who had known Marie Antoinette for twenty years and had almost certainly been intimate with her at some point, organized the escape. They had made elaborate arrangements, but in Varennes, the postmaster, Jean-Baptiste Drouet, recognized the king when they passed through. Drouet made arrangements for them to be detained in the next town.

THE GREAT GLOBE ITSELF

He earned eternal fame for this, but he was finished in 1796, when he got mixed up with the radical communist Gracchus Babeuf.

Bouille had to flee into Belgium, and he joined the émigrés. Louis and Marie Antoinette were detained in Varennes until units came to escort them back to Paris. Six thousand National Guardsmen were enough to ensure that there would be no interference from foreign Armies. Von Fersen eventually returned to Sweden and gained high office. He was killed by a mob in Stockholm on June 20, 1810, during the funeral march of the Swedish crown prince, as the mob blamed von Fersen for the crown prince's death. The cause of von Fersen's death was having his rib cage crushed by someone in the mob jumping on it from a high distance.

Louis had left a note behind him in Paris repudiating all of his actions during the period of the assembly, calling it a sham of royalty. He had no say in the appointment of judges, ambassadors, or commanders. He had no power to control the clubs or the press, which were allowed to print or say anything they wanted about him and his wife. These were all perfectly legitimate points to bring up, and no chief executive in French history, before or since, has ever been at such a disadvantage. He was escorted into Paris on June 25. The mob was uncharacteristically silent when the king's carriage returned to the Tuileries Palace. The assembly posted signs reading, "Anyone who applauds the king will be beaten. Anyone who insults him will be hanged."

In the assembly, Barnave had begun stepping up into the role that Mirabeau had been playing. He and a few other assemblymen accompanied the royal family. They had brought the situation in Paris under control. Now it was Barnave's turn to be put under Marie Antoinette 's spell. He became the biggest advocate of a more powerful monarchy between now and the end. The prime topic of political discussion in France was not how much power the king should have but whether Louis would remain king, or whether he should be deposed. Those favoring Louis were called Feuillants, and those wanting Louis deposed were called Girondists. Girondists were split on what should replace him, with some favoring a republic, but the most common idea put forward was to put the Dauphin on the throne with the Duke of Orleans as regent or lieutenant general. The king's brothers Artois and Provence had disqualified themselves by virtue of their emigration. Brissot wrote a pamphlet declaring that the king had deposed himself by his flight and that if the monarchy should continue, it should be under another monarch.

There was still a royalist faction in favor of a more powerful monarchy and a republican faction in favor of no monarch, but these were both on the fringes of politics for now.

By virtue of his attempted escape, Louis's power was suspended, and the assembly authorized ministers to execute decrees without obtaining the his signature. The Comte de Provence, having escaped to Belgium, declared himself the regent-in-fact. On June 28, it was proposed in the assembly that the Duke of Orleans be elected to the position of regent of France for Louis XVII, although it did not actually call for deposing Louis XVI, which sounds like the lawyers were busy editing proposals into nonsense. The next day, the duke published a statement in a journal stating:

> I am ready to serve my country on land and sea or as a diplomat, in other words in any position where my zeal and commitment to the people can be of use. But as for the Regency, I renounce the offer formally and finally, preferring to humbly continue my work for the liberty and freedom of the common people. I repeat, I seek neither high office nor reward. I trust that this statement will finally silence my detractors who have sought for years to condemn my actions, which were only taken in the best interests of the people.

This declaration had a serious deflating effect on the Orleanist cause.

Although I haven't been able to find anything written about it, I suspect that Leopold II and the other powers of Europe had opened communications with France and, presenting a united front, had

THE GREAT GLOBE ITSELF

made it clear to France that deposing Louis and replacing him with the Duke of Orleans would make France a pariah, isolated, and outcast in European affairs, so the duke issued his statement, and the rehabilitation of Louis began. Such a statement might have been accompanied by a promise to make the duke king of Belgium after all.

The fall of Lafayette and Bailly, July 1791: On July 14, the second anniversary of Bastille Day, the altar was again set up on the *Champs de Mars*, but Talleyrand couldn't say Mass this year, having been excommunicated a few months before. Lafayette, in disgrace for letting the king escape, was keeping a low profile. He would not be leading a parade on horseback this year. The speeches were not as good with Mirabeau dead. The king and queen would not be publicly renewing their oaths to the people, being prisoners in their palace. None of the people who had made the celebration of 1790 so memorable were available in 1791, making it the worst Bastille Day ever.

On July 17, a massacre occurred. The Cordeliers had organized a petition at the altar calling for the removal of Louis XVI, the abolition of the monarchy, and the formation of a republic. Two men were hiding under the altar. The reason they were there has never been determined because they were strung up before being able to explain themselves. Most historians have concluded they were a couple of perverts who were just there to look up women's dresses. The National Guard troops, under Mayor Bailly and General Lafayette, opened fire on the mob when it became unruly, and fifty people were killed. The popularity of Lafayette and Bailly went up in smoke, and after that, they were nothing but a stench in the nostrils of the people of Paris.

The Declaration of Pillnitz, August 1791: Having suppressed the Brabant Revolution in September 1790, Leopold II consolidated his gains in Belgium. Revolutionary France was alarmed at the large Austrian Army on its border. In July, after the Flight to Varennes, Leopold II issued the Padua Circular, calling on his fellow sovereigns to join him in demanding the freedom of Louis XVI and his family. In August, the Treaty of Sistova ended the war between Austria and the Ottomans. Austria gained a small area along the border but had to end its occupation of Belgrade. Having secured his eastern and southern flanks, Leopold then went to Pillnitz in Saxony to meet with Frederick William II, and the two of them issued the Declaration of Pillnitz on August 27, declaring the joint support of the Holy Roman Empire and the Kingdom of Prussia for Louis against the revolutionaries. For fifty years, Prussian-Austrian antipathy had been axiomatic in European diplomacy, and on the rare occasions when they were on the same side, it was bad for France.

Russia, Great Britain, and Spain also disapproved of what was happening in France to Louis and Marie Antoinette. There were those in France who asked, "Why shouldn't we have the leaders that we want?" And "Who do these foreign tyrants think they are to suggest otherwise?" Regardless, the hostility that France was generating from the rest of Europe was enough to make them pause and think.

The Constitution of 1791: The text of the Pillnitz Declaration made it to Paris in September, spurring the assembly to complete its constitutional work. On September 3, they passed the Constitution of 1791, to be effective October 1, after which date the Constituent Assembly would now go by the name Legislative Assembly. The Declaration of the Rights of Man served as the preamble. On September 14, Louis XVI swore an oath to the Constitution and was invested in his new reduced powers. When that happened, Leopold retracted his support for the Pillnitz Declaration. The Constitution of 1791 had the following features:

- The executive branch to be a hereditary monarchy. The assembly to vote him his expenses. The king to be deposed if he leaves the country without the permission of the

THE GREAT GLOBE ITSELF

assembly. The king to appoint and dismiss his ministers. Each minister to report monthly to the assembly on his expenses. The king to be the commander of the Army and the Navy. The king could not declare war or sign a treaty without the consent of the assembly. The king to have the right to veto legislation, but the legislation will become law if passed by the assembly three sessions in a row.

- The legislative branch to be a unicameral assembly. The assembly to have 747 members, 9 from each of the 83 departments. To prevent the formation of a House of Lords, all hereditary titles and privileges to be abolished, except for the king's. The citizenry to be divided into active citizens (adult males who pay the equivalent of three days' wages in taxes) and passive citizens (all others). This is to separate the bourgeoisie from the artisans and the peasants. The legislature to be elected by active citizens, which numbered 4,300,000 men out of a total population of 25 million. The legislature to be elected every two years and cannot be dissolved or extended by the king. Legislators are limited to one term.
- No member of the current Constituent Assembly can sit in the first legislature (this was the self-denying ordinance, which turned out to be a mistake).
- France to be divided into eighty-three departments of roughly equal size, and the departments to be divided into communes. A total of 43,360 communes were established. Internal tolls to be abolished. Cruel and unusual punishments such as branding or the pillory are outlawed, but the death penalty is kept. Dr. Guillotine perked up hearing that. The parlements, which had been trying to be a counterweight to the power of the crown before 1789, to be abolished in favor of a new judiciary, appointed by the assembly.

Elections were held for the new Legislative Assembly. Among the new assemblymen was Jean Roland. He and his wife, Manon,

229

moved to Paris from Lyon. They soon become influential members of revolutionary society, with Manon running one of the most influential salons in the city. Roland was soon dominating the Girondists, the group that kept getting disappointed by the Duke of Orleans. Manon, known to history as Madame Roland, was a sophisticated and educated woman of whom it was said that you knew she was intelligent before she opened her mouth. She liked to tell the story of being invited to a party with some aristocrats, only to be asked to dine with the servants. I'd like to hear the aristocrats' version of that event.

The ideas that had been so radical in 1789 had now been implemented, and the new Legislative Assembly promised further changes. We can start to see the relay race nature of the revolution, where a group comes into power, establishes change until they are satisfied, and are replaced by a new group wanting more change. This will occur about every two years.

The election of 1791 returned factions of Cordeliers, Girondists, and Feuillants, as well as some traditional royalists who wanted the throne reestablished in its former powers. This last group had no support structure within Paris. On October 1, the Legislative Assembly convened: 136 Girondists took their seat on the left side of the hall, 264 Feuillants sat on the right, with the other 347 members making up the other factions. The tradition of liberals being on the left and conservatives being on the right may have occurred at this time, although there are competing tales. At the top of the agenda was how to deal with the threat of the émigrés, who, by all accounts, were forming counterrevolutionary Armies on the other side of the Rhine and what to do with the priests that refused to swear, who were fomenting the superstitious country bumpkins to do the same thing.

France on the road to war: On October 14, the assembly passed a law that made service in the National Guard mandatory for all active citizens and their sons over eighteen. On that day, Brissot, who was not foreign minister but was head of the committee on foreign affairs in the assembly, delivered a speech, noting that the Russians had ended their wars against the Ottomans and Sweden, and the

THE GREAT GLOBE ITSELF

Austrians had ended their war against the Ottomans. Archenemies Prussia and Austria had set aside their differences, signed a treaty at Reichenbach, and issued the Pillnitz Declaration as a warning to France. These actions on the part of Russia, Prussia, and Austria were as much in response to what was happening in Poland as they were to events in France, but Brissot had a valid point.

Brissot's speech made no proposals of support to Poland or to the Ottomans. There was nothing about reaching out to the British. His solution was to raise an Army, destroy the émigré Army in Trier, and kick the Austrians out of Belgium. At least we can say that France was making the right first move by organizing a bourgeoisie Army. The Feuillants were initially against a war with Austria, but to their surprise, Louis and Marie Antoinette were in favor of one. Louis calculated that he had nothing to lose from a war. If it went well, he gained power as commander in chief. If it went bad, the Prussian and Austrian Armies would destroy the Paris mob. On November 9, the assembly decreed that all émigrés that had not returned to France by January 1, 1792, would be sentenced to death. The king vetoed this decree on November 12. On November 29, priests were given one week to swear loyalty to the government or face loss of job and pay. The king vetoed this decree on December 19. The Paris mob was very upset about these vetoes.

Bailly's term as mayor of Paris ended in November. Lafayette ran for the office but lost to Girondist Jerome Petion. Bailly retired from politics and moved to the country to write his memoirs. He was still there in October 1793, when the Terror started and came to arrest, try, and behead him. Petion was one of the Girondists proscribed in June 1793, and he escaped to Bordeaux. The Terror caught up with him in June 1794, and he committed suicide rather than face arrest and the guillotine. As far as the mayoral election, Marie Antoinette was delighted to see Lafayette go down to defeat. Lafayette retired to his estates in Auvergne and began lobbying for a military command, which he soon got but without a marshal's baton, the excuse being that he was too young, only thirty-four this year.

Feuillant War Ministry, December 1791–March 1792: In December, the Comte de Narbonne-Lara, a Feuillant, was appointed war minister. This man was allegedly the son of Louis XV, and so uncle to, but the same age as, Louis XVI. He actively planned for war against the Austrians in Belgium and the émigrés in Trier, who were in the process of forming an Army under the command of Louis Joseph de Bourbon, the Prince of Conde. He was able to raise a force of twenty-five thousand men. Trier is located between Luxembourg and Koblenz. Narbonne had to flee France after August 1792 but was cleared to return in 1801, thanks to Talleyrand's intervention. In 1809, Napoleon called on him to serve as a high-level diplomat, engaging in important assignments at critical times in Vienna, Munich, Berlin, and Vilna. He had much of the charm and grace that had gone missing when Talleyrand resigned. He died of typhus while commanding a Saxon stronghold in November 1813.

Soon after taking office, Narbonne established three field Armies: the Army of the North under Rochambeau; the Army of the Center under Lafayette; and the Army of the Rhine under Luckner. Rochambeau and Luckner were made marshals. A fourth Army, the Army of the Midi, was also established under General Montesquoi. Over the next seven years, the French Revolutionary Armies would undergo divisions, expansions, and reorganizations, most of the time under the direction of Lazare Carnot, the Organizer of Victory.

At the same time that Narbonne took over at the War Ministry, Montmorin was replaced at the Foreign Ministry by a man named Claude Antoine de Lessart, both of whom would die in the 1792 September Massacres.

CHAPTER 4

The French Convention, 1792–1794

1792: L'Audace, et Encore de l'Audace, et Toujours de l'Audace

The United States

Money matters: The US Congress passed the Coinage Act of 1792 in April, establishing the dollar as the standard unit of currency, which I don't how it was different than what Robert Morris had done ten years before. The value of the dollar was pegged to the widely circulated Spanish dollar.

In May, the New York Stock Exchange opened for business at Forty Wall Street, two doors down from the Bank of New York at Forty-Eight Wall Street. The 40 Wall Street was later the site of Aaron Burr's Manhattan Company. The current building on the site is a seventy-story building that was completed in 1930. It has been known as the Trump

Building since 1995. Twenty-four stockbrokers made an agreement under a buttonwood tree. The agreement read as follows:

> We the Subscribers, Brokers for the Purchase and Sale of the Public Stock, do hereby solemnly promise and pledge ourselves to each other, that we will not buy or sell from this day for any person whatsoever, any kind of Public Stock, at less than one quarter of one percent Commission on the Specie value and that we will give preference to each other in our Negotiations. In Testimony whereof we have set our hands this 17th day of May at New York, 1792.

The first stock sold was that of the Bank of New York, and the second stock was the Bank of the United States.

Money matters were the leading cause of political factionalism in 1792. In May, Alexander Hamilton wrote, "Mr. Madison, cooperating with Mr. Jefferson is at the head of a faction decidedly hostile to me and my administration." Congressman Madison had led the fight against the establishment of the Bank of the United States. Although the sectional differences between New England, the South, and the mid-Atlantic states were present from the beginning, the bank was the issue that first marked the division of the country into factions. Despite the factions, federal elections in November went smoothly. In contrast to the chaos in France and Poland, George Washington was peacefully and unanimously reelected president.

The western frontier, 1792: In June, General "Mad" Anthony Wayne, General Saint Clair's replacement, established the headquarters of the Legion of the United States at Fort Lafayette, which he built near Fort Pitt because Fort Pitt was dilapidated. Wayne had been a major general during the revolution, had negotiated with the Cherokee Indians in Georgia, and had been a resident in and congressman for Georgia between 1784 and 1792. President Washington now appointed him to command the force that would avenge the loss at the Wabash. The legion was organized into four sublegions that consisted of three infantry battalions, one troop of dragoons, and an artillery battery. The legion remained at the fort until November 1792, when it moved to Legionville, twenty-two miles west of Fort Lafayette. This was where they were at the end of the year 1792.

Negotiations with the Indians of the Northwest Confederacy were conducted by Secretary Knox in person. The Canadians provided support to the Indians, who were divided among themselves and never conveyed a coherent message to the US of what they wanted from them. There were hard-liners who wanted no white settlements north of the Ohio River, even though there were already several, and there were assimilators who had concluded that the white man's coming was unstoppable, and it was best to learn to live in that reality. At the end of 1792, the negotiations continued.

Also in June, Kentucky was admitted to the Union as the fifteenth state. Kentucky had seceded from Virginia because of the long distance to the state capital and the fact that the Virginians did not recognize the importance of the Ohio and Mississippi Rivers to Kentucky. That secession had been formalized when Congress passed the Southwest Ordinance, a companion to the 1787 Northwest Ordinance that asserted federal ownership of all land west of the Appalachian ridgeline. The barrels of bourbon whiskey continued to flow down the Ohio River to New Orleans.

Eastern Europe

On March 29, Gustav III of Sweden was assassinated at the age of forty-six. He had engaged in power struggles with the Swedish nobility since his accession in 1771, and it was a plot planned and executed by some very angry nobles that got him. He was shot at a masquerade ball at the Royal Opera House in Stockholm. He was succeeded by his fourteen-year-old son, Gustav IV. This occurred only four weeks after the untimely death of Leopold II.

Poland had a divide between the crown and the nobility similar to the one in Sweden. The May 3, 1791, Polish Constitution was supported by King Stanislas and the Polish bourgeoisie, but the nobles despised it as it stripped them of many of their privileges. In January, a delegation of nobles traveled to Saint Petersburg to ask Catherine to intervene. They issued a proclamation critical of the constitution as a contagion of democratic ideas following the fatal example set in Paris. The nobles were all still in Saint Petersburg when on May 14, 1792, the declaration of the Targowica Confederation was published in Targowica, a town in Prussian Silesia not far from Breslau but a long way from Saint Petersburg. The Prussians were definitely weighing in against the Poles.

Europe goes to war, 1792

Preliminaries, January to April 1792: At the same time that the Polish nobles were appealing to Catherine, France prepared to fight Austria while, at the same time, trying to avoid war with Prussia. France and Austria were still technically bound by an alliance. Louis was still king, so the diplomacy that preceded this war was conducted in the old style, like the letters that gentlemen sent to each other preparatory to fighting a duel. In January, diplomatic notes from Vienna to Paris asked for clarification of the status of properties in Alsace owned by the Austrian emperor or by princes of the empire. Notes from Vienna to the Army in Belgium directed them to cooperate with the ruler of Koblenz (the bishop elector of Trier) to thwart any French invasion. This meant that he was authorized to support the Prince of Conde 's French émigré Army.

Talleyrand, now a diplomat, went to London to meet with Pitt and his foreign minister Grenville. It was his first foray into the field of international diplomacy, and he, like the Duke of Orleans, had very little success. He was there to assure the British that Louis XVI was firmly on the throne, that the new constitution was working, and that France wanted an alliance with Great Britain in the event of a war with Austria, which was likely. The British weren't interested in an alliance with France for many reasons related to both historical and current events. An alliance with France wasn't going to prevent another partition of Poland; it was only going to embroil them in a war against Austria. Pitt and Grenville told Talleyrand there was no

THE GREAT GLOBE ITSELF

chance of an alliance but that Talleyrand could count on British neutrality, and maybe more if stability did return to France.

On January 15, 1792, France sent an ultimatum to Austria demanding they explain why they were supporting the émigrés. The deadline for Austria to respond was March 1. Vienna replied with a demand that German lands in Alsace be restored, that the royal family be liberated, and that Avignon be returned to the pope. On February 7, Prussia and Austria signed a formal alliance. Their partnership would last three years and was tense while it endured.

Death of Leopold II, accession of Francis II, March 1792: The French ultimatum deadline passed, and Leopold II died on the same day, certainly one of the most inopportune deaths in history. For once, we see an inopportune death that doesn't directly benefit British foreign policy. Well, maybe it did somehow. Whenever Talleyrand is involved, motives get murky, and you can never be sure why anybody does anything. For two years, since the death of his brother Joseph II, he had been shoring up local and foreign support, and the strain of constant travel may have wrecked his health. It is also suspicious that his wife, Marie Louise, died less than three months later. They were both in their forties. It makes you think that someone in Vienna was poisoning the imperial food.

The new emperor, Francis II, son of Leopold II, was twenty-four years old at the time of his accession. He had no real sympathy for his aunt Marie Antoinette, whom he had never met, so saving the French royal family was not as important to him as it had been to Leopold. Francis's career would be defined by the five wars he fought against France. He lost the first four rounds. Austria signed treaties yielding land and population to France in 1797, 1801, 1805, and 1809. Finally, Francis was victorious in 1814, and Austria retrieved almost everything they had lost with the notable exception of Belgium, the original cause of the war in Europe that lasted twenty-three years.

Rise of the Girondists, March 1792: On March 10, the Feuillant Ministry collapsed just as the war was about to get underway. War Minister Narbonne and Foreign Minister Lessart were perceived to be wobbly as far as carrying out the task of destroying the émigré Army. They could not withstand the attacks from the Girondists in the assembly. A mostly Girondist cabinet was appointed, including Charles Dumouriez and Jean Roland. Dumouriez was a Feuillant at heart, but he vowed to run the military establishment with honor. The bourgeoisie Girondists in the assembly were mostly lawyers, and there was no one in their faction with a résumé that included any significant military service. The Girondists had heard of the myth about the Continental Army being composed of farmers who had defeated the British with their squirrel guns and believed it. The way they got ready to fight this war in 1792 shows clear signs that they thought soldiering was a matter of putting on a uniform and marching, their ardor would do the rest, and if they failed, it was because of treason in the form of French royalists in their ranks sympathetic to the enemy.

In April, Dumouriez addressed the assembly in a long speech listing all that Austria had done to deserve war. The assembly drafted a declaration of war against Francis, the king of Bohemia and Hungary, not Francis the Holy Roman emperor. The Girondist lawyers in the assembly thought this would do to keep the Prussians out of the war. Louis XVI addressed the assembly, saying, "Gentlemen, you have just heard the results of the negotiations in which I have been engaged with the court of Vienna. The conclusions of the report have been unanimously approved by my council. I have adopted them myself. They are conformable with the wish the Legislative Assembly has several times expressed and with the sentiments communicated to me by a great number of citizens in different parts of the Kingdom. All would rather have war than see the dignity of the French people insulted any longer. Having done my best to maintain peace, as I was in duty bound to do, I have now come—in conformity with the terms of the Constitution—to propose war to the Legislative Assembly." This was not what I would call a day-of-infamy speech, but the declaration of war passed the assembly with only seven nays.

Meanwhile, in Strasbourg, an engineer officer named Rouget de Lisle wrote the "*Chant de Guerre de l'Armee du Rhin*," soon to be known as "The Marseillaise." He dedicated it to his commander Marshal Luckner. It's interesting that a song that talks about irrigating the fields of France with the impure blood of foreigners would be

THE GREAT GLOBE ITSELF

dedicated to an officer of German birth, but Luckner had served the king of France for his entire career. At the same time, a robber named Nicolas Pelletier became the first person to die by the guillotine. The execution was over in seconds, and the crowd felt cheated of a day of entertainment. They yelled, "Bring back the gallows!" When the Terror started in October 1793, the government did their best to increase the entertainment value of these executions with tumbril rides and drummers.

French advance and retreat in Belgium: The French objective was to conquer Belgium and destroy the émigré Army. Rochambeau's Army of the North was to invade western Belgium toward Brussels, while Lafayette's Army of the Center was to invade eastern Belgium toward Liege. Luckner's Army of the Rhine would guard the right flank to hold against the Prussians and the émigré Army. Each of the three French Armies had about fifty thousand men, all containing a mix of regulars and National Guards, and the National Guards distrusted the regulars from the beginning.

On the other side of the line, the Austrian governor of Belgium was Prince Albert of Saxony, and he was also in command of the Austrian Army. He was cooperating with the French émigré Army under the command of the Prince of Conde and, soon, with Prussian Army, under the command of the Duke of Brunswick.

On April 28, Rochambeau's Army of the North advanced toward Brussels in two columns under General Dillon and General Biron. The National Guards were undisciplined and insubordinate and suspected a trap. At the first sight of the enemy, they turned tail and fled, shouting, "Every man for himself! We are betrayed!" General Dillon attempted to stop the retreat and was murdered for his trouble, the shooters accusing him of treason. General Biron advanced toward Mons, but he considered the place too well fortified and returned to his starting point. I'm surprised he hadn't done any recon. On April 30, Rochambeau resigned. Lafayette, to Rochambeau's right, called off advances on Liege and Namur. There were noisy demonstrations in Paris after these setbacks.

In May, Lafayette wrote to Prince Albert, requesting a truce. Luckner took command of the Army of the North, keeping command of the Army of the Rhine through a subordinate. On May 21, Prussia declared war on France. Command of the allied Austrian-Prussian émigré Army was given to the Duke of Brunswick, who had commanded the Prussian Army since 1786.

Russia invades Poland: Three weeks after the disastrous debut of the French citizen-soldier, on May 18, Russia invaded Poland in support of the Polish nobles and the sentiments of the Targowica Confederation. Prussia, technically still an ally of Poland, made it clear where its interests were by refusing to support the Polish Army and then declaring war on France on May 21. At that point, they probably considered the defeat of France to be a matter of marching.

On May 29, the Great Sejm of Poland adjourned in the face of the Russian invasion and turned over all power to King Stanislas, whose regime and Army were also the creation of the bourgeoisie. Ninety-seven thousand Russian troops were opposed by seventy thousand Polish troops. The Russians advanced in two columns from the north and the south. The southern column faced stiff resistance from the king's nephew Joseph Poniatowski and American Revolution veteran Thaddeus Kosciuszko (a protégé of the Czartoryski family), but the northern column advanced steadily. In addition to the invading Russians, Poland faced the internal threat of the forces raised by the nobles of the Targowica Confederation. The Prussians were mostly on the Rhine, but at the time, it was thought that they would crush the revolutionaries in Paris as quickly as they had the ones in the Netherlands in 1787. In July, King Stanislas opened negotiations with the Russians. Being convinced that resistance was futile, he abandoned the bourgeoisie and joined the Targowica Confederation. There is a lot of debate among Polish historians about whether King Stanislas was right or not about his judgment of Poland's chances. At the time, he agreed with the conventional wisdom that Armies run by the bourgeoisie had no chance against the professionals and made his decisions from there.

Kosciuszko resigned his commission in September. He had not lost any battles, traveled through what remained of Poland, and even ventured into Austrian-held Lvov (Lemberg to the Austrians) in Galicia, where crowds gathered to see the famed commander.

THE GREAT GLOBE ITSELF

The Austrians offered him a commission, which he turned down. Eventually, he made it to Leipzig in Saxony, where the Polish émigrés were plotting an uprising, and he was soon leading it.

Joseph Poniatowski also resigned his commission and traveled to Vienna, where his mother's family resided. The Austrian capital was filled with Polish nobles that had been part of the Targowica Confederation. As he was constantly challenging them to duels, he was asked to leave Vienna and went into exile. He may have been in Paris in 1793. He was asked by his uncle King Stanislas to return to Warsaw, as Thaddeus Kosciuszko was organizing an uprising in the spring of 1794.

Frederick William II had approached Catherine with a proposal for a Second Partition of Poland as a reward for having abandoned his supposed ally. He wanted Poznan and Gdansk (Posen and Danzig in German). Catherine thought it was a good idea but needed to get a rubber stamp from the Poles, so she ordered the convening of another Sejm in Grodno in 1793. Austria was to be left out of the Second Partition of Poland, as discussed below.

The overthrow of the monarchy in France

Journee of June 20: The French military reverses in April 1792 touched off a new and more radical phase of the revolution. Up until now, the bourgeoisie had controlled events, but now the working class of Paris made their voice heard. Their straight-legged pants gave them the name *Sans Culottes*. The *Sans Culottes* generally adhered to what was soon to be called the Cordeliers and were urban workers, artisans, minor landholders, and associated Parisians. They were generally just as hostile to the bourgeoisie as they were to the clergy and the nobility. Now they were in terror that the road to Paris was open, that the generals were betraying them at the king's command, and that the National Guards were being deliberately slaughtered by being the first troops sent against the enemy.

Marat and his *Friend of the People* had been shut down by the Feuillant government in December 1791 but was back in business in April 1792. This publication and Hebert's *Pere Duchesne* had field days denouncing the crown and the traitors who were lying down for the Austrians. *Pere Duchesne* was considered by the *Sans Culottes* to be delightfully vulgar and radical. Hebert published 385 issues between September 1790 and March 1794, about 2 per week. Its themes were that the powerful were unable to provide enough food in the markets, couldn't win on the battlefield, and were in cahoots with the Austrian Committee. Their overthrow was at hand! The red cap of liberty, an idea taken from the Romans who issued red Phrygian cap to freed slaves, now became their emblem to distinguish good from evil. It would become famous in June 1792, when Louis XVI was forced to put one on his head. Since it was also the emblem of the Tammany Society in America, it's a good question of who was copying whom.

While there was a truce in effect in Belgium, Louis and the assembly, rather than try to figure out what was happening on the battlefield, renewed their struggle. On May 27, the assembly decreed that any nonjuring priest could be deported on the word of twenty citizens. Louis vetoed it. On May 30, Louis allowed the dismissal of his six-thousand-man Constitutional Guard. This was a new organization established in October 1791 that Louis had no interest in, except to view it as a threat. He kept the Swiss Guards around the palace. He vetoed a decree of the assembly to establish a twenty-thousand-man National Guard camp in Paris. The two royal vetoes were unpopular even among Louis's ministers. Dumouriez supported the veto of troops around Paris, needing them for the front, but the *Sans Culottes* suspected treachery, leaving Paris unprotected.

On June 13, Louis was emboldened by the criticism of the Girondist ministers to dismiss them. The ministry positions were taken over by Feuillants. Roland had, in print and to the king's face, denounced his vetoes. Most of his objections had been written by his wife, Manon. Christopher Hibbert writes:

> Jean Roland, urged on by his wife who had become the guiding force of the Ministry, publicly condemned the King's [vetoes], reading out the sharply worded condemnation in His

Majesty's presence and reminding him that he would have to choose between the Revolution and its opponents. The King, already exasperated by the rudeness of Roland who insisted on appearing at Court with laces in his shoes instead of the prescribed buckles, responded by dismissing him.

Dumouriez took on the job of war minister in addition to his function as foreign minister but soon resigned from his ministries and headed for a command under Luckner in the Army of the North.

On June 20, the third anniversary of the Tennis Court Oath, the forty-eight sections of Paris organized a demonstration, to protest the way the government was handling the war and especially to protest the king's vetoes. This was organized and led by the Girondists, who had been kicked out of the ministries and now turned to the Cordeliers, who were not prominent in the assembly but had a great deal of control over the Commune of Paris. Eight thousand people set out on the morning of June 20 to plant a symbolic tree, but the crowd turned violent, and it broke into the Tuileries Palace. Louis confronted them bravely. His heart was at rest as he demonstrated by placing someone's hand on it to check. It was either one of his aides or, as the picture indicates, one of the National Guards. The picture also shows a man holding a red cap of liberty, which Louis donned, and a bottle of wine from which Louis took a drink, straight from the bottle, to toast the people's health. After dispensing several hours of abuse, the mob left.

Mayor Jerome Petion was suspended from his duties for failing to react to the mob that day. Louis gained some respect for facing down this threat, but his personal courage and bearing in this incident were not enough to offset the indecisiveness and artful slyness of the last several years. Personal courage is no substitute for a well thought out plan. As Talleyrand's biographer Duff Cooper said, revolutions are suppressed with force, not trickery. One thing we can say is that the Duke of Orleans was not involved with this event, having forsaken his ambitions back in June of 1791, after Varennes. Maybe he was being told by Louis that he would be king of Belgium after France conquered it in 1792. There is some evidence of this, as his nineteen-year-old son, the future King Louis Philippe, was given a division command in Belgium at this time.

Bonaparte, who was in Paris at the time, was appalled at this display of royal weakness. If he had been king, he later said, he would have fired into the mob with cannon and dispersed them at the first volley. This is something he actually did three years later, with the result that Paris remained mob-free for the next thirty-five years.

Lafayette was dismayed at the *journee* of June 20 and returned from his headquarters at the Army of the Center to Paris on June 28 for the purpose of arranging a coup, but he failed to generate enough support. The people still recalled his negligence in allowing the king to escape to Varennes in June 1791 and his role in the massacre at the Champs de Mars the following month. Marie Antoinette was not his friend and preferred to take her chances with the *Sans Culottes*, saying, "Better to perish than be saved by Monsieur de Lafayette." The ministers and the deputies pointedly asked Lafayette what he was doing in Paris and why he was not at his post. So he returned to his command.

The Brunswick Manifesto: By early July, the combined Prussian-émigré force was organized and began marching Koblenz to Luxembourg under the command of the Duke of Brunswick. At the same time, command of the French Armies was shuffled, with Lafayette taking command of the Army of the North, Luckner taking command of the Army of the Center, and Biron taking command of the Army of the Rhine. This was rearranging the deck chairs on the *Titanic*. The king and his ministers were dealing with the aftereffects

THE GREAT GLOBE ITSELF

of the journee of June 20, and it was the assembly that took the lead in responding to the enemy's advance. On July 11, the assembly issued the declaration of *La Patrie en Danger,* which read in part:

> Citizens, the Fatherland is in danger. May those who will obtain the honor of marching first to defend what they hold most dear always remember that they are French and free; may their fellow citizens maintain the safety of persons and property in their homes; let the magistrates of the people watch attentively; let all, in calm courage, the attribute of true strength, wait to act for the signal of the law, and the fatherland will be saved.

Weapons were distributed to the passive citizens of Paris, and they were admitted to the National Guard. The assembly summoned National Guards from around France, who are sometimes called fédérés, to Paris to defend the capital. These were the troops that would be used to attack the Tuileries and dethrone Louis. The terms *National Guards* and fédérés are conflated and are used inconsistently in the record, especially in the early phases of the war. As the shooting war got underway, the distinctions between National Guards, fédérés, and regulars were lost, as were the distinctions between active and passive citizens.

The troops began trickling into Paris. On July 14, the third anniversary of the storming of the Bastille, the king was made to burn a symbolic tree of feudalism. He did so and returned to the Tuileries, not to be seen in public again until the day of his execution in January 1793. On July 25, the Duke of Brunswick published the Brunswick Manifesto. It had been written by the Prince of Conde and included an inflammatory paragraph, reading:

> The city of Paris and all its inhabitants without distinction shall be required to submit at once and without delay to the King, to place that

prince in full and complete liberty, and to assure to him, as well as to the other royal personages, the inviolability and respect which the law of nature and of nations demands of subjects toward sovereigns...Their said Majesties [Francis and Frederick William] declare, on their word of honor as emperor and king, that if the chateau of the Tuileries is entered by force or attacked, if the least violence be offered to their Majesties the King, Queen, and royal family, and if their safety and their liberty be not immediately assured, they will inflict an ever memorable vengeance by delivering over the city of Paris to military execution and complete destruction, and the rebels guilty of the said outrages to the punishment that they merit.

Needless to say, the people of Paris were not cowed by this document, using copies of it in various disrespectful fashions. On July 30, Brunswick sallied from the fortress of Luxembourg and advanced to the fortress of Longwy, which fell shortly. Paris resounded with howls of betrayal. The same day, five hundred fédérés from Marseilles entered Paris singing the song, written in Strasbourg, that was forevermore known as "The Marseillaise."

"The Marseillaise" was made the national anthem in 1795, losing that status in 1799 under Bonaparte. Bonaparte preferred a song called "*Veillons au Salut de l'Empire*" (Strive for the Safety of the Empire). It was again the national anthem for a brief period in 1830. It gained international status in 1848, when mobs in every city

THE GREAT GLOBE ITSELF

in Europe sang it. The Paris Commune sang it in 1871. The Third Republic officially adopted it in 1879.

Allons enfants de la Patrie,	Arise children of our fatherland,
Le jour de gloire est arrivé!	[For] the day of glory has arrived!
Contre nous de la tyrannie,	Against us, tyranny,
L'étendard sanglant est levé, (bis)	Has raised its bloody flag, (1)
Entendez-vous dans les campagnes	Do you hear in the fields
Mugir ces féroces soldats?	The howling of these fearsome soldiers?
Ils viennent jusque dans vos bras	They are coming into your midst (2)
Égorger vos fils et vos compagnes!	To slit the throats of your sons and wives!
Refrain	Chorus
Aux armes, citoyens,	To arms, citizens!
Formez vos bataillons,	Form your battalions!
Marchons, marchons!	Let us march, let us march!
Qu'un sang impur	Let impure blood (of our enemies)
Abreuve nos sillons!	Soak the furrows (of our fields)

The day of the communists, August 10, 1792: The presence of all those National Guard troops in Paris singing "The Marseillaise" encouraged those in Paris who now felt like they had the means (the troops), the motive (the Brunswick Manifesto), and the opportunity (regular Army troops gone to the front) to dethrone Louis XVI, present the deed to the assembly as a *fait accompli*, and let them decide what to put in place as a national government. On August 3, Mayor Petion, restored to his duties, presented a demand to the assembly in the name of the forty-eight sections of the Commune of Paris for the deposition of the king. On August 6, a petition signing, calling for the abolition of the monarchy, was staged at the Champs de Mars, probably on that same altar from 1791. This was the Cordeliers, who were responsible for the similar petition drive that took place after Varennes in 1791, now joined by the Girondists, who were more and more republican in outlook. The assembly resisted.

On August 8, the assembly refused to indict Lafayette for his attempted coup of June 28. Brissot had led this prosecution, but Lafayette's friends defeated it. On August 9, Paris girded for the upcoming assault on the Tuileries Palace. Up to the last minute, it appeared that Louis XVI would defend the place. This was the big showdown between the Feuillants versus the Girondists-Cordelier alliance.

Starting very early in the morning, the Central Committee of the Paris Commune Sections proclaimed an Insurrectionary Committee. The tocsin started ringing early to summon the troops. They took possession of the Hotel De Ville. Mayor Petion was kept locked in his office to give him plausible deniability for not intervening. Petion resigned as mayor in October 1792 and joined the assembly, where he voted for the death of the King with reservations, ending his career. He committed in 1794 while on the run from the Terror, so at least he avoided the guillotine.

The commander of the Paris National Guard, a Feuillant named the Marquis de Mandat, had only recently succeeded Lafayette. That morning, he was arrested and executed on the steps of the Hotel de Ville, as a rumor had spread that he had authorized the guard to fire on the mob. Antoine Joseph Santerre, a Cordelier National Guard general was appointed to command it. Santerre had been a brewer, gaining popularity by distributing his product in his district. He then became a leader in the National Guard. Upon taking command, he issued the order to advance on the Tuileries Palace.

The movement was organized in two columns: One was led by Santerre, approaching from the *Faubourg Saint Antoine* to the east. The other was led by a man named General Francois Westermann, approaching from the *Faubourg Saint Marceau* to the south. These areas were both east of the Hotel de Ville on the north side of the Seine.

THE GREAT GLOBE ITSELF

Santerre and Westermann were both proclaimed heroes and later got commands in the Revolutionary Armies with undistinguished results. They were both arrested during the Terror. Westermann was guillotined, and Santerre was released after Thermidor and retired from public life.

Louis knew they were coming and reviewed his troops at 5:00 a.m., a sword buckled around his fat waist, but soon he and his family departed for the assembly for protection. This did not stop the march on the Tuileries, which began at 6:00 a.m., no doubt with the troops singing "The Marseillaise." The Tuileries was defended by nine hundred Swiss Guards and about two hundred servants and functionaries of various kinds. After defending the place for about an hour, the Swiss Guard was overwhelmed. Many of those who surrendered were killed, their red coats waved about as ensigns, inspiring generations of revolutionaries, including the Russian and Chinese Communists of the twentieth century, to use red flags as their symbols. About six hundred Swiss Guards were killed in action or massacred at the Hotel de Ville after surrendering. About three hundred National Guards were killed in action.

Georges Danton, a Cordelier serving in the municipal government of the Paris Commune, was front and center for the whole thing, and he emerged from the situation as justice minister and the most powerful man in the country. Camille Desmoulins, a former Girondist who, three years before, had incited the Bastille riots, became his secretary general. After August 10, the danger in Paris to anybody associated with the old order was so great that most of the Feuillants left the city, and the foreign embassies all closed down.

There are historians, most of them Marxist in orientation, who deny that the communists of the modern day have anything to do with these revolutionaries who overthrew the French monarchy. I disagree because if you read about Marx, you see that he studied these events and based his revolutionary theories on the absolute necessity to repeat them in order to affect a successful revolution. Marx added that the 1789 revolution overthrew a feudal system controlling an agricultural society but replaced it with a bourgeoisie system controlling an industrial society. Therefore, the inevitable progression was a second revolution to overthrow the bourgeoisie, and a postindustrial society run by the working class, the workers' paradise, would ensue. The problem with his theory is that every society will have elites, whether they are called nobility or bourgeoisie or whatever it is that the Chinese and Russians called their communist elites. In their day, the Nazis would say that Marx intended for Jews to replace the bourgeoisie but that Marx was too sly to admit it.

From August 10 to September 20, the Commune of Paris was the effective government of France. It was firmly in control, as the assembly had been reduced to a rump by the departure of anyone who thought the king should continue to sit on the throne. For six weeks, the assembly passed whatever the Commune told it to pass. It ended all control of education by the church, forbade the public wearing of religious vestments, and suppressed all religious orders that had survived previous purges. They viewed the Catholic Church as their prime enemy. The assembly appointed new ministers, including Danton, as mentioned above. The Commune demanded the abolition of the monarchy, but the lawyers pointed out that there was nothing to take its place.

The assembly suspended the monarchy and ordered a universal manhood election for a convention to meet on September 20 for the purpose of writing a republican constitution and to govern France in the meantime. There was no self-denying ordinance here, and one-third of the members of the convention would consist of men who had been part of either the 1789 or 1791 Assemblies. Voter turnout was understandably low, given the amount of time there was to organize it. The royal family was taken into custody and imprisoned in the temple.

September Massacres: The Commune already had enemy lists made up. Suspected priests and other treasonous persons were rounded up, and the prisons of Paris were soon filled with political prisoners. Marat wrote of the necessity to exterminate these vermin.

Dumouriez had been ordered on August 18 to arrest and replace Lafayette, order Luckner to organize a new Army of the Interior to cover Paris, and find someone to replace Luckner at the Army of the Center. Lafayette attempted to rally his troops "in support of the Constitution of 1791" but to no avail. He crossed enemy lines and was soon arrested by the Prussians, who considered him to be a dangerous revolutionary. Lafayette had managed to infuriate everyone. He pointed out to his captors that he had American citizenship. The American minister in The Hague came to see him but could do nothing for him since Lafayette was serving as a French officer, and that outweighed all other considerations. He would be a prisoner for five years until, from out of the blue, Bonaparte had him released as part of the 1797 Treaty of Campo Formio. I am sure that in 1797, people were telling Bonaparte, "Lafayette was supposed to be the military hero, not you." I think that Bonaparte's unexpectedly generous deed squared him with the cosmos.

News from the front continued to be bad, with Brunswick moving on from Longwy to capture Verdun. At the news of the fall of Verdun, Danton called for thirty thousand volunteers from Paris to go to the front. The *Sans Culottes* said they could not leave for the front and leave their families as prey for these evil priests and royalists. Paris must be cleansed before troops departed the city. The arrests continued, and the prisons were so full that abandoned monasteries were put in service as prisons.

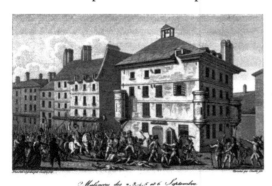

On September 2, Danton made the most famous speech of his career, saying, *"Il nous faut de l'audace, et encore de l'audace, et toujours de l'audace, et la France est sauvee!"* (We need audacity, and again more audacity, and always audacity, and France is saved!) This is the line in the movie *Patton* that is incorrectly attributed to Frederick the Great. I can see Francis Ford Coppola sitting at his typewriter, thinking that it was a cool line but that no one knew who Danton was. Or maybe he thought that it would be out of character for Patton to be quoting revolutionaries. Danton had to allow summary justice on the prisoners. For the next two weeks, the September Massacres were inflicted on enemies of the revolution, resulting in the deaths of approximately 1,400 people.

This was made legal with some sections of the Paris Commune passing resolutions that suspects be put to death prior to the departure of volunteers to the front. The affair went from street mobs tearing suspects to pieces to informal summary courts guarded by National Guards. Once found guilty, the suspects were turned over to executioners who killed them in ways that spectators found amusing. For their services, the participants were paid six francs a day, three meals, and of course, as much wine as they could drink. In France, the wine never runs out. Danton soon resigned as justice minister to take a seat in the convention.

Marat wrote in *Friend of the People,* "Let the blood of the traitors flow, this is the only way to save the country." Danton said, "I don't give a damn for the prisoners. Let them look after themselves as best they can." Later, he said, "It often happens, especially in time of revolution, that one has to applaud actions that one would not have wanted or dared to perform oneself." Danton and the rest of the government were preoccupied with an enemy invasion.

Talleyrand, who was a Feuillant, was among the people who escaped France at this time. He went to live in Great Britain, where he found himself in the same position as Lafayette, hated by both the émigrés for starting the revolution and the revolutionaries for supporting Louis. He was expelled in March 1794, along with all other French undesirables. He then migrated to the United States. He lived in New York and was friends with both Aaron Burr and Alexander Hamilton, so he was well-connected in America. He pursued business ventures in commodities trading, land speculation, and banking. He returned to France in September 1796 after his name was removed from the list of suspected émigrés. He became foreign minister in July 1797.

One of the most prominent victims of the September Massacres was Princess Marie Louise of Lamballe, a close friend of Marie

Antoinette's. As an intimate of the court, she had been held prisoner since August 19 in La Force prison. She was hauled before a summary court, refused to take an oath to the republic, and was turned over to a group of men in the street, who killed her within minutes. Among the atrocities cited concerning her death included rape; cutting off her breasts; putting her head on a pike, taking it to a hairdresser, and displaying it under Marie Antoinette's window; cutting off her genitals for display; ripping out, roasting, and eating her heart; and cutting off one of her legs and discharging it out of a cannon.

Military operations and political developments in France, July to December

French advance in Belgium: General Dumouriez took command of the Army of the North on August 18. Luckner, commanding the Army of the Center, was relieved on September 1 and told to raise a new Army of the Interior in Chalons sur Marne that would cover Paris. Chalons sur Marne thus began a long career as the main training base of the French Army, and it remains an Army base to this day. Luckner was replaced at the Army of the Center by Francois Kellerman, who, up to that time, had been content to serve quietly but was now thrust into the spotlight, and he would come through for his country. The Army of the Rhine continued to be commanded by Biron. In October, it was split into the Army of the Rhine and the Army of the Vosges, which was commanded by General Adam Philippe Custine, known as General Mustache for his Ambrose Burnside-style facial hair.

Austrian foreign minister Prince Wenzel Kaunitz resigned at this time. He had been in office since 1756 and had been the chief architect of the France-Austrian Alliance. His duties had been restricted for several months by this point as he watched his life's work come crashing down. Well, I suppose that happens to us all in some fashion. Either you watch your life's work come crashing down, or your life's work watches you come crashing down. He was eighty-one now. His replacement, Philipp von Cobenzl, only lasted until

March 1793, having failed to prevent, or even detect, the Second Partition of Poland by the Russians and the Prussians.

Brunswick's Army, which by now had added an Austrian contingent, moved west toward Paris through the Argonne Forest. He was moving at an incredibly slow pace as the allied Army carried a significant logistical tail as they went. Dumouriez moved southeast toward him from Lille, while Kellerman advanced west from Metz. Luckner was at Chalons standing between Brunswick and Paris. Brunswick saw himself about to get surrounded and decided to turn back east, get past Kellerman, and return to Luxembourg. On September 20, in Valmy, a town about halfway between Metz and Paris, Brunswick's Army underwent the famous cannonade of Valmy, got around the French forces, and retreated out of France. General Luckner was criticized for not sallying from Chalons to trap and destroy Brunswick, leading to his retirement in January 1793, his eventual arrest, and his execution in January 1794. His German birth had led to his allegiance to France being questioned. There's a good possibility that his accusers were correct.

The First French Republic, September 1792: On September 21, the last day of summer, the convention assembled, and its first decree was to abolish the monarchy and to declare France a republic, effective September 22, 1792, which later became New Year's Day of year 1 of the French Revolutionary calendar. The convention developed executive committees as mechanisms to govern the country until a constitution was written and peace restored. Initially, the convention sat in the Tuileries Palace. The royal family had been removed from the Tuileries to the temple, the old fortress that the Templars ran back in the fourteenth century and used as their Paris headquarters. Later, the convention sat in the Salle du Manege, presumably after the completion of some renovations, which is where the assembly

THE GREAT GLOBE ITSELF

had also met. The convention achieved its objectives of writing a constitution, fending off France's enemies, and restoring some stability, although at the cost of inflicting the Terror on the nation. Marat now changed the name of his publication from *Friend of the People* to *Journal of the French Republic*. As time went by, he turned on the Girondists, calling for confiscation of estates and death to the bourgeoisie.

The convention soon split between the Girondists, representatives of the bourgeoisie, and the more radical Montagnards, representing the *Sans Culottes*. There is some conflation in the record of the terms *Montagnard*, *Jacobin*, and *Cordelier*, and we will use the term *Montagnard*. The convention debated the fate of Louis XVI. One of the Montagnards, Louis de Saint Just, a future *eminence grise* of the Terror, gained fame for his eloquent demands for the trial and execution of the king.

The monarchy and the rest of the feudal system had been shed from France like a snakeskin, revealing a complete republican society underneath, a social structure familiar to the people of the United States. The Girondists were obliged to defend property, while the Montagnards were in favor of higher taxes and easy money, and this was main political dividing line now.

Operations in Southeast France, September to December 1792: In southern France, in late September, General Montesquoi successfully invaded Piedmont-Sardinia and occupied Savoy, the land south of Lake Geneva. France soon annexed Savoy as the Department of Mont Blanc. Montesquoi was accused of royalist leanings, and he escaped to Switzerland in November, to be replaced by Kellerman. It was the first step in France gaining control of the alpine passes, which would eventually enable France to dominate Italy. Further south, one of Montesquoi's subordinates, General Anselme, captured Nice. He was an insubordinate subordinate and unilaterally called his command the Army of the Var, after the name of a river that ran through the area. This command was eventually, after several expansions and reorganizations of the Army, recognized as a separate command and named the Army of Italy, which Bonaparte led to victory in 1797.

Operations on the Rhine and Main, 1792: General Custine was in command of the Army of the Vosges, which was located west of Strasbourg. In late September, he advanced north and east to Speyer, on the west bank of the Rhine, across from Heidelberg. The Prussians were so surprised they failed to blow up any bridges before retreating, allowing Custine to cross the Rhine into Germany. By the end of the year, Custine was in Frankfurt am Main, issuing proclamations and emptying the pockets of the nobles and high clergy. Mainz was declared a republic, the first of the so-called sister republics that France would use as a precursor to annexation.

In 1797, Goethe published an epic poem called "Herman and Dorothy," which had this campaign as a backdrop. Herman is a wealthy innkeeper's son, in a village on the east bank of the Rhine, who falls in love, against his father's wishes, with a compassionate girl named Dorothy from the west bank. Dorothy is a refugee from Custine 's Army but spends most of her effort helping others. The father wants Herman to marry a local girl with a dowry but is eventually brought around to approving of Dorothy. The point of the story was that people should marry for love, not economics, a radical point of view at the time.

Dumouriez conquers Belgium: In September, Dumouriez had attempted to support Kellerman at Valmy, but as soon as Dumouriez left Lille, the Austrians under Prince Albert captured it. After Valmy, Dumouriez turned around and expelled the Austrians from Lille in October and then advanced on Mons. The Austrians met them at the Battle of Jemappes, not too far from Mons. Louis Philippe, the nineteen-year-old son of the Duke of Orleans, later King Louis Philippe, showed some ability commanding one of the French divisions. The Austrians were greatly outnumbered and retreated to Antwerp, leaving the door open to Brussels, which Dumouriez occupied on November 13. Upon the capture of Brussels, there was dancing in the streets of Paris, and France joyfully annexed Belgium, in accordance with Danton's pledge that France would expand to its natural frontiers. Belgium remained a part of France until 1814.

THE GREAT GLOBE ITSELF

Many of Dumouriez's troops passed through the town of Waterloo on the way to Brussels. The war started in 1792 with French soldiers advancing through Belgium against German forces, soon to be joined by the Dutch and British. The war ended in 1815 at Waterloo, with German, Dutch, and British forces advancing the other way. Belgium remained a potential flash point through the nineteenth century. There was a delay of ninety-nine years, but in 1914, the Germans continued the advancing through Belgium into Frances, only now the British were on the other side of the line. Then in 1918, that war ended with the British advancing the other way through Belgium toward Germany. The cycle was repeated in 1940 and 1944, and hopefully, we have seen the last of Belgium being used as a highway for France, Great Britain, and Germany to get at each other.

Enough cannot be said about the extent to which the victories of Dumouriez and Custine bolstered the convention in Paris with the courage to put Louis on trial for treason. Custine was strictly military and had no political friends or ambitions, but Dumouriez, who had been appointed to his command by the king, was dismayed that his victory in Belgium was being used to have the king tried. He attempted to oppose the convention in various ways; for example, objecting when they attempted to direct military strategy as civilian interference in military operations. Over the next several weeks, he stayed in Belgium, was insubordinate, was reprimanded, threatened to resign, and was appeased by a visit from Danton, who told him that a declaration of war against Great Britain and the Netherlands was imminent and to begin planning an invasion of the Netherlands now. I don't know if Danton told him that the king was going to be tried and guillotined, but he probably did.

On December 15, the convention issued a decree authorizing French forces to loot (maybe the word *forage* was used) in enemy territory. Dumouriez was displeased, stating that such a decree was bound to hurt his Belgium campaign by costing him the support of the locals. The looting clause might have been part of the Edict of Fraternity, which stated, in part:

> From this moment the French nation proclaims the sovereignty of the people in all cooperating regions, the suppression of all civil and military authorities which have hitherto governed you, and of all the taxes which you bear, under whatever form; the abolition of the tithe, of feudalism, of serfdom; it also proclaims the abolition among you of all noble and ecclesiastical corporations, and of all prerogatives and privileges as opposed to equality. You are, from this moment, brothers and friends, all are citizens, equal in rights, and all alike are called to govern, to serve, and to defend your country.

The French Army occupied Antwerp, completing the takeover of Belgium. The Austrians had evacuated to the fortress of Luxembourg. They must have considered Antwerp to be indefensible for some reason. To gain the support of the merchants of Antwerp, the convention decreed that the Scheldt River in Belgium was now open to all navigation. For 150 years, it had been open only to the Dutch, per the 1648 Treaty of Westphalia. The Dutch protested, but suddenly their Prussian protectors became evasive in their dealings with the Dutch. The Second Partition of Poland was in the works and was going to require the transfer of a lot of Prussian troops from west to east.

The trial of Louis XVI: As stated above, the convention directed that Louis be tried for treason. On November 20, the *Armoire de Fer* was found in the royal family's Tuileries apartments, where correspondence of the king and queen revealed much embarrassing information about the king's private machinations with many people. One result was the removal of Mirabeau 's corpse from the Pantheon. There does not seem to have been any correspondence with the

THE GREAT GLOBE ITSELF

enemy found. But Roland had the papers filed with the convention, and there was no way to delay the trial of the king at this point.

In early December, Custine was forced by the Duke of Brunswick to retreat from Frankfurt to Mainz. Custine offered to resign, but the convention, already in a tiff with Dumouriez, refused. He was ordered to defend the Rhine boundary. Future marshals Soult and Saint Cyr were serving in his Army at this time. Things slowed down on the military operations front for a few months now, until spring.

On December 11, "Louis Capet" was summoned by the convention to answer the charge of "having committed various crimes to reestablish tyranny on the ruins of liberty." Louis pointed out that Capet was not his name; it was the surname of one of his ancestors. Louis was charged with thirty-three offenses, a long list of accusations recounting the history of France from the day of the Tennis Court Oath to the fall of the monarchy. He was guilty of the things he was accused of. For example, here's number 8:

> An agreement was made at Pillnitz, on 24 July 1791, between Leopold of Austria and Frederick William of Brandenburg, who pledged themselves to restore to France the throne of the absolute monarchy; and you were silent on that agreement up to the time when it was known to all Europe.

The author of these charges was future Committee of Public Safety member Robert Lindet. I wonder if he could have cited the statutes that had been violated. Probably not. Lindet got all of the insanity out of his system for a few years after Louis was found guilty because his service on the committee was productive for the economy like Lazare Carnot 's service was productive for the Army.

On December 23, Louis XVI made his second appearance in court. His lawyers' refutation of the charges was ineffective and his conviction a foregone conclusion. The only suspense was whether the convention would vote death, prison, or some form of exile.

PETER HARDY

1793: Tambours (Drums)

The United States, 1793

The Neutrality Proclamation: The United States was torn by events in Europe. The Northern and Southern states were very different places, with the North being majority nonslave, mercantile, federalist, and generally pro-British, and the South being majority slaveholding, agricultural, Republican, and generally pro-French. Of course, there were pro-French people in the north (like Aaron Burr) and pro-British people in the south, but the yin and yang generally held. George Washington began his second term on March 3, 1793. He was a Southerner, but most of the people who agreed with his policies were Northerners. He had wanted to retire but was urged to run for reelection by both Jefferson and Hamilton, one of the few things the two men agreed on these days. They symbolized their two sections of the country perfectly. Technically the country was still allied to France.

Having led a revolution himself, Washington, at one level, had sympathy with the one happening in France, but on many other levels, he disliked it. For one thing, he disapproved of the execution of Louis XVI, which occurred on January 21. The United States would not have gained independence without the ships and men provided by Louis. Lafayette had been forced to defect by his enemies in France and was now, as far as anyone in the US knew, either a refugee or a prisoner in Prussia or Austria. Being an aristocrat, Washington disliked the *Sans Culottes* rabble that seemed to be increasingly in charge in Paris. Nevertheless, he needed to be president of the whole country, not just the anti-France part.

War between France and Great Britain was declared on February 1. Washington convened the cabinet, which agreed that a Neutrality Proclamation was in order. As we recall, Jefferson had written the Declaration of the Rights of Man that had been included as the preamble of the French Constitution of 1791, and his heart was with France and the revolution. He was half-hearted in the notion of a neutrality proclamation, suggesting delay or making the proclama-

THE GREAT GLOBE ITSELF

tion unofficial. He was overruled. The proclamation was issued on April 22 and read as follows:

> Whereas it appears that a state of war exists between Austria, Prussia, Sardinia, Great Britain, and the United Netherlands of the one part and France on the other, and the duty and interest of the United States require that they should with sincerity and good faith adopt and pursue a conduct friendly and impartial toward the belligerent powers:
>
> I have therefore thought fit by these presents to declare the disposition of the United States to observe the conduct aforesaid toward those powers respectively and to exhort and warn the citizens of the United States carefully to avoid all acts and proceedings whatsoever which may in any manner tend to contravene such disposition.
>
> And I do hereby also make known that whosoever of the citizens of the United States shall render himself liable to punishment or forfeiture under the law of nations by committing, aiding, or abetting hostilities against any of the said powers, or by carrying to any of them those articles which are deemed contraband by the modern usage of nations, will not receive the protection of the United States against such punishment or forfeiture; and further, that I have given instructions to those officers to whom it belongs to cause prosecutions to be instituted against all persons who shall, within the cognizance of the courts of the United States, violate the law of nations with respect to the powers at war, or any of them.
>
> In testimony whereof I have caused the seal of the United States of America to be affixed to these presents and signed the same with my hand.

> Done at the city of Philadelphia, the 22nd day
> of April, one thousand, seven hundred and nine-
> ty-three, and of the Independence of the United
> States of America the seventeenth.

Citizen Genet, April to October 1793: Between the time that war was declared in Europe and the Neutrality Proclamation was issued, the Girondists, who, until June, were firmly in charge in France, sent Edmond-Charles Genet, a.k.a. Citizen Genet, to the US as the minister. He arrived in Charleston on April 8. He had previously been the French minister in Saint Petersburg but had been ejected in 1792 for his antimonarchial attitude, with Catherine II calling him "superfluous and intolerable." Instead of traveling to Philadelphia to present his credentials, he stayed in Charleston, where he was honored as the manifestation of the French Revolution incarnate. Genet and the local French consul general began recruiting ships and men to harass British shipping and invade Spanish Florida. France hadn't declared war on Spain until March, which explains why they weren't mentioned in the Neutrality Proclamation. Genet finally arrived in Philadelphia in May, where he raised great excitement among the Republicans and great alarm among the Federalists. When his privateers began attacking British shipping, Washington and Hamilton demanded that Jefferson expel Genet. Jefferson filed a request with the French government to recall Genet but did not expel him.

The Girondists were overthrown in June by the Montagnards, who sent a commission to Philadelphia to bring Genet back under arrest. The Terror was now underway in Paris, and Washington realized that Genet would certainly be guillotined if he were taken back to France. Attorney General Edmund Randolph worked it out with the commission to allow Genet to stay in the US, where he married the daughter of New York governor, George Clinton, spent the rest of his life farming, and died in 1834. Washington was highly displeased with Jefferson's performance of his duties regarding neutrality and Genet, and this was a major factor in Jefferson losing his job.

The western frontier, 1793: In the Ohio Valley, negotiations continued between the American delegation of Benjamin Lincoln

THE GREAT GLOBE ITSELF

and Timothy Pickering and the British-supported Northwest Confederacy. Once again, the Indians failed to present a unified front, some demanding white evacuation of the northwest and others trying to be more accommodating. The delegation gave up in April, and General Wayne was authorized to move against the Indians. Washington was disappointed at the failure of diplomacy and placed most of the blame on Jefferson, who loathed the British and never negotiated with them in earnest, and this was the final nail in the coffin for Jefferson's career in the State Department, where his last day was December 31, 1793. He was replaced by Edmund Randolph at state, with William Bradford of Pennsylvania replacing Randolph as attorney general. Jefferson returned to Monticello and began plotting his 1796 run for the presidency.

General Wayne moved his force down the Ohio River from Fort Lafayette (Pittsburgh) to Fort Washington, which is now the site of the city of Cincinnati in southwestern Ohio. Both the fort and the city had been established in 1788. On the west side of Lake Erie, near present-day Toledo, was Fort Miami, the British base that had been supporting the Northwest Confederacy with weapons and supplies. The British had been happy to torment the United States, but now that hostilities with France had commenced, the British needed to put this aid to the Indians on the back burner. Wayne's force moved north from Fort Washington to Fort Jefferson, northwest of the present city of Dayton, close to the site of Saint Clair's defeat in 1791.

The British were, at that very moment, in the process of sending an expeditionary force to Flanders. Eventually, a force of twenty thousand British soldiers was deployed. Little Turtle had been unable to convince his allies that without British support, they were doomed. He stepped down from command and another chief named Blue Jacket (of the Shawnee) took over. I couldn't find out for certain how Blue Jacket got the name, but in the 1870s, a story was published that Blue Jacket was a white man with the excellent name of Marmaduke Van Swearingen, captured by the Shawnee while out hunting in a blue jacket. The story seems plausible, although DNA testing of his descendants indicates that Blue Jacket was not white.

263

Eastern Europe, 1793

The Second Partition of Poland: On January 23, Prussia and Russia signed a treaty that set the conditions for the Second Partition of Poland. Although it appears that the Prussians betrayed the Poles, the Prussians didn't see it that way. Their view was that it would have been inconsistent to be fighting radicals in France while supporting their like-minded peers in Poland. Prussia and Russia both knew the territories that they desired. The Russians had already occupied their desired areas during the 1792 campaign, and now the Prussians did likewise in Danzig and Posen. Some accounts say that Danzig resisted and that the Prussians had to lay siege to it for seven weeks. My guess is that the folks in that part of the world were neighbors, who knew each other, and it was more of a negotiation than a siege. It probably wasn't apparent, at first, to the Polish nobles of the Targowica Confederation that large chunks of sovereign Polish territory were going to be lost. The Russians attempted to organize a Sejm that would throw out the Constitution of 1791 and ratify the territorial concessions, but it took several months and what Polish historians call coercion and bribery to do so. The Russians would have called it persuasion and monetary incentives.

Francis II was displeased that his foreign minister Philip Cobenzl had been caught flat-footed by news of the Second Partition of Poland. Cobenzl had replaced Kaunitz less than a year before and was still trying to figure out the best route to commute to the office. Francis II replaced him with Johann von Thugut in March 1793. Thugut remained in office until 1800, pursuing a policy of avoiding cooperation with Prussia while staying at war with France. He attempted to gain support from Russia and Great Britain, not always successfully, as he had to negotiate his way through their differences. Thugut's downfall came when the Austrians were defeated at the Battle of Hohenlinden in December 1800, and he was replaced with Cobenzl 's cousin Ludwig.

Since 1792, the Prussians had committed all of their combat units to the campaigns against the French in Flanders and the Rhineland, but now in July 1793, they reduced their Flanders and

Rhineland contingents, needing troops in Poland to secure the lands newly acquired in the Second Partition. This would have a negative effect on both campaigns. The reason that the Prussians were comfortable moving troops from the Rhineland to Poland was that the French Committee of Public Safety, which was being run by Danton at the time, had sent peace feelers to the Prussians and the British, who thought the end of the war with France was imminent. The British had gone off to besiege Dunkirk, and the Prussians had gone off to secure Poland. Then to their discomfort, Danton was kicked off the CPS by Robespierre and other hardcore revolutionaries who inaugurated a policy of no peace until victory.

The Sejm could not meet in Warsaw, as the Russians, probably citing the conditions in Paris after the overthrow of the monarchy in August, deemed it unsafe. Thus the session was called at Grodno, in a facility known as New Castle, which was one of the residences of King Stanislas, who, as we recall, had joined the Targowica Confederation. The Sejm was in session from June 17 to November 23 and passed the following acts:

- Poland and Russia to maintain an eternal alliance
- Territorial transfers to Prussia (58,000 square kilometers) and Russia (250,000 square kilometers), reducing the population of Poland from nine million to four million
- Abolition of the 1791 Constitution, although some rights granted to the bourgeoisie were retained
- Restoration of the Polish Permanent Council, a council of state that would now include the Russian minister
- Reduction of the Polish Army to fifteen thousand men

Kosciuszko plots an uprising: Kosciuszko spent most of 1793 in Leipzig, Saxony, plotting with other émigrés to conduct an uprising against the Russians. Early in the year, he traveled to Paris in an attempt to gain support, but the French had bigger fish to fry and didn't see the point in parting with resources in a year when every border was threatened. He returned to Leipzig empty-handed. Just as the British had nothing to spare for the Ohio Valley Indians, the French had nothing to spare for the Poles.

Kosciuszko crossed the border into what was left of Poland and had some clandestine meetings with some sympathetic Polish officers, but the Polish Army was being dismembered as per the direction of the Grodno Sejm, with what was left being incorporated into the Russian Army. Poles unsympathetic to the new order were being rounded up. By the end of the year, Kosciuszko was being pressured to execute his uprising in the spring of 1794. Although the leaders seem to have been based in Leipzig, when the uprising occurred, it took place in Krakow, five hundred miles away, which may have been the reason that progress was slow when it came to building up a force. All the traveling would have to be done through the Austrian territories of Bohemia and Moravia, which shows that Austria was happy to inflict some punishment on the Russians and Prussians for leaving them out of the Second Partition of Poland. Or it may be symptomatic of the weakness of the Austrian government that they couldn't detect these activities. For the record, the Austrians denied all knowledge of the activities of Kosciuszko and his confederates.

King Stanislas Poniatowski wrote to his exiled nephew, Joseph, asking him to participate in the uprising, to which Joseph reluctantly agreed. In the 1792 campaign, Kosciuszko had been Poniatowski's subordinate, but in 1794, roles would be reversed. I haven't read anything about jealousy between the two, but we can presume it was there and was detrimental to the cause.

Czartoryski and Poniatowski rivalry in Poland: One other thing we can say about Poland now is that the royal family was the Poniatowskis (King Stanislas had been elected in 1764), but there was another highly regarded family—Czartoryskis, who were Kosciuszko's patrons. Adam Kazimierz Czartoryski had been a candidate for the throne in 1764 but had lost out to Stanislas Poniatowski. He was on the bourgeoisie side of the political divide in these days and declined to support the Russians and the Prussians. His son was Adam Jerzy Czartoryski, who, as we shall see, was happy to serve the Russians in various high-level capacities. It was just the opposite with the Poniatowskis, with King Stanislas submitting to the Russians and

THE GREAT GLOBE ITSELF

his nephew Joseph so opposed to the Russians that he was eventually made a marshal of France. It seems that the rivalry between the Poniatowskis and the Czartoryskis begins now.

There are some interesting coincidences between the American Adams family and the Polish Czartoryski family. The first thing one notices is the first name of both Czartoryskis was Adam. The two fathers were about the same age, and the two sons were about the same age. The Polish father was Adam, and his son was Adam Jerzy. The American father was John, and his son was John Quincy. The American father served in the Continental Congress. and the Polish father served in the four-year Sejm. The American son served as the first ever US minister to Russia. The Polish son was the Russian foreign minister. The American son and the Polish son must have been well acquainted with each other in Saint Petersburg. The Polish father and son were on opposite sides of the line in 1812, with the father on the French side and the son on the Russian side. The American father and son were on the opposite sides of the line in 1812, with the father generally pro-British and the son working for the pro-French Madison administration. It's strange that four careers at opposite ends of the western world could arc in such a way.

France, Flanders, Mainz, and the Pyrenees, January to June 1793

Louis XVI executed: Louis XVI was tried and found guilty by the convention on January 15. No one voted not guilty, but twenty-three abstained. Well, if you say the king committed a crime by locking the National Assembly out in June 1789, and there's no question that he did it, and you don't have the option of pointing out that this action is not a crime, then you have to conclude the king committed a crime. I still say that the charges need to cite statutes that have been violated. The next day, there was a vote on the sentence, a much more divisive event, with 361 deputies voting for death, 72 voting for death with reservations, and 288 voting against death. Among the regicides was the Duke of Orleans, who must have wondered what he had wrought at this point. The duke was surely dismayed at the declaration of a republic. He'd had his chances, but when he walked up to the bell, he never rang it. Now he was a not-too-influential member of the convention, although his son was serving with distinction in the field, commanding a division under Dumouriez. The close vote regarding the death sentence indicated the future of internal strife in France, as the revolutionary government would soon find itself fighting internal as well as external enemies.

Louis was executed on January 21 at 10:15 a.m. Louis's arms were bound behind him, and his hair was cut, as was done with all citizens condemned to the guillotine, although not many had been by this date. His final speech of forgiveness and justification was drowned out by order of General Santerre, the man who had led the August 10 *journee*. When Louis began speaking, Santerre ordered the drums to start beating by shouting, "*Tambours!*" (Santerre's descendants have denied this story.) After the blade fell, many dipped their handkerchiefs in the blood as it poured on the scaffold. Later, the process would be improved with the addition on the scaffold of a man with a bucket. The Girondist leader, Roland, resigned from office the next day. He had been the one to order the publication of the information in the Armoire de Fer but had not expected it to result in Louis's death or in the end of the monarchy. Prior to the execution, Dumouriez had returned to Paris from the front to try and use his victory at Jemappes to save the king somehow, but it was hopeless and only raised suspicions about his loyalty. He returned to Belgium to find that his Army was starting to share those suspicions.

Three days after the regicide, William Pitt dismissed the French minister, a man named the Marquis de Chauvelin, who did not make much of a mark in politics but inspired a character of the same name in *The Scarlet Pimpernel*. Great Britain's entrance into the war against France was now inevitable. The issue was not about killing or exiling kings, as Great Britain had done both. It was about France occupying Belgium, especially the port of Antwerp, and now being a threat

THE GREAT GLOBE ITSELF

to the Netherlands, long Great Britain's entry point into Europe. The convention preemptively declared war on Great Britain and the Netherlands. Piedmont-Sardinia, which had Savoy and Nice taken from it in 1792, was already at war with France, as were Austria and Prussia. France would declare war on Spain in March. Longtime British ally Portugal joined the war and sent units to serve with the Spanish. France was now fighting in Belgium, Germany, Piedmont, and Spain.

The guillotining of the king caused an uproar in every country in Europe. Danton said that France "responds to the challenge of war by throwing down the head of a King." He also declared that France would extend to its natural boundaries, the Rhine, the Alps, and the Pyrenees. The series of campaigns that now started against France have been, in retrospect, called the First Coalition, which is said to have run from now until October 1797, when France and Austria signed the Treaty of Campo Formio. The nomenclature has been developed by British historians, so the campaign of 1792, in which the British were not involved, doesn't count.

Campaign in Flanders, 1793: The British Army sent troops to Belgium at once, starting with a regiment under George III 's second son, Frederick, Duke of York, in northern Belgium, a.k.a. Flanders. The British were on the continent, but it would take a while for them to be ready to conduct operations. The Duke of York would serve as the British commander in Flanders until March 1795, when the French Army overran the Netherlands. Overall command of the allied force was given to the Austrian commander Prince Josias of Saxe-Coburg-Saalfeld, referred to in history as Prince Coburg. As we recall, Prince Coburg had teamed up with Suvorov in the Balkans in 1789, and they had been very successful against the Ottomans there. If not for this pesky revolution in France, they would have been in Constantinople by now. Coburg now took over command of the Army in Belgium from Prince Albert of Saxony, as he and Maria Christina had moved back to Vienna after the Battle of Jemappes. Albert and Maria Christina 's son Archduke Charles was twenty-two this year and served under Prince Coburg with distinction.

269

The convention decreed a levy of three hundred thousand men as Dumouriez began his invasion of the Netherlands in February, supposedly against the advice of the representatives on mission that accompanied the Army. We say *supposedly* because we only hear about this advice after Dumouriez failed. The levy produced about half the required number by August, which was not bad for a draft in those days. The decree was generally obeyed in most of the country, but in the Vendee region, west of Paris, it sparked a revolt that would take many years to quell. The region was conservative, and the people had deep ties to their nobles and their churches. In March, the Vendee repulsed an Army sent from Paris to quell their rebellion.

In March, Dumouriez was defeated by Prince Coburg at the Battle of Neerwinden, a town thirty-five miles east of Brussels. Future marshal Michel Ney participated in that battle. Subsequently, the representatives on mission began an inquiry into Dumouriez's conduct of the battle. His previous attempts in Paris to intercede for the king had raised suspicions that he might be losing on purpose. Dumouriez blamed the convention's December 1792 looting decree for his problems, asserting that it cost him local support. He had the representatives on mission arrested and turned over to the enemy. They were held until December 1795, when they were exchanged for Marie Antoinette 's daughter Marie-Therese.

Dumouriez's troops were displeased by his actions, and when he ordered a march on Paris to overthrow the Montagnards, they refused to obey. Much of the resistance to Dumouriez was led by a young officer named Lazare Hoche, who would soon make a name for himself. Before the troops could mutiny, Dumouriez and Louis Philippe defected to the Austrians on April 5. The convention soon responded by rounding up all of Louis XVI's relatives, including the Duke of Orleans. The Girondists, who had long association with the duke, began to feel that events were slipping out of their control and soon began maneuvering in Paris to depose the Montagnards and end the war.

For the next few years, Dumouriez would travel to every court in Europe, intriguing against the revolution. He was supposedly in contact with the Duke of Enghien at the time of the Pichegru

THE GREAT GLOBE ITSELF

Conspiracy in the spring of 1804. In that same year, he would settle in England and be paid as an adviser to the Third Coalition. Louis Philippe would similarly wander Europe and the United States, settling in London from 1799 to 1815. Dumouriez returned to France in 1815 at the age of seventy-six and retired. Dumouriez's command was turned over to General Auguste de Dampierre, who was killed in action on May 9 and replaced by General Francois Le Marche, who was defeated at Famars on May 23 by the Duke of York. Le Marche resigned but survived, indicating that he held the correct political views. France had begun the year by invading the Netherlands and now, in May, had been completely driven out of Belgium. Custine then took over command of the Army of the North.

Establishment of the Committee on Public Safety, April 1793: The convention had been fearful of enemies of the revolution, and the defection of Dumouriez and Louis Philippe lent weight to that fear. On April 6, the convention established the Committee on Public Safety, which was given broad executive powers over the Army, Navy, the ministries, and the judicial system. The duties of the CPS included the conduct of the war (including the appointment of generals), the appointing of judges and juries for the Revolutionary Tribunal, the provisioning of the Armies and the public, the maintenance of public order, and oversight of the state bureaucracy. The CPS was also responsible for interpreting and applying the decrees of the National Convention and thus for implementing some of the most stringent policies of the Terror; for instance, the levée en masse, passed on August 23, 1793; the Law of Suspects, passed on September 17, 1793; and the Law of the Maximum, passed on September 29, 1793. Initially, Danton controlled the CPS and led it through the May 31–June 2, 1793, insurrection that expelled the Girondists from the convention (discussed below), but that was as far as Danton was willing to go, and he began to call for compromise and peace and was replaced when the committee was reorganized in July 1793.

Siege of Mainz, 1793: On the Rhine, the Prussians approached Mainz on April 14 and laid siege to it. The town was under the command of Custine until he left in May to take over the Army of the North. He turned over command to Alexander de Beauharnais, who

271

defended Mainz with twenty thousand troops. Frederick William II was present on the Rhine, while the Prussian Army was commanded by General Dagobert Wurmser. On July 23, the siege ended in a French surrender. The French troops were released with the promise that they wouldn't fight for a year. The promise was kept as these men were used in the Vendee. They marched off singing "The Marseillaise."

In March 1794, Beauharnais was accused of incompetence and arrested. He was guillotined on July 23, 1794. If he had been able to hang on another week, his wife, Josephine, would not have become an empress and her children, Eugéne and Hortense, would have lived relatively normal lives. After the departure of Beauharnais, the Prussians consolidated their gains in Mainz. The remaining French forces occupied the Lines of Wissembourg, a defensive line in Alsace on the west side of the Rhine. It appeared that the Prussians could attack anytime, and a sense of urgency prevailed in Paris, with the CPS frequently inserting themselves into operations there in the form of firing generals and haranguing the troops to increase their revolutionary zeal.

Spain, 1793: In October 1792, the Army of the South was split into the Army of the Alps and the Army of the Pyrenees. The Army of the Alps maintained control of Savoy. In the Pyrenees, the Spanish Army invaded Rousillon, the southernmost district in France, on April 17. Rousillon had belonged to Spain until 1659 and was still, even in 1793, distinctly Spanish in outlook. The French then divided the Army of the Pyrenees into eastern and western halves. The western Pyrenees was commanded by General Joseph Servan, while General Mathieu de la Houliere commanded in the east. This year, most of the action was in the east. Houliere suffered a defeat in April and blew his brains out a few weeks later when told he would be removed and arrested. He was replaced by General Claude Suchon, who was arrested after three weeks in command because of his Girondist leanings. He was transported to Paris and languished in prison until he was guillotined in April 1794. Suchon was replaced by General Louis-Charles de Flers, who performed credibly but was removed from command in August, when his close relation with Dumouriez

THE GREAT GLOBE ITSELF

was discovered. He was guillotined in July 1794. General Hilarion Barbantane replaced de Flers but was removed three weeks later for displaying cowardice in the face of the enemy. He was arrested but managed to avoid the guillotine, probably because he held the correct political views. The merry-go-round continued for the rest of the year, with commanders dying, intriguing, and losing until General Jacques Dugommier, the victor of Toulon, took command at the beginning of 1794. To be fair, these generals were under the thumbs of the representatives on mission to an extent unknown elsewhere, and Dugommier's appointment solved that problem because he was both competent and prorevolution.

In the western Pyrenees, Servan was in command until he was purged as a Girondist, and a merry-go-round of command ensued until October, when General Jacques Muller was appointed, and he lasted for eleven months. There was some combat but nothing of a decisive nature.

The fall of the Girondists, June 1793: Back in Paris in May, the Girondists made attempts to arrest their enemies—the journalists Marat and Hebert. Marat was taken before the Revolutionary Tribunal, which acquitted him three days later. A week later, the convention established the short-lived Commission of Twelve, which was disbanded after one week, after attempting unsuccessfully to arrest Hebert. About the same time, Camille Desmoulins published *History of the Brissotines* (another name for Girondists), severely undermining their position by portraying them as being in the pay of foreign countries. The Montagnards in the convention retaliated against the Girondists' Commission of Twelve by implementing forced loans from the bourgeoisie to finance the war. This was Girondists' political base, and they resisted the law and its implementation. Marat and Hebert used their journals to denounce "the protectors of the rich."

From May 31 to June 2, the Montagnards staged an insurrection in Paris demanding the arrest of twenty-two Girondists, the names picked by Marat, Hebert, and Pache, the last being a former Girondist and now mayor of Paris, looking for some retribution against the former colleagues who had expelled him. One of the names on the list was Brissot, once the chief propagandist for the

Duke of Orleans. They organized a march on the convention, which was sitting at the Tuileries. Pache handed the list of names to General Francois Hanriot, the commander of the Paris National Guard, and ordered him to arrest them. Hanriot had replaced Santerre, who had been given a command subduing the revolt in the Vendee. He was a favorite of the *Sans Culottes* and claimed to be the man who disemboweled the Princess de Lamballe in September 1792.

It is inexplicable to me that the convention still allowed the mayor of Paris to control large bodies of troops after what the Paris National Guard had done in August and September of 1792, but they did. I would hope that they fixed that problem after this incident in June 1793. Hanriot marched to the Tuileries and demanded that the twenty-two Girondists be given up. A standoff occurred, but on the third day, they were surrendered. Having secured his prisoners, Hanriot left the Tuileries. He kept them in jail until the start of the Terror, when they were all executed in a single day.

Now that it was clear that the Girondists were no longer welcome there, many of them fled back home to foment uprisings against the convention under the name of Federalism, an attempt to decentralize power, and to keep the bourgeoisie from being ruined. In an interesting conjunction of names, Federalists in the United States were the faction that wanted more central power, not less. The French Federalists became proponents of what the United States would call states' rights. Many cities in southern France would soon be engaging in armed resistance against Paris. Former minister Roland was able to flee, but his wife, Manon, sure that she would not be arrested because she held no office, stayed in Paris and even went to the convention to protest the arrest of the twenty-two. To her surprise, she, too, was arrested and thrown in jail, where she stayed until her trial and execution in November.

Paris was now in the hands of the Montagnards. Hebert went back to his journal and began espousing even more radical views. Marat had served his purpose, and his influence began to wane. That is to say, he was good at writing about executing people but not so much when it came to actually doing it. Besides, he was ill with a skin disease that kept him in a bath all day. For now, the driving spirit on the CPS was Danton, but Robespierre gradually gained influence in the next two months at Danton's expense. The reason that Danton began to lose influence was that he, too, began trying to end the war and to find a compromise with the Girondists, convinced that it was foolish to fight so many foreign enemies while the country was so divided internally. It was a reasonable conclusion to draw, but there was a faction that was still ready to live and die by his catchphrase *"toujours l'audace"* and was ready to take on all enemies, foreign and domestic, convinced that the revolution itself was at stake.

On July 13, the Girondist Charlotte Corday murdered Marat in his bath. She had gained admittance to his house by claiming to have  the names of Girondist conspirators. It didn't hurt that she was young and attractive. She had a dagger hidden in her bra and stabbed Marat in the heart. David would paint one of the iconic images of the revolution now—Marat dead in his bath. The painting shown here is not David's but must have been painted in the days before movies talked. Because of the murder, there were no official events on July 14, making it the worst Bastille Day ever. At her trial, Corday asserted that Marat had caused the massacres of September 1792. Challenged for proof, she said, "I can give you no proof; it is the opinion of all France." She stated that she had killed one man to save a hundred thousand. Charlotte Corday was guillotined four days later, on July 17. Much later, she was dubbed "the angel of assassination." Marat was interred in the Pantheon on September 21, 1794, and then disinterred in February 1795, when the political winds shifted.

With the Girondists gone, the convention began to consider the fate of Marie Antoinette and her eight-year-old son, Louis XVII. Exile, prisoner exchange, and trial were all considered. Louis XVII was separated from his mother in early July and turned over to Antoine Simon, a cobbler, who was assigned to give the boy some exposure to the working class. It was decided that guillotining Marie Antoinette would provide a vivid display of French resolve in the face of the enemy. In early August, Marie Antoinette was transferred to a prison called the Conciergerie and tagged as prisoner number 280. There were a few unsuccessful attempts to break her out.

France, June to October 1793

Lyon: In June 1793, the news from the front wasn't good for France. The Austrians, Dutch, and English were on the move in the north, invading France and capturing the town of Valenciennes. The Prussians were laying siege to Mainz in Germany, and the Spanish were moving north in the eastern Pyrenees. The Piedmont-Sardinians were crossing the Alps to retake Savoy and Nice. The Vendee was in full-blown revolt. Even in Corsica, the faction that the Bonapartes were opposing, led by the British stooge Paoli, condemned the regicides and declared independence from France. This soon resulted in the expulsion of the Bonapartes and others of like mind to metropolitan France. The convention passed a very democratic constitution, the Constitution of 1793, which was immediately suspended until such time as the national emergency passed. It never went into effect, as it was superseded in 1795 by the Constitution of the Year III, which established the directorate.

At the same time that Charlotte Corday was being guillotined, the Montagnards in Lyon were arrested, tried, and guillotined by the now-counterrevolutionary Girondists who had taken over there and were in opposition to the radicals in Paris. The convention was outraged that anyone but themselves was using the guillotine *pour encourager les autres*. They ordered General Kellerman, commanding the Army of the Alps since December 1792, to restore central government authority in Lyon. The hero of Valmy did not fail to answer the call. He moved the bulk of his force to Lyon and named it the Army before Lyon, keeping a screen in the Alps that must have fooled the Piedmontese, as their attempts to retake Savoy were feeble this year. CPS member Couthon soon joined Kellerman to oversee operations.

THE GREAT GLOBE ITSELF

On August 10, Kellerman began a siege. The city surrendered on October 9, and the convention began rooting out the enemies of the state, beginning with those who had guillotined the Montagnards in July. Although the convention issued a decree that the city would be destroyed and rebuilt as Liberated City, it eventually settled for a few demolitions and massacres. Kellerman's service at Lyon would not do him much good, as he and Couthon had been slow to implement the order to destroy the city. In October, Kellerman was arrested, Couthon returned to Paris, and they were replaced by Joseph Fouche and Jean Collot d'Herbois, along with two thousand Parisian National Guards, to execute the Carthaginian sentence against the city. Fouche had made his reputation in the Vendee and in Nievre. It was in Nievre that he ordered signage installed at the cemeteries that said "Death is an eternal sleep."

Robespierre's Committee of Public Safety, September 1793: In late July, the Committee on Public Safety was reorganized, and the twelve men who led France until the Thermidor Reaction (July 28, 1794) were appointed, including Robespierre. Robespierre was not the head of the committee (all members had equal power), but he would bring focus to it and death to anyone suspected of wavering. It's too easy to say that he led through fear. Terror could scare people into moving in the same direction, but it seems that they were already scared by the knowledge that the failure of the revolution, whether it was due to either internal or external foes, meant their destruction. There were twelve members of the committee as it was constituted from September 5, 1793 to July 31, 1794.

The High Hands, the ones who pursued the Terror to the utmost and were outlawed and executed in July 1794 in the event known as 9 Thermidor:

1. Maximilien de Robespierre (1758–1794) was the face of the CPS and, to the country, was the CPS. His activities will be extensively described below until his execution, along with Couthon and Saint Just on 10 Thermidor.
2. Georges Couthon (1755–1794) was sent to Lyon to assist Kellerman with the siege there in August 1793 but couldn't

carry out the task of destroying the city and was replaced by Collot. He suffered from meningitis and had to use a wheelchair. He blamed his medical problems on the frequent sexual experiences of his youth. I would think the man was joking if he weren't French. He wrote the law of June 1794 (22 Prairial) that deprived counsel to those accused of treason in order to increase the pace of executions. He was guillotined with Robespierre and Saint Just on 10 Thermidor, although it took fifteen minutes to place him on the board because of his disability.

3. Louis Antoine de Saint Just (1767–1794) was sent to the Army of the Rhine after the surrender of Mainz and did a lot of purging. After Alexander Beauharnais departed for the Vendee, the Army of the Rhine needed rebuilding. There was a merry-go-round in the office of commander of the Army of the Rhine until Saint Just found General Pichegru in October. Saint Just also found General Hoche, whom he appointed to the Army of the Moselle, so give him some credit for being able to spot talent. He was just twenty-six when he was guillotined with Couthon and Robespierre on 10 Thermidor.

The True Revolutionaries, more radical than the High Hands but not as bloodthirsty, who were all exiled to Cayenne in March 1795 in the wake of the penultimate Montagnard uprising, known as the riots of 12 Germinal:

1. Bertrand Barère (1755–1841) advocated a national system of education that would inspire patriotism, which he called *la religion de la patrie*. He was something of a weathervane, playing both sides of every issue, and managed to be on the right side of the line when they came after the High Hands on 9 Thermidor. He was arrested after 12 Germinal, transported to Cayenne, escaped, was pardoned, and had a long public career during the empire, the restoration, and the July Monarchy.

THE GREAT GLOBE ITSELF

2.   Jacques Nicolas Billaud-Varenne (1756–1819) understood more than anyone that the revolution was an all-or-none proposition that had to succeed 100 percent, and anything less meant failure and death. He spent his time developing the administrative apparatus that got of the orders of the CPS transmitted and executed down the line. He, along with Collot, survived 9 Thermidor by turning on Robespierre at the last minute. He was transported to Cayenne in March 1795, escaped, and died in Jamaica in 1819.

3.   Jean-Marie Collot (1749–1796) had a philosophy similar to that of his colleague Billaud-Varenne. Collot spent a lot of time outside of Paris, conducting the Terror in Nice, Nievre, Compiegne, and Lyon. He and Joseph Fouche would conduct the terror in Lyon in ways that would go down in infamy. He also survived Thermidor by turning on Robespierre. He was transported to Cayenne in March 1795, where he died.

The Experts, those who focused on winning the war. They were all arrested or went into hiding in the course of the last Montagnard uprising in Paris in May 1795, known as the Riots of 1 Prairial, by which time the Committee of Public Safety had been defanged:

1.   Lazare Nicolas Marguerite Carnot (1753–1823), the Organizer of Victory. Before the revolution, he had a distinguished career as a military engineer. He had his tyrannical moments, such as when, in a fit of jealousy, he accused General Jourdan after the Battle of Wattignies in October 1793. He would take charge of and organize the Revolutionary Army. The Army would grow from 650,000 men in June 1793 to 800,000 in September 1794. He received a large share of the credit for the victories that ensued, which was a great source of political protection for him. He was arrested after 1 Prairial but was amnestied and became a director, the only person to serve on both the

279

PETER HARDY

committee and the Directory. He even served Bonaparte until Marengo, after which he restricted his public duties to the Senate.

2. André Jeanbon Saint André (1749–1813) focused on naval affairs. Based in Brest, he purged the Navy of royalists and implemented reforms to educate the sailors. He was able to increase the output of ship construction, and the French Fleet performed adequately on the Glorious First of June in 1794. Brest is not far from Nantes, but he managed to steer clear of the atrocities committed by Jean-Baptiste Carrier in Nantes. He was denounced and arrested after 1 Prairial. After his amnesty, he had a minor diplomatic and governmental career, being named a Baron of the Empire in 1809.

3. Robert Lindet (1746–1825) was the author of the insane charges used against Louis XVI in his trial. Lindet served as a sort of a commerce or economics minister, focusing on labor, food, clothing, and transportation, both for the Army and the general population. He deserves a lot of credit, as much as Carnot, I think, for developing the sinews of war. He was denounced and arrested after 1 Prairial. His political insanity returned as he got involved with Gracchus in 1796, and then he had minor successes until Bonaparte took over the government in 1799, after which he refused to serve.

4. Claude-Antoine Prieur-Duvernois (1763–1832) aligned himself with Carnot in the military realm, overseeing ordnance, munitions, and even exploring technology, such as observation balloons and steamboats. Later, he helped found the *Ecole Polytechnique* and the *Institut Français* and helped to roll out the metric system. He went into hiding after 1 Prairial and then was amnestied. He was a member of the Council of Five Hundred until Bonaparte took over, when he retired from politics.

5. Pierre-Louis Prieur (1756–1827) directed reprisals against the Federalists in Normandy and then went to Brittany to establish the Reign of Terror there. He was seldom in

THE GREAT GLOBE ITSELF

Paris and was out of town during 9 Thermidor. He went into hiding after 1 Prairial and had no further involvement in public affairs. He was banished in 1816 and died in Brussels in 1827.

There was one more member of the CPS who was originally considered one of the High Hands: Jean Hérault de Séchelles. He was sent to Savoy in 1792 to organize the new department of Mont Blanc. He and Saint Just were sent as commissioners to the Army of the Rhine at the same time, where Saint Just began to suspect Herault's devotion to the revolution as Herault began sounding like Danton, always talking peace and compromise. Saint Just arranged for Herault to be purged at the same time as Danton and Desmoulins and guillotined in April 1794.

Whether you agree with the aims of the Montagnards or not, it cannot be denied that they led France through a very difficult period when it was taking on every power in Europe except Russia, even while a significant portion of the French people opposed the revolution. Victor Hugo summed it up when he said, "1793 was the war of Europe against France, and of France against Paris. And what was the Revolution? It was the victory of France over Europe, and of Paris over France. Hence the immensity of that terrible moment, 1793, greater than all the rest of the century." Future generations of Frenchmen would be exhorted in the trials of their days to, once again, be the France of 1793.

The Levee en masse: In late July, Valenciennes fell to the allies. The enemy was now in France. General Custine, who had formerly commanded the Army of the Rhine at Mainz, had been given command of the Army of the North in May but had not moved against the enemy. After the fall of Valenciennes, General Houchard replaced him. Custine was summoned to Paris in July to face the Revolutionary Tribunal and was guillotined on August 28, 1793.

On August 10, the first anniversary of the fall of the monarchy, the Louvre opened as a museum. It had ceased to be a government office building when Louis XIV moved the court to Versailles in 1682. Ideas to turn it into a museum had been kicking around since then. The museum was renamed the Central Museum of the Republic and was free to the public three days a week. As the French Revolutionary Armies spread across Europe, loot from their victories began to be deposited there. It was close in 1796 for structural repairs and reopened on July 14, 1801, making it the best Bastille Day ever. The man behind this effort was Francois Neufchateau. Neufchateau later was arrested by Robespierre, released after Thermidor, became a director and interior minister (1797–1798), senator in 1800, a member of the French Academy in 1803, count in 1808, retired in 1814, and died in 1820.

On August 23, the convention decreed the *levee en masse*, which was written in part by Carnot. The first paragraph was an exhortation that every person in France was now working to drive the enemies of France out of the country and is very stirring, and even the old men would serve by going to the public squares and preaching hatred for kings and the unity of the republic. The rest of the decree was more prescriptive, with actual assignments and funding that provided specific direction to implement the decree. There was enough guidance in it for the CPS to actually raise, feed, equip, train, and fight Armies to defend the north, the Rhine, the south, the Pyrenees, and the coasts.

It is common to say that the French Revolutionary Armies numbered 1.5 million men at their peak, but that is a misconception. The Army had about 600,000 men in August 1793, and the *levee en masse* probably did end up drafting 800,000–900,000 men into the Army between 1793 and 1797, but they were not all in the Army at the same time. Looking at the orders of battle for the various Armies, we see that most of them peaked at between 70,000 and 100,000 men, so the maximum end strength of the Army and the Navy during these years was probably about 850,000 men. This was still enough troops to dominate on every battlefield.

There was a massive demonstration in Paris on September 4 and 5, led by Hebert, fueled by food shortages and battlefield losses. This resulted in new laws passed in September that fixed the price of grain (making it disappear from the public markets) and a "law of suspects," authorizing the government to arrest anyone who, by word or deed, showed himself or herself to be friends of tyranny and enemies of liberty. September 5 marked the start of the Reign of Terror.

Flanders, July to September 1793: Up until now, the allies in Flanders had been cooperating, but in July, Danton and others sent out peace feelers to the British and the Prussians. Everyone but Austria thought this was a good idea, as the British were casting their gaze upon the sugar islands of the West Indies, and the Prussians were casting theirs upon Poland. Thirty-three thousand British troops would soon be in the Caribbean, occupying Saint Dominique and other islands. Pitt directed the Duke of York to detach his command from the main body and take Dunkirk as a port of entry and bargaining chip at any negotiations. The Prussians in Flanders also left, assigned to occupation duties in Posen and Danzig. Coburg could have made a lot of progress if the allies had focused, but a combination of French reinforcements and shiny distant objectives intervened. What the British and Prussians didn't know was that Danton and his friends were soon unable to follow through on their peace proposals as they were removed from their positions on the CPS and replaced by more zealous revolutionaries.

In early September, the Army of the North under General Houchard defeated the Duke of York at Hondschoote, lifting the siege of Dunkirk. Houchard was rude to the commissars who were embedded with his Army. They complained about his lack of follow-up, and he told them they had no business telling him how to conduct operations because they were not military. This was the same mistake Dumouriez had made. After Houchard was defeated at the Battle of Menin on September 13, he had to move his Army back to its starting point inside France. Houchard was relieved of command and replaced by future marshal Jean-Baptiste Jourdan on September 25. Houchard was arrested, tried, and guillotined on November 17, 1793. At his trial, he was accused of cowardice. He ripped off his shirt, showing many scars from previous battles. He said, "Read my answer!"

The Austrians and the Prussians were more successful against the French: On September 11, Prince Coburg's Austrians were victorious at Le Quesnoy. About the same time, the Duke of Brunswick was victorious in Alsace. Coburg headed to Mauberge to lay siege there. In response, the CPS sent Carnot to oversee General Jourdan in his prosecution of the war in Flanders.

General Jourdan, with Carnot in tow, lifted the siege at Mauberge and defeated Prince Coburg on October 16 (the same day that Marie Antoinette was guillotined) at Wattignies. Carnot's presence was, on balance, a positive influence on the battle, although controversy exists even today as to how exactly he had contributed to the victory. Legend has it that he shouldered a musket at some point. After the battle, Carnot and Jourdan disagreed on strategy. This may or may not have been a case of civilian meddling, as the generals called it. You never see Carnot referred to as a general, but pictures of him at the time show him wearing epaulets on his shoulders. When Jourdan's forces met with reverses after he split them up to chase the enemies' also divided forces, Carnot accused Jourdan before the convention, which ordered his relief and arrest in January 1794. He was replaced by General Pichegru, who transferred from the Army of the Rhine after he and Hoche had driven the allies out of the Rhineland, as described below. Jourdan was cleared in March 1794 and replaced Hoche, who had been accused and arrested, as commander of the Army of the Moselle.

Jourdan would earn a marshal's baton in 1804 for his victory at Wattignies and the next year at Fleurus. Carnot was also employed by Bonaparte in 1800, when Minister of War Berthier was on campaign in Italy. Carnot's son was one of the great thinkers of thermodynamics, and his grandson was president of France.

Houchard, Custine, and Luckner were all under arrest for their inadequate performance commanding the Army of the North. Lafayette and Dumouriez had defected to the Austrians. Rochambeau had retired. The Flanders campaign had been difficult for France, but Jourdan was the one who made it work. He was lucky because the reinforcements, the increasing number of volunteer units that were gaining experience, started to have an impact, so he had the advantage of numbers and fighting spirit that his predecessors did not. At the same time, the Austrians were finding themselves with fewer and fewer troops among their Prussian and British allies.

THE GREAT GLOBE ITSELF

The Rhine, July to September 1793: On the Rhine, the French Army there had been demoralized since the fall of Mainz in July. They were in defensive positions in Wissembourg. The command was a merry-go-round with generals lasting weeks or days. CPS member Saint Just would arrive in October. Another CPS member, Herault de Séchelles, accompanied him. Saint Just recruited Jean-Charles Pichegru to command the Army of the Rhine and Lazare Hoche to command the Army of the Moselle. Give credit to Saint Just for spotting and promoting talent. Also give Saint Just credit for spotting weakness, as Herault de Séchelles was spending too much time with the Prussians engaging in diplomacy that bordered on treason, at least in Saint Just's mind. Most of the writing about Saint Just is hostile, because he was merciless to his enemies, but he was good at his job.

Toulon, July to September 1793: On August 28, the city of Toulon allowed a British and Spanish force to occupy the city. Toulon was a major French naval base that was home port to twenty-six ships of the line. This revolt, like the one in Lyon, was inspired by Girondists driven from Paris in June and was as serious a threat as the revolt in the Vendee. A French force was detached from the Army of the Alps under the command of Jean Francois Carteaux, a former painter (one of his portraits was of Louis XVI), and laid siege to Toulon. Bonaparte, recently ejected from Corsica, came by to pay his respects to one of the representatives on mission there, a fellow Corsican named Saliceti. Bonaparte took a look around at the French positions and shared his thoughts, and he was soon appointed artillery commander. His plans to lay in artillery and blow up the British positions and ships was not forcefully executed by the overwhelmed Carteaux. By November, Carteaux was dismissed and replaced by General Dugommier. A career soldier, Dugommier recognized Bonaparte's ability and accepted his plan, giving Bonaparte all the resources he needed to carry it out, which he did with a high degree of energy.

PETER HARDY

The Reign of Terror begins, October 1793

As previously mentioned, the first use of the guillotine against political foes (not counting the execution of Louis XVI) had been by the Girondists in Lyon in July 1793. Then in the same month, Charlotte Corday murdered Marat and was guillotined for it. In August, General Custine was executed for his failures on the battlefield in Flanders. Now the CPS, armed with the Law of Suspects that had been passed in September, decided it was time to try and execute Marie Antoinette. The gray eminence conducting these prosecutions was Antoine Quentin Fouquier-Tinville.

She was told on October 13 that her trial would start the next day. She was accused of sending massive amounts of money to Austria, orchestrating orgies at Versailles, ordering the assassination of the Duke of Orleans, massacring the National Guards in August 1792, and, most shockingly, committing incest with her son. Her son, eight, had been coached to testify against her. Fouquier-Tinville compared Marie Antoinette to Messalina, the evil wife of the Roman emperor Claudius. For all of the evil she was thought to have committed, she was still thought of as a decent mother, and now they wanted to take that from her too. The trial lasted one day, and she was convicted and sentenced to death, to occur on October 16.

As we recall, the first public execution by guillotine in 1792 had been a brief affair that had taken seconds, a great disappointment to the crowd that day. Even when Louis was executed, he had been driven to the guillotine in a coach. Now the execution of Marie Antoinette was to be made into a spectacle. She was transported from the Conciergerie prison to the guillotine, at the *Place de la Revolution*, in an open tumbril, a ride which took an hour, and she was jeered at

THE GREAT GLOBE ITSELF

by huge crowds the entire way. A priest accompanied her in the cart, but she ignored him as he was a juring priest whom she had never met before. The revolutionary government wanted to execute her in as publicly humiliating a fashion as possible. In such a manner did they intend to show the resolve of the Republic of France.

The CPS had a lot of priests, Girondists, and failed generals waiting in the queue behind Marie Antoinette, and they wanted them executed in just as public and spectacular fashion as Charlotte Corday, General Custine, and the queen. The message was "join us or die" in a very grim way; it was loudly broadcast and widely received.

To show that some of the motivation for initiating the Terror was directed toward achieving military victory, in October, a poet named Augustine Ximenez, a Frenchman of Spanish descent, published a book the included the line *"Attaquons dans ses eaux la perfide Albion"* (Attack in its waters perfidious Albion). The definition of *perfidious* is deceitful and untrustworthy. This was not the invention of the term *perfidious* Albion, but it now became a popular pejorative used by Great Britain's enemies to refer to them over the years, usually with great justification.

In late October, the twenty-two Girondists that had been arrested at the Tuileries in June were tried. They were all found guilty and guillotined on October 31, singing bravely, *"Plutôt la mort que l'esclavage!"* (Death rather death than slavery!) as they were driven in tumbrils to their execution. One of them had killed himself the night before. His corpse was loaded in the tumbril and beheaded with the rest.

A week later, the Duke of Orleans was tried in one day and guillotined the next. According to Hibbert, he was allowed to go home, have a final feast—which he consumed with exceptional avidity—and return the next day to have his head removed. He was probably somewhat satisfied knowing that Marie Antoinette, who had labeled him as a coward after the Battle of Ushant in 1778, had preceded him to the guillotine. His final words were, "Let's get on with it." He was the sorcerer's apprentice of the revolution. He was the one who lit this candle, but the fire got out of control on him. The government confiscated his fortune, which was the largest in France.

The Orleanist faction survived, however, and his son would be king of the French, from 1830 to1848, so the duke's efforts were not a complete waste of his time.

The day after the Duke of Orleans's death, Madame Roland was tried and guillotined. Her "I'm only the wife" defense had  been ineffective, as her enemies replied that Marie Antoinette had just tried the same plea. She had been writing her memoirs since her arrest in June. When the monarchy had fallen in August 1792, the statue of Louis XV in the Place had been replaced with a Statue of Liberty, which eventually inspired the one in New York Harbor. From the scaffold, it was one of the victims' last sights. When Madame Roland climbed the scaffold, she saw the statue and said, "Oh, Liberty, what crimes are committed in your name!" Word of his wife's death soon reached Roland, who was in Normandy. Depressed, he committed suicide in the woods. His half-eaten corpse was discovered several weeks later.

On November 12, former Paris mayor Jean Bailly was guillotined, having fled his home, been captured, arrested, and tried in the last week of his life. I'm surprised he lasted this long, as he should have been rounded up with the other Feuillants in August 1792. The last mistress of Louis XV, Madame du Barry, was guillotined on December 8. As we recall, she had been shown the door at Versailles two days after the death of Louis XV in 1774. She was now accused of helping émigrés and sentenced to death. She was terrified on the scaffold, saying, "One more moment, Mr. Executioner! I beg you!" Dostoevsky later philosophized about this clinging to life.

General Houchard was guillotined on November 17. His refusal to take the direction of representatives on mission, and then his subsequent defeat in battle, described above, led to his relief, arrest, trial, and execution. Marshal Luckner was guillotined on

THE GREAT GLOBE ITSELF

January 4. He was accused of collusion with the enemy, with his lack of elan in the field and his German heritage lending credence to those accusations.

The guillotine at the *Place de la Revolution* was not the only source of Terror, as the representatives on mission carried it out in the provinces. In Nantes, a man named Jean Baptiste Carrier loaded counterrevolutionaries onto barges that he intentionally sank in the Loire. By this and other means, he eliminated four thousand undesirables in four months. In Lyon, the terror was directed by Joseph Fouche and Jean-Marie Collot. At one point, they executed three hundred prisoners by the expedient of moving them into a small space and shooting them with grapeshot from cannon. The technique was ineffective, and about half of the prisoners had to be sabered. Nearly two thousand enemies of the state would eventually die in Lyon by May 1794. It was at this time that Fouche said, "Terror, salutary terror, is the order of the day here…" and paraphrased Thomas Jefferson and "The Marseillaise," saying, "The impure blood of criminals fertilizes the soil of liberty and establishes power on sure foundations." Collot and Fouche were known from now on as the *mitrailleurs* of Lyon. Before the invention of the machine gun, this meant a user of grapeshot shot from cannons.

The pendulum reaches its amplitude: The French Revolution has been described as a swinging pendulum as it became more and more radical, from May 1789 to November 1793. At that point, the radicals peaked in popularity, and then they were suddenly no longer in fashion. The point at which the pendulum begins to swing the other way is called the amplitude, and that point was reached in November 1793.

In the midst of the mayhem of the Terror, the revolutionary calendar was implemented on October 24, 1793. The first day of the first month of year 1 was September 22, 1792, making the first revolutionary day 3 Brumaire An II. Each month consisted of three ten-day weeks, which proved highly unpopular, as it meant people had to work nine days to get one off. I suppose they compensated for that by inserting sixteen additional days off through the year.

PETER HARDY

The months of the new calendar, along with the British nicknames, are:

French month	Old month (approximate)	British nickname
Vendémiaire (grape harvest)	22 Sep–21 Oct	Wheezy
Brumaire (fog)	22 Oct–20 Nov	Sneezy
Frimaire (frost)	21 Nov–20 Dec	Freezy
Nivose (snowy)	21 Dec–19 Jan	Slippy
Pluviose (rainy)	20 Jan–18 Feb	Drippy
Ventose (windy)	19 Feb–20 Mar	Nippy
Germinal (seed)	21 Mar–19 Apr	Showery
Floreal (flower)	20 Apr–19 May	Flowery
Prairial (pasture)	20 May–18 Jun	Bowery
Messidor (harvest)	19 Jun–18 Jul	Wheaty
Thermidor (heat)	19 Jul–17 Aug	Heaty
Fructidor (fruit)	18 Aug–16 Sep	Sweety
Five (or six) complementary days at the end of the year	17–21 Sep Note: On leap years of the old calendar, 1 Ventose would be 18 February	Virtue (vertu), talent (genie), labor (travail), convictions (l'opinions), rewards (recompenses), and every leap year, revolution

There were those who viewed the Terror as a duty, and then there were those who viewed it as a cathartic expiation. These people were called Enragists, and Hebert was their leader. Atheism was at their core, and now they aspired to nothing less than the destruction of the Christian faith. On November 10, Hebert, who was assisted

THE GREAT GLOBE ITSELF

by an antireligious radical named Pierre Chaumette, supervised a nationwide festival of reason, an attempt to replace the Catholic church with an atheistic substitute. Churches across France were transformed into modern Temples of Reason. Notre Dame de Paris hosted the largest ceremony of them all. The Christian altar was dismantled, and an altar to Liberty was installed; the inscription "To Philosophy" was carved in stone over the cathedral's doors. The proceedings took several hours and concluded with the appearance of a Goddess of Reason who, to avoid idolatry, was portrayed by a living woman named Sophie Momoro, the beautiful wife of another Enragist named Antoine Momoro. Hostile contemporary accounts reported the Festival of Reason as a "lurid, licentious affair of scandalous depravities." The reviews were not good and helped drive the Thermidor reaction forward. Even dedicated Montagnards like Robespierre began to publicly separate themselves from the Hebertist faction.

On November 21, Danton returned to Paris after a long absence, thinking that the revolution had gone too far, and he might help correct the course. He and Camille Desmoulins soon began publishing *The Old Cordelier*, criticizing radicalism and the Terror. They became known as the Indulgents, to differentiate them from the Enragists. Robespierre initially approved of *The Old Cordelier* because it directed its initial attacks against Hebert and the Enragists. Desmoulins attacked Hebert for bringing the French Republic into disrepute through his writings, claiming that "when the tyrants of Europe wish to vilify the Republic, to make their slaves believe that France is covered with the darkness of barbarism," they reprinted *Le Père Duchesne*. Hebert responded by quoting some of Desmoulins' radical writings from back in '89, when he was inciting mobs to attack the Bastille. *The Old Cordelier* came out weekly for the next six weeks, but to Robespierre's dismay, it began attacking the government and calling for an end to the Terror. At the end of the year, the CPS found itself under attack from the Indulgents on the right and the Enragists on the left. But it could be argued, the Terror was producing results on the battlefield, as we shall see below.

French military operations, October to December: In Flanders, Jourdan pursued the retreating allies after Wattignies, splitting his force. The allies turned and faced him in late October, forcing the French to fall back. That was the end of the 1793 campaign in Flanders. Carnot accused Jourdan before the convention, and Jourdan was relieved of command in January 1794, but he was eventually cleared and placed in command of the Army of the Moselle in March 1794, which he led in Flanders alongside Pichegru's Army of the North.

Most of the action in the fall of 1793 was in the Rhineland. A mostly Austrian force under General Wurmser attacked Wissembourg on October 13. The French lost three thousand men and retreated. Saint Just sacked the commander of the Army of the Rhine, who avoided the guillotine as he held the correct political views. Saint Just then appointed Pichegru to command the Army of the Rhine and ordered Hoche, whom Saint Just had just appointed to the Army of the Moselle, to take up an area on Pichegru's left. The two Armies operated against Wurmser's Austrians and Brunswick's Prussians, with Hoche attacking the Prussians at Kaiserslautern and Pichegru attacking the Austrians at Haguenau. Hoche and Pichegru failed to work harmoniously, so Saint Just put Pichegru under Hoche's command. Despite the friction between Hoche and Pichegru, the French were victorious over the Prussians at the second Battle of Wissembourg, on December 29. The Prussians retreated to Mainz, thus maintaining a foothold on the left bank of the Rhine for now. The Austrians crossed the Rhine and retreated to Worms.

Pichegru turned over command of the Army of the Rhine to General Claude Michaud, went to Paris to file charges against Hoche, and was appointed commander of the Army of the North to replace Jourdan. Hoche was removed from command of the Army of the Moselle in March 1794 and replaced by Jourdan. Hoche remained in prison until August 1794 and was released after Thermidor.

In Toulon, Dugommier and Bonaparte applied some organization and energy to kicking the British and the Spanish out of the city. Dugommier provided leadership, resources, and timely decisions, while Bonaparte provided the plan and the energy to carry

THE GREAT GLOBE ITSELF

it out. Batteries were placed at strategic high points, and the British were blown out of the water. They were forced to evacuate Toulon on December 19, but they were able to destroy half the French ships of the line. The British headed to Corsica and got into contact with their stooge Paoli, who had been back since 1790.

The French victory in Toulon led to bitter recriminations between Spain and Great Britain and was a leading cause of Spain leaving the First Coalition in 1795. After the allies departed Toulon, eight hundred counterrevolutionaries were rounded up and executed. In his report, Dugommier said, "I have no words to describe Bonaparte's merit: much technical skill, an equal degree of intelligence, and too much gallantry..." I'm sure it sounds better in French. In another reality, Dugommier might have been France's George Washington, with Bonaparte relegated to the role of Hamilton, getting shot by Moreau or Bernadotte in a duel.

Another representative on mission, Paul Barras, took notice of Bonaparte as well. Barras had been in the Army in India, held legislative and judiciary positions in the lower levels, and had been a commissar in the Army that took Savoy in 1792. He would soon be introducing Bonaparte to important people in Paris, including one of his mistresses, Josephine de Beauharnais. Bonaparte was promoted to brigadier general at the age of twenty-four and was assigned as the artillery commander in the Army of Italy, where he would serve with future marshal Massena. Dugommier was assigned to command of the Army of the Eastern Pyrenees, where future marshals Perignon and Augereau commanded divisions of the Army, and Lannes and Victor commanded brigades. Nothing of importance had occurred in the Pyrenees in the last three months of the year.

In Northwest France, the Vendean revolt was suppressed by a combination of the Terror implemented by Carrier and the arrival of General Beauharnais and the troops that had surrendered in Mainz at the beginning of the year. The rebels would be inactive through most of 1794.

PETER HARDY

1794: Terror Is the Order of the Day

The United States

Andrew Jackson enters politics: Andrew Jackson had married Rachel Robards in August 1791 after her husband left her, but he never finalized the divorce. At first that was an unimportant detail to the Jacksons and the community they lived in, but now his increasing prominence in public life made him aspire to public office, and bigamy was both a crime and a sin. They married again in January 1794, as Jackson joined the Republican Party and threw his hat in the ring to serve as a delegate to Tennessee's constitutional convention in 1796. There are those who give Jackson credit at this convention for both coming up with the name Tennessee and establishing the capital in Nashville, and I can see the possibility of both being true, even though the facts are unclear. It comes from a true place.

When Tennessee achieved statehood, Jackson was elected as the sole congressman from December 1796 to September 1797. As soon as he turned thirty, he was elected US senator and served from September 1797 to April 1798. He found the work of the Senate to be obscure, involving votes on motions and amendments that he didn't see the point of but were, to the senators, critical elements of legislative strategy. He did not have a legislative temperament. While he was in Washington, Rachel made it clear that she wished he was home. He decided the work he was doing wasn't worth the separation, so he resigned and went back to Nashville. He was appointed as a judge of the Tennessee superior court and was able to stay home in Nashville.

We won't really be interested in Jackson again until the War of 1812, so a quick summary of his career until then is that in 1801, he was appointed as the judge advocate general (JAG) of the Tennessee militia, making him a colonel, and then in 1802, he defeated John Sevier, a Revolutionary War hero, for election as major general in command of the state militia. Their relationship was bitter, and there were some public shouting matches, but no duels. In 1804,

THE GREAT GLOBE ITSELF

he resigned his judgeship to concentrate on private business and his militia command.

Jackson did fight a duel in May 1806, where he shot and killed a man named Charles Dickinson. Dickinson shot Jackson in the chest, but the bullet did not strike his heart. It was too close for removal and was in Jackson's body for the rest of his life. An examination of the events surrounding the duel indicates that the honor of Rachel was not involved, but that the argument stemmed from personal rivalry and the outcome of a horse race. His body and his reputation suffered greatly for many years afterward. Jackson said, "I should have hit him if he had shot me through the brain." Dickinson had published a piece in a Nashville newspaper calling Jackson a poltroon and a coward.

Later in 1806, he was involved in Aaron Burr 's scheme to detach Texas from Mexico or whatever he had in mind, but Jackson avoided Thomas Jefferson 's wrath. Jackson covered himself by producing a lot of documentation showing that he was acting within the bounds of his office. Burr seems to have enticed Jackson by drawing his gaze to Florida, an idea which stayed in Jackson's mind until he conquered it in 1818. We don't hear much more about his activities until 1812, the year the Tennessee volunteers went to war.

Jackson had become a Mason in 1800, joining Saint Tammany Lodge No. 1 in Nashville. In the 1830s, when Jackson was the face of Freemasonry, a movement loathed by a large minority in the country, being anti-Mason became synonymous with being anti-Jackson. Jackson doesn't have seem to have been fanatical about the organization, but it was one of the straws his enemies grasped at to do him harm.

The cotton gin, 1794: In March, Eli Whitney received a patent for the cotton gin, a mechanical device to remove seeds from cotton. Eli Whitney was born in 1765 in Massachusetts. He graduated from Yale in 1792 and moved to South Carolina to be a tutor. On the ship en route to Charleston was the widow of the Revolutionary War general Nathaniel Greene, Catherine Littlefield Greene. She invited Whitney to visit her plantation near Savannah. At the plantation, he developed a machine that stripped the seeds from the cotton boll.

This increased the productivity of a slave from one pound of cotton a day to twenty-five pounds, as one cotton gin could produce fifty pounds of cotton but needed two men to operate it. Whitney said he was inspired when he observed a cat attempting to pull a chicken through a fence but was only able to pull a few feathers through.

Most historians believe that the cotton gin allowed the American slavery system to become sustainable just when it was close to going out altogether, but I think that something would have stimulated the production of cotton because there was a demand for it. The "satanic" cotton mills of England, as William Blake would call them, had been operating their water frames since 1771, and they hungered for more and more cotton to turn into cloth. Now there were mills all over, including New England. Cotton exports increased from a half million pounds in 1793 to 93 million pounds in 1810. Cotton exports represented 50 percent of the value of all American exports between 1820 and 1860, which is why the South was confident that "King Cotton" would win the war for them in 1861. It didn't because the textile industry purchased more expensive cotton from Egypt and other places. The reason for the increase in cotton demand was a combination of people wanting more clothing, American cotton being much cheaper than other sources, and a growing population.

Whitney didn't make a lot of money on the cotton gin and went broke filing lawsuits on people who infringed on his patent. In 1798, war was in the air, as the US was taking on France in the Quasi-War. Whitney signed a contract to produce ten thousand muskets. He produced the muskets and is credited with the idea of interchangeable parts. It's a good story, but the government had been issuing ten thousand musket contracts for years. The history of manufacturing is much more complicated than the idea of one guy thinking up and executing the idea of interchangeable parts. For example, we can read about the first war between Rome and Carthage in 264 BC and find the story of the Romans building a Fleet from scratch and using a single plan to manufacture five hundred ships. They manufactured all the parts and then just put them all together on an assembly line. Nevertheless, we have to say that Eli Whitney was a great success in life.

THE GREAT GLOBE ITSELF

The United States Navy: Since the end of the American Revolution, American shipping had been interdicted on the coast of North Africa, known as the Barbary Coast. The three centers of gravity on the Barbary Coast were the beylics of Tunis, Algiers, and Tripoli. A beylic was an Ottoman satrapy ruled by a bey that was largely autonomous from Constantinople. They have gone down in American history as the Barbary Pirates, although they were not, strictly speaking, pirates, being lawfully authorized servants of their governments.

Secretary of state Thomas Jefferson, being pro-French, had used the issue to beat the drums for an American Navy that could defend against the Barbary pirates and incidentally could also be used to fight the Royal Navy. Jefferson was ignored until 1793, when France and Great Britain went to war, and the British began interdicting American merchant shipping with impunity. As we have seen, Great Britain in 1793 had also armed and incited the Indians of the Northwest Confederacy, and although the British had ceased this activity by the end of 1793, the Indians had determined to proceed against the Americans anyway, in which case the Americans would have presumed that the Indians still had British support. Legislation was introduced in January 1794, authorizing the construction of six frigates and the purchase of twenty sloops. The terms *frigate* and *sloop* are used in various ways over the years and in different ways by different navies, but in this case, a frigate is a ship carrying thirty-eight to forty guns on a single deck. The deck with the guns was called the upper deck, and below that deck was crew berthing, and it was called the gun deck. Today in the Navy, gun decking is the term used when people create false records to be shown at inspections. I don't know if there's a relation or not. Frigates were able to travel faster than larger ships and had enough firepower to take on whatever they were chasing. A sloop is a ship carrying twenty guns or less and is suitable for low-intensity conflict.

In April 1794, Congress passed an authorization for six frigates to be constructed in Portsmouth, New Hampshire (USS *Congress*), Boston (USS *Constitution*), New York City (USS *President*), Philadelphia (USS *United States*), Baltimore (USS *Constellation*), and

297

Gosport, Virginia (USS *Chesapeake*). President Washington picked the six names from a list of ten provided by the secretary of war, who oversaw naval affairs at the War Department until the Department of the Navy was established in 1798.

The government also purchased twenty merchant ships, fitted them out with cannon, and christened them as sloops of war. The legislation further provided pay and sustenance for sailors and Marines, including officers, to man the ships. Because there was a sharp political divide between pro-British Federalists and pro-French Republicans, the legislation was strictly worded so that construction of the Fleet would halt if peace were made with the bey of Algeria, who presumably was thought to be able to influence the beys of Tunis and Tripoli.

In 1796 an agreement was reached with the bey of Algeria to pay tribute that would protect American shipping, which happened to coincide with the Jay Treaty going into effect and the subsequent end of British seizures of American shipping. Construction of all six frigates was duly halted, and Washington asked Congress for instructions. New legislation was passed in April 1796, allowing completion of *United States, Constellation*, and *Constitution*, as they were the furthest along. They would be christened in 1797, just as John Adams came into office with a new belligerence toward France.

The conquest of Ohio and the Jay Treaty, 1794: In the spring, the Legion of the United States moved out from its base at Fort Jefferson and moved north in the general direction of the Indian base at Fort Miami. Along the way, they built Fort Recovery on the site of the battlefield known as St Clair's Defeat. The British had their hands full between the fighting in Europe and their new policy of taking over Saint Dominique and the other French sugar islands. They were well aware that Washington, though officially neutral, preferred Great Britain over revolutionary France, especially after the Terror started in September. But they also had made promises to the Indians in the Northwest Confederacy, so they managed to put 120 men in Fort Miami and at least pretended to support them.

On June 30, the Indians attacked Fort Recovery and were repulsed. The legion continued marching north and got to the

Maumee River, not far from Fort Miami, on August 9. They constructed Fort Defiance. There was a battle on August 20, known as Fallen Timbers, in which the Indians were able to muster 1,300 warriors against the legion's 3,000. Tecumseh, twenty-six years old this year, participated in the fight. It took an hour for the Indians to be scattered, and the British refused them entry into Fort Miami. The Indians claimed it was a betrayal, but I would guess that the British had made it abundantly clear that they could not expect any sanctuary in Fort Miami. The Indians, who had their families encamped nearby, departed, and the Americans let them depart. They then set up camp within sight of Fort Miami. There was a standoff, but nobody on the ground was willing to start an Anglo-American War, and so the Americans withdrew after a week to Fort Recovery. Wayne spent the rest of the year building forts (including Fort Wayne, Indiana, on the site of the Miami capital of Kekionga) and suppressing small bands of resistance. He had secured Ohio.

JOHN JAY BURNED IN EFFIGY.

Immediately upon receiving word of Fallen Timbers, Washington sent Chief Justice John Jay to London to negotiate the Jay Treaty. Jay had overseen foreign affairs in the days of the Articles of Confederation and was reliably pro-British. Washington and Hamilton did not trust Jefferson's replacement at state, Edmund Randolph, who was too friendly with France. The Jay Treaty was signed in London on November 19. Washington submitted it to the Senate, and it was ratified after a rancorous debate on June 24, 1795, by a 20–10 vote. Jefferson, Madison, and Burr all argued against the treaty and were hardened in their determination to organize politically against the Federalists, of whom they considered Washington one. At some point, the text of the treaty was published and caused an uproar. Jay joked that he could travel at night by the light of his burning effigies. The treaty took effect on leap day, February 29, 1796. The treaty gave the Americans a free hand to establish settlements in Ohio but made them a British ally for all intents and purposes.

Jay, who still held the post of chief justice, had stayed in London after sending the treaty to Philadelphia in November, as an opportunity had presented itself for the United States to settle their western and southern borders with Spain. Jay kept an eye on things in London, while the American minister to Great Britain, Thomas Pinckney, went to Madrid to negotiate the Treaty of San Lorenzo (a suburb of Madrid). Jay was still in London when he was elected governor of New York in May 1795, presumably before all those effigies of him started burning. There were a couple of reasons for Spain to want to settle their border issues with the United States. Primarily, they would be worried that with the United States having settled the dispute in Ohio, they would bear the full brunt of American pressure on the question of border disputes. Secondly, with more settlement in the Ohio Valley, a lot more product would come floating down the river to New Orleans. The Americans would want New Orleans to receive their products with as little problem as possible. Thirdly, Spain was, by the end of 1794, ready to end the war with France in the Pyrenees and had a general desire to end all their conflicts.

The Whiskey Rebellion: The Whiskey Act, an excise tax on distilled spirits, was passed by Congress in March 1791. Washington had set up a bureaucracy to collect the tax by November. Over the next three years, opposition to the tax became more organized, and in western Pennsylvania, it eventually became violent. Western Pennsylvania farmers considered the tax to be especially onerous because distilling was found to be a very efficient way to process and transport their excess grain and because money in the form of coinage, or specie, was the only allowed means of payment of the tax and was always in short supply on the frontier. Many of the farmers viewed the tax as a deliberate plot to ruin them, as it was widely believed that Hamilton always favored the big businesses of the east at the expense of the farmers of America.

By July 1794, there was enough rage in western Pennsylvania to provoke a march of seven thousand farmers on Pittsburgh. One of the rebel leaders, David Bradford, began comparing himself to Robespierre and called for a guillotine to be set up in Pittsburgh to execute the wealthy. Future treasury secretary Albert Gallatin, who had been elected to the Senate from Pennsylvania but was unseated because he had not been a citizen long enough, was in Pittsburgh and was sympathetic to the rebels but tried to curb their excesses.

Word of this activity reached Philadelphia, and Washington  ordered the call-up of thirteen thousand militia, which concentrated in two groups in Cumberland, Maryland, and Carlisle, Pennsylvania. Washington reviewed the troops, on horseback and in uniform, on October 3 and 10, the only time a president has done so. Contrary to what you might read, he didn't command the troops or direct operations. The Cumberland review is illustrated here. Washington was satisfied, turned command over to Dan Morgan and Light-Horse Harry Lee, and returned to Philadelphia. I am sure that Washington wouldn't have minded going to western Pennsylvania, a trip down memory lane to relive the days of his youth when he was causing international incidents and finding the sound of bullets flying over his head charming.

The two columns marched to Pittsburgh. The rebels melted away without a shot being fired. Maybe they had got the word that Robespierre had been guillotined himself, which put a new light on David Bradford's ambitions. Order was restored, and there were only about twenty-five trials resulting in two death sentences, both of which were reversed by pardons from Washington. Having proved his point about the futility of resistance to the federal government, Washington and his successors became very lax about collecting the whiskey tax, at least from the poor farmers on the frontier. David Bradford escaped down the Ohio River and settled in New Orleans, whence he called for his family to join him. Adams pardoned him in 1799, which allowed him to return to Pittsburgh and reclaim his property. He died in 1808, forty-six years old.

Washington's administration was nearing the end of six years at the end of 1794. There was an election coming up, and Washington wasn't going to be participating, although he made no announcements until September 1796. At the end of 1794, Hamilton resigned from the Treasury Department, and Knox resigned from the War Department. Oliver Wolcott took over at Treasury and Timothy Pickering took over at war. Hamilton still had some important goals that he pursued until Burr killed him in 1804, at the age of forty-seven. Knox retired from public life and died in 1806, aged fifty-six, having acquired a lethal throat infection caused by swallowing a chicken bone. Knox left office on a sour note, Washington having been disappointed in his performances in Ohio and Pennsylvania and letting Knox know it. The relationship between the two men was never the same.

Eastern Europe

Kosciuszko's Uprising, 1794: At the beginning of the year, the Polish Army was in the process of being amalgamated with the Russian Army. The Greater Polish National Cavalry Brigade refused to demobilize and took the field in a town named Ostroleka, located

120 kilometers northeast of Warsaw and not far from the Prussian border. Riots broke out across the country. You have to give the Poles some credit for organization here. There was a Russian Army unit located in Krakow, and they took the field and headed for Ostroleka. On March 24, Kosciuszko crossed the Vistula River from Polish Austria (Galicia) into Krakow, announced a gen-

THE GREAT GLOBE ITSELF

eral uprising, and conducted a *levee en masse* of sorts by impressing all the local males, aged eighteen to twenty-eight, into his new Army, amounting to about 1,400 men. He also took up a collection—nonvoluntary of course—to fund it. Weapons were collected, and the new recruits were given scythes, axes, and pikes. Kosciuszko was able to link up with the cavalry brigade, and they advanced toward the enemy. On April 4, they were able to fend off a Russian unit at Raclawice, which was touted as a victory. Several Polish units that were being demobilized now joined the uprising.

The uprising in Warsaw, led by a shoemaker named Jan Kilinski, drove the Russians out by April 19. He turned the city over to Kosciuszko in May and was rewarded with the rank of colonel and a prominent command. Other cities fell to the Poles about the same time. On May 7, Kosciuszko proclaimed the guarantee of civil rights and the end of serfdom in Poland and continued to build up his forces. On May 27, Joseph Poniatowski arrived in Warsaw take a division command in Warsaw near his uncle the king. This was a fine arrangement since Kosciuszko didn't want Poniatowski near him, and Poniatowski didn't want to be near Kosciuszko. As we recall, Kosciuszko was an agent of the Czartoryski family, who were rivals of the Poniatowskis. The Poles distrusted each other from the beginning.

The Russian forces all retreated to the Prussian and Russian borders to regroup and get reinforcements, backing up to strike a bigger blow, and the Russians called on the Prussians to assist. Eighteen thousand Prussians crossed the border from Silesia into Poland and linked up with nine thousand Russian troops. Kosciuszko moved south from Warsaw with fifteen thousand troops and was defeated on June 6 by the Russian-Prussian force. Kosciuszko was wounded, the Poles retreated to Warsaw, and Krakow was captured by the Russians. The Austrians now joined the war, apparently have explained to the satisfaction of the Russians how they had failed to keep Kosciuszko from entering Krakow in the first place.

In July, a force of forty thousand Russians and twenty-five thousand Prussians laid siege to Warsaw. The siege was broken in September by the Greater Poland uprising, but the Russians brought in another corps under Suvorov, and the Polish forces were snuffed out one by one. Kosciuszko himself was wounded in action again and taken prisoner in October. Now Polish defeat was a matter of marching to Warsaw, where King Stanislas and the remaining Polish forces under his nephew were barricaded. Another siege was successful in November. Polish historians claim that when the city surrendered, the Russians pillaged it and killed twenty thousand civilians, a claim refuted by most Russian historians.

King Stanislas was exiled to Saint Petersburg, where he spent the rest of his life. He formally abdicated in November 1795, after the Third Partition of Poland, there being nothing left to govern. He died on February 12, 1798. He had never married, so Joseph was his heir. Paul I sponsored a state funeral in Saint Petersburg. In 1938, his body was transferred to his hometown in Poland. In 1995, his body was transferred from there to a cathedral in Warsaw. His nephew was ejected from Warsaw, his estates confiscated, and he moved to Vienna. He was allowed to return to Warsaw in 1798, after the death of his uncle, where he was idle until 1807, when Napoleon made him minister of war for the Duchy of Warsaw.

As for the Czartoryskis, they were invisible during the 1794 uprising, making all of their contributions through their agent Kosciuszko. After the Polish defeat, the father, Adam Czartoryski, remained in Poland, but his estates were confiscated, while his sons Adam Jerzy and Konstanty joined the Russian Army, served in the Imperial Guard, and became friends with future emperor Alexander I. In 1804, Adam Jerzy would be the Russian foreign minister and the driving spirit behind the Third Coalition. The Czartoryskis would hitch their wagon to Russia, while the Poniatowskis would hitch theirs to France. Their choices didn't work out for either one of them or their country.

After his capture, Kosciuszko was sent to Saint Petersburg in chains. He was pardoned in 1796 by Paul I and traveled to the United States, where he was distrusted by John Adams and the Federalists but embraced by Jefferson. He traveled to France in 1798 but found no employment there. When Bonaparte took over in November 1799, the two men met. Kosciuszko explained his plan for Polish freedom

THE GREAT GLOBE ITSELF

to Bonaparte, who listened impatiently. Bonaparte thought that Kosciuszko was living in a fantasy world, as he was convinced that the Poles were firmly under the thumbs of the partitioners. There were no more meetings and Kosciuszko called Bonaparte "the undertaker of the French Republic." After that, he couldn't get arrested in Paris and left. He was an adviser to Adam Jerzy Czartoryski in the days of the Third Coalition but retired after that. He died in 1817, seventy-one years old.

France, 1794

Fall of the Enragists and the Indulgents: Success on the battlefield led to questions from various quarters in Paris regarding continuation of the Terror. These had started in December 1793, with publication of *The Old Cordelier* by Desmoulins, who, along with Danton and the other Indulgents, were attempting to put an end to the Terror. On the other side of the argument was Jacques Hebert, publisher of *Pere Duchesne,* and his associates the Enragists. As we recall, he had organized the atheistic Festival of Reason, the point in the swing of the revolutionary pendulum where it started swinging back the other way. Robespierre and his allies were more worried about the Enragists than the Indulgents. They believed that the Terror was still necessary because the government needed to defend itself against counterrevolutionaries, the enemies of the people, to whom only death was owed, as Robespierre said. However, they did relent in some instances. For example, when word of the excesses of Jean Baptiste Carrier in Nantes came to the CPS in February, they recalled him to Paris, although he was not arrested until September. Word also came from Lyon about the similar excesses of Joseph Fouche and his mitrailleuses, but Fouche had the CPS member Couthon, who was equally guilty, cover for him, so he was not recalled until April.

The Indulgents had launched their initial attacks against the Enragists, which Robespierre encouraged, but then the Cordeliers attacked the CPS, resulting in Desmoulins' expulsion from the Jacobin Club. Robespierre and Desmoulins had been close friends and colleagues for years and now found themselves in a life-or-death struggle with each other. The stress of dealing with Indulgents and Enragists made Robespierre so ill that he absented himself from government business from February 13 to March 13. During his absence, Hebert and Carrier called for a general uprising, but the response was weak. I would imagine that the reason for that was that either the mayor of Paris didn't agree with Hebert and Carrier or that he didn't have an Army of National Guards to do his bidding anymore. I hope it was the latter.

Robespierre returned to work, encouraged. On March 13, the CPS ordered the arrest of Hebert, Chaumette, Momoro, and about twenty other Enragists. Carrier remained free for some reason, possibly because he was a member of the convention. It was the atheistic Festival of Reason that did them in. They were all tried on the same day, March 24, and went to the guillotine that evening. There was some follow up to get rid of some of Hebert's associates, including Hebert's widow, but his radical agenda was finished in France. I don't know whether Momoro's widow, who had played the goddess of reason in the November 1793 Festival of Reason, suffered a similar fate, but it was a step forward of a sort that women were receiving equal treatment, at least when it came to the guillotine.

Robespierre and Saint Just and their allies now turned to the problem of Danton, Desmoulins, and the rest of the Indulgents. Danton was warned to get out of town, but he didn't think they would have the nerve to arrest him. He was wrong because a warrant for the arrest of the Indulgents was issued on March 31. The warrant included the name of CPS member Jean Herault de Sechelles, whom, as we recall, Saint Just had suspected of being soft on counterrevolution since their days together as representatives on mission on the Rhine in 1793. Maybe Saint Just arranged to be in the room when they arrested Herault just to see the look of surprise on his face. That would have been in keeping with his evil reputation in history. The Indulgents were accused of corruption, taking bribes, and counterrevolutionary conspiracy. They were tried from April 3 to 5, with a decree of the convention preventing them from calling witnesses or otherwise defending themselves. Fifteen Indulgents were executed on April 5. Danton told the executioner, "Show my head to the people. It is worth a look." Desmoulins' wife attempted, on April 5, to organize a mob to free her husband from prison. She was arrested and tried, then guillotined on April 13, the same day as the widow Hebert and maybe the widow Momoro.

The pace of executions in Paris increased, as the convention passed decrees on suspending Revolutionary Tribunals in the provinces and bringing all political cases to Paris, where the prisons soon filled up. There were prominent victims. William Malesherbes had been Louis XVI's minister of the *Maison du Roi* in the 1770s and later was defense counsel at the king's trial in January 1793. He and his family were accused of helping émigrés and were all guillotined. Madame Elizabeth, sister of King Louis XVI, had been detained in August 1792, along with the rest of the royal family and was now accused of helping her brother. Well, she couldn't very well argue about that. She was guillotined along with twenty-five others on May 10. To her credit, she spent her last hours comforting her fellow victims.

On April 21, former commander of the Army of the Rhine Alexander de Beauharnais and his wife, Rose, were arrested. Rose was released in July, but Alexander was guillotined on July 23, only five days before Robespierre and his associates were guillotined themselves. Rose married Bonaparte in 1796, who rechristened her Josephine and adopted her children Eugéne and Hortense, who both made their marks on history. Executed along with Beauharnais was a German prince named Frederick von Salm. Salm's residence was confiscated by the government and converted into the Palace of the Legion of Honor in 1804, and if you want to know what it looks like but don't want to fly to Paris, go to Lincoln Park in San Francisco and visit the Fine Arts Museum there, as it is a three-quarter replica built in 1924 as a World War I memorial. Or you can go to Paris and see the original at full scale, and it still serves as the headquarters of the Legion of Honor to this day.

Robespierre thought that the atheism of the Enragists was presumptuous, as they were claiming knowledge of things they couldn't possibly know. He thought the God of the Bible was a fairy tale, but his approach was that God was a real being, and he wanted to present Him in a more modern, scientific, and abstract way. In May, he gave a speech describing his Cult of the Supreme Being. Robespierre believed that Hebert's "reason" was only a means to an end, as the purpose of reason was to lead men to virtue. Belief in a living God and a higher moral code were constant reminders of justice, and justice was essential to a republican society.

The two principles of the Cult of the Supreme Being were a belief in the existence of God and the immortality of the human soul, which are Masonic ideas. He scheduled a festival for June 8. The artist JL David got to work and came up with a program of activities for the day. Not coincidentally, the festival occurred on Pentecost, the day that the Holy Spirit came upon the apostles in Jerusalem. The festival occurred, but Robespierre seems to have offended as many people as he reached. He was mocked as a new Moses coming down from the mountaintop with a new religion for the people given to him directly by the Almighty. The fatal flaw in his religious program was that the man of no compromise had compromised. If he had guillotined the Indulgents for their willingness to compromise on the revolution, then he himself was guilty of trying to compromise between the atheistic cult of reason and the old Christian religion, and he would pay the same price as the Indulgents.

To remedy the problem of Paris prisons overrun with political prisoners, on June 10, which was 22 Prairial, the convention passed a law streamlining the process for accusing, arresting, trying, and guillotining counterrevolutionaries. The only two verdicts were acquittal or death. Soon thirty people a day were being guillotined. Members of the convention were not made immune from the law of 22 Prairial, and those who had supported Danton and Desmoulins started to get nervous. The men who had carried out the Terror in the provinces were especially vulnerable to being accused, as there were plenty of survivors ready to accuse them. We've talked briefly about men like Carrier, Fouche, and Barras, who served in provinces, and there was another, Jean-Lambert Tallien, who had performed similarly in Bordeaux, although his murderous instincts had been tempered by a beautiful young local woman by the name of Theresa Cabarrus, whom Tallien married and brought to Paris, where she

THE GREAT GLOBE ITSELF

made quite a splash. Theresa saved so many lives in Bordeaux by sweet talking her husband that she earned the name of Our Lady of Thermidor. Tallien was accused of being a moderate and told to stand trial. He and others began looking to their safety, but at the end of June, Robespierre, Saint Just, and their allies seemed to be in firm control.

Naval operations, 1794: In February, Great Britain successfully invaded and occupied the French island of Martinique. They had come at the invitation of French plantation owners who had been told that the freeing of their slaves by the convention was imminent. The French defense was nominal, consisting of nine hundred militia. The British rewarded the planters for their inept defense by allowing them to keep their slaves. It goes to show you that the British posturing in the American colonies about freeing the slaves was just that. They cared nothing about remedying the servile condition of Negroes unless it benefited them somehow. Sugar islands had historically been very lucrative, but for various reasons, including new technology that allowed sugar to be extracted from beets, which could be grown in Europe, and the increasing discomfort Europeans felt about consuming things produced by slaves, the sugar islands began declining as the years went on. The British held onto Martinique until 1802, when they returned it in the peace of Amiens. A similar British attempt in Guadeloupe was repulsed by December 1794, while a third assault on Sainte Lucie succeeded until the British were driven out in 1795.

Almost erased from the history books is what happened in Saint Dominique in 1794. An anti-French rebellion had been going on since 1791, which is to say a rebellion of the slaves, free blacks, and mulattos against the whites, who constituted an artisan class of shopkeepers and a bourgeois class of plantation owners. The blacks made no distinction between the white bourgeois and artisan classes. The convention in Paris thought that the answer was to free the slaves. Toussaint Louverture came to prominence at this time, when he sided with the French government. The whites on Saint Dominique disagreed with the French government and turned to Great Britain for help, which led to the British operations in Martinique, Guadeloupe,

309

PETER HARDY

and Saint Lucie. Most of the thirty thousand troops they deployed went to these three locations, but they also landed about six hundred Marines in Saint Dominique, enough to give the whites hope but not enough to make a difference in the conflict. By now it was the summer of 1794, and the allies were in full retreat in Flanders, as described below. The writing was on the wall, and Pitt decided that the best use of the British Army was not in Flanders but in Saint Dominique, the largest sugar island in the world.

In April, France and the United States organized a large convoy of grain ships (about 170) intended to sail from Hampton, Virginia, to France. This was before the Jay Treaty and may have been a factor in why the Jay Treaty soon came about. The convoy set sail on April 2 and was protected by a Fleet under the command of Louis Villaret, who had served under Suffren in India in the 1780s. The Royal Navy was commanded by Richard Howe, who was still in active service eighteen years after his and his brother's time in the American Revolution. On the Glorious First of June, the two Fleets engaged as Howe attempted to interdict the convoy. Villaret's force was well thrashed by Howe, losing seven ships, but the convoy got through unmolested. Thus, both sides claimed victory. Howe served until 1797 and died in 1799. Villaret died in 1812 while serving as governor of Venice.

The British force that had been in Toulon in 1793 spent the year 1794 in Corsica, helping Paoli to reduce French garrisons on the island. While participating in an attack on the garrison at Calvi, Lord Horatio Nelson was blasted in the face and lost sight in one eye. We will be hearing more from him as he spends his life losing body parts by engaging in reckless behavior. The pro-British sources say the British were helping Corsica fight for independence, but in reality, after eliminating all the French forces on the island, they added it to the domains of George III with the same status as Ireland, which is to say that Ireland, Corsica, and Great Britain were all kingdoms in personal union with George III. At the end of 1794 and well into 1795, there was a great deal of confusion as to who was in charge, as Paoli still thought that he was running a republic, even though the British had installed a viceroy by the name of Baronet Gilbert Eliot.

THE GREAT GLOBE ITSELF

I've never seen anything written about the impact of this move on the thinking of Napoleon Bonaparte. If the British had played fair with Corsica at this point, perhaps Napoleon's ambitions wouldn't have been incited to the extent that they were.

Flanders and the Rhineland, 1794: During the fall of 1793, in the Army of the North in Flanders, General Jourdan and Lazare Carnot had disagreed on strategy. Carnot accused General Jourdan, and for a while, it looked like Jourdan's career, and maybe even his life, was over. General Pichegru had resigned from the Army of the Rhine to go to Paris to accuse Hoche and was successful. Hoche was arrested and jailed in March. The Army needed successful generals, so Carnot relented on Jourdan, and he was given Hoche's command, the Army of the Moselle.

I don't know what had happened in the relationship between Saint Just and Hoche, as Saint Just had been the one to discover Hoche and advance him. He had even made Pichegru subordinate to Hoche in the previous campaign against the Prussians. Maybe Saint Just was too busy supervising the executions of the Enragists and Indulgents to notice, or maybe Hoche's misfortune was the result of people who were nervous about Saint Just wanting to send him a message. Anyway, Hoche stayed in jail until August 1794, where he caught the tuberculosis that would kill him three years later.

In Flanders, Carnot decided on a two-pronged offensive under Pichegru and Jourdan. Jourdan moved his headquarters north from the left flank of the Rhine to the right flank of Flanders with a portion of the Army of the Moselle, incorporated the Army of the Ardennes and a portion of the Army of the North into his command, and renamed it the Army of the Sambre-et-Meuse. To Jourdan's left, Pichegru was in command of the remainder of the Army of the North, which was still a very large force. On the other side of the line, Emperor Francis II joined Coburg at allied headquarters. The Austrian general opposing Pichegru was Francois Clerfayt, with help from the Duke of York. The general opposing Jourdan was Prince Coburg himself, with help from the Prince of Orange, the son of the Dutch Stadtholder William V. The prince who would later be King William I of the Netherlands.

In the Rhineland, the portion of the Army of the Moselle that remained there continued as a separate command from the Army of the Rhine during 1794, but the two were combined into the Army of the Rhine and Moselle in April 1795. In 1794, these forces remained on the defensive. On the allied side of the line, the Duke of Brunswick had resigned from command of the Prussian forces. He was replaced by Wichard von Möllendorf. Maybe Brunswick was needed in Poland. Wurmser remained in command of the Austrian forces, with an assist from von Hohenlohe. They also remained mostly on the defensive, although they did conduct an attack on Kaiserslautern as a diversion when the pressure in Flanders got too high.

Great Britain now signed a new agreement with the Prussians, offering a lump sum of £300,000, plus £50,000 a month thereafter to maintain sixty thousand troops in Flanders. The Prussians took the money, but there were delays in getting the troops there, and then of course the Polish uprising came along. The Prussians failed to comply with the agreement but told Great Britain that it was due to unforeseen circumstances. I assume they kept the £300,000 and any £50,000 payments to date, but the money stopped flowing. After France conquered the Netherlands, there were serious repercussions between Prussia and Great Britain for this lack of Prussian performance. Prussia scoffed at the enraged British, pointing out that the British had frittered away their resources pursuing their interests in Corsica and the West Indies. I can see Frederick William II saying something like, now I know why my Uncle Frederick the Great couldn't stand you people. The Prussians would pursue peace with France and neutrality in Europe for the next ten years.

On May 17, at the Battle of Tourcoing, the Army of the North was attacked by Clerfayt's force. Francis II was present to observe operations, the only time he ever spent in the field. Future marshal MacDonald, one of the Wild Geese, participated in the battle. British or Irish people and their descendants who were exiled because of involvement in rebellion settled in France or Spain and serve in the French or Spanish Army are called Wild Geese. There may be some connection between the Wild Geese and the expression wild goose chase, but I wasn't able to find any documentation of it. The Army of the North managed to hold its ground and, on the next day, counterattacked and made the allies retreat. The French pursued, and the allies turned and stood, four days later, at Tournay. The allies held their position, but for the first time, the weight of French numbers began to be felt, with subsequent effects on allied morale. Pichegru was in command, but one of his division commanders, Jean Moreau, distinguished himself. The fact that Kosciuszko had, earlier in the month, started his uprising in Poland didn't help the allies. Russia sent a request to Austria and Prussia for help, and Prussia withdrew twenty thousand troops from the west and sent them east to Poland. Francis II departed Flanders on May 29 to attend to matters in Poland, ending his only personal experience of war.

The allies attempted a distraction on May 23 when they attacked Kaiserslautern in the Rhineland. Prussian commander Möllendorf and Austrian commander Hohenlohe attacked with forty-five thousand men against a French force of twenty thousand. The French retreated but counterattacked in July, wiping out all of the Prussian gains. Laurent Saint Cyr and Nicolas Oudinot were two future marshals of France at the battle.

By early June, Jourdan and the Sambre-et-Meuse were ready to join in. Saint Just accompanied Jourdan. In early June, while Pichegru laid siege to Ypres, Jourdan laid siege to Charleroi. Prince Coburg attacked Jourdan on June 26 in the Battle of Fleurus, a French victory, which turned out to be the tipping point in the Flanders campaign. An observation balloon was used in the course of the battle, the first use of the third dimension in the history of warfare. After the battle, Saint Just returned to Paris for a brief hero's welcome, until finding out that his political position had dangerously deteriorated, as described below. Jean Bernadotte, Jean-de-Dieu Soult, and Francois LeFebvre, as well as Jourdan himself, were four future marshals participating in the battle, which was a pretty intense fight.

The demoralized allies, facing two French Armies each the size of their one, retreated across the Meuse by July 15 and were in Germany by July 24. The British and Dutch were soon in the Netherlands. French victory in Belgium was now a matter of marching. Pichegru was in Brussels on July 11 and Antwerp on July 27. Jourdan was in Namur on July 15 and Liege on July 27. At the same time, the Prussian and Austrian Armies in the Rhineland moved to the east bank of the Rhine. The only allied forces left on the west side of the Rhine were in the fortresses of Mainz and Luxembourg. There were recriminations between the Austrians and Prussians, although these didn't stop the Third Partition of Poland from happening. An Austrian-Prussian alliance was as unnatural as one between Great Britain and Spain. Great Britain was looking to Austria like a better prospective ally than Prussia.

Eastern Pyrenees, Western Pyrenees, Alps, and Italy, 1794: General Jacques Dugommier, the hero of Toulon, was in command in the eastern Pyrenees. Future marshals Dom Perignon, Pierre Augereau, Jean Lannes, and Claude Victor served under him. On the other side of the line was General Luis de Carvajal. Dugommier launched his offensive in April and made steady progress through the year. On November 17, Dugommier launched the Battle of Black Mountain but was killed in action on November 18, struck by a cannonball. Bonaparte later honored his memory by granting his son a hundred thousand francs. Perignon assumed command and resumed

THE GREAT GLOBE ITSELF

the attack. Carvajal led a counterattack at the head of 1,300 horses, and he, too, was killed in action. The Spanish retreated to the Roses Fortress on the Ebro River that Perignon laid siege to, and it surrendered in early February 1795, which was the end of operations in the eastern Pyrenees.

General Jacques Muller was in command of the western Pyrenees. Future marshal Bon-Adrian Moncey served under him. On the other side of the line was General Ventura Caro. The Spanish attacked one of Muller's camps, the *Sans Culottes* Camp, in February 1794, and they were repulsed. Muller commenced his advance in June, and like Dugommier, he was unstoppable. In September, he was transferred to the Army of the Alps but only as a division commander. The representative on mission in the western Pyrenees, Jean-Baptiste Cavaignac, had, for a while, been questioning Muller's devotion to the revolution and forced his resignation. Cavaignac then made Moncey commander of the Army of the Western Pyrenees. Muller was commanding the Army of Mainz in 1799 during the War of the Second Coalition and was defeated by Archduke Charles at Mannheim. He was replaced in command but continued to serve under Bonaparte in various low-profile posts until his retirement. Cavaignac was a zealous pro-Terror revolutionary but turned on Robespierre in time to avoid sharing his fate. His son Louis-Eugéne Cavaignac served in the Army with distinction in Algeria for years and, in 1848, was, for several months, dictator of France after Louise Philippe was dethroned, but he was defeated by Louis Napoleon in the 1848 presidential election.

Moncey continued operations with just as much success as Muller. However, the French were unable to annihilate the Spanish forces before winter set in. As on every other front, the French Armies outnumbered their enemies in the Pyrenees. By the end of the year, Spain, like Prussia, was looking to end the war with France but kept fighting into 1795 to try to gain a better position at the negotiating table.

The Army that had retaken Toulon was technically a detachment of the Army of Italy that was returned after Toulon was retaken. The commander of the Army of Italy this year was General Pierre

Dumerbion, a career officer. Serving under him were Bonaparte and future marshal Andre Massena. The Army of Italy inflicted two defeats on the Austrian-Piedmont allies. In April 1794, they won the Battle of Saorgio, and in September, they won the Battle of Dego. Bonaparte did a lot of the battle planning, and Dumerbion gave him a lot of the credit in his reports to Carnot, but Bonaparte never stepped out of line and perfectly played the part of the supportive subordinate. After Thermidor, Bonaparte was briefly arrested, having been an associate of Robespierre's brother Augustine at Toulon. He was cleared and returned to duty. The Army of Italy was on defense per instructions from Carnot, who rejected the Army of Italy's proposals, drafted by Bonaparte, for more aggressive action. Dumerbion was fifty-seven this year and in ill health, retiring in 1795 and dying in 1797. Will Bonaparte's bosses all fare as poorly as Dugommier and Dumerbion? Let's find out.

The Army of the Alps was based in Grenoble under the command of Thomas-Alexandre Dumas. In April and May, Dumas launched several attacks on Mount Cenis, which controlled the Little Saint Bernard Pass between France and Italy. He was successful in June, but that month was called before the CPS to answer questions about his conduct. He was able to delay this interview long enough for Thermidor Reaction to eliminate the folks who wanted to question him. Dumas was born in 1762 in Saint Dominique, son of a French aristocrat and his enslaved Negro concubine. Before leaving Saint Dominique in 1778, his father sold his mother and sisters but brought him to France. He got a nobleman's education and lived well. He enlisted in the Army in 1786 as a private. He was commissioned in October 1792 into a unit of free men of color called the Saint George Legion serving in the Army of the North. He was made a brigadier in July 1793 and a general of division in August. He briefly commanded the western Pyrenees until given the command of the Army of the Alps, which he held until his recall by the CPS in June 1794. He served in various capacities, including in Egypt (where he got on Bonaparte's wrong side), until he was captured and held prisoner in Naples from 1799 to 1801. After his release, he struggled because Bonaparte did not forgive. He married in November 1792,

THE GREAT GLOBE ITSELF

and his son, the author of *The Count of Monte Cristo* and *The Three Musketeers,* was born in 1802. He died of stomach cancer in 1806. I don't know why they defile history by making television programs that fantasize about Cleopatra and George III 's consort, Charlotte, being black and ignore Dumas. I suppose they sell the stories they think people want to buy.

The Thermidorian Reaction, July 1794: The Battle of Fleurus on June 26 led to the decision of the allies to evacuate Belgium. There was great rejoicing throughout France as Pichegru and Jourdan had now made Dumouriez's 1792 conquest of Belgium permanent. Nevertheless, in Paris the guillotine continued to rise and fall forty times a day. It was moved from the *Place de la Revolution* to the *Faubourg Saint Antoine* (east of the Bastille) to make it less conspicuous, as if the government was now ashamed of what it was doing. Maybe it was because the *Faubourg Saint Antoine* was more working class, and it was that class that enjoyed the spectacle the most.

The whole point of the guillotine had been to make it a very public way of killing enemies of the revolution in the most gruesome way possible. It was starting to seem cruel that people were still being killed for sticking to their religious beliefs or speaking of the king or a nobleman nostalgically. The Terror was putting a damper on what should have been a great celebration of victory in Belgium. There began to be talk and whispering about amnesty for the accused and accountability for the perpetrators of the Terror.

The Committee of Public Safety now began to realize that the Terror was becoming unfashionable. The members who could say that they weren't the drivers of the Terror now began to say so loudly, and the blame began to settle on Robespierre, Saint Just, and Couthon. These three responded by planning to use their powers to round up and kill their accusers. The atmosphere at the CPS was dark, with nobody quite sure who to trust and who was on what side of the line. Robespierre, for his part, took frequent absences from work, as he did not like being called a dictator by his colleagues, whom he thought had all been pulling together with him as a team, but now they were making noises about being dragged along. Saint Just, feeling some

317

sense of ownership of the decisive victory at Fleurus, felt confident that his status as hero would protect him. As far as Couthon, the man who had written the law that denied "counterrevolutionaries" like Danton the right to defend themselves at trial, I suppose he thought that perhaps his disability might provide him some protection. The three appeared to make some concessions to their colleagues as far as stepping down from their positions and sharing power with other committees, but at the same time, they were drawing up additional charges against their enemies. Comparisons to the Roman triumvirate of Antony, Octavian, and Lepidus, who, in their day, had seized power and unleashed a proscription of their enemies, were made. A *proscription* is when the people in authority condemn their opponents to death by the expedient of publicly posting their names and offering rewards for their deaths without trial.

Because of all the tension, July 14 rolled around again with little fanfare, making it the worst Bastille Day ever. The fact that Camille Desmoulins, the man who had incited the events of that day, had just been executed was no small factor in the manner in which the day was not commemorated. One event that was recorded was Fouche showing up that day at the Jacobin Club where Robespierre berated him for his atheism, saying, "So, Fouche, who told you to tell the people there is no God?" As we recall, Fouche had had signs posted in cemeteries stating, "Death is an Eternal Sleep." Fouche proceeded to make himself scarce, although from the shadows, he worked hard to bring the triumvirate down.

On Saturday, July 26, Robespierre made a two-hour speech to the convention in his best suit, the same one he had worn in May when discussing his Cult of the Supreme Being. We dress up for what we think is important. The convention was now meeting in the renovated *Salle du Manege*. He denied being a dictator or a tyrant, said the revolution was in danger, and declared that a purge of counterrevolutionaries needed to be conducted. Asked to name names, he refused. The cool response of the convention was to order the speech to be printed and referred to the relevant committees. That evening, Robespierre gave the same speech at the Jacobin Club, where it was warmly received, except by Collot and Billaud-Varennes, who, as a

THE GREAT GLOBE ITSELF

result, were expelled from the club, an event which saved their lives. Later that night, they and the other five other members of the CPS (one was out of town), along with Tallien, Barras, probably Fouche, and others, met and agreed that if they wanted to survive, the triumvirate had to die.

The next day, July 27 (9 Thermidor), the same day that Pichegru entered Antwerp, and Jourdan entered Liege, Saint Just made a speech to the convention in support of Robespierre, attempting to place the blame on three other members of the CPS: Billaud-Varenne s, Collot, and Carnot of all people. Saint Just had just spent three months in the field with the victorious Jourdan, who had been Carnot's enemy, which may explain that. He was interrupted by Tallien, and then by thirty-five more speakers, all of whom denounced the triumvirate. While the accusations began to pile up, Saint Just remained silent. Robespierre then attempted to secure the tribune to speak but was shouted down. Robespierre soon found himself at a loss for words after one deputy called for his arrest, and another gave a mocking impression of him. When one of the deputies realized Robespierre's inability to respond, he shouted, "The blood of Danton chokes him!"

The triumvirate, along with their enforcers and associates, were arrested, but the mayor of Paris, a man named Jean Baptiste Fleuriot-Lescot, attempted to come to their rescue, ordering the jailers not to accept any member of the convention into the prison. He offered them protection at the Hotel de Ville, so that's where they went. The convention then declared them to be outlaws, which had the advantage of allowing them to be shot on sight or arrested and executed without a trial. More shades of the Roman triumvirate as the Senate had declared Antony and Lepidus to be outlaws as well. As the night went on, the forces of the convention under the command of Barras gradually massed around the Hotel de Ville, while those of the Commune gradually dispersed. Before the convention moved in, some of the outlaws attempted suicide. Robespierre was wounded in the jaw with a pistol shot, although accounts vary as to whether he shot himself or was shot by a soldier. Eventually, the prisoners were brought to the Conciergerie, the same prison where Marie Antoinette had been held. Among those taken into custody was the mayor of Paris.

The next morning, the triumvirate and their associates were guillotined. The device itself had been retrieved from the *Faubourg Saint Antoine* back to the *Place de la Revolution*, France being no longer ashamed of who they were executing. Fifteen others were executed as well, including General Francois Hanriot, the commander of the Paris National Guard, who had been the muscle behind the fall of the Girondists in June 1793; the mayor of Paris; and the cobbler Antoine Simon, who had been Louis XVII's guardian and had coached him to accuse Marie Antoinette of teaching him to masturbate.

The day after the guillotining of Robespierre and the others, the CPS ordered the arrest of the seventy members of the Paris Commune that had defied the orders of the convention and protected the outlaws. I don't see where there was a trial, but they were all sentenced to death, which, for the record, was in accordance with legal procedures of the law of 22 Prairial. The convention then ordered the CPS to be disbanded, and their duties were transferred to other committees. The CPS was reconstituted on September 1, 1794, with fewer duties and different members (with the notable exception of Carnot, who was thought to be as indispensable as George Washington).

The prisons in Paris held eight thousand political prisoners who had been marked for the guillotine, and most of them were released. They immediately began accusing their former captors. Many of the men who had been involved in overthrowing the triumvirate had spent the last year vigorously carrying out their policies and were on the receiving end of these accusations. It was decided that they would offer one of their own as a scapegoat to assume the sins of all the others. Subsequently, Jean-Baptiste Carrier, the man who had drowned all those people by loading them on barges in the Loire and sinking

THE GREAT GLOBE ITSELF

them, was arrested, and a tremendous show trial took place for the next three months. Carrier defended himself by saying:

> I took but little share in the policing of Nantes; I was only there in passing, being first at Rennes and later with the Army. My principal task was to watch over and see to the victualing of our troops, and for six months I supplied two hundred thousand men there without its costing the State a halfpenny. Hence, I have little information to offer in the matter.

The survivors of Nantes were dumbfounded at such a declaration, which the word *false* did not do justice to. He and two accomplices were found guilty and guillotined on December 16, 1794. The public desire for vengeance seemed satisfied, although something called the White Terror continued in France for several months.

In November, the convention decreed that all the Jacobin Clubs would be closed permanently. There was no debate, and the vote was unanimous. The winds of fashion are whimsical. For the next few years, the standard of radicalism would be carried by Francois "Gracchus" Babeuf, radical communist who published *Journal of the Freedom of the Press*, soon to be called *The Tribune of the People*. He vigorously attacked the leaders of Thermidor as well as the poor economy and its impact on the proletariat. He would be frequently arrested until his downfall in May 1797. In December, seventy-three of the Girondist deputies who had been scattered in June 1793 were reseated in the convention. This was a sign that the *Sans Culottes* had been firmly repressed, but there would be attempts to revive their radical program. For now, the bourgeoisie were back in control. The radical economic and judicial laws, including 22 Prairial, were revoked.

Military operations in Northern Europe, July to December 1794: When Paris emptied the prisons after Thermidor, one of the prisoners released was General Lazare Hoche, and he was welcomed back to the Army with open arms, given command of Army of the Coasts of Cherbourg and the Army of the Coasts of Brest. He happened to take command while Carrier was on trial, which put the people of Nantes in a good mood. He and his bosses, the convention representatives on mission, were soon negotiating with the Vendean insurgents. Pichegru had not forgotten his 1793 dispute with Hoche and disagreed with Hoche's rehabilitation, but for now, the Army was big enough for both of them. It was when Hoche achieved acclaim in 1795 that Pichegru decided to become a royalist.

The Prussian and Austrian Armies in the Rhineland retreated east of the Rhine in October. The French Armies of the Rhine and the Moselle—not yet combined—converged on Mainz and began a siege in December that would last for the next ten months. General Kleber, who had distinguished himself at Fleurus under Jourdan, was in command. In November, they began a siege of Luxembourg that lasted for seven months. General Moreaux (not Moreau), who was a modest man for a French general, was in command. Rhine-Moselle even managed to cross the Rhine and capture Mannheim on December 24. This was all done under General Michaud, who was just as modest as Moreaux.

Meanwhile, Jourdan had consolidated the French position in southern Belgium and was able to advance to Cologne and Koblenz, while at the same time, Pichegru had done the same in Brussels and Antwerp and, in October, crossed the border into the Netherlands. In December, the Waal River (which is what the Rhine River is called when it enters the Netherlands) froze, and Pichegru's Army crossed it in force. The British retreated into Hanover and left the Dutch to fend for themselves, one more reason for the Prussians to dislike them. Encouraged by the success of the Army in the frozen Netherlands, the convention ordered the French Navy to attack Great Britain, hoping to catch them off guard. The *Croisière du Grand Hiver,* "Campaign of the Great Winter," resulted in severe damage to several French ships. The British mostly watched in amazement as it happened, as the series of events until early February was a clinic of French bad luck and poor seamanship.

CHAPTER 5

The Directory, 1795–1799

1795–1796: Young Bonaparte

The United States, 1795–1796

The Pinckney Treaty: Just as Jay had settled most of the major disputes with Great Britain in 1794, so Thomas Pinckney, US minister to Great Britain, traveled to and negotiated a similar treaty with Spain. It declared that neither side would interfere with the other's shipping, established the northern border of West Florida, and guaranteed free navigation of the Mississippi River, all the way from its source in the north (they weren't sure where that was yet) to the Gulf of Mexico in the south. The United States was given rights of deposit in New Orleans, meaning they didn't have to pay Spain any import duties when all those products started floating down the Mississippi and Ohio Rivers. Americans used this right to transport and store products such as flour, tobacco, pork, bacon, lard, feathers, cider, butter, cheese, and of course, whiskey. Both sides also promised not to incite the Indians against the other. Soon the future began to be as doubtful for the Choctaw and Chickasaw in Mississippi as it was for the Shawnee, Miami, and Lenni Lanape of the Ohio Valley.

The Pinckney Treaty was signed in October 1795, ratified by the Senate in February 1796, and declared in effect in August 1796. Spain temporarily revoked it during the Quasi-War of 1798, when they were France's ally. Other than that, it was in operation until the Louisiana Purchase in 1803 made it moot west of the Mississippi and the Adams-Onis Treaty nullified it in Florida in 1819. Spain was negotiating at the same time with France in Basel, signing a treaty ending the wars in the Pyrenees in July 1795.

In the wake of the Jay Treaty, starting in June 1796, the French Navy began seizing United States merchant vessels. As far as France was concerned, the US and Great Britain were allies. It was at this time that the US repudiated its debt to France from the American Revolution, claiming that the government to which the money was owed no longer existed. Tensions between the United States and France increased.

Pinckney received enough acclamation for his achievement to earn the Federalist nomination as John Adams ' running mate in 1796. Vice presidential candidates were not referred to as running mates until 1916, when Woodrow Wilson dubbed Vice President Thomas Marshall that. Before that, a running mate was a horse entered in a race to set the pace for a horse of the same owner or stable.

At the beginning of 1795, Hamilton resigned as secretary of the Treasury. He returned to New York, where he had some work to do as far as mending his family relationships and finances. He may have done some politicking for John Jay, who was elected governor of New York in May. His home in Manhattan stills exists today in Saint Nicholas Park at 135th Street and Saint Nicholas Avenue. He continued to advise Washington and the cabinet on any and all matters, although he and Adams never got along, and he took no part in the 1796 presidential election, as all the action took place in Philadelphia.

Colonization west of the Appalachians: In Ohio, General Wayne had constructed a series of forts along what would become the western boundary of Ohio. At one of these, Fort Greenville, Wayne summoned the Indian chiefs to negotiate a treaty based on earlier treaties. A dozen chiefs showed up, with Blue Jacket of the Shawnee advocating signing and Little Turtle of the Miami wanting different terms, as the Miami had not been party to the previous treaties. On

THE GREAT GLOBE ITSELF

the American side, Wayne was assisted by William Henry Harrison, Meriwether Lewis, and William Clark, among others. The Indian negotiating position was severely weakened when Wayne revealed that the British had signed the Jay Treaty and would no longer be supporting the Indians. Little Turtle, the last holdout, then signed the treaty in August, and it was ratified by the Senate in December 1795. The treaty established a line of settlement (which was soon being repeatedly violated by the whites) between whites and Indians. The Indians received about $20,000 in blankets, utensils and animals, plus annual gifts of money, clothing, and supplies. The line of settlement ceded about two-thirds of present-day Ohio to white settlement.

After the treaty was signed, the Legion of the United States was reduced to four regiments of eight hundred men each and was renamed the United States Army. Wayne was still in command when he died on December 15, 1796. He was traveling back from Ohio to Pittsburgh and succumbed to an ulcer while stopping in the newly established settlement of Erie, Pennsylvania. Wayne's deputy, General James Wilkinson, took command.

Tecumseh had been a follower of Blue Jacket during the war, and with peace, he married three women, established himself as chief of a Shawnee tribe of 50 warriors and 250 people, and moved from spot to spot in what is now central Indiana. He lived like this for ten years, until the Jay Treaty expired, and Great Britain and the United States resumed their hostility. One can imagine the sense of dread hanging over these people, where they tried to go about their lives in the ways of the elders, while on the other side of the line, more and more whites were showing up. As time went on, they became more dependent on the gifts from and trading with the whites as the forests became increasingly hunted out. The whites used whiskey for currency among themselves and with the Indians. Before Columbus, the Indians had brewed beer, but they didn't have the technology to build stills. Since the arrival of stills and rum and whiskey in the 1500s, the detrimental effects of hard liquor on Indians had been constantly and consistently observed. Laws were passed, often at the request of Indian leaders, to outlaw the sale of hard liquor to Indians, which, in every case, were as futile as Prohibition in the 1920s. To this day, the death rate among Indians due to alcohol-related causes is four times that of the general population.

In addition to the terrible effect of alcohol on Indians, we can also discuss another aspect of Indian culture of the time, which was its extremely violent nature that shocked the Europeans from the first days of contact, starting with the reports of the massive human sacrifices performed at Tenochtitlan. This aspect of Indian culture is almost completely ignored today as it conflicts with the popular picture of Indians as victims, but it certainly existed, and the reason for its existence was not that the Indians were a more violent species of humanity than the Europeans. It existed because the Indians had no government or church to give them any sense of religious identity, national identity, or social obligation.

The English philosopher Thomas Hobbes, who lived from 1588 to 1679 and must have read a lot about the Indians in the Americas, wrote a book called *Leviathan* in 1651. To him, humanity without society was a *bellum omnium contra omnes*, a war of all against all, writing:

> Hereby it is manifest that during the time men live without a common Power to keep them all in awe, they are in that condition which is called War; and such a war as is of every man against every man...In such condition there is no place for Industry, because the fruit thereof is uncertain: and consequently no Culture of the Earth; no Navigation, nor use of the commodities that may be imported by Sea; no commodious Building; no Instruments of moving and removing such things as require much force; no Knowledge of the face of the Earth; no account of Time; no Arts; no Letters; no Society; and which is worst of all, continual Fear, and danger of violent death; And the life of man solitary, poor, nasty, brutish, and short.

THE GREAT GLOBE ITSELF

In July 1796, Cleveland was founded, being named after Connecticut militia General Moses Cleaveland, who had fought in the revolution as a young man and had stayed in the Connecticut militia. Having established the new town, he went back to Connecticut, never to return, so he wasn't around to make corrections when the townsfolk began spelling his name wrong. Cleveland and Cincinnati, which, as we recall, was founded in 1788, both experienced steady growth.

In Kentucky, Daniel Boone widened the trail through Cumberland Gap in 1775 to accommodate wagon traffic on what was soon called the Wilderness Road. Settlers began pouring in. Boone remained active in Kentucky until 1799, when he moved to Missouri. The Cherokee resisted from 1776 to 1794, with some help from the British, until the Jay Treaty was signed. Lexington and Louisville had been established in the 1770s, and Kentucky achieved statehood in 1792. The Treaty of Holston was signed in 1791, defining the Cherokee hunting grounds, but the chiefs that weren't there to sign it didn't recognize it. Because the Indians were nomadic, it wasn't certain that there were any *permanent* Indian residents in Kentucky at all. To entice immigration, land speculators published claims that Kentucky was Indian-free. Anyway, by the year 1796, the Kentucky militias were capable of neutralizing any threat the Indians might pose to the whites.

Tennessee and Georgia experienced low-level conflict with the Indians on the same level as Kentucky, which had been generally neutralized by 1796. Tennessee entered the Union on June 1, 1796, as the sixteenth state.

The Supreme Court, 1795–1796: In June 1795, John Jay resigned as chief justice after his election as governor of New York. Congress was out of session, and Washington used a recess appointment to make John Rutledge chief justice of the United States. A month later, Rutledge made a speech critical of the Jay Treaty. Among other things, he said he hoped that Washington died rather than sign it and that he preferred war with Great Britain to signing the treaty. Well, he was a Southerner from South Carolina, and Southerners tended to prefer France to Great Britain. The Federalists held a large majority in the Senate, and Rutledge became a stench in their nostrils.

Despite the unflattering things Rutledge had said against him, Washington submitted Rutledge's name to the Senate for permanent appointment when Congress convened in December 1795. Rutledge was voted down. He could have stayed on until June 1796, but he resigned in December 1795, having been chief justice for 138 days, the shortest tenure of any chief justice. The court decided two cases during his time in office. Soon after his rejection by the Senate, he attempted suicide by jumping off a pier in Charleston, but he was saved by two of his slaves. He died in 1800 at the age of sixty.

After Rutledge was rejected, Washington nominated Associate Justice Cushing, who declined the appointment even though he was confirmed by the Senate in one day. Washington then nominated Connecticut senator Oliver Ellsworth on March 3, 1796. Ellsworth was confirmed on March 8, 1796, and served until resigning on December 15, 1800. He was replaced by John Marshall.

1796 presidential election: The original concept of the electoral college was that each elector would cast two presidential votes for two presidential candidates, who had to be from different states, and that whoever had the most votes would be president and the runner-up would be vice president. This had worked fine when Washington would be the candidate, but 1796 would be an election contested by two parties that differed widely on many issues. Washington had spent 1795 and 1796 on the Jay and Pinckney Treaties that had done much to secure the western borders as well as the sea trade routes, but Congress got little done, as the Senate was dominated by Federalists, while the House was dominated by Republicans, as the two factions were already calling themselves.

Washington prepared his farewell address, which was published in newspapers in September 1796. I couldn't find anywhere that he

THE GREAT GLOBE ITSELF

delivered it as a speech. It was not until then, only three months before the election, that it was clear that he was not running for a third term. The address did not mention entangling alliances but said:

> The great rule of conduct for us, in regard to foreign nations, is in extending our commercial relations, to have with them as little political connection as possible. Europe has a set of primary interests, which to us have none, or a very remote relation. Hence, she must be engaged in frequent controversies the causes of which are essentially foreign to our concerns. Hence, therefore, it must be unwise in us to implicate ourselves, by artificial ties, in the ordinary vicissitudes of her politics, or the ordinary combinations and collisions of her friendships or enmities.

It was Jefferson's 1801 inaugural address that used the phrase "entangling alliances."

Washington's sudden retirement only three months before the election led to a scramble where the Federalist Congressional Caucus nominated Adams and Thomas Pinckney (of Pinckney Treaty fame), while the Republican Caucus nominating Thomas Jefferson and Aaron Burr. Presidential nominating conventions that occur now didn't start until 1832. John Adams was elected president, and Jefferson, was elected vice president, thanks in part to the intrigues of Alexander Hamilton, who attempted to manipulate the electoral college vote in South Carolina by suggesting that their electors vote for Jefferson and Pinckney, which would make Pinckney president and Adams vice president. The Federalists in the north found out about this intrigue and manipulated *their* votes by voting for Adams and anyone but Pinckney. Jefferson ended up coming in second and became vice president. There must have been talk about changing the rules of the electoral college, but it didn't get done before the

Eastern and Central Europe

Prussian withdrawal from the war and Third Partition of Poland, 1795: Prussia and Austria had been strange bedfellows in the 1793–1794 campaigns in Flanders and on the Rhine. There were serious recriminations on both sides for their defeats, and by the beginning of 1795, all Prussian troops had withdrawn from the Rhine and Flanders, and Prussia, along with Spain and Hesse-Kassel, began negotiating with France. Austria continued the war against France for reasons of their own but engaged in diplomacy with Prussia and Russia throughout 1795, to settle the fate of Poland. One interesting note about Austria's position was that the Austrian emperor's brother Ferdinand, the Grand Duke of Tuscany, broke with the Austrians in early 1795 and declared Tuscany to be neutral, a maneuver which added a couple of years to his tenure in Florence.

Poland remained under Prussian and Russian occupation, while this diplomacy occurred. While Prussia was engaging with France in Basel, in January 1795, the Austrians and the Russians signed an agreement to partition Poland, with Catherine and Francis advising Frederick William of the agreement in February. Frederick William was understandably upset by this arrangement made behind his back, but Francis had just as much cause to be upset with Frederick William for negotiating the Second Partition of Poland without him, withdrawing from Flanders and the Rhine, and negotiating with France. Prussia and Austria therefore stowed their mutual resentments and began negotiating the Third Partition of Poland with Russia.

There was a lull in both military and political activity in Poland until October 1795, when Austria, Russia, and Prussia signed a treaty dividing the remaining territories of the Commonwealth of Lithuania and Poland. The Russian part included 115,000 km² and 1.2 million people, including the city of Vilnius; the Prussian part included 55,000 km² and 1 million people, including the city of Warsaw; and the Austrian part included 47,000 km² and 1.2 million, including the cities of Lublin and Krakow. These divisions lasted until 1807 when Bonaparte created the Duchy of Warsaw at Prussia's expense. The next month, November 1795, King Stanislaus Poniatowski, already in exile in Saint Petersburg, formally abdicated.

While conducting their business in Poland, Austria concluded an alliance with Great Britain and Russia. At the same time, Prussia was making peace with France, although not going so far as to conclude an alliance with them. Great Britain began planning an invasion of France, which occurred mostly using French émigré troops, in June 1795. The result, a French Republic victory, is discussed below. Russia's main contribution to the alliance was to recognize the Comte de Provence as Louis XVIII after the death of the Dauphin. The alliance sputtered to a halt in 1796 with the death of Catherine II and the victories in Italy of Bonaparte. The new lineup of enemies of France was still considered the First Coalition, said to last from 1793 to 1797.

Death of Catherine II: With its borders secure against Sweden, Poland, and the Ottomans, in April 1796, Russia launched an expedition into the Caucasus. They called it a punitive expedition as they claimed portions of the Caucasus as a protectorate, and the new Shah of Persia, Aga Mohammad Khan, had been challenging that claim. Catherine II put Valerian Zubov in command of a fifty-thousand-man Army that occupied the Caucasus, and by November, he was poised to invade Persia and topple the Shah and replace him with the Shah's more pliable brother. Unfortunately for Zubov, Catherine II died on November 16, 1796, and she was succeeded by Paul I, who was now forty-two years old. Paul I's nineteen-year-old son, Alexander, took no steps to prevent his father's accession. The Russian Army in the Caucasus was withdrawn, the first of many reversals of policy in store for Russia for the next five years. The aggressive Persian Shah was assassinated in 1797, which eliminated the threat to Russia on that front. Zubov and his brother would later lead the assassination of Paul I in 1801.

The cause of Catherine II's death at the age of sixty-seven was determined to be a stroke. Soon there were fantastic accounts in the French and British satirical press claiming she died from trying to have sex with her horse. The idea of bestiality among the eastern barbarians had been expressed for many years in western publications to show how uncivilized the Russians were. Catherine II ruled for thirty-four years and was one of the most successful monarchs in European history. The stories about how her court favorites were always her lovers should be taken with a grain of salt in my opinion, coming mostly from people she had defeated politically or militarily or had punished for some crime or deficiency. There may have been some truth to her being wild in her younger days, but during her reign, she behaved with dignity and wisdom.

France

French operations in France, Germany, and the Netherlands, 1795: Pichegru's Army of the North began an invasion of the Netherlands in January, crossing the frozen Waal River. On January 18, 1795, Pichegru captured Amsterdam, which, anticipating a French victory, had established a revolutionary committee that opened the city up to the French. Guided by Abbey Sieyes and Jean-Francois Rewbell, two future directors under the directorate, the revolutionary committee followed the process established by the Paris Communists in August 1792 and proclaimed the Batavian Republic, deposing Stadtholder William V. The Dutch Fleet was captured in port by Pichegru, intact, on January 24. Pichegru was summoned to Paris to be hailed as the savior of his country. He turned command of the Army of the North over to General Jean Moreau. Moreau oversaw the final operations in the conquest of the Batavian Republic. In May, France concluded a treaty of alliance with the Netherlands, which included a requirement for the Dutch to support a twenty-five-thousand-man French Army of occupation.

While Pichegru was in Paris, the *Sans Culottes* organized an uprising against the convention. Pichegru was called upon to suppress it, which he did, as described below. Pichegru was then given command of the Army of the Rhine and Moselle, which he led from March 1795 to March 1796.

THE GREAT GLOBE ITSELF

The Prussians had pulled the plug on the war in Flanders and the Netherlands, and they were back in Prussia (and Poland) by the end of 1794. Prussia and Spain began negotiating with France in Basel, Switzerland. The Prussians made peace with France in April 1795, while the Spanish did the same in July 1795. The Portuguese forces that were embedded with the Spanish Army were sent home. Although Portugal technically remained at war with France, they had no means to come to grips with the enemy. Austria remained the only power facing France on the continent, aided by Piedmont-Sardinia and a few minor German and Italian states. Catherine had been negotiating to join the alliance, and if she had not died this year, a Russian force, probably under Suvorov, would have been on the way.

The Austrians, with the exception of the garrison in Luxembourg, had all moved east of the Rhine, so the troops that Pichegru, and then Moreau, faced in the Netherlands were British, Dutch, and Hanoverian, who were hopelessly outnumbered. Soon the Dutch began worrying about their homes and families, while the Hanoverians began to forget that George III was their sovereign. The British troops, for their part, were most interested now in getting to Bremen so they could get on ships home themselves. British historians do their best to spin these operations as a fighting retreat, but it wasn't really. The British force embarked at Bremen in April 1795. Hanover declared itself neutral and sought the protection of Prussia to enforce that neutrality, which was fine by France, having signed a peace agreement with Prussia in April.

The Duke of York was widely ridiculed for his failure in the Flanders campaign, an unfair criticism, as he had performed his duties to the best of his ability given the resources available. He would keep his job as commander in chief of the British Army for many years, but because of Flanders, he gets a mention in a British nursery rhyme, which goes:

> The grand old Duke of York, he had ten thousand men,
> He marched them up to the top of the hill and he marched them down again,

And when they were up, they were up. And
when they were down, they were down,
And when they were only halfway up, they
were neither up nor down.

Stadtholder William V fled to London, where the first thing
he did was send out letters to all the Dutch colonies, telling them
to surrender to the British. Having done so, he was ignored by the
British until 1799, when there was a British-Russian invasion that
was repelled after a few months. As compensation for the loss of the
Netherlands, his son was given a few territories in Germany during
the mediatization process in 1802. After France's defeat in 1815,
the son was returned to the throne in the Netherlands as king, not
stadtholder.

Luxembourg had been under siege since November 1794.
Capturing the fortress was a precondition to French offensive operations on the east side of the Rhine. Luxembourg had plenty of
ordnance but ran out of food in June 1795 and surrendered. The
Austrians were allowed to leave the fortress with honors. France
dubbed Luxembourg the Gibraltar of the North, stealing that nickname from Fort Ticonderoga. Now only Mainz remained on the
west side of the Rhine, but the area was defended by Austrian Armies
under the command of Wurmser and Clerfayt. Jourdan and Pichegru
prepared to kick the Austrians out of Mainz. France had completed
the conquest of Belgium, the Netherlands, and all of the land west
of the Rhine. It was a great achievement, and the people of France
expressed great joy and satisfaction. There were those in France who
began advocating for peace and the restoration of the king. Others
were opposed, and conflicts occurred.

Meanwhile in northwest France, in February 1795, the French
government finalized an agreement with the Vendeans, guaranteeing
them their property and freedom of worship. In return, they recognized the sovereignty of the French Republic. Hoche was given the
credit for this, as he had instituted policies favorable to the Vendeans.
Hoche was a diligent officer and prepared the area for a British invasion, which was not long in coming.

There were some die-hard counterrevolutionaries in northwest France, known as Chouans, who were begging the British to invade. On June 27, 1795, a Royal Navy squadron appeared at Quiberon Bay, which, as we recall, was the site of a decisive naval battle in 1759 during the Seven Years' War. An Army of about ten thousand émigrés and British troops disembarked, joined forces with the Chouans, and moved inland. They brought enough war material to equip an Army of forty thousand men, but before they could do any recruiting, General Hoche engaged this force, defeating it decisively on July 21. Soon, 750 prisoners (many were former French naval officers in English uniforms) were shot, and a thousand more were held in prison, where they didn't last long. The rest were released. Hoche was now the big thing in Paris. Pichegru, remembering when he had accused Hoche and put him within days of the guillotine, was now worried about his future and decided that he could secure his safety—not to mention fame, fortune, and power—if he arranged a restoration of the monarchy.

Louis XVII died on June 10, 1795, and his uncle was proclaimed Louis XVIII by the émigrés. In August 1795, Pichegru, commanding the Army of the Rhine and Moselle, contacted the émigré forces to discuss restoring the monarchy. In September 1795, Jourdan and Pichegru began a campaign of sorts against the Austrians. One of the objectives was to force the surrender of Mainz, which General Kleber had been blockading with little success since December 1794. Jourdan crossed the Rhine near Dusseldorf and moved south toward Mainz. Two Austrian Armies under Clerfayt and Wurmser moved to meet him. Pichegru crossed the Rhine south of Mainz, near Mannheim, but then stalled. Jourdan wanted to combine their forces, advance between the two Austrian Armies, and defeat them in turn, but Pichegru had other ideas, so all they could do was send to Carnot in Paris for instructions. Jourdan began a siege of the east side of Mainz, while Pichegru remained inactive around Mannheim. Rumors of his betrayal of the revolution soon made the rounds.

In October 1795, Austrian maneuvering around Mainz forced Jourdan to retreat north toward Dusseldorf. He was strung out between Mainz and his crossing site two hundred miles north. Mainz still remained under siege on the west side of the Rhine by Kleber's forces, but now it could be resupplied more easily. The Austrians reinforced the city and launched a sortie on October 29, 1795, defeating the French in the Battle of Mainz. In November, the Austrians retook Mannheim. The Armies then called a truce for the winter. For the next three months, charges of conspiracy, some of them from Jourdan, were directed Pichegru's way, and Pichegru offered to resign, which, to his surprise, was accepted. Moreau took command of the Army of the Rhine and Moselle in March 1796, turning the Army of the North over to General Pierre de Ruel. Jourdan retained command of Sambre and Meuse. Pichegru was not arrested or tried, probably because he could have named the names of his cohorts in Paris. He soon went into politics, as he was now committed to the restoration of the monarchy as his destiny.

Spain and France renew their alliance, 1795–1796: In February 1795, the last action of the War of the Pyrenees took place as the Spanish garrison at Roses surrendered to General Perignon. Although the Spanish sued for peace, the convention relieved Perignon anyway for failing to get at the enemy forces south of Roses. He returned to politics and diplomacy. Napoleon made him a marshal in 1804, and he served in Parma and Naples. In Naples, he became Murat's chief of staff.

Spain ended all their conflicts in 1795, negotiating the Basel treaty with France in July and the Pinckney treaty with the US in October. Spanish prime minister Godoy earned the title of Prince of Peace for his achievements. In August 1796, Spain signed a defensive alliance with France, the Second Treaty of San Ildefonso, and declared war on Great Britain. This alliance led to momentous events in American history, including the Quasi-War and the Louisiana Purchase. The alliance between Spain and Great Britain had not been a good one. Relations between Spain and Great Britain had been generally hostile since the days of the Spanish Armada in the 1500s. In 1779–1783, there had been an epic Spanish siege of Gibraltar, while at the same time, the Spanish were seizing West Florida from the British. The recent Spanish-English operation in Toulon, foiled by Bonaparte, had resulted in mutual recriminations and distrust.

From the standpoint of Spanish-Portuguese relations, Portugal was always the ally of Great Britain, and Spain was always the ally of France, although Spain and Portugal rarely went to war against each other. France and Spain had been on the same side in just about every major European conflict since the War of the Spanish Succession. The American Revolution had shown that combined French-Spanish naval operations could be effective against the Royal Navy. Even so, Spain frequently chafed under the arrangement and was constantly reminded that they were the junior partners in this scheme. They stuck with it because the alternatives had been tried and were worse.

When Spain declared war on Great Britain in August 1796, the British panicked, as they were worried about the Spanish Fleet blocking Gibraltar, and evacuated their bases in Corsica and Elba to Portugal. The British presence in the Mediterranean vanished overnight. The British had struggled in Corsica. After declaring Corsica to be a kingdom under the rule of George III in 1794, giving it the same status as Ireland, the Corsicans had been rebelling ever since, aided by France. Hopefully, when the British cut and ran from Corsica, they took their supporters with them. Anyway, Great Britain never got another chance with Corsica, and when they returned to the Mediterranean in 1798, they elected to reestablish Minorca as a base instead of Corsica. By then, the Corsicans were so proud of Bonaparte that their allegiance to France became assured.

Spain and the United States were on good terms at this time. The Pinckney Treaty between Spain and the United States had just been publicly proclaimed two weeks before. France would put pressure on Spain over the next couple of years to distance itself from the United States. Spain had the power to hurt the United States a lot, because all the farm and factory products from the west had to get to market by floating down to New Orleans. The causes of the Quasi-War began to foment. General Moncey, a future marshal of France, was the French ambassador to Spain that negotiated the treaty of 1796.

The Constitution of 1795: At the beginning of the year in Paris, the first sightings of exotic, pleasure-loving youth cavorting about the streets of Paris were reported in the sources. The offspring of

PETER HARDY

the bourgeoisie, the *Jeunesse Doree* (gilded youth), spent money, and dressed provocatively. The men were called *Encroyables,* and the women were called *Marvelouses.* Thanks to Theresa Tallien, it now became a fashion for women to use see-through material in their dresses. The men began wearing top hats, which were provocative for some reason. Top hats came out at the same time that soldiers started wearing shakos. The men were organized into militia units that terrorized the Jacobins, even shutting down clubs. These units were called *Muscadins* because of their perfumed smell. The name had first been applied pejoratively to similar groups that had defended Lyon when they had rebelled against Paris in 1793. They carried canes that they used as weapons and called them "constitutions."

Tallien's husband, who had earned his stripes as a revolutionary knee-deep in blood in August and September of 1792, was riding the wave of reaction and profiting greatly by it. High society in Paris was at a stage where it believed in nothing. The only thing in the country that seemed to be working was the armed forces.

In March 1795, in what was to become known as the riots of 12 Germinal, Paris once again broke out in *journee* over the price of bread. The winter had been harsh, and food prices had doubled since January. The slogan of the rioters was "Bread and the Constitution of 1793!" The Thermidorian government held the Montagnards responsible for the riots, and by April 1, many of the remaining Montagnard leaders, including former Committee of Public Safety members Barere, Billaud-Varenne, and Collot, had been arrested and transported to Cayenne. As stated above, Pichegru was in town being honored for his conquest of the Netherlands, and he was tasked with suppressing the riots, which he did. He may have been approached by royalists now, although he didn't show any signs of having signed on until August 1795, when he was leading the Army of Rhine and Moselle, as described above, after his rival Hoche had defeated the British invasion at Quiberon, also as described above.

In April 1795, the convention passed the Law of 18 Germinal, establishing the metric system, with standards for the meter, the are (area of 100 m^2), the stere (1 m^3 of stacked wood), the liter (1/1000 of an m^3 of water), and the gram (1/1000 of the weight of a liter of

THE GREAT GLOBE ITSELF

water). The word *gram* comes from mille-grave [gra(m)]. A grave was the weight of a liter of water, 2.2 pounds, but it fell out of use because it was also a noble title (as in margrave), so it was replaced with kilogram. A meter was one ten-millionth of the distance at sea level from the equator to the North Pole through Paris. The metric system would be officially adopted on December 10, 1799, one of Napoleon's first acts as first consul. The US doesn't use the system, but US Army soldiers, to this day, have to know the metric system for distances in order to navigate on a map or call artillery in on a target. When I was in the service, we called a kilometer a click but didn't know why. It turns out that click was first used in World War II and was related to the operation of dials on military machinery, possibly mortars or jeeps. The dials are gone, but the term remains.

Another important scientific/technical event occurred in May 1795 when Georges Cuvier arrived in Paris to work at a natural history museum. Cuvier was the father of vertebrate paleontology and was the first to demonstrate that mass extinctions among animals had occurred. He developed the geological column, establishing the relative time periods that species suddenly appeared, thrived, and then suddenly disappeared. His work remains unchallenged to this day.

On May 7, 1795, Antoine-Quentin Fouquier-Tinville was guillotined after a forty-one-day trial. He had been the prosecutor for many people guillotined during the Terror, starting with Charlotte Corday and climaxing with Hebert and Danton. He was one of the most sinister figures of the Terror, giving the appearance of legal form to political murders. He had turned on Robespierre and the others and survived Thermidor for a couple of days but was soon arrested. His trial had been delayed until March 1795. His defense was that he had followed the orders of the CPS, words to inspire a generation of Nazis. At the end of the day there was a pile of headless corpses, as he was decapitated along with fifteen of his accomplices from the Revolutionary Tribunal.

On May 20, 1795, 1 Prairial an III, the final Montagnard uprising, known as the *journee* of 1 Prairial, occurred in Paris. A general named Jacques Francois Menou commanded the force that quelled this last gasp effort of the radicals. The Montagnard leaders were all arrested and either were executed or managed to kill themselves. Of the twelve CPS members who had overseen the reign of Terror, four had already been guillotined, and three had been sent to Cayenne, already known as the "dry guillotine." The convention ordered the arrest of the remaining five, including even Carnot. Three were arrested, and two went into hiding, although they were all soon amnestied or released. They weren't the only ones arrested, as Menou went into the working class neighborhoods and arrested thousands. A new command under Menou, the Army of the Interior, was created in July 1795 to keep Paris under control. This is the last time we will refer to the radicals as Montagnards, a faction which can be said to now be extinct. Radicals in the future will be referred to as Jacobins.

As stated above, Louis XVII died on June 8, 1795, of tuberculosis. To me, his death seems suspicious, given the planning that was going on among the exiles. Someone in the French government who was part of the plot arranging a restoration may have assassinated him or at least exposed him to disease. Given that he had been brainwashed for the last three years, he might not have been fit to rule as king anymore. There would eventually be over a hundred men claiming to be him over the years. One of the characters in Huckleberry Finn claimed to be the "Dolphin," swindling people along the Mississippi River in the 1840s. His sister Marie-Therese was finally released on December 18, 1795 (her seventeenth birthday), and was sent to Vienna. For a time, she was a pawn in the dynastic marriage game, including talk of her marrying the Austrian general Archduke Charles and making him the monarch of France with the title of grand elector. She eventually married her cousin, the son of the Comte de Artois, later Charles X. She would have become queen of France if Charles X had not been deposed in 1830. She never had children. Maybe her husband needed as much instruction in the act of reproduction as her father had.

Upon receiving word of Louis XVII's death, the Comte de Provence named himself Louis XVIII and issued the Declaration of Verona, declaring that when he was restored, he would restore the monarchy as it had been before 1789, which must have been

THE GREAT GLOBE ITSELF

quite amusing to the French Republicans. But the tone and words of Verona were understandable; appeasement was what had cost Louis XVI his head. The Bourbons had more than just a declaration. Even though it didn't work out, they had a fairly well-coordinated plan, including British-supported landings in the west and contact with the number one general in the east, Pichegru.

In June, in response to the Paris riots in March and May, the convention introduced the proposed Constitution of the Year III. It was a conservative document written in the spirit of the times, intended to correct radicalism. The convention debated it for the next two months. It established a bicameral legislature with the upper body known as the Council of Ancients and the lower body known as the Council of Five Hundred. The unicameral bodies that had governed France since 1789 had passed laws in fits of passion, and it was intended to slow down the legislative process.

All taxpaying French males over twenty-five were eligible to vote in primary elections, as long as they had been residents in their district for at least a year. The residency requirement was aimed at the *Sans Culottes,* who, by the nature of their work, found it difficult to maintain the same residence over a long period of time. There were about five million men who qualified to vote. They selected thirty thousand electors who were over thirty and had income equivalent to 150 days' taxes, and these in turn voted for the Council of Five Hundred. I'm not sure how the Council of Ancients was appointed. Possibly three men were appointed from each department. An ancient had to be at least forty years old. The ancients appointed the five members of the Directory from a list developed by the Council of Five Hundred.

The Directory constituted the executive branch. The central government retained great power, including emergency powers to curb freedom of the press and freedom of association. A new preamble, the Declaration of Rights and Duties of Mankind, included an explicit ban on slavery: "Every man can contract his time and his services, but he cannot sell himself nor be sold; his person is not an alienable property."

On July 14, in honor of the sixth anniversary of Bastille Day, the convention adopted "The Marseillaise" as the French national anthem, lasting until Bonaparte revoked it in 1799, picking another song, "Strive for the Well Being of the Empire," and it would fade away until 1848, when it became an international song of working class revolution. The Third Republic adopted it for good in 1879.

On August 22, 1795, the Constitution of the Year III was ratified by the convention, establishing the Directory and remaining in effect until November 1799. At the same time, the convention decreed that two-thirds of the members of the convention would serve either as ancients or as members of the five hundred. They were worried that new representatives might be too eager to move toward restoration of the monarchy, and they were right to be worried. On September 23, both the new constitution and the two-thirds rule were approved after a September plebiscite. The royalists were outraged at the rigging of the system and commenced a march on Paris.

14 Vendemiaire: In late 1794 or early 1795, Bonaparte had been ordered to depart his artillery command in Italy and take command of an infantry unit in the Vendee. He had time to fall in love with the sister of his brother Joseph's wife, a woman named Desiree Clary, to whom he became engaged in April 1795. He didn't want to take the command in the Vendee, viewing it as a demotion and was posted temporarily in the Topographic Bureau in Paris, the office overseeing the production of military maps. He volunteered to go to Constantinople to help the sultan's artillery, but he was annoying the powers that be, who were in the process of removing his name from the list of generals. My theory is that he was distracted by what was happening in Corsica at the time, which, as we recall, had just been proclaimed by the British as a kingdom under the rule of George III.

In response to the march of the royalists on Paris, the convention ordered General Menou to crush them as he had crushed the Montagnards, but Menou's response was weak. Suspecting his loyalties, the convention fired Menou and replaced him with Barras, who hadn't been in uniform for twenty-five years (in Corsica when the French invaded it). Barras remembered Bonaparte from their days in Toulon and made him his number two. Bonaparte ordered his sub-

THE GREAT GLOBE ITSELF

ordinate and future brother-in-law, Joachim Murat, to get some of Menou's cannon and set it up in areas of Paris selected by Bonaparte. Menou was helpful enough in the process that Bonaparte never ceased to employ him after that.

On October 5, 1795, 14 Vendemiaire an III, a two-hour engagement between Bonaparte's force and the royalists resulted in three hundred corpses and the end of the royalist uprising. Thomas Carlyle later wrote that Bonaparte dispersed them with "a whiff of grapeshot." The royalists weren't finished, though, as the activities of Pichegru over the next several months would show. It was also at this time that Paris was reorganized into twelve *arrondissements* that we know today. The joke at the time was that nonmarried couples who were living in sin were said to have been married at the town hall of the thirteenth *arrondissement*. When the city annexed the area inside the Thiers wall in 1859, eight more *arrondissements* were formed. Since they happened at the same time, I wouldn't be surprised to find that the new civic organization was Bonaparte's idea since he was mathematically inclined and knew maps, but I haven't read anywhere whose idea it actually was.

Bonaparte was promoted to major general and given command of the Army of the Interior. Barras introduced his mistress, Rose Josephine de Beauharnais, to Bonaparte. Rose was having to use a stick to keep the generals away, as she had also been seeing Hoche since he had gained fame in July. Maybe Hoche's tuberculosis was in evidence by now. Bonaparte soon forgot about his engagement to Desiree Clary, although he didn't break it off until just before his wedding to Josephine, in March 1796. It was (and still is) widely believed among the people of France that Bonaparte's fortune started the day he met her and ended the day he divorced her. The marriage was a civil ceremony. When Pope Pius VI I came to Paris in December 1804 to crown them, one of his conditions was that he had to perform a marriage ceremony for them beforehand so that they would be married in the church. The couple agreed.

Bonaparte's jilted fiancée, Desiree Clary, later married Jean Bernadotte, who became a marshal of France and then king of Sweden, which made Desiree queen. Their son Oscar, also future king of Sweden, was born in 1799. She enjoyed living in Paris and rarely moved to visit her husband during his long absences. She even remained in Paris during the period when her husband was leading Sweden as part of the Sixth Coalition against France in 1813. She finally moved to Sweden in 1823, five years after her husband became king.

During the six months that he commanded the Army of the Interior, which was responsible for security in the Paris region, Bonaparte would often take security measures without consulting the Directory or the minister of war. The minister of war happened to be the former deputy of Hoche, a man named Jean Baptiste du Bayet, and he may have been put there for the purpose of keeping Bonaparte in check. Bayet didn't like being ignored or bypassed by Bonaparte and would bring him before the Directors to accuse him, at which point Bonaparte would explain everything he was doing and why he hadn't waited for permission, and his arguments were unassailable. Bayet was sent to Constantinople in February 1796 as the minister, spending his time equipping and training the Ottoman artillery. As we recall, Bonaparte had volunteered for that assignment and had been refused. Bayet died of a fever there in December 1797, aged thirty-eight. He was not replaced because of the impending French invasion of Egypt. When peace was made in 1802, General Brune was sent to Constantinople and continued to help improve the Ottoman artillery.

Even now, Bonaparte had a lot of irons in the fire, and his second scheme after Constantinople was to ask for the command of the Army of Italy, presenting to the directors the plan he had been working on since commanding the artillery there in 1794. This was approved, and so a month after Bayet left Paris, Bonaparte married Josephine and departed for Italy, having secured what funds and troops the Directory had to spare. He was replaced as commander of the Army of the Interior by a General Hatry, whose task it was to decommission that force and send it elsewhere, which he accomplished in August 1796, by which time Bonaparte was famous. The duties of the Army of the Interior were taken over in Paris and even-

THE GREAT GLOBE ITSELF

tually the rest of the country by the Ministry of Police, which had been formed in January 1796.

The Directory, 1795: The Directory went into effect in November 1795. It superseded the very democratic Constitution of 1793, which had never been put into effect. It goes without saying that all five directors were regicides. The directors were:

Seat A:

Etienne-Francois Le Tourneur (November 1795– May 1797) gained attention during the siege of Toulon and, subsequent to that, was involved with the reorganization of the Toulon Fleet. He admired and followed Carnot. He stepped down from the Directory in May 1797 and was replaced by Barthelemy, a man of like-minded viewpoint, as part of the normal rotation specified in the Year III Constitution.

Francois-Marie, Marquis de Barthelemy (May 1797–September 1797) was part of the team that negotiated the Prussian and Spanish Peace Treaties in 1795 in Basel, Switzerland. He took Le Tourneur 's place and conspired with Carnot and Pichegru for a Bourbon restoration and, with Carnot, was deposed from office on September 4, 1797, and replaced by Neufchateau. He was transported to Cayenne, escaped, and in 1800, Bonaparte made him a senator.

Francois de Neufchateau (September 1797– May 1798) was known for inaugurating the canal system in France. Well, canals had been around for a while; he systemized it at the national level. He also turned the Louvre into a museum, and it opened as such on August 10, 1793, exactly one year after the fall of the monarchy. He served for eight months until May 1798. He became a senator in 1800 and a member of the French Academy in 1803.

Jean-Baptiste Treilhard (May 1798–June 1799) replaced Neufchateau. He would have a major role in drafting the Napoleonic Code, but his deeds in the Directory were few, as he was swept out with Merlin and Revelliere-Lepaux in June 1799.

Seat B:

Lazare Nicolas Marguerite Carnot (November 1795–September 1797), the Organizer of Victory, served on the CPS from August 1793 and oversaw the establishment of the greatly expanded French Revolutionary Armies. He had been arrested after the May 1795 riots but was soon amnestied. He got along with everyone but Jourdan. Unfortunately, Jourdan had to execute Carnot's 1796 campaign plan. On September 4, 1797, it was Carnot and Barthelemy versus the rest of the directors when Augereau was sent by Bonaparte to help the other directors crush the royalists. Because of who he was, he was allowed to escape to Switzerland, where he wrote a treatise on calculus. In 1800, Bonaparte made him war minister, but Carnot resigned after Berthier returned from Italy and took up the war ministry again. His two sons Sadi and Hippolyte were both distinguished in their fields and his grandson Sadi (the son of Hippolyte) was president of France, 1887–1894, until an anarchist assassinated him.

Philippe-Antoine Merlin (September 1797–June 1799) replaced Carnot in September 1797. He had been minister of police at the start of the Directory and knew who all the royalist sympathizers were. He was one of three directors who resigned in June 1799. He held minor positions of honor during the empire.

Seat C:

Jean-Francois Rewbell (November 1795–May 1799) was best known for having opposed the September 1791 law granting Jews equality. He was the force behind the Directory's aggressive military policies, especially in 1798, but was blamed for the defeats in 1799 and was turned out of office in the regular course of the elections of May 1799, just before the storm hit in June 1799.

Abbey Sieyes (May 1799–November 1799) was well known from the days of 1789 and was greeted as another savior of his country, having lain low since the early days. He plotted the overthrow of the Directory but was unable to control Bonaparte after the coup of November 1799.

Seat D:

Louis Marie de La Revelliere-Lepeaux (November 1795–June 1799) had been a Girondist and so had hidden from June 1793 until Thermidor. He was the author of the December 1792 Edict of Fraternity that offered French support to the oppressed of all nations and authorized French troops to loot in foreign countries. For some reason, he despised his fellow director Carnot. He desired to use his power to advance a new religious sect, the Theophilanthropists. He was ousted in June 1799 along with Trilhard and Merlin, after which, he took no further part in public affairs.

Seat E:

Paul Francois Jean Nicolas, Vicomte de Barras (November 1795–November 1799) was the only director to serve all the way through the period of the Directory. He was shameless in his display of sexual and financial corruption to the point where even Paris disapproved. He encouraged the relationship between Rose De Beauharnais and Bonaparte because she had been too demanding of a mistress. Rose may have pleaded for leniency for Barras when the end of the Directory came in 1799.

There were three other short-termed directors from June to November 1799 named Moulin, Gohier, and Ducos.

The decline of Tallien: Jean-Lambert Tallien had done much to end the Terror and had been the toast of Paris since July 1794, but his ride was ending. He had been the idol of the top-hat wearing gilded youth and the husband of Theresa Tallien, the queen of the Paris salons, "Our Lady of Thermidor." He and his wife were now in 1795 deemed frivolous, and he was not named to the Directory. He soon lost influence within the Council of Five Hundred, where he still had a seat. Bonaparte took him to Egypt with him in 1798, where he edited Bonaparte's journal, which means he may have been the originator of the Army bulletins that Bonaparte used to such effect over the years. He was captured by the British while trying to get back to France and was released by them in 1802. Theresa divorced him that year, and he floundered for a few years until Fouche and Talleyrand got him a sinecure as the French consul in Alicante, Portugal. He went blind in one eye after getting yellow fever, was medically retired on half pay, and ended his days as a charity case of Louis XVIII, which was unexpected given his deeds in August and September of 1792. He died in 1820 at the age of fifty-three. I would not be surprised to find that he had a drinking problem.

Gracchus Bebeuf and the Conspiracy of the Equals, 1795–1796: One of the first actions of the Directory was to issue a new currency

THE GREAT GLOBE ITSELF

called the *mandat* to replace the *assignat*. Initially, 800 million francs in *mandats* were issued to replace 24 billion francs in assignats, a 30:1 ratio. Within a year, the *mandat* was worth nothing, as the nation had no faith in this scheme. The resulting economic chaos spelled trouble for the Directory and strengthened the royalist faction. Practically the only income the government got in 1796 was from Bonaparte's Italian campaign.

Another thing that the Directory did at the start was to separate the police into a separate ministry, established in January 1796. The resources to stand up this ministry were taken from the Army of the Interior, still commanded by Bonaparte at this time, so we can give him some credit as one of the primary founders of the French Police State. Its primary function was to establish a centralized national database of criminals and offenders, but of course, it was soon seized upon by the politicians to develop dossiers on rivals. To its credit, it was able to detect conspiracies as they hatched and kept the peace. As the position had the potential to make the office holder as powerful as a Praetorian prefect or an FBI director, the turnover was high until Joseph Fouche was appointed to the office in June 1799. He *did* become as powerful as a Praetorian prefect or an FBI director, and even Bonaparte was afraid of him.

Francois Noel Babeuf had been active in Jacobin journalism since after 9 Thermidor and had been jailed twice, in October 1794 and February 1795. Since then, he had gone underground, awaiting his opportunity. He called himself "Gracchus" Babeuf in honor of the land-reforming brothers who ignited the Roman Revolution in the second century BC. When the Directory announced the end of the system of subsidized bread and meat in Paris in February 1796, it caused a huge outcry, and the plan was canceled. Gracchus and his fellow conspirators saw their opportunity. They had delusions that they constituted a "secret Directory" that could depose the directors and take over the government. In what became known as the Conspiracy of the Equals, they issued a manifesto and hung posters around Paris with pithy slogans such as "Nature has given to every man the right to enjoyment of an equal share in all property," "Let all the arts perish, if need be, as long as real equality remains!" praised the massacres of September 1792, saying "a more complete September" was needed, and called for the restoration of the Constitution of 1793, which, as we know, had never been enforced due to the war and had now been superseded anyway.

By May 1796, with Bonaparte gone to Italy, the directors began worrying that some police and Army units in Paris might be getting infected by Gracchus's propaganda. They decided that the new Ministry of Police was ready to deal with the situation. Led by Carnot, they acted, and that month, hundreds were arrested and held for trial. Riots were conducted in attempts to gain freedom for the suspects, but the directors held firm. One of those arrested was Jean Baptiste Drouet, the postmaster who had spotted and detained Louis XVI in Varennes when he had attempted to escape in 1791. To sidestep the potential for riots, trials were held outside of Paris and did not start until February 1797, probably after more purges of Jacobins had been undertaken in Paris. Babeuf and one other man, Augustin Darthe, were sentenced to death, with some sentenced to transport to Cayenne and others acquitted.

The day after his conviction, Gracchus Babeuf was guillotined. It was the last public execution in Paris until 1804. The execution of Gracchus marks the end of the Thermidor Reaction, and the pendulum started swinging to the left again. One of Babeuf's statements was, "Society must be made to operate in such a way that it eradicates once and for all the desire of a man to become richer, or wiser, or more powerful than others." I can think of at least two things wrong with that. Here's another: "The French Revolution was nothing but a precursor of another revolution, one that will be bigger, more solemn, and which will be the last." His doctrine would have its followers over the years and became the seed of the ideology of communism starting in the 1830s. Karl Marx and Friedrich Engels called the Conspiracy of the Equals "the first appearance of a truly active Communist party." The 1830s were years of dissatisfaction in Europe that spawned movements that were variously messianic, revolutionary, or utopian.

The return of Talleyrand, 1796: Talleyrand, as we recall, had escaped France in September 1792 during the Paris massacres. He had been a Feuillant who had supported the Bourbons in a constitutional monarchy and, in his heart, remained so, although he thrived under all the regimes for the next twenty years. He had lived in Great Britain until March 1794, when France and Great Britain went to war. He then moved to New York, where he was Aaron Burr 's houseguest for a time. Burr was then a United States senator. He was also a friend of Hamilton's. With friends like those, it is no wonder that he got along so well with Bonaparte, as all three had despotic temperaments. In New York, Talleyrand was in the banking business. Since Thermidor, he had been petitioning the convention, and then the Directory, to remove his name from the list of banished émigrés. He had many influential friends in France, including Germaine de Staël, and they arranged his return to France in September 1796.

He would soon gain a position in the government, but for now, he renewed his friendships and acquaintances in Paris. The Directory and Paris society remembered the man who had saved the revolution in 1789 by nationalizing the church and thought he might be able to once again be of service. He was, using what he had learned in the US by giving information and insight to the government in how to deal with the increasingly hostile US in the wake of the Jay Treaty.

French military plans, 1796: Since the resignation of Pichegru in March 1796, the Army of the Rhine and Moselle had been commanded by Jean Moreau, who had played an important role in the Battle of Tourcoing in May 1794. Jourdan had been commanding Sambre and Meuse since June 1794, and he had won two important battles: Wattignies in October 1793 and Fleurus in June 1794. Now Bonaparte was the new commander of the Army of Italy. These three men—Bonaparte, Moreau, and Jourdan—all had the aura of victory around them, standing in more or less equal stead in the eyes of the public. Director Carnot, no friend of General Jourdan, was still in charge of the war in the Directory and drew up the 1796 campaign plan against Austria and their allies. It was expected that all three generals would advance against the enemy, link up in the Tyrol, and end the war by dictating terms in Vienna. Jourdan was the most prestigious of the three, but in hindsight, he had peaked and could be said to be suffering from burnout. He should have been able to give Moreau orders, but he was not. Perhaps Carnot retained some resentments from Wattignies. Carnot should have either taken the field himself or given Jourdan supreme command over all the forces in Germany.

Operations in Ireland, 1796: Not to be left out of the equation at this time was Hoche, who had pacified the Vendee revolt in Brittany and thrown back an émigré invasion at Quiberon. In December 1795, all the northern and western coastal Armies had been combined into one Army, which was placed under Hoche's command. Despite the settlements made in the Vendee in 1795, there were still rebel forces out there that Hoche ran to ground by June 1796. The Directory then ordered him to invade Ireland, teaming him up with an admiral named Justin Morard de Galles and an Irish revolutionary named Wolfe Tone. Tone was a former Dublin lawyer who had gotten involved in radical politics and was exiled to Philadelphia in 1795. The US had just signed the Jay Treaty, and they were in no mood to support any anti-British operations, so he went to Paris in February 1796 and convinced Foreign Minister Delacroix and Director Carnot that twenty thousand Irishmen, an organization known as the United Irishmen because they had Protestants and Catholics as members, were ready to rise up and drive the British out of Ireland, which was true.

The plan was for fifteen thousand French troops to land in Bantry Bay in the southwest corner of Ireland with weapons and supplies for the twenty thousand United Irishmen, who would converge on Cork after the French established a base. The combined force would then overthrow the Irish government and proclaim a republic. Future marshal Emmanuel Grouchy was a member of the French force. The British were so worried about it that they sent an assassin after Hoche in Rennes in October, who got off a shot but missed. On December 15, 1795, the French Fleet sailed from Brest into some of the worst weather in years. The Royal Navy retired to their ports and let nature go to work. The French ships were scattered, and although some made it to Bantry Bay, none landed any men or material. By January 13, 1796, all the surviving ships had made it back to Brest, with the loss of twelve ships and two thousand sailors and Marines.

THE GREAT GLOBE ITSELF

Hoche was not blamed for the disaster and was given command of the Sambre and Meuse in February 1797. Wolfe Tone said that the British had had their luckiest escape since the days of the Spanish Armada two centuries before.

Archduke Charles of Austria, 1796: By June 1796, Bonaparte had been fighting in Italy for two months, as described below, but the French Armies in Germany were only now ready to move. The Army of the Sambre and Meuse, commanded by Jourdan, with future marshals Francois Lefebvre and Jean Bernadotte commanding divisions, was ready near Koblenz. A force in Dusseldorf under General Kleber protected Jourdan's left flank. Facing Jourdan was the Army of Austrian marshal Wilhelm Wartensleben. Further south, General Moreau commanded the Army of the Rhine and Moselle. Future marshal Laurent Saint Cyr commanded a division, as did General Louis Desaix, the man who, in 1800, would be killed in action while marching to the sound of the guns and saving Bonaparte at Marengo. General Moreau was facing the other Austrian Army led by Marshal Latour.

Archduke Charles had his headquarters collocated with Wartensleben and had overall command of both Austrian Armies. He was only twenty-five, younger than Bonaparte! As we recall, he was the son of Emperor Leopold II but had been adopted and raised in Belgium by his aunt Maria Christina and her husband, Prince Albert of Saxony. He had seen action at Jemappes, Neerwinden, and Fleurus. He had seen a lot of the Austrian lands, so he had a cosmopolitan outlook and wasn't really attached to Belgium, but he did want to avenge the loss of Belgium for the sake of his adoptive parents.

Charles proved to be a good commander, one of the best of the age and one of the few to defeat Bonaparte in battle. Charles knew that the two French Armies were operating independently, and his strategy was to maneuver such as to get them far apart enough from each other so that he could combine his forces against one Army or the other. Easy to say, hard to do.

At one point in 1799, Talleyrand and Sieyes drafted a scheme to wed Charles to Marie Therese, the daughter of Louis XVI and Marie

353

Antoinette, and make her queen and him prince consort of France, giving him the title of grand elector. That makes him a doppelgänger for the Duke of Orleans, who also had ambitions in both France and Belgium. If that had worked out, France and Austria would have avoided war, and then what would the history of Europe have looked like?

Operations in Germany, 1796: Jourdan's Sambre and Meuse crossed the Rhine near Bonn on June 4 and was met by Wartensleben, so his advance soon stalled. Moreau 's Rhine and Moselle crossed the Rhine near Strasbourg on June 24 and inflicted a defeat on Latour on July 9, at the Battle of Ettlingen. Latour retreated to Stuttgart. Jourdan was encouraged and moved forward to Frankfurt am Main, reaching it by the end of July. Moreau kept moving east and won another victory over Latour at Neresheim in Bavaria on August 11. Latour withdrew to the south bank of the Danube and was now far enough apart from Wartensleben that a gap formed between Jourdan's and Moreau 's Armies. It was the opportunity Charles had been looking for. Charles was able to lead his reserve force toward Jourdan's rear, which was unprotected. On August 24, he and Wartensleben inflicted a defeat on Jourdan at the Battle of Amberg. As expected, Moreau was too far from Amberg to come to Jourdan's defense and continued to march east. That same day, August 24, he defeated Latour at the Battle of Friedberg. Charles said that it didn't matter if Moreau made it all the way to Vienna once he had beaten Jourdan. On September 3, he did just that at the Battle of Wurzburg. Jourdan's Army fell back to its starting position near Bonn by mid-September. Jourdan resigned his command on September 23, turning it over to Pierre Ruel, who turned over command of the Army of the North to Jean Francois Dejean. Hoche returned from the failed Ireland expedition in January 1797 and took command of Sambre and Meuse in February 1797, as Ruel was better suited to diplomacy than field command. Jourdan left the Army and went into politics, joining the Council of Five Hundred.

Subsequent to the Battle of Wurzburg, Moreau conducted a fighting retreat back up the Danube Valley and was across the Rhine by the end of October. He was ordered to transfer troops to the Army

THE GREAT GLOBE ITSELF

of Italy, which, by now, was having a great deal of success, as described below. Moreau brought five thousand prisoners back with him, so his campaign was spun as a success. One of Moreau 's subordinates, General Francois Marceau, was killed in action leading the rear guard that was covering the Army's retreat over the Rhine. For some reason, a frieze sculpture of his funeral on September 20, 1796, was deemed a fitting subject for the *Arc de Triomphe*. Archduke Charles won an excellent reputation for his handling of the campaign and, today, is mentioned in the same breath with the likes of Bonaparte, Suvorov, Nelson, Blücher, and Wellington.

Victory over Piedmont, March to April 1796: Bonaparte's Army of Italy had been assigned a supporting role in the campaign of 1796, as it was decided in Paris that the main effort ought to be in Germany. On March 26, Bonaparte arrived at his new headquarters in Nice. He made a poor initial impression, showing everyone pictures of his wife. They all knew who she was: a Paris salon queen who would drag him down like Theresa Tallien had dragged her husband down. As a matter of fact, after Bonaparte left Paris, she had immediately started an affair with an officer named Hippolyte Charles. Bonaparte heard rumors when he returned from Italy in 1797, but she denied them. Later he got confirmation of the rumors and considered divorce, but by that time, he was about to become first consul. The people loved Josephine, so the affair ended, the two stayed married, and we hear nothing further of any infidelity on the part of Josephine Bonaparte. Her husband, on the other hand, would father children with three different women, possibly including the queen of Prussia, between 1805 and 1809.

In Italy, Bonaparte relieved General Barthelemy Scherer, who was not a bad commander but was a victim of Paris politics. He was almost old enough to be Bonaparte's father and said some regrettable things to him on the way out. Scherer went to Paris and was assigned as inspector general of the Army of the Interior, which, in those days, was transitioning resources to the new Ministry of Police. He was minister of war from July 1797 to February 1799 and, as such, approved the expedition to Egypt. In 1799, he commanded in Italy again but was defeated by Suvorov and ordered to turn over his command to Moreau. When Bonaparte took over the government at the end of 1799, Scherer was finished. He died in 1804, aged fifty-six.

Under Bonaparte's command for his first campaign were eleven of the twenty-six future Napoleonic marshals of France: Berthier, Murat, Brune, Lannes, Bessieres, Marmont, Suchet, Massena, Augereau, Victor, and Serurier. Augereau, Serurier, and Massena, all men older than him, commanded his three divisions. Berthier was chief of staff, the first of many such collaborations over the next eighteen years. Berthier's skill was absorbing the general intentions of Bonaparte and translating them into detailed orders. That starts with good maps, which is what Berthier had been doing for most of his career, as had his father before him, and where Bonaparte had just come from. Berthier had three brothers who served in the Army, two of who became generals.

Bonaparte issued a bulletin to his troops which read:

> Soldiers, you are naked, ill fed! The government owes you much; it can give you nothing. Your patience and the courage you display in the midst of these rocks are admirable; but they procure you no glory, no fame is reflected upon you. I seek to lead you into the most fertile plains in the world. Rich provinces, great cities will be in your power. There you will find honor, glory, and riches. Soldiers of Italy, will you be lacking in courage or constancy?

He then put on his general's hat, possibly put his hand inside his waistcoat, stated there would be an inspection tomorrow, and the day after that, he would attack the enemy.

On the other side of the line, there was an Austrian Army of thirty-two thousand men under the command of General Johann Peter Beaulieu, with a Piedmont Army of twenty-five thousand men under General Michelangelo Colli to his north. The two men were friends, but Beaulieu had been warned not to cooperate too closely with the unreliable Piedmontese. Bonaparte's attack consisted

THE GREAT GLOBE ITSELF

of him getting his Army between the two forces and pummeling the Piedmont Army while the Austrians were blocked from coming to their aid. After losing three battles in ten days, King Victor Amadeus III of Piedmont-Sardinia was informed by Bonaparte that Piedmont was about to become the Republic of Alba. To prevent such a catastrophe, the king left the war, even though two of his daughters were married to the counts Artois and Provence (a.k.a. Louis XVIII), and his oldest son and heir was married to their sister. He signed an armistice at Cherasco on April 28, 1796. He kept Piedmont, but Nice and Savoy became permanent parts of France. In 1802, France annexed Piedmont, but the king kept Sardinia, as it was under British control.

For the next two years, Piedmont was an open highway for French troops heading into Italy, but the king kept his capital in Turin. He died six months later at age seventy from apoplexy. He was succeeded by his son Charles Emmanuel IV, who was Stuart claimant to the British throne after the death of Cardinal York in 1807. In 1802, Bonaparte would pitch the idea of making him king of Great Britain, or at least Ireland, and Charles Emmanuel was convinced enough of its plausibility that he abdicated his throne and moved to Rome to live with Cardinal York. The War of the Third Coalition and the Battle of Trafalgar closed the door on that opportunity in 1805.

Speaking of Louis XVIII, he had been living in Italy, whence he had delivered the Declaration of Verona in 1795, but with the French Army now only 180 miles away in Turin, he had to depart for Blankenburg in Brunswick and then had to leave there for Latvia after Frederick William II died in 1797, as Frederick William III said he could not guarantee his safety.

Bonaparte's destiny: Turin had, and still has, a noted museum dedicated to ancient Egyptian artifacts. The museum had been established in 1753, thanks to the interest of King Charles Emmanuel III. It's possible that this museum played a part in inspiring Bonaparte with the idea of a campaign in Egypt. The famous Shroud of Turin had been in the city, in Saint John's Cathedral, since 1578. Its existence can be documented to the year 1357, when it was in Lirey,

357

north central France, southeast of Paris. Carbon dating of the shroud in 1988 yielded a manufacture date of the cloth of between AD 1260 and 1390. There are some Freemasons who speculate to this day that the shroud is imprinted with the image of the body of Jacques de Molay, last grand master of the Knights Templar, who was burned at the stake in 1314, by order of the king of France. The method of how the image was produced remains uncertain, as no one has been able to replicate the process. Glad to see there's still a little mystery left in the world.

Bonaparte in Turin, just as the campaign that made him famous was getting underway, is reminiscent of Alexander the Great at the oasis of Siwa in the Nile Delta at the dawn of his fame. Alexander went to Siwa early in his career, and it was there that the priests told him he was a god and invincible on the battlefield. Now Bonaparte, in a city with a museum of Egyptian artifacts and a miraculous shroud, was experiencing something similar. Did something in Turin tell him of his future fortune? What would Bonaparte have concluded from this juxtaposition of Christian and pagan memorabilia? Bonaparte may have dreamed he might be a new Alexander, so it's altogether fitting and proper that his career was ended by the emperor of Russia, whose name actually was Alexander.

One other point about Bonaparte's state of mind in April 1796 is that the British were still referring to the land of his birth as the Kingdom of Corsica, whose ruler was King George III of Great Britain. As we recall, the British had evacuated the Mediterranean, including Corsica, in the wake of the renewed Spanish-French alliance of August 1796. I think that all of Bonaparte's actions up to that point were geared toward the goal of eradicating the British presence in Corsica. When that goal was achieved by others through diplomacy, he must have, at first, felt that he had been cheated of his destiny but then concluded that he had a greater destiny, perhaps not to recreate the empire of Alexander but that of Augustus. That idea makes most of his actions over the next eighteen years make more sense. We will see him taking over the entire peninsula of Italy, then attacking Malta and Egypt, beating Austria and then making peace with them by slicing up the Republic of Venice (including the Ionian

Islands and the Dalmatian Coast), obsessing over the island of Sicily, and dethroning the king of Spain. These were all areas that were very important to Augustus in his time as emperor. That would make his conflicts with Great Britain and Russia nothing but obstacles to be overcome in his quest to recreating the Augustan realm.

Operations in Italy, May to December 1796: Reaction in Paris to Bonaparte's feat of driving Piedmont-Sardinia out of the war was one of pleasant surprise, that a man of whom nothing was expected had performed such a service, although he was criticized by the directors for having engaged in diplomacy with the Piedmont government. As far as we know, the government didn't send any political or diplomatic staff to oversee Bonaparte's engagements, but maybe they did. For now, he wasn't behaving much differently than his peers Jourdan, Moreau, and Hoche on that score.

The Directory in Paris duly noted Bonaparte's achievement and reinforced his Army to fifty thousand men, mostly from the Army of the Alps. Jourdan and Moreau hadn't even started across the Rhine yet. Bonaparte now turned his attention to the suddenly outnumbered Austrians under Beaulieu. On May 10, the same day that Gracchus Babeuf and his fellow communists were being arrested in Paris, the Army of Italy was victorious over the Austrians at Lodi. Beaulieu called for reinforcements and retreated to the fortress of Mantua. He prepared for a siege there and sent the main body to Trento, where, in June, they linked up with twenty-five thousand Austrian troops under Wurmser.

The French pulled up to Mantua on July 4. The siege would last until February 1797. In the meantime, the French occupied the city of Milan, with its magnificent cathedral. It was ceded by Austria in 1797 and was the capital of the Cisalpine Republic, then the Italian Republic, and finally the Kingdom of Italy as time

went on. On August 5, the French defeated a relieving force at the Battle of Castiglione. On September 5, they defeated a relieving force at the Battle of Bassano. For the next two months, the main Austrian effort was in Germany as Archduke Charles was beating up on Jourdan and Moreau. In October, with the French out of Germany, both sides began sending reinforcements to Italy.

On November 17, the Austrians sent a third relieving force to Mantua. They were defeated at the Battle of Arcola, with Bonaparte himself hoisting a battle flag and running across a bridge at the head of a unit. At the end of the year, the Austrians remained under siege, and a fourth relief force was being readied.

The Cape Colony, 1795–1796: As stated above, after Dutch stadtholder William V was deposed in January 1795, he wrote letters to all of the Dutch colonies, advising them to surrender to the British. In June 1795, a British squadron arrived at the Cape Colony, South Africa. The Dutch resisted, and the new republican government in Amsterdam sent a squadron to assist. The Dutch foundered as the qualified sailors were all pro-monarchy and generally pro-British. The Dutch lost seven warships before surrendering in September. A better use of the ships would have been to sail them to Brest and let Hoche use them for the invasion of Ireland. The British controlled the Cape Colony for seven years, returned it to the Dutch in 1802, and then took it over permanently in 1806. By the 1830s, the Dutch settlers there were fed up with British policies on race and language, and twelve thousand of them went on the Great Trek to the interior and founded Johannesburg and the Boer Republics. They were motivated by many of the same things that the American pioneers on the Oregon Trail were.

The Mediterranean, 1795–1796: After Spain and France sealed their alliance in August 1796, the Royal Navy had exited the Mediterranean in a panic. At the same time, the Army of Italy was occupying Piedmont (Turin) and Lombardy (Milan). As a result of being abandoned by the British, Ferdinand and Maria Carolina of Naples ended their war with France in October 1796. They had been at war with France since the days of Toulon in August 1793. They paid France an indemnity of eight million francs. Maria Carolina

THE GREAT GLOBE ITSELF

was Marie Antoinette 's sister and ran the country with the passive acceptance of her husband. They had the loyal assistance of Lord Acton, a British subject who had been serving the Neapolitan crown since 1778. He had previously served as Leopold II 's admiral when Leopold was Duke of Tuscany. Like the Emperor Claudius, Acton was married to his niece, his brother's daughter. This was considered incest in Great Britain but not in Naples, where it had the harmless-sounding name of avuncular marriage. They were the grandparents of the Lord Acton, who said that power corrupts, and absolute power corrupts absolutely.

In 1796, the British relocated their Mediterranean forces to Portugal and maintained their position in Gibraltar, which had proved to be impregnable during the epic four-year siege by Spain in 1779–1783. Tensions rose between Spain and Portugal, but that was normal for the region, and the two countries stayed at peace.

British invasion of Saint Dominique, 1795–1796: The British force that had been sent to the West Indies in 1794 was too small to have any decisive effect. They withdrew from most of the islands they had occupied in 1794 and based themselves in Jamaica and Barbados. In Saint Dominique, the British retained control of, or at least access to, Port-au-Prince. Pitt wanted British control of Saint Dominique and had signed an agreement with the whites there that he would intervene on their behalf and restore their power and their slaves to them. Most of 1795 was spent gathering and training a thirty-thousand-man expeditionary force to extirpate France from the West Indies. In November 1795, two hundred ships under the command of Admiral Hyde Parker embarking thirty-thousand men under the command of General Ralph Abercromby sailed from Portsmouth to the West Indies for what Pitt called the big push. Abercromby had experience in the Seven Years' War but had avoided service in the American Revolution because he had favored the American cause. He had spent the years 1775–1783 in Ireland with an infantry regiment.

The British performed the same moves that they had tried in the American Revolution, occupying Port-au-Prince in March 1796 and attempting to spread out from there. In America, they had occupied the major ports of New York and Charleston and attempted to spread out from there. Parker and Abercromby, having no experience of the war in America, must have thought their strategy was unique and brilliant. Toussaint Louverture had pledged allegiance to France, so he was committed to fighting what he considered a British invasion. The course of events for the next two years was also similar to the American Revolution in that the British would attempt sorties out of Port-au-Prince that Louverture would beat back. The British had learned enough not to engage in any Saratoga- or Yorktown-style campaigns, so there were no defeats suffered per se. The British public despised the Saint Dominique invasion as something that would restore slavery to a freed nation and was a constant drain on manpower due to the yellow fever that was rumored to be rife among the British troops.

Some people who have closely examined the British and French campaigns in Saint Dominique believe that the death toll from yellow fever has been exaggerated, and I myself am skeptical. After all, the white natives in Saint Dominique had been there for generations and don't seem to have been unduly affected by it. Also, the other islands in the West Indies should have been just as susceptible to yellow fever as Saint Dominique, but they weren't. Josephine Bonaparte herself had been born and raised in Martinique. I view most of the literature related to yellow fever deaths in Saint Dominique as Marxist-inspired hysteria, driven by fear of the tropical climate and the view among the European masses and even some of the elites, that blacks were not affected by heat or yellow fever because they were a different species of humanity than whites.

1797: God Save Emperor Francis

The United States, 1797

The new Duke of Orleans in the US, 1797: Since the guillotining of the Duke of Orleans in 1793, his son Louis Philippe now held that title. As we recall, he and Dumouriez had defected to the Austrian in April 1793. Unlike Lafayette, they did not get arrested and had been traveling since then. This year, the duke visited the

THE GREAT GLOBE ITSELF

United States and lived there from February to September, traveling widely and meeting all the important people. In Philadelphia, he was able to meet up with his two brothers, who had moved there after their release from prison. We imagine a February 1797 White House reception in Philadelphia where the duke, Washington, and Tennessee congressman Andrew Jackson, present and future leaders of their countries, meet. President-elect Adams and Vice President-elect Jefferson would be there too.

The Orleans brothers spent the next seven months touring New York, Boston, Maine, and even made it to Jackson's Nashville. Upon hearing of the Coup of Fructidor (September 4, 1797), discussed below, and that their mother had been exiled to Spain, they decided to meet her in Spain. They got on a boat in Nashville and floated downstream to the city named for their ancestor, where they intended to sail to Havana and then Spain. They ended up spending a lot of time in Cuba and then got diverted to Canada, where they became good friends with the Duke of Kent, Queen Victoria's father. They never did make it to Spain, landing in Great Britain in January 1800, where they stayed. The duke's brothers would die in 1807 and 1808 from the tuberculosis that they had contracted while in prison in 1793. They never saw their mother again. She died in 1821.

The land boom busts, 1797: There was a financial panic that had begun in 1796 as speculators had driven up the price of western land, but there was too much land for the number of pioneers available to settle it. Nor was there sufficient money to pay for it as the governments of Europe were buying everything they could for their Armies and Fleets, constricting the amount of credit available worldwide. Land prices plummeted. Robert Morris fell victim to the bursting bubble and ended up in debtors' prison from February 1798 to August 1801. He lived quietly after his release and died in 1806 at the age of seventy-two. He was only the most prominent casualty of hundreds. The panic showed how the British and American economies were already interlinked, as one element of the panic was the Bank of England halting withdrawal of specie (silver and gold coin) by depositors. This constriction of the money supply had the effect of increasing the downward pressure on prices, including land prices.

John Adams takes over, 1797: John Adams entered office in March 1797 and soon found out that his biggest threat was not from his vice president and electoral opponent, Jefferson, but from his supposed fellow Federalist Hamilton. In June 1797, vitriolic pamphleteer James Callender, the same man who, in 1802, would accuse Jefferson of having Sally Hemings as a concubine, published a pamphlet accusing Hamilton of an extramarital affair with a Marie Reynolds in 1791 and 1792 while serving as secretary of the Treasury. He further accused Hamilton of corrupt financial dealings with Reynolds' husband. Hamilton wrote a pamphlet in response admitting to the affair but denying the corruption. The scandal blew over but made him unelectable. It was a truly salacious scandal, where the husband pimped his twenty-three-year-old wife to Hamilton. Hamilton used the Clinton defense, stating that his sexual weakness did not interfere with the honest execution of his duties. Hamilton's wife left him, although they reconciled after a year. The incident almost led to a duel between Hamilton and James Monroe, with Hamilton as the instigator as he was convinced that Monroe had leaked the information in retaliation for Hamilton having a hand in Monroe's recall as minister to France in September 1796. After Hamilton was killed by Aaron Burr in 1804, Hamilton's friends attempted to paint Hamilton as a man who hated dueling, but clearly this wasn't the case.

Charles Pinckney, older brother of Thomas Pinckney of Pinckney Treaty fame, was named as Monroe's successor as minister in Paris. When he presented his credentials to the French government, they were refused. The Directory was concerned about the state of French-American relations. Monroe had been recalled, so they heard, because he was too friendly to France. The Directory was angry that the US had decided to stop paying France the debt on war loans they had taken out during the American Revolution on the grounds that the money was owed to the king of France, not the republic. It was apparent that the US had allied themselves with Great Britain, as witnessed in the Jay Treaty. President Adams was well-known in France from his diplomatic days as disliking France and preferring the British. And now Adams had sent to them, as his minister, the brother of the man who had negotiated the Pinckney

THE GREAT GLOBE ITSELF

Treaty that was now tying the hands of their ally Spain. These were all issues that needed to be straightened out before a US minister could be credentialed in Paris. France, in retaliation for the US loan default, was already in the process of seizing every American merchant ship they could in the West Indies, over three hundred between October 1796 and June 1797.

Pinckney returned to the United States and reported the situation to Washington and Adams in February 1797. It was true that Adams had never been a big fan of the French, and we recall when he gave it to Vergennes with the bark off back in 1780. The French fully expected the US under Adams would develop even closer relations with the British and were acting accordingly. A lot of this information and advice that the Directory was getting was coming from Talleyrand, who had just come back from exile in New York City, and his American insights were about to lead him to the job of foreign minister in July 1797, as discussed below.

Meanwhile, France was pressuring Spain to contribute in other ways to the anti-US cause. France suggested to Spain that they revoke some of the conditions of the 1795 Pinckney Treaty, including the right of deposit in the city of New Orleans. Since the people in Ohio, Tennessee, and Kentucky got their goods to market by floating them down the river to New Orleans, it was a drastic thing France was asking. But France was strong, Spain was weak, and Spain would eventually succumb to the pressure.

When Adams reported to Congress on the tiff with France in May, he proposed sending a commission to Paris while, at the same time, building up the Army and the Navy. The idea of the commission was to restore neutrality by signing a French version of the Jay Treaty with France. Subsequently Charles Pinckney, John Marshall, and Elbridge Gerry departed for Paris in July 1797. Adams also proposed defensive treaties with Prussia and Sweden, two countries that were neutral but tilted toward France. By the time the commission arrived in Paris in October 1797, Talleyrand was foreign minister, and the Directory had just suppressed a royalist coup, removing two directors and replacing them with men more aligned to revolutionary principles, as discussed below. Talleyrand slow-rolled the Americans,

365

only provisionally accepting their credentials and arranging back channel meetings with intermediaries later known in published reports as X, Y, and Z. This is where it stood at the end of 1797.

The frigates that had been ordered in 1794 started coming down the ways, starting with USS *United States* in Philadelphia in May, USS *Constellation* in Baltimore in September, and USS *Constitution* in Boston in October 21. For now, the War Department managed the construction and operations of US naval vessels, as the Department of the Navy was not established until 1798. *Constitution* got its nickname *Old Ironsides* during the war of 1812 in a fight with HMS *Guerriere*. It was the subject of a famous poem by Oliver Wendell Holmes Sr. in 1830 that saved it from the boneyard. When it was refitted in 1832, a figurehead of President Andrew Jackson was placed on the bow. It is still in commission today.

Eastern and Central Europe

Paul I takes over, 1797: Paul I succeeded to the Russian throne upon the death of his mother, Catherine II in November 1796. His first act was to get the biggest bone out of his throat, passing a law regulating the imperial succession, which, until now, had been a matter of whatever was in the current sovereign's will. Now the throne would pass to the eldest male heir. His second act was to get the second biggest bone out of his throat. As we recall, his father, Peter III, had been deposed in 1762, then had died while in custody and was buried without fanfare. Paul now had his father reburied with great fanfare and even had the one of the few surviving conspirators of his father's assassination, Alexei Orlov, carry the imperial crown in front of the coffin during the procession. Paul conducted a coronation ceremony for the corpse before the burial.

Paul canceled Zubov 's Persian expedition, and he also canceled another agreement that Catherine had made with Austria just before her death to provide sixty thousand troops to fight France. This turned out to be a good decision because the troops would not have arrived in time to make any difference on the battlefield. The Austrians were being pummeled by Bonaparte, and they asked

THE GREAT GLOBE ITSELF

for an armistice in April 1797. Paul was dismayed by both France and Austria when he learned that the centerpiece of the French-Austrian peace agreement was the dismemberment of the Venetian Republic, with several islands in the Ionian Sea that Russia coveted being turned over to France. As we recall, Russia had established the Black Sea Fleet in Sevastopol in 1783 and now had interests in the eastern Mediterranean that France was beginning to encroach upon. Subsequent French actions in Malta and Egypt led to Paul entering the Second Coalition in 1798.

Like his father, Peter, Paul had a pro-Prussian outlook, but he was unable to convert that outlook into an alliance this year, mostly due to the death of Frederick William II, described below, but also due to Prussia's desire to stay on the good side of France in hopes of acquiring Hanover. Prussian neutrality toward France was as fictional as American neutrality toward Great Britain.

Deutschland Über Alles, 1797: Austrian composer Joseph Haydn had spent most of his career in the service of the important Hungarian Esterhazy family, who were good old-fashioned landowning and military-serving aristocrats. In 1790, family patriarch Nicholas Esterhazy died, and his son dismantled the musical establishment of the family. Haydn went on tour in England from 1791 to 1795, and everywhere he went, he heard crowds singing "God Save the King." This inspired him to write a similar song for his sovereign Emperor Francis II. On February 12, 1797, Francis's twenty-ninth birthday, Haydn debuted, for the first time, at court "*Gott Erhalte Franz Den Kaiser*" ("God Save Emperor Francis"). The original lyrics were written by Lorenz Leopold Haschka, who was now running the University of Vienna library. When the Holy Roman Empire was dissolved in 1806, the song became the official anthem of the new Austrian Empire, with the name of the emperor to be changed as circumstances dictated. The current lyrics, beginning with the line "*Deutschland, Deutschland über alles*" were written in 1841 by August Heinrich Hoffman von Fallensleben, a popular poet from Breslau in Prussia. The lyrics were considered liberal and revolutionary for the time, and he lost his job and had to go into hiding. German troops were singing it in 1914 as they marched on Paris, and the song became popular in Germany,

367

even though it was still the song of the Austrian emperor. It became the German National Anthem in 1922, part of a compromise where German conservatives got the song, while liberals got the black-red-and-gold flag of the 1848 revolution, not the red-white-and-black Hohenzollern flag. Here are the lyrics:

Deutschland, Deutschland über alles,	Germany, Germany above all,
Über alles in der Welt,	Above everything in the world,
Wenn es stets zu Schutz und Trutze	When always, for protection,
Brüderlich zusammenhält,	We stand together as brothers.
Von der Maas bis an die Memel,	From the Maas to the Memel
Von der Etsch bis an den Belt -	From the Etsch to the Belt -
Deutschland, Deutschland über alles,	Germany, Germany above all
Über alles in der Welt.	Above all in the world.
Deutsche Frauen, deutsche Treue,	German women, German loyalty,
Deutscher Wein und deutscher Sang	German wine and German song,
Sollen in der Welt behalten	Shall retain in the world,
Ihren alten schönen Klang,	Their old lovely ring
Uns zu edler Tat begeistern	To inspire us to noble deeds
Unser ganzes Leben lang.	Our whole life long.
Deutsche Frauen, deutsche Treue,	German women, German loyalty,
Deutscher Wein und deutscher Sang	German wine and German song.

Death of Frederick William II, 1797: Exactly one year after the death of Catherine the Great, Frederick William II died on November 16, 1797. During his reign, from 1786 to 1797, Frederick William developed an interest in mysticism and Rosicrucianism. Much of his policy was influenced by a mystic high priest named Johann Christopher von Wöllner. After the age of fifty, his health began running down, but he continued his lifestyle as long as his body let him. The king was known to the people as *Der dicke Lüderjahn* (the fat sack of s———). We shouldn't be too surprised to note that Frederick William's death occurred just after he had enraged the British by taking a lot of money from them, promising to defend the Netherlands

THE GREAT GLOBE ITSELF

with sixty thousand troops, then failing to deliver one soldier. We can't discount the idea of assassination, because when the British struggle militarily, monarchs unfriendly to them seem to drop dead suddenly. As a result of Prussia's perfidious conduct, since April 1795, France controlled the Netherlands, Prussia controlled Hanover, and the British no longer had any place in continental Europe where they could hang their hat. Instead of assassinating kings, Great Britain should have been looking in the mirror to reflect on the decisions they had made to strip troops from Flanders and send them on wild goose chases to Saint Dominique and Corsica.

Frederick William II was succeeded by his twenty-seven-year-old son, Frederick William III, whose wife, Queen Louise, daughter of the Grand Duke of Mecklenburg Strelitz, was one of the most beautiful women ever to sit on a throne. Her aunt (her father's sister) was Queen Charlotte of Great Britain. Louise was the mother of Prussian king Frederick William IV and German emperor William I. She died in 1810 at the age of thirty-four but gave birth to nine children altogether. Not as fertile as her royal aunt Charlotte but still pretty good. Louise and Frederick William III married on December 24, 1793, in a double wedding, as Frederick William III's brother Louis married Louise's sister Frederica on December 26, making it the best Christmas ever. Yes, Frederick married Louise, and Louis married Frederica. This was the first time in a long time that the king and queen of Prussia seemed to be interested in each other outside of their official duties. The queen was very popular with the people and had a lot of influence over her husband. For years, she publicly supported her husband's desire for Prussia to stay neutral, which is to say pro-French, but she would advocate for war against France in 1806, to her subsequent sorrow.

Louis XVIII leaves Prussia for Russia, 1797: One of the side effects of the death of Frederick William II was that Louis XVIII, who had been living in Prussia, was now forced to leave the country. Frederick William III told Louis that Prussia, as a neutral country, could not guarantee his safety. Since arriving in Prussia from Italy, Louis had not been living in a palace but in a two-bedroom apartment over a shop in the town of Blankenburg in Brunswick, under a false identity. Paul I offered Louis the use of a huge palace in Latvia called Jelgava, where Louis and his courtiers were able to reinstate some of the old routines of Versailles. He was there until 1807, when Russia and France concluded a peace agreement at Tilsit. That year, Alexander told Louis that Russia, as an ally of France, could not guarantee his safety, so Louis went off to live in Great Britain.

Western Europe, 1797

French victory in Italy: All eyes were on Italy as the French pressed the siege of Mantua, and the Austrians continued to send relief forces. Three relief forces had been thwarted in 1796, and on January 14, 1797, the Army of Italy defeated the Austrians a fourth time at the battle of Rivoli. Today, the Rue de Rivoli in Paris runs from the Place de la Concorde to the Place de la Bastille, passing the Tuileries Gardens, the Louvre, the Palais-Royal, and the Hotel de Ville along the way. This is as close as it comes to a shrine to Bonaparte in the city of Paris today. Mantua surrendered on February 2, and the road to Austria was now open. General Bernadotte crossed the Alps from France with twenty-thousand men as reinforcements, arriving in Milan in March. Bonaparte made him a division commander, beginning a long and often-contentious relationship. After Campo Formio, Bernadotte was made French minister to Vienna. While there, he flew the tricolor over the embassy, which caused offense and some riots, partly because Louis XVI's daughter Marie Therese was then living in Vienna. Being supremely self-confident, Bernadotte could be insufferably arrogant, which was what made him a successful king of Sweden.

With the Austrians temporarily disposed of, Bonaparte sent a division down to invade the Papal States, which had been passively hostile for the last year. Pope Pius VI didn't want to fight and signed the Peace of Tolentino, ceding Avignon and the Romagna to France. Subsequently, Joseph Bonaparte was named French minister to the Vatican. His presence there led to some incidents at the end of 1797 that would give France an excuse to occupy Rome, take the pope prisoner, and bring him back to France. As part of the Peace of Tolentino, Pius had to pay 36 million lira or 15 million francs. Much art was transferred from Italy to France. Not the *Mona Lisa*, though, which had been in the possession of the kings of France since Da Vinci finished painting it in 1519. It was already hanging in the Louvre on public display, probably in the same room where it is today. Bonaparte gained a reputation for looting art, and it was the biggest criticism of him in Paris when he became famous in 1796. Most of what he sent from Italy to Paris was returned after 1815.

Bonaparte formed a special unit he called the Guides to be his bodyguard on the march to Vienna. The Guides, originally numbering about 1,500, were the seed of the Imperial Guard, which, by 1812, numbered around 100,000 men. They were commanded by cavalry officer and future marshal Jean Baptiste Bessieres. The Guides were all cavalry troopers, but as the guard grew, it came to embrace all of the military arms, including engineers, sailors, and Marines.

Leoben and Campo Formio, 1797: The Austrians put Archduke Charles in charge of the Army that stood between Bonaparte and Vienna, but the French were in pursuit mode, and the Austrians had no chance to dig in anywhere. General Barthelemy Joubert distinguished himself commanding the detached left wing of the Army of Italy as it advanced through the mountainous terrain of the Tyrol. On April 18, ten weeks after and three hundred miles east of Mantua, in Leoben, Bonaparte sent a note to Charles offering to split the Republic of Venice with Austria in exchange for Austria ceding Lombardy (Milan) and Belgium to France. Bonaparte seems to have thought this up all on his own as he passed through Venice while in pursuit of the enemy. This was the bargain that later disturbed Paul I, as mentioned above. An armistice between France and Austria was agreed to, as both Bonaparte and Charles had to send to their governments to gain concurrences for making peace on the basis of splitting Venice between them. These were eventually obtained, and negotiations followed in the town of Campo Formio where a treaty was signed on October 18.

One of Massena 's brigadiers, Charles Leclerc, was sent off to Paris in April to announce the armistice. On France's eastern front, Hoche's Army of the Sambre and Meuse and Moreau 's Army of the

Rhine and Moselle had both crossed into Germany, and Hoche had already fought a battle, but when Leclerc announced the news in Paris, all French operations in Germany halted. As described below, Paris was about to go through some political turmoil related to royalists and a looming war with America. As far as I have been able to find, Paris left all the negotiations to Bonaparte, who may have brought in his brother Joseph to help. When Leclerc returned to Milan, he was surprised to be offered the hand of Bonaparte's sister Pauline. Josephine was in Milan with her husband during this period (they were living like royalty), and she might have been doing some matchmaking. Pauline and General Leclerc were married in Milan Cathedral on June 14, on the same day that another Bonaparte sister, Elise, conducted a religious wedding ceremony there with her civilly married husband, Felix Baciocchi. I think double weddings are great, and they are how many of Shakespeare's comedies end. I can also imagine Josephine asking her fourteen-year-old daughter, Hortense, what she thought of Bonaparte's brother Louis and Hortense sticking out her tongue and gagging.

One of the unexpected provisions of Campo Formio was for Lafayette to be released from his Austrian prison, which was pretty thoughtful of Bonaparte, as no one in Paris seems to have given Lafayette a thought in years. Lafayette wrote a thank you note to Bonaparte, but he refused to swear loyalty to the French Republic, as his other country, the United States, was in a state of Quasi-War with France. For the next three years, he lived in Hamburg on the estate of a relative. The people like Edmund Burke, who, years before, had predicted that the French Revolution was going to end in a Cromwellian military dictatorship had once cast Lafayette as the new Cromwell, but now Bonaparte, the actual new Cromwell had set Lafayette free.

The war with Austria came to an end on October 18, 1797, as the Peace of Leoben was formalized in the Treaty of Campo Formio. Great Britain had no more allies, so this was the end of the line for the First Coalition. Bonaparte turned over command of the Army of Italy to Berthier in December, who was ordered to lead the Army into Rome at the beginning of 1798. A portion of the Army of Italy

THE GREAT GLOBE ITSELF

was separated under Massena's command to garrison the Ligurian Republic.

The Cisalpine Republic, 1797: In late June, Bonaparte combined Lombardy and the Romagna into one land and decreed the birth of the Cisalpine Republic, later to be the Kingdom of Italy, with him as king and Josephine's son Eugéne de Beauharnais as viceroy. The capital was Milan. At the same time, he converted Genoa into the Ligurian Republic, which was later annexed into Metropolitan France. Bonaparte took advantage of the fact that he currently occupied Venice and sent one of his brigadiers to the Ionian Islands with the Venetian Fleet to establish French government there. He intended to annex them to France, not the Cisalpine Republic, early evidence that he envisioned himself as the new Augustus.

In July, Barras sent a communication to Bonaparte requesting that he send some troops to Paris that were needed to save the revolution from Pichegru and the royalists, a repeat of what Barras and Bonaparte had done in Paris in October 1795. Bonaparte's division commanders at the time were Massena, Joubert, Augereau, Serurier, and someone named Gabriel Rey, who, after 1799, had no more personal contact with Bonaparte, although he was in the French Army until 1820. Bonaparte sent Augereau, who accomplished his mission as described below.

Planning the expedition to Egypt: Bonaparte was still in Italy but getting ready to take over the Army of England when he proposed an expedition to seize control of Egypt as the best way to get at Great Britain—by blocking their access to India across Suez. More early evidence of his identification as the new Augustus, as Egypt had been critical to Augustus's early success, not because he had fought and deposed Antony and Cleopatra there but for its wealth and grain. Because it was important to Augustus, it was important to Bonaparte, even though in 1798, it wasn't wealthy, and Europe had plenty of grain. Bonaparte had read about what Augustus had conquered, but he didn't know why Augustus had conquered it.

A French expedition to Egypt as a way of getting at the British didn't make much sense, since the Mediterranean was empty of British ships, so they weren't communicating with India via Suez anyway.

373

Great Britain had occupied the Cape Colony since September 1795 and were finding that route to India adequate, being longer but more secure and all on the water. Not only was the Mediterranean empty of British ships, but French naval strategists could have pointed out that the quickest way to get British ships to reenter the Mediterranean was to concentrate the French Fleet in Egypt at the opposite end of the Mediterranean from Gibraltar.

Moreau, Pichegru, and Hoche, 1797: As stated above, operations on the Rhine ceased after the armistice of Leoben was announced. Moreau 's career was derailed when it came to light that Pichegru had been in "treasonous" correspondence with the French-émigré Army commander, the Prince of Conde. This cannot have come as much of a surprise to anyone, as Pichegru was currently running for office as a royalist and would soon be president of the Council of Five Hundred. Treason is a matter of dates, as Talleyrand would later say. Moreau had been Pichegru's deputy but denied any knowledge of his dealings with royalists, an assertion many found hard to believe. Moreau resigned as commander of the Army of the Rhine and Moselle and was without a command for two years. He was replaced by future marshal Augereau.

The generals were almost all antiroyalist and began putting their fingers on the scales when it came to the elections. If Louis XVIII were restored, the days of Bonaparte and other generals living like kings and dictating peace to the likes of the Habsburgs would be over. They would be reduced to being lackeys to a bunch of effeminate wimps with law degrees. They had risked their lives, fortunes, and sacred honor for the revolution, and they had won. They were the products of natural selection, survival of the fittest, and they were prepared to defend their position, regardless of the will of the people, whom they regarded as fickle and fond of change, favoring a republic this year and an absolute monarchy next year.

Hoche was in Paris for a week to fill in as minister of war but soon returned to Sambre and Meuse, where the tuberculosis finally did him in on September 19, 1797. Peace negotiations were ongoing and the Austrians stood down, so the French did likewise. Sambre and Meuse and Rhine and Moselle were combined into the Army of

THE GREAT GLOBE ITSELF

Germany on September 27 under the command of Augereau, who was tasked to dismantle it and send the troops to other theaters. On December 9, the remnants of the Army of Germany were split into the Army of the Rhine and the Army of Mainz. In March 1798, the Army of the Rhine was renamed the Army of Switzerland.

Battle of Cape Saint Vincent, 1797: Subsequent to the failure of the 1796 French invasion of Ireland, in February 1797, the Spanish Fleet that was based in Cartagena in the Mediterranean departed in order to link up with the French Fleet at Brest. The British Mediterranean Fleet, based in Portugal, which is not in the Mediterranean, got wind of this, and the commander Admiral Jervis determined to meet them as they rounded Cape Saint Vincent at the southwest-most corner of Portugal. On February 14, Jervis engaged the twenty-seven Spanish ships with his fifteen. Horatio Nelson, missing an eye but still possessing two arms for now, was commanding a squadron and managed to board and capture two ships, a major factor in securing a British victory. This was the battle where he yelled, "Westminster Abbey [that is, death] or Glory!" In all, the British captured four ships and took three thousand prisoners. The remaining Spanish ships pulled into Cadiz and were blockaded until the end of the War of the Second Coalition in 1802. The significance of the battle was that the British once again had access to the Mediterranean, so they were later able to destroy the French Fleet while it was riding at anchor at Aboukir in August of 1798. Jervis was, afterward, given a victory title: Earl of Saint Vincent.

After the Battle of Cape Saint Vincent, Lord Nelson was promoted to rear admiral and, in July, was conducting operations against the Spanish in the Canary Islands, which are off the coast of Morocco. He heard that there was a horde of Spanish gold on one of the islands and decided to personally lead a raid to get it. The Spanish were ready for him, and the raid was repelled. Nelson was shot in his right arm, and it had to be amputated. He went through a period of depression, as he believed his career was over, and went through phantom limb syndrome, which he said was proof of the existence of the soul. He was considering retirement when he was called back to duty in March 1798, after it became apparent that

375

Bonaparte was gathering a large Army and Fleet in Toulon for some unknown purpose.

French raid on Fishguard, Wales, 1797: Also in February, Lazare Hoche and Wolfe Tone had been sent to Sambre and Meuse, with the Army of the Coasts of the Ocean liquidated and replaced by the Army of England, which was, for now, an organization only on paper. Someone, presumably Admiral de Galles, ordered four ships and 1,400 men to conduct a landing on the west coast of the island of Britain. Apparently the plan was to land in Bristol, destroy it, then march on Chester, destroy it, and finally march on Liverpool and destroy it too. About half the men were French grenadiers, but the other half were prisoners. Maybe the grenadiers were there to guard the prisoners. Unable to land near Bristol, they landed in a town called Fishguard, about as far west in Wales as it gets. The name of the unit was the Black Legion, as they wore British Army coats that had been dyed black. The commander was an Irish-born American by the name of Colonel William Tate. Tate had gotten involved with one of Citizen Genet's projects in 1793, a plot to take over New Orleans, which was controlled by Spain at the time. In 1795, when Spain and the United States signed the Pinckney Treaty, the state of South Carolina came to arrest him, so he fled to France.

On February 22, the four ships dropped off the Black Legion near Fishguard and skedaddled back to France. The locals soon mobilized, forming units with names, like the Pembrokeshire Yeomanry, the Fishguard and Newport Volunteers, and the Cardiganshire Militia. The crews of two revenue cutters, which is what the coast guard was called in those days were called in. The lord lieutenant of Wales was alerted and appointed Baron Cawdor, who was an MP and also commander of the Pembrokeshire Yeomanry, to overall command. The prisoner half of the Black Legion was soon looting farms and getting drunk. A few broke into a church and, to keep warm, lit a fire, blasphemously using pages from the Bible as kindling and pews as firewood. The British militia units surrounded the place and convinced Tate that he was hopelessly outnumbered, which included a ruse involving dressing local women up in what appeared, from a distance, to be uniforms and having them march up and down a hill.

THE GREAT GLOBE ITSELF

There is a plaque in Fishguard commemorating Jemima Nicholas, the woman who came up with the idea. Tate surrendered on February 24. He and the grenadiers were eventually repatriated to France, and the British justice system probably took care of the rest. A book on the subject was written by a man named Phil Carradice, who probably has sold the movie rights, which I would pay money to see if they ever produce it.

Mutinies at Spithead and Nore and the Battle of Camperdown, 1797: In April, the Spithead and Nore mutinies took place in Great Britain, paralyzing the Royal Navy for the entire summer of 1797. Spithead is located near Portsmouth, on the south coast, and Nore is in the Thames Estuary on the east coast. Sailors' wages had not kept pace with wartime inflation, while improved technology (the coppering of ships' hulls, for example) allowed longer deployments, as ships no longer needed to have the barnacles scraped from their hulls. The admiralty handled the munities with a mixture of concession and severity and only hanged one man. The crews were back at work by the end of May, but there could be no operations of any size that year. The Royal Navy had expanded greatly since 1793, and the new sailors, whether they were willing or unwilling recruits, were not going to be satisfied with the conditions of service as they were. Word of the mutinies soon arrived in France. The French Fleet was still recovering from the Ireland expedition, but Wolfe Tone was soon in the Netherlands readying a raid using the Dutch Fleet. Fortunately for the British, the North Sea Fleet in Great Yarmouth had been unaffected by the mutinies.

In October, the British North Sea Fleet under Admiral Adam Duncan fought the Dutch Fleet under Admiral Jan Willem de Winter in the Battle of *Kamperduin* (Camperdown). The Dutch Fleet, with Wolfe Tone and his United Irishmen aboard, had attempted to emerge into the North Sea to conduct a raid on the English coast and was severely pummeled by the British, losing by capture eleven of their twenty-six warships. Nelson declared that he would have given his other arm to have been there, a line which might have inspired that black knight scene in *Monty Python and the Holy Grail.* Although the Dutch still had many warships and immediately went back to work constructing new ones, the Dutch sailors were demoralized and never recovered their spirit. British pride in their brave boys knew no bounds. A popular rhyme went:

> Saint Vincent drubbed the Dons, Earl Howe he drubbed Monsieur,
> And gallant Duncan now has soundly drubbed Mynheer;
> The Spanish, French and Dutch, though all united be,
> "Fear not," Britannia cries, "my tars can beat all three. Monsieurs, Mynheers and Dons, your country's empty boast, Our tars can beat all three, each on his native coast."

Saint Dominique, 1797: In Saint Dominique, the British attempted a sortie into the countryside, in which they found that there was nothing to be gained but being surrounded by the enemy. They got about forty miles from Port-au-Prince before Louverture was able to do just that, and they scampered back to safety. The British commanders at the time, who were not Abercromby or Parker (they knew a career-killing assignment when they saw one), got on a ship to London and recommended a halt to all operations and evacuation of the British Army and all of the whites who wished to depart. Before they left for London, they notified Louverture that they would not be conducting any major military operations. If you read the biographies of the British commanders involved, they invariably gloss over this part of their résumé. By the end of the year, no decision had come from London, as Pitt still viewed possession of Saint Dominique as potentially useful in peace negotiations.

The Coup of 18 Fructidor, 1797: The Constitution of 1795 called for elections of one-third of the members of each legislative chamber, and these occurred in April 1797. Of the 216 members of the Council of Five Hundred that ran for reelection, 205 were defeated, replaced mostly by royalists.

General Pichegru was among those elected and was soon president of the Council of Five Hundred. He, along with two directors, Barthelemy and Carnot, were soon plotting a restoration of the monarchy in the style of 1660 Stuart England. Barthelemy had just become a director this month after his predecessor, Le Tourneur, was term limited. Carnot supported a restoration because he was satisfied that the Army had achieved what it needed to and that the generals were on the verge of getting out of control. To him, it was alarming that Bonaparte was conducting diplomacy and negotiating peace terms with the enemy, with the approval of the other three directors.

In July 1797, Talleyrand entered office as minister of foreign affairs. He had seen Bonaparte's potential in 1796 and had been writing him letters to encourage his political career. Talleyrand had lived in America from March 1794 to September 1796 and had been friendly with both Aaron Burr and Alexander Hamilton, two men who would prove to have traits similar to Bonaparte. Talleyrand's predecessor at the Foreign Office was Charles Delacroix, and it was rumored that Talleyrand had fathered Delacroix 's son Eugéne, as Charles Delacroix had a tumor removed in September 1797. and Eugéne was born in April 1798. Well, according to the math, Delacroix could have been the father. Eugéne Delacroix became a prolific painter and is best known today as the painter of *Liberty Leading Her People*.

The other three directors—Barras, Rewbell, and Lepeaux — were opposed to any restoration of the monarchy. They were supportive of the generals because they worked hard, got results, and supported the revolution. In July, Barras sent the abovementioned request to Bonaparte in Milan for military support against the royalists, probably at Talleyrand's suggestion. In September, Augereau and his division arrived in Paris and were encamped outside the city. Moreau and Bonaparte had both already sent evidence of Pichegru's premature communications with the Prince of Conde to use as evidence against him.

On September 4, 18 Fructidor, Directors Barras, Rewbell, and Lepeaux declared martial law in Paris with General Augereau ready to support that decree. Director Barthelemy, president of the Council of Five Hundred Pichegru, and president of the Council of Ancients, a man named Francois Barbe-Marbois, were arrested, along with over two hundred members of the Council of Five Hundred. Carnot was allowed to escape to Switzerland. Barthelemy and Carnot were deposed and replaced. The reason that the Ministry of Police hadn't done anything to stop the coup was that one of the new directors was Philippe Antoine Merlin, former minister of police. The other new director was Francois Neufchateau, the man who had transformed the Louvre from a government office building into a museum. Barthelemy, Pichegru, and Barbe-Marbois were transported to Cayenne along with sixty-five legislators. The elections were annulled, émigrés were sentenced to death, and nonjuring priests were deported, making it seem like 1791 again. The Jacobins were once again welcome in Paris.

Carnot spent his time in exile working on a treatise on calculus. Bonaparte would rehabilitate him and make him minister of war in 1800. Pichegru would escape and continue to torment Bonaparte for the next several years until his death by suicide (allegedly) in a French prison in 1804. Barthelemy escaped from Cayenne and made his way back to France by 1800, where he submitted. Bonaparte made him a senator. Barbe-Marbois was pardoned in 1800, appointed by Bonaparte as director of the Public Treasury in which capacity he negotiated the terms of the Louisiana Purchase with Robert Livingston in 1803.

In an echo of the de-Christianization campaigns of 1794, Director Lepeaux now began pushing the idea he called theophilanthropy, which means something like God being a friend to man. Henri Gregoire wrote in his *Annales de la Religion*:

> Theophilanthropism is one of those derisive
> institutions which pretends to bring to God those

THE GREAT GLOBE ITSELF

> very people whom they drive away from Him by estranging them from Christianity... Abhorred by Christians, it is spurned by philosophers who, though they may not feel the need of a religion for themselves, still want the people to cling to the faith of their fathers.

The tenets of this faith were Masonic in origin and were developed by Thomas Paine and others based on the writings of Rousseau. No dogmatic creed was imposed on the adherents of the new religion, but it had two fundamental tenets: the existence of God and the immortality of the soul, as they were beliefs deemed necessary for the preservation of society and the welfare of individuals. Today in Masonry, they publicly state their belief in "the fatherhood of God, the brotherhood of man, and the immortality of the human soul." When Bonaparte came into power, he scattered the adherents of this sect as part of his concordat with the Catholic Church. There were some attempts at revival over the years that came to nothing. In France, people were either devoted to the Catholic Church, or they weren't. The government had learned its lesson about imposing new religions from the experiences with Hebert 's and Robespierre's attempts in 1794. Religion is a matter of revelation, not legislation. God shows Himself to us; we don't describe Him in a statute.

The struggle between royalists and revolutionaries had an economic component because on September 30, the Directory, having vanquished the royalist threat, repudiated two-thirds of the public debt. The numbers get fuzzy when you are dealing with government budgets, but in general, the public debt amounted to 4 billion francs, and the French government was overspending by 25 million francs per month. It can be presumed that the royalists had fought so hard to get back into power, in part, because it was to them that the money was owed, and it can be again presumed that the repudiated debt was that portion of the debt owed to royalists.

The XYZ Affair, 1797: It was about this time, October 1797, that the American commissioners Charles Pinckney, John Marshall, and Elbridge Gerry arrived in Paris, and one of their explicit instructions from Adams was to refuse to entertain any requests from the French government for loans. They met with Talleyrand, who asked them for an explanation of the speech to Congress made by Adams in May, where he had asked for a military buildup. They weren't prepared for that, and the meeting ended. Soon "X" (Jean-Conrad Hottinguer) asked for a meeting with Pinckney, who relayed French demands for a loan and for £50,000 for Talleyrand. X then introduced them to "Y" (Pierre Bellamy), identified as a member of Talleyrand's inner circle, who suggested that the United States purchase French currency at inflated prices. Talleyrand then sent "Z" (Lucien Hauteval) to meet with Gerry, who was an old friend of his, and Z assured Gerry that if the Americans paid the money, then France would stop seizing American merchant vessels. By now, France had signed the Campo Formio agreement with Austria and was at peace in Europe. X and Y met with the commission to point this out with the implication that they could focus on a war against the United States if they didn't get the money. Pinckney replied with the line, "No, not a sixpence," which was later expanded into the catchphrase "millions for defense, not a cent for tribute!" This was while the US was paying tribute to the beys in Algiers, Tunis, and Tripoli to protect their shipping on the Barbary Coast, so it was a little hypocritical. Talleyrand noticed that Gerry was less intransigent than Pinckney and Marshall and began efforts to split the commission up; for example, having Z ask Gerry to keep secrets from the others. Gerry, to his discredit, played along. This is how it was at the end of 1797. The credentials of the US commission were never accepted, and all communications were through the back channels of X, Y, and Z.

Bonaparte returns to France, December 1797: On December 3, Bonaparte may have been initiated into a Masonic lodge in Nancy. If he was, he was never serious about it for himself, just as he was never serious about religion in the sense of needing salvation. The Freemasons claim he was initiated, although they have no evidence of where or when and can only guess. Nancy, in December 1797, is the earliest opportunity, and it would have had the advantage of being a relatively private matter, known only to his generals, who were, for the most part, Freemasons themselves and might have been encour-

THE GREAT GLOBE ITSELF

aging him to take the plunge, so to speak. Bonaparte did appreciate the positive impact that Freemasonry and religion had and was convinced that they made men better citizens.

On December 5, Bonaparte entered Paris in triumph after ending the war with Austria. He was greeted by adoring crowds. Germaine de Staël, Necker's daughter, met him during this time. She knew everyone in Paris and had been instrumental in getting Talleyrand his job at the Foreign Office. It was during these days that she asked him who the greatest woman was. He responded that it was the one who had the most children, which made her clutch her pearls. Her later writings of her impressions of him at this time are worth quoting at length, as they express the awe in which he was held:

> He foresaw that peace would be popular in France because the passions were subsiding into tranquility, and the people were becoming weary of sacrifices; he therefore signed the treaty of Campo-Formio with Austria. But this treaty contained the surrender of the Venetian Republic; and it is not easy to conceive how he succeeded in prevailing upon the Directory, which yet was in some respects republican, to commit what, according to its own principles, was the greatest possible enormity. From the date of this proceeding, no less arbitrary than the partition of Poland, there no longer existed in the government of France the slightest respect for any political doctrine, and the reign of one man began when the dominion of principle was at an end.
>
> It was with this sentiment, at least, that I saw him for the first time at Paris. I could not find words to reply to him, when he came to me to say, that he had sought my father at Coppet, and that he regretted having passed into Switzerland without seeing him. But, when I was a little recov-

ered from the confusion of admiration, a strongly marked sentiment of fear succeeded. Bonaparte, at that time, had no power; he was even believed to be not a little threatened by the captious suspicions of the Directory; so that the fear which he inspired was caused only by the singular effect of his person upon nearly all who approached him. I had seen men highly worthy of esteem; I had likewise seen monsters of ferocity: there was nothing in the effect that Bonaparte produced on me that could bring back to my recollection either the one or the other... Far from recovering my confidence by seeing Bonaparte more frequently, he constantly intimidated me more and more. I had a confused feeling that no emotion of the heart could act upon him...

Every time that I heard him speak, I was struck with his superiority; yet it had no similitude to that of men instructed and cultivated by study or society, such as those of whom France and England can furnish examples. But his discourse indicated a fine perception of circumstances, such as the sportsman has of the game that he pursues. Sometimes he related the political and military events of his life in a very interesting manner; he had even somewhat of Italian imagination in narratives, which allowed of gaiety. Yet nothing could triumph over my invincible aversion for what I perceived in him. I felt in his soul a cold sharp-edged sword, which froze the wound that it inflicted; I perceived in his understanding a profound irony, from which nothing great or beautiful, not even his own glory could escape; for he despised the nation whose suffrages he wished, and no spark of enthusiasm was mingled with his desire of astonishing the human race.

It was in the interval between the return of Bonaparte and his departure for Egypt, that is to say, about the end of 1797, that I saw him several times at Paris; and never could I dissipate the difficulty of breathing which I experienced in his presence. I was one day at table between him and the Abbé Sieyès; a singular situation, if I had been able to foresee what afterwards happened...

The Abbé Sieyès conversed during dinner unaffectedly and fluently, as suited a mind of his degree of strength. He expressed himself concerning my father with a sincere esteem. "He is the only man," said he, "who has ever united the most perfect precision in the calculations of a great financier to the imagination of a poet." This eulogium pleased me, because it characterized him. Bonaparte, who heard it, also said some obliging things concerning my father and me, but like a man who takes no interest in individuals whom he cannot make use of in the accomplishment of his own ends...

He already took delight in the art of embarrassing, by saying disagreeable things; an art which he has since reduced into a system, as he has every other mode of subjugating men by degrading them. At this epoch, however, he had a desire to please, for he confined to his own thoughts the project of overturning the Directory and substituting himself in its stead; but in spite of this desire, one would have said that, unlike the prophet, he cursed involuntarily, though he intended to bless [a reference to Numbers 23–24].

Bonaparte emitted an aura of invincibility and infallibility as he took command of the force designated to invade England. Even in Italy, he had realized the difficulty involved in invading Great Britain and, as mentioned above, was in the process of convincing the Directory to turn the force toward Egypt. His nominal boss, the minister of war, was Barthelemy Scherer, the man he had replaced as commander of the Army of Italy in March 1796. The two of them were willing to let bygones be bygones, and Scherer enthusiastically supported the Egyptian expedition, seeing no downside to it whether Bonaparte won or lost. Talleyrand supported it for the same reason.

1798: The Principle of Population

The United States, 1798

The Mississippi Territory, 1798: In April 1798, the United States organized the Mississippi Territory, later divided into the states of Mississippi and Alabama, from land ceded by Georgia and Spain. It ran between the Chattahoochee and Mississippi Rivers and between latitudes 31.00 degrees and 32.28 degrees. Georgia still claimed the land to the north of latitude 32.28 up to the Tennessee border. They would finally cede that in 1802. The white population of Georgia in 1798 was limited to the Savannah River Valley, including Savannah, Augusta, and the surrounding small towns and plantations. On the frontier near what is today Macon, the Creek Agency had been set up to interact with the Creek Indians of Georgia and Alabama since 1796. The Indian agent there was Benjamin Hawkins, and he was sincere in his desire to uplift the Creek Nation and was moderately successful at convincing them to forsake the old ways and take up the ways of the white man.

Most of the Mississippi Territory was in the hands of the US, but it was originally landlocked, as the Gulf Coast, known at the time as West Florida, was still under Spanish control. This included Baton Rouge, Gulfport, Biloxi, Mobile, and Pensacola. The US would challenge this in the days of the Madison administration before and during the War of 1812. White population growth in

THE GREAT GLOBE ITSELF

the territory was stifled due to the fact that millions of acres of land were part of the Creek Nation's hunting grounds. The Creeks had to cede the land in 1814 in compensation for siding with the British and Tecumseh, after which the white and slave populations boomed.

XYZ Affair, 1798: By the beginning of the year in Paris, Talleyrand had frozen Marshall and Pinckney out of all communication as they refused to budge regarding any loans or bribes. They asked for their passports, but there was a delay over the question of whether they would formally leave on their own or had been told to leave. Eventually, Talleyrand formally told them to leave, putting the onus for failure on him. Talleyrand told Gerry to stay in Paris, telling him that as long as he stayed, France wouldn't have to declare war, which is a lot of pressure to put on somebody.

As a result, when Marshall and Pinckney left in April, Gerry stayed behind until October. Release of the commission's dispatches to the public with the names changed to X, Y, and Z led to a clamor to spend "millions on defense but not a cent on tribute," as the saying went. Congress authorized the completion of the rest of the original six frigates—*Congress, President,* and *Chesapeake*—and authorized the construction of six more (funded in part by the British) to serve in the newly created Department of the Navy. *Congress* was launched August 15, 1799; *Chesapeake* was launched December 2, 1799; and *President* was launched April 10, 1800. *Chesapeake* was the ship that Captain James Lawrence was commanding in 1813, and his dying order was, "Don't give up the ship!" The order could not be obeyed, and the ship surrendered. The lumber from the ship was later used for a building in Wickham Hampshire called Chesapeake Mill that you can visit to this day.

In May, Congress nullified the alliance with France and authorized the recruitment of an Army to be used to conquer Florida. The next time the United States would be part of an alliance would be when they formed and joined NATO in 1949. Adams addressed the Congress about XYZ, seeming to recall his own mistreatment by the British in 1785 as one of the things he said in his message was "American ministers shall be treated as representatives of a great nation."

In June and July, Congress passed four laws that were collectively known as the Alien and Sedition Acts. The Federalists controlled Congress, as they had since the beginning of the Washington administration and were becoming high-handed.

The Naturalization Act repealed and replaced the Naturalization Act of 1795 to extend the duration of residence required for aliens to become citizens of the United States from five years to fourteen years. It was superseded in 1802, when the residency period was restored to five years.

The Alien Act authorized the president to deport any resident alien considered "dangerous to the peace and safety of the United States." It was activated June 25, 1798, with a two-year expiration date.

The Alien Enemies Act authorized the president to apprehend and deport resident aliens if their home countries were at war with the United States. Enacted July 6, 1798, and providing no sunset provision, the act remains intact today.

The Sedition Act made it a crime to publish "false, scandalous, and malicious writing" against the government or its officials. It was enacted July 14, 1798, with an expiration date of March 3, 1801 (the day before Adams' presidential term ended).

These laws would inspire Madison and Jefferson to write the Kentucky and Virginia Resolutions, which laid the philosophical foundation for the nefarious doctrine of nullification. Some states that were controlled by Republicans threatened not to execute the laws.

On July 4, Adams offered George Washington the position of commander in chief of the United States Army with the rank of lieutenant general, a rank that would not be conferred on anyone else until Ulysses Grant in 1864. Well, the Confederate Army had a few full generals in it. With France and Spain having become allies in 1796, the United States had its eyes on Spanish-controlled territories to the south and west. They were also concerned about free navigation of the Mississippi River, the current border between the United States and Spanish America. Washington accepted, along with Hamilton, who was made a major general and given the title

THE GREAT GLOBE ITSELF

of inspector general, making him once again Washington's deputy. Washington was now sixty-six years old and delegated most of the responsibility to Hamilton. Washington rarely left Mount Vernon, and Hamilton raised and trained this Army in New Jersey.

Jefferson and his faction declared their concern that this Army might be turned on them as they protested the Alien and Sedition Acts. Hamilton indicated that he was indeed willing to use the laws against Jefferson and his friends. When we first took note of Hamilton in 1776, we saw his similarities to Bonaparte as far as the intellect, the ambition, the foreign birth, and the service in the artillery. Now that Bonaparte was famous, Hamilton might have noticed the same things and thought to himself, *Why not me?* Jefferson and Madison, and Adams for that matter, were all calling him an aspiring Bonaparte in these days. So was Aaron Burr, himself another aspiring Bonaparte.

In addition to the Army being raised in New Jersey, we recall that the Legion of the United States, now named the United States Army, was in the west, four regiments strong. Hamilton ordered the commander there, General James Wilkinson, to establish a reserve corps in the vicinity of the confluence of the Mississippi and Ohio Rivers in order to be ready to attack Spanish settlements on the west side of the Mississippi. Things moved slowly and the base, Cantonment Wilkinson, wasn't established until September 1800 in what is now Pulaski County, Illinois. This was long after Adams had shut down the Quasi-War. The base operated for two years before it closed.

As we recall, Wilkinson had been put in command of the Army after the untimely death of General Wayne in December 1796. Wilkinson has a bad reputation in the history books, being accused of being a paid Spanish agent, a charge which was never proven during his lifetime. After Hamilton resigned from the Army in 1800, Wilkinson was the commanding general of the Army for the next twelve years. He was a longtime friend of Aaron Burr's (1775 in Quebec) and Benedict Arnold 's (1777 in Saratoga). Burr and Wilkinson would engage in some shadowy operations in the west in the days after Burr's term as vice president, the purpose of which was never clear. Burr also engaged with the likes of Jackson, Clay, and Harrison during his time out west.

The Quasi-War, July to December 1798: In July 1798, Congress authorized the Navy to attack French shipping, military and civilian, in the West Indies. Spain, egged on by France, revoked the right of deposit for American goods in New Orleans. It would not be restored until 1801. The Quasi-War was underway. It was not a declared war, and no combined operations with Great Britain were ever contemplated. However, the Royal Navy and the US Navy shared the same signal system and allowed each other's merchant vessels in their convoys. The war was popular in the United States and helped the Federalists in the 1798 elections. The French public was dismayed at the anger toward their country in America, which was cascading on top of other troubles they were having at the end of 1798 with Great Britain, Austria, Russia, the Ottoman Empire, Naples, and the pope. In late 1798, the directors called Talleyrand to account. He was able to wriggle free from the situation with the help of Gerry, who backed up Talleyrand's false claims that he didn't even know X, Y, or Z and that he had been pursuing a French version of a Jay Treaty all along. Gerry left Paris in October 1798, and his report to Adams was that France desired peace. Adams addressed Congress to that effect in December 1798. At the beginning of 1799, Talleyrand and the US began a long diplomatic process to end the war, which dragged on at decreasing levels of intensity until October 1800.

In November, the state of Kentucky passed the Kentucky Resolutions, condemning the Alien and Sedition Acts. They were ghostwritten by Thomas Jefferson and stewarded through the Kentucky legislature by a state representative named John Breckinridge, who later served as Jefferson's attorney general and was the grandfather of US vice president and, later, Confederate states general John Breckenridge. In the days before *Marbury v. Madison*, there was no mechanism by which laws passed by Congress could be determined to be in violation of the Constitution, so nullification by the states was thought to be the way. The idea was that the states would act as tribunes, vetoing laws they might disagree with. In December, the state of Virginia passed the Virginia Resolutions, also condemning the Alien and Sedition Acts. They were openly authored by James Madison, using the word *interposition* instead of *nullification*.

Kentucky and Virginia submitted their resolutions to the other states for concurrence, but they all rejected, disapproved, or ignored them. The states who took notice of them generally said they viewed the courts as the best way to determine the constitutionality of federal laws, but some of them may have been eyeing the Army that Hamilton was building when they said that. *Marbury v. Madison* was decided in 1803 by John Marshall's Supreme Court, and that killed the nullification debate for years. Jefferson and Madison even used the Alien and Sedition Acts against their enemies during their years in power, as they were never declared unconstitutional. The idea of state nullification lived on after *Marbury v. Madison*, leading to the Nullification Crisis in South Carolina in the days of Andrew Jackson.

Egypt, 1798

Preparations for invasion, 1798: Bonaparte evaluated the condition of the French Navy in Brest and the Dutch Navy in the Netherlands and concluded that the idea of invading Great Britain or Ireland was unfeasible. He continued to press for his idea of conquering Egypt and thus bestriding the shortest line of communication between Great Britain and India. After conquering Egypt, he supposedly would then make contact with a Mysore nabob named Tipu Sultan and send fifteen thousand men to Mysore to help drive the British out. I don't know how he convinced the Directory to go along with this, which reinforces the idea that they and their ministers were all happy to get Bonaparte not just out of France but Europe entirely. There are several problems with the strategy involved in a French invasion of Egypt:

- The British had evacuated the Mediterranean in 1796, so they weren't using it as a line of communication to India. As we recall, when France conquered the Netherlands, the British went on to seize control the Cape Colony in South

Africa, and that was the primary line of communication to India.

- Sending the entire Toulon Fleet to Egypt would reopen the Mediterranean to the Royal Navy again, which is exactly what happened as Nelson started chasing it as soon as it weighed anchor and started moving east. Then after destroying the Toulon Fleet, the Royal Navy set up bases in Sicily, Naples, and Minorca.
- France was at peace and had diplomatic relations with the Ottomans, who were the rulers of Egypt. In 1798, the Ottomans were not part of any alliance with any of the great powers, so why didn't France conclude an alliance with the Ottomans so that their expedition would be welcomed in Cairo instead of being fought? Talleyrand told Bonaparte that he would inform the Ottoman ambassador in Paris of the operation, but he never did.
- When the French invasion of Egypt became known, Paul I immediately concluded an alliance with the Ottomans, a country that the Russians had, for years, been dominating in a way matched only by the treatment of Mexico by the United States in the 1840s. Russia soon concluded an alliance with Austria and Great Britain as well, sending large Armies to Switzerland, Italy, and the Netherlands as part of the War of the Second Coalition.
- Mesopotamia and Persia inconveniently lay between Egypt and India. Today it is a six-hour flight from Cairo to Mumbai, a longer distance than between New York and LA. France might have gone through the Red Sea, except for the fact that all the French ships were in the Mediterranean, and the Suez Canal wasn't built until 1869.
- The Ottoman Fleets had been eliminated from the Indian Ocean by the Portuguese in the 1500s. They had a presence in the Red Sea, but nothing that could sail the ocean or withstand the British if they could.

THE GREAT GLOBE ITSELF

In March, the Directory approved the Egyptian expedition, allocating 40,000 troops, 22 ships of the line, and 120 transports, almost the entire Mediterranean Fleet. They also sent a large number of scientists and scholars to document what they found and collect samples. Presumably their credentials as Egyptologists were kept under wraps. As stated above, the British had evacuated the Mediterranean in 1796, and their nearest base was in Portugal. However, the Spanish-Mediterranean Fleet had also left their base in Cartagena and been defeated at Cape Saint Vincent and was now bottled up in Cadiz. The massive amount of military activity taking place in Toulon soon became known to the British, but the purpose of it remained a mystery. Guesses as to its objective included Ireland, Italy, the Ionian Islands, even the Crimea. The French were planning diversions in Ireland to keep the British out of the Mediterranean, but that wasn't enough. Admiral Jervis asked for one-armed, one-eyed Nelson to take command of the squadron assigned to follow the Toulon Fleet. Nelson spent the next three months searching the Mediterranean for him.

Malta, May to June 1798: The French expedition departed Toulon on May 19 and arrived in Malta on June 9. The commander of the Knights of Malta was hostile to the French, probably because he had received word that the French had occupied Rome and arrested his boss, Pope Pius VI, so he tried to make life difficult for them; for example, only allowing two French ships into the harbor at a time. Bonaparte didn't have time for that and ordered an assault, which was aided by the Maltese knights of French extraction, and he conquered Malta in three days. It was now that Bonaparte informed his troops that they were going to Egypt. The conquest of Malta would have major consequences. In October, Paul I got himself elected grand master of the Knights of Malta, although I'm not sure who the voters were. As such, he claimed to be duty bound to respond to French aggression in Malta and points east. Paul declared war on France at the end of 1798. Later, Britain starved the French out of Malta and occupied it, promising to leave as part of the Peace of Amiens. They didn't, which led to a resumption of the war between France and Great Britain in 1803.

By June 22, Nelson found out that Egypt was the French objective, and he arrived in Alexandria on June 28, two days before the French. Seeing nothing there, he continued the search for the French Fleet. With a little more patience, he and Napoleon would have faced off in a sea battle. Nelson would have won, and Bonaparte's name, whether he lived or died, would have been added to the growing list of French generals who had their moment and then were gone.

Cairo, July 1798: On July 1, the French landed in Alexandria. This was a major event in history for reasons far beyond the war that was underway now. Bonaparte landed with scientists, who intended to study the ruins of Egypt to match it up against the ancient literature. Egyptology, the Rosetta Stone, the *Book of the Dead*, King Tut, and all the archaeology that followed and echo down to the present day proceed from this event. The French moved toward Cairo, which is where the Sphinx and the Great Pyramid of Giza are located.

Egypt was under the control of a duumvirate of Mamluks named Ibrahim Bey and Murad Bey. Bey is a title, not a name, that means "Satrap." On July 21, they brought a force up to face the French in what was to become known as the Battle of the Pyramids. In his order of the day, Bonaparte said, "Soldiers! You came to this country to save the inhabitants from barbarism, to bring civilization to the Orient and subtract this beautiful part of the world from the domination of England. From the top of those pyramids, forty centuries are contemplating you." The Mamluks were scattered, with

Murad Bey heading south up the Nile and Ibrahim Bey heading east toward Sinai. Neither of them ever managed to restore their fortunes.

Cairo surrendered, and Bonaparte made it his headquarters. He preached tolerance of religion and even participated in some Islamic rituals, while the Egyptian imams preached to the people that the French were evil demons. Bonaparte sent notes to Sultan Selim III in Constantinople to the effect that even though he had invaded his empire, he was not his enemy. Everyone else in Europe convinced the sultan otherwise. Bonaparte incorporated some Mamluk units into his Army. These units would still be in the French Army, serving in Spain in 1808, although by that time, most of those Mamluks were French soldiers in Muslim costumes. They would be a symbol to the Spaniards of the righteousness of their cause against France, a godless (or even worse than godless—Muslim!) nation. Religion was a powerful force that France's enemies were always able to use against them.

Battle of the Nile, August 1798: It took Nelson four weeks to find out that he had missed a rendezvous with the Toulon Fleet in Alexandria by two days. As soon as he found out, he went there with

all speed, arriving in the afternoon of August 1. Nelson did not pause but went directly from convoy to battle formation. The French Fleet was at anchor and lost thirteen of seventeen ships, four destroyed, nine captured. The highlight of the battle was when the French flagship *L'Orient* caught fire and blew up. Nelson suffered a head wound, but he didn't lose any body parts. When word got out that the French Fleet was destroyed, all the enemies of France, as well as the French enemies of Bonaparte, took comfort in knowing that the French expedition to Egypt was doomed. General Bernadotte celebrated in Paris by marrying Desiree Clary. Paul I sent Nelson a gift. Selim III awarded him the Order of the Turkish Crescent, invented for this occasion because all the other Ottoman orders were for Muslims only. Pitt wanted to give Nelson an earldom like the one given Jervis, but Spencer, the first lord of the admiralty, reduced it to a barony because Nelson was only a squadron commander, not commander in chief of a Fleet, so he became Baron Nelson of the Nile.

The victory at the Nile had repercussions all over Europe since it enabled the formation of the Second Coalition. Bonaparte in Egypt was compared to Hannibal in Italy, as a flame that would be spent soon for lack of fuel. Austria was getting nowhere in the mediatization process at the Congress of Rastatt, as described below, and was ready to get back in the fight. The Russians, annoyed at the French incursion into the Eastern Mediterranean, especially Malta and the Ionian Islands, were also ready to take on France. The Ottomans, for once, were on the same side as the Russians and the Austrians, although this was as unnatural as a Spanish-English or an Austrian-Prussian alliance. Austria and Russia had only recently been executing the Greek Project to kick the Ottomans out of the Balkans, and now they were all allies. Naples was worried about the French Army that had just occupied the Papal States, as described below, and they signed on. Even the US was fighting France in the West Indies, although they were not part of the Second Coalition.

France had everyone but Spain and Prussia lined up against them. Talleyrand was presiding over a complete failure of diplomacy, but there isn't too much that diplomacy can do after the enemy destroys your Fleet and strands your best general. Talleyrand must not have considered the possibility that the Toulon Fleet could be destroyed so easily. Well, he wasn't a naval strategist, but I can't see that the men who were had been consulted much, as the directors, and everyone else in the government, had been bedazzled by Bonaparte, including the ones who sent him to Egypt praying for him to fail. One thing Talleyrand got to work on immediately was lowering the heat with the United States, as described above.

For the rest of the year, Bonaparte issued proclamations from his headquarters in Cairo, proclaiming the freedom of the Egyptians, which brought him some a degree of local popular support. He also sent General Desaix south to terminate Murad Bey 's command. Imams were constantly preaching against the French infidels, inciting numerous riots and revolts. They were suppressed. Bonaparte reinstated local government control. He took a trip to Suez to see if a canal was indeed feasible there. In Constantinople, Selim III prepared to move on Egypt, with one force concentrating in Rhodes and coming by sea and the other concentrating in Syria and coming by land. By the end of the year, Bonaparte had gotten word of these plans and prepared to go on offense.

Italy, 1798

France arrests the pope, 1798: Joseph Bonaparte had been named as the French minister to the Papal States, but he was really there to incite a revolution that would turn them into another French sister republic. On December 28, 1797, there was a riot at Joseph's palace in response to a republican festival he held there. A French brigadier named Leonard Duphot was shot and killed by papal troops. Duphot had been engaged to Desiree Clary, Joseph's sister-in-law and former fiancée of Bonaparte, after which she met and married General Bernadotte. Pope Pius VI personally apologized for the shooting. Most of the Army of Italy under Berthier was renamed the Army of Rome and was soon on the march to that city with nine thousand men. Berthier left a small force behind in Milan under General Joubert that kept the Army of Italy name. On February 10, the Army of Rome entered Rome unop-

posed. Berthier proclaimed the Roman Republic and demanded that the pope renounce his temporal authority over the Papal States, which the pope refused to do. The pope was then arrested and exiled to Tuscany, where the Habsburg grand duke Ferdinand was attempting to maintain his state's neutrality. The history books say the pope was a prisoner, but that doesn't seem to be the case; he was an exile, free to go anywhere but Rome.

Berthier turned over command of the Army of Rome to General Etienne MacDonald, the son of a follower of Charles Stuart, the Young Pretender, who settled in France after the collapse of the 1745 coup in Scotland, making him one of the Wild Geese. In May, Austria and Naples signed an alliance to restore the pope to his temporal throne. The arrest and exile of Pius VI shocked the sensibilities of the good Catholics of the world and was an important factor in the development of the Second Coalition.

North Italy, 1798: A French-inspired republican uprising in the Kingdom of Piedmont (Turin) in April was suppressed, but eventually King Charles Emmanuel IV was ousted by General Joubert, who was commander of the Army of Italy in Milan, which, at this point, was a subordinate command of the Army of Rome. Joubert occupied Turin, but the status of Piedmont remained in flux, while the war of the Second Coalition was underway. At some point, the French force evacuated Piedmont and joined Scherer in Verona, while Joubert went to Paris to get married. Tuscany still had a Habsburg grand duke, and Parma still had a Bourbon duke, but these two must have had serious concerns about the future at this point.

Lord Nelson in Naples and Sicily, 1798: After reporting his destruction of the Toulon Fleet, Nelson sailed to Naples, arriving on September 22. Nelson had spent time in Naples before and had a low opinion of the country, describing it as "a country of fiddlers and poets, whores, and scoundrels." Nevertheless, he was greeted as a hero by the royal couple Ferdinand and Maria Carolina, as well as the British minister to Naples, William Hamilton. Hamilton had been the minister since 1764 and was now sixty-nine years old. He had observed eruptions at Etna and Vesuvius in the 1760s and written scientific papers on volcanoes, which got him elected as a Fellow of

THE GREAT GLOBE ITSELF

the Royal Society in 1770. He was widowered in 1782. In 1791, he married his second wife, known to history as Lady Emma Hamilton. She was thirty-four this year. Nelson, who was married, now demonstrated that his recklessness was not limited to sea fights and began an affair with Lady Hamilton that they did little to conceal. William Hamilton knew about the affair and, at the very least, tolerated it. Nelson's fame and glory overshadowed all, for now.

We also recall that John Acton had been serving as the prime minister of Naples since 1779. At the direction of Jervis, who was planning an invasion of Minorca, Acton, Hamilton, and Nelson began discussions with Ferdinand and Maria Carolina regarding taking action against the French Army of Rome. Ferdinand and Maria Carolina were more than willing to do just that, having signed an alliance with Austria in May 1798. Austria sent Karl von Mack, a veteran of the Flanders campaign, to take command of the Neapolitan Army, and it was he who now led it into the Papal States in October.

The Army of Rome under General MacDonald (remember, he's French) responded. Neither the Army of Rome, which was mostly former Papal States troops nor the Neapolitan Army were cohesive or disciplined, and they both frequently mutinied against their foreign commanders. When the Army of Rome advanced, the Neapolitan Army simply evaporated rather than face the enemy. MacDonald was then able to get the Army of Rome, reinforced with French troops, to march toward Naples. Mack had been abandoned by most of his troops and didn't trust the ones who remained. MacDonald took him prisoner and transported him to France, where he was eventually released. Some histories read that he voluntarily turned himself over to the French, fearful of his own troops, something which may not be true but comes from a true place. With the French marching on Naples and no Army to defend it, at the end of the year, Ferdinand and Maria Carolina fled to Palermo, on the island of Sicily, at the end of the year. MacDonald entered the city of Naples on January 20, 1799, and proclaimed the entire country of Naples, which extended all the way down to the heel and toe of Italy, to be the Parthenopean Republic, a tribute to the Greek colony established there around 700 BC and named for one of the sirens mentioned in the "Odyssey." *Parthenos* is also the Greek word for "virgin" and was applied by the ancient Greeks to Athena and, later, by Christians to Mary, the mother of Jesus. The Army of Rome was renamed the Army of Naples in January 1799.

The Royal Navy returns to Minorca, November 1798: In November, Admiral Jervis captured Minorca and reestablished Royal Navy presence in the Mediterranean. Minorca was returned to Spain in 1802 as part of the Peace of Amiens, something which the Royal Navy establishment bitterly opposed. The British made no attempt to reestablish any presence on Corsica or Elba, which had been their primary Mediterranean bases until 1796. Despite the cooperation of the Austrian, Neapolitan, and British governments in Italy in the year 1798, the War of the Second Coalition is not said to have begun until Russia signed an alliance with Austria and Naples on November 29, 1798.

Switzerland, the bridge between Italy and France, 1798

As a result of Bonaparte's conquests in Italy, France now had substantial interests there. French military strategists knew that it was important to secure the passes in the Alps between France and Italy, so it is not surprising that agitation began in Switzerland to replace the fervidly neutral Swiss government with one that was more inclined toward France. Already in 1797, the pro-French faction began advocating for the French Army to enter the country and replace the decentralized Swiss Confederation with a more centralized republic. The Army of the Rhine, commanded by future marshal William Brune, was renamed the Army of Switzerland, and it marched into Bern in March 1798. Brune had distinguished himself in command of a division under Bonaparte in Italy in 1797. Brune was a competent soldier, but his independence, ambition, and political activity were a little too blatant for Napoleon to ever completely trust him. In April, Brune declared the Helvetic Republic. Switzerland would be a main theater of operations during the War of the Second Coalition. After securing Switzerland in May, he turned over command to Massena and returned to France. He was in the

THE GREAT GLOBE ITSELF

Netherlands in 1799, performing credible work defending against the British-Russian invasion.

There would be tensions in Switzerland over the next five years between the Unitaires, who favored the new centralized order, and the Federalists, who favored the old decentralized order. In 1803, Bonaparte, by then first consul, detached Neuchatel, the portion of Switzerland where the Alpine passes were, made it an independent state, and restored the old Swiss Confederation.

Great Britain and Ireland, 1798

Malthusian economics: In June, economist Thomas Malthus published *An Essay on the Principle of Population, as it affects the Future Improvement of Society with Remarks on the Speculations of Mr. Godwin, M. Condorcet, and Other Writers.* William Godwin had published his utopian works *Enquiry Concerning Political Justice* in 1793 and *Of Avarice and Profusion* in 1797. He was also the father of Mary Wollstonecraft Godwin Shelley. The Marquis de Condorcet had published his utopian vision of social progress and the perfectibility of man, *Esquisse d'un Tableau Historique des Progres de l'Espirit Humain* (*The Future Progress of the Human Mind*) in 1794. Malthus's essay was in response to these utopian visions, as he argued:

> This natural inequality of the two powers of population and of production of the earth, and that great law of our nature which must constantly keep their effects equal, form the great difficulty that appears to me insurmountable in the way to the perfectibility of society.

This means that the limitations of the food supply will eventually make nations, ever growing in population, turn on each other in a struggle for survival. Malthus later became a professor of history and political economy (which was what economics was called in those days) at the British East India College, which I didn't know they had one. He was known by his students as "Pop" Malthus, with Pop being short for population.

Although advances in agriculture and industry have temporarily staved off Malthus's predictions of catastrophe, Malthusianism is still advocated today in revised forms, as it seems inevitable that one day, the population bubble will burst. These days, the idea of running out of food is accompanied by the idea of running out of energy as stated in the Olduvai theory, which is that our growing civilization is only made possible by burning finite fossil fuels, and when they are gone, an event which, for the last forty years, has been ten years away, the global population will be reduced catastrophically to about one billion people living in a world reduced to the technologies of the year 1860. Time will tell.

The Irish Rebellion of 1798: The Treaty of Campo Formio in October 1797 had left Great Britain as France's only enemy, and the British were fully expecting a French invasion in 1798, with the most likely scenario being a repeat of Hoche's 1796 Bantry Bay invasion of Ireland. Hoche was lined up to take command, but he died in September 1797. The cause of death, tuberculosis, is uncontested in the history books, but the British are notorious for using assassins when cornered and, in fact, had sent one to kill Hoche before Bantry Bay. They were not comforted when the victorious Bonaparte was put in Hoche 's place.

Before the British figured out that Bonaparte was intending to do something in the Mediterranean rather than in the British Isles, the Irish government, under John Pratt, the Marquess Camden, preemptively began a purge of suspected French collaborators, that is, the United Irishmen, starting with the arrest of the leaders on March 10 and then declaring martial law on March 30. Suspects were publicly flogged, contributing to an atmosphere of terror, at least according to the Marxist-oriented Irish historians who dominate the field. The United Irishmen had no idea whether France was coming to Ireland or not but were in a situation where it made sense for them to rebel in either case.

The plan was to take control of Dublin and the surrounding counties, which is an Irish province traditionally known as Leinster. The United Irishmen raised the standard of rebellion there on

May 24, having heard that Bonaparte had shoved off from Toulon the week before. They might have been assured by their French contacts that Bonaparte was headed to Dublin, who were only saying that as part of the French plan to disguise his true objective, Egypt, which seems pretty cold to me. Lord Camden was ready for them in Dublin, and they were defeated in two weeks. The rebels were arrested and, in many cases, executed after summary trials. British Army forces were never used against the rebellion. It was the Irish government forces using portable gallows to hang hundreds of rebels, as per the illustration. The word was passed among the United Irishmen in Leinster to rally in Enniscorthy, County Wexford, in the southeast corner of Ireland. They may have thought that a French expeditionary force was going to land there, hopefully not more deception from French agents. Soon there were sixteen thousand poorly armed and trained United Irishmen concentrated in Enniscorthy, led by a man named Anthony Perry, known as the Screeching General, who had managed to avoid detection by the government before May 1798.

In London, an Irish-born Whig MP named George Tierney spoke against the government's harsh policies in Ireland, and William Pitt replied to Tierney that he obviously wasn't a patriot. Tierney challenged Pitt to a duel, which Pitt accepted, and it occurred on May 27. Fortunately, no one was injured. It seems incredible that the leader of the country would risk himself in such a reckless fashion, but the spirit of Lord Nelson was permeating the nation. The country agreed that it was too reckless, and there was a deep sense of shock that it had happened. It shows the high level of emotion revolving around Irish-British relations.

Marquess Camden stepped down as lord lieutenant of Ireland and was replaced by none other than Lord Cornwallis of Battle of Yorktown fame. He arrived in Dublin on June 21, and on that same day at Enniscorthy, the Irish Army, under Camden's military commander, a man named Viscount Lake, attacked the United Irishman at a place called Vinegar Hill. Lake's force was able to inflict significant casualties on the United Irishmen with their artillery. About one thousand rebels were killed and five thousand captured, with about ten thousand falling back to Wexford. Lake fully intended to inflict a memorable punishment on his captives, but Cornwallis said it was time to start thinking about reconciliation and amnesty, which was granted to men who returned to their villages. Perry and his remaining force were run to ground at Edenderry in County Offaly (a.k.a. County King) on July 21, and Perry was hanged, screeching as he went.

The Castlebar Races, 1798: When word of the Irish Rebellion came to Paris in May, the Directory felt obligated to support it somehow and made a few gestures, or maybe they had these diversions lined up ahead of time, starting with sending a regiment under the command of Jean Joseph Humbert to land in Killala, County Mayo, in the northwest corner of the island. By the time Humbert landed, it was late August, and Cornwallis and Lake had broken the back of the rebellion with a combination of concession and severity. Nevertheless, when Humbert landed, he recruited five thousand Irishmen to the cause. He declared the Republic of Connaught, which was the name of the traditional province in the west, like Ulster in the north or Leinster in the east. Lake's forces moved to scatter what they thought was a mob of potato farmers and were shocked to see French troops. The ensuing battle became known as the Castlebar Races because of the speed with which Lake's troops retreated, having no idea of the size of the enemy force. Humbert pursued with his regiment and one thousand Irish rebels, two thousand men in all. Lake, joined by Cornwallis, turned and stood at a town called Ballinamuck, County Longford, with thirty thousand men altogether. The French surrendered. It sounds like Cornwallis led them into a trap. Some of Humbert's officers were Irish-born but had been made French citizens, and Humbert pled that they be treated as such. They were all hanged, including Wolfe Tone's brother Matthew. The rebel Irish knew they were doomed and futilely resisted. The ones who weren't killed in action were summarily hanged. Lake and Cornwallis moved into County Mayo and put an end to the Republic of Connaught.

Humbert and his French-born troops were transported to Dublin, where they were exchanged. Humbert later served in the expedition to Saint Dominique, where he was sent home after being accused of sleeping with Pauline Bonaparte. He was dismissed from the Army in 1803. In 1810, he immigrated to New Orleans and had a business relationship with the pirate Jean Lafitte. He took part in independence movements in Mexico in 1813 and Argentina in 1814, commanding a corps at some point. In 1815, he enlisted as a private in the Army commanded by Andrew Jackson at the Battle of New Orleans. He made quite a show dressed in his French brigadier's uniform, earning a thank you from Jackson. After that, he lived the rest of his life as a schoolteacher until his death at the age of fifty-six.

The capture and execution of Wolfe Tone, 1798: On September 16, a French squadron escorting three thousand men under General Jean Hardy and Wolfe Tone departed France, intending to land in Donegal, County Donegal in western Ulster. I don't know if Hardy was one of the Wild Geese or not, but I doubt it since the name appears in both Great Britain and France over the centuries. When my father retired, he took to studying genealogy and read variously that our name was derived from England, Scotland, and the Huguenot region of France,

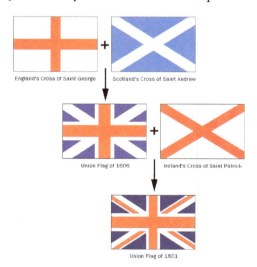

where *hardi* means bold. Wolfe Tone was intending to rally the Irish rebels. The squadron was intercepted by a Royal Navy force, and it attempted to escape, but only three of the ten ships made it back to France. Tone, Hardy, and his remaining force were taken captive. They were exchanged by December 1798. Hardy later commanded a division in Germany under Moreau in 1800, then commanded a corps in Saint Dominique, where he died of yellow fever in May 1802, one of the first such deaths in Saint Dominique, at the age of forty. I saw his name on the *Arc de Triomphe* when we visited Paris in 2014 but only just now read up on his career.

Wolfe Tone was taken to Dublin, tried, and sentenced to death by hanging, being refused a firing squad. The day before his hanging, he managed to get ahold of a knife and slit his own throat. The Irish Rebellion was at an end. It was a primary cause of the law passed in 1801, creating the United Kingdom of Great Britain and Ireland. The Union Jack had to be modified to include the diagonal cross of Saint Patrick. Before, the diagonal stripes were white, but since 1801, there were white-and-red diagonal stripes.

Income taxes in Ireland and Great Britain: Because of all the raids and incursions into Ireland in 1798, at the end of the year, Pitt announced that the government would be implementing an income tax starting in 1799. The tax was abolished in 1802 with the Peace of Amiens, reinstated in 1804, then abolished again in 1816. There were no further income taxes in Great Britain until the start of World War I in 1914.

British withdrawal from Saint Dominique, 1798: In July, the British decided to abandon Port-au-Prince. With the coming of the Second Coalition, British ground forces were now committed to an Anglo-Russian invasion of the Netherlands. General Abercromby, who had declined to stay in command of the Army while it was in Saint Dominique, was once again placed in command for the Netherlands operation. Many of the whites in Saint Dominique went with the British as they left, and the plantation system was on the verge of collapse, but Louverture succeeded in convincing enough of them to stay to temporarily stave off the destruction of the sugar industry there.

THE GREAT GLOBE ITSELF

Louverture now had to compete with a former colleague, Andre Rigaud, for power. Rigaud was a mulatto, and the mulattos constituted a separate class from the blacks, generally favoring continued association with France in the same way that Canada was associated with Great Britain. They mostly lived in the south peninsula of Saint Dominique. Louverture represented greater autonomy and only nominal dependence on France. Louverture and Rigaud engaged in what has been dubbed the War of the Knives until Rigaud was defeated and exiled in October 1800. Rigaud would later return with the French expedition when they invaded Saint Dominique in February 1802.

The issues related to class, race, slavery, exploitation of labor, and miscegenation have not been heavily explored in this discussion of the British attempt to occupy Saint Dominique. These are topics in which the facts matter less than how people feel about those facts. The field is heavily dominated by Marxists, whose assertions generally go unchallenged. One writer, for example, describes a French general as follows:

> Rochambeau ordered six hundred pit bulls from Cuba and forbade anyone to feed them. The pit bulls were to live by eating only "negro meat." That led to larger revolts against the French, as a submissive slave diligently working in the fields would suddenly be devoured by dozens of hungry pit bulls. Today, the saying *"manger la viande des nègres,"* eat the meat of the negros, still resounds deeply in Haiti and the world.

This is the kind of polemic (a debate point framed in such a way as to purposely invite an angry response) that one should avoid giving any credence to, and there are lots of them in the literature surrounding the campaigns in Saint Dominique.

PETER HARDY

France, Eastern and Central Europe, 1798

Failed German mediatization, 1798: One of the terms of the treaty of Campo Formio was that a Congress would assemble to develop a plan that would give compensation to the German princes who had lost lands west of the Rhine. This is called mediatization, because there would be a lot of princes and bishops who had formerly had a direct line to the Holy Roman emperor that would now have a grand duke or an elector between them and the emperor. Ten German states came to Rastatt, a lovely town near Karlsruhe, in November 1797 to meet with three French delegates. Austria was present, but Prussia was not, having lost no territory west of the Rhine. The Congress sat for fifteen months without result until the War of the Second Coalition put an end to it at the end of 1798. A new compensation Congress reconvened in Paris after the Second Coalition collapsed in 1801. Twenty-four-year-old Clemens von Metternich, future chancellor of Austria, got his first exposure to European politics as his father's secretary at this Congress. He was a younger German version of Talleyrand and lasted as chancellor from 1806 to 1848. The period of European history from 1815 to 1848 is often called *The Age of Metternich.*

The Second Coalition, December 1798: France had occupied and then annexed the Ionian Islands in November 1797, as described above. After France invaded Egypt in July, Russia and the Ottomans formed an alliance, also as described above. Paul I was not as annoyed about Egypt as he was about the Ionian Islands and, later, Malta. Russia sent Admiral Feodor Ushakov to the Mediterranean, and he began liberating the Ionian Islands from French rule, conquering Corfu in March 1799. The Ionian Islands were independent until 1807, when France regained control of them per the Treaty of Tilsit. In 1814, they were occupied by the British as a protectorate, which they remained until 1864, when they became part of Greece.

By December 1798, Russia, Great Britain, Austria, the Ottomans, and Naples formed the Second Coalition. It was not a full-fledged alliance, as Austria and Great Britain had no formal agreement with each other, only an informal one to cooperate as cir-

THE GREAT GLOBE ITSELF

cumstances dictated. Russia promised sixty thousand troops to support Austria and forty-five thousand troops to support Great Britain. Austria planned for two Armies: one in Germany under Archduke Charles and another in Switzerland under General Friedrich von Hotze, who had ably assisted Charles in 1796 and 1797. Hotze had the added advantage of being a Swiss citizen. Suvorov was called out of retirement to take a Russian Army to Italy. Another Russian force, under General Ivan von Fersen, would be combined with a British force commanded by General Abercromby under the overall command of the Duke of York that would invade the Netherlands.

French interference in the Netherlands, 1798: After turning over the Foreign Office to Talleyrand in July and then having surgery, Charles Delacroix was sent to The Hague as minister in December 1797 and incited the Dutch radicals to stage a coup in January 1798. A new constitution was passed in April that was in line with the one in France. When the Directory tilted back to the right in May 1798, there was a similar turn to the right in the Netherlands. France completely dominated the Netherlands, and for the next seventeen years, when Paris sneezed, The Hague caught a cold. This was a big bone in the throat of Great Britain, who had dominated the Netherlands since 1688.

Events in Paris, 1798: The elections of 1797 in France had gone heavily in favor of the royalists, and the Directory's response was to nullify it. The elections of 1798 had then gone heavily in favor of the Jacobins, which, to the Directory, was just as bad. Whether you're falling on your face or your back, you're not standing up. The Council of Five Hundred had 104 newly elected Jacobin deputies. In May, the government passed a law—the Law of 22 Floreal—depriving these deputies of their seats, awarding them to persons favorable to the Directory. It must have been frustrating for the bourgeoisie that the electorate only seemed to be able to think in terms of royalists or Jacobins. Unlike 1797, when Augereau had provided military support to the Directory, no general was needed to back up this action, as the Jacobins had no access to any military or police power. One election that was not nullified was that of Jean Baptiste

Treilhard, elected as a director to replace Neufchateau, who had only served for a year.

France prepares to fight the Second Coalition, December 1798: After resigning from the Army in 1796, Jourdan had been elected to the Council of Five Hundred. In September 1798, Jourdan's conscription law was passed. The law regulated the age and number of men that could be called up annually. It extended to recently annexed areas in Belgium, Luxembourg, and the Rhineland. Some resistance occurred there and was quickly put down. The law would be in effect until the end of the empire in 1815.

As 1798 went on, it became clear to the Directory that Austria and Russia would be fielding Armies in Germany and Italy soon. With Bonaparte in Egypt and Moreau still suspected as a royalist, Jourdan was needed to grab his sword and saddle up. In November, he arrived on the Upper Rhine to take command of the Army of Observation, the main force along the Rhine. He would face his old nemesis Archduke Charles. To his right was the Army of Switzerland under Massena. He would face Marshal Bellegarde. Brune was commanding in the Netherlands, and he would face a British-Russian force under the Duke of York. In February 1799, General Scherer left the War Ministry and took command of the Army of Italy, where he would face Suvorov. Moreau was incorrectly suspected as a royalist, but like Jourdan was needed, so he was given a job in Italy as one of Scherer's division commanders. Scherer was replaced as minister of war by a civilian named Louis de Mureau, who was replaced by General Bernadotte in July 1799. General MacDonald retained command of the Army of Naples.

1799: Let's Throw All the Lawyers in the River

The United States, 1799

Winding down the Quasi-War: John Adams was convinced that France was in a bind in Europe and that they sincerely desired peace with the United States. In February, he authorized his minister to the Netherlands, a man named William Vans Murray, to reopen formal communications with Paris. Murray was favorably received by Talleyrand, which was a start. There were objections from the cabinet and from the Federalists in Congress, mostly quibbles about Murray's qualifications, which Adams appeased by appointing two additional commissioners to join Murray. Taking a page from Washington's Jay Treaty playbook, Adams nominated the chief justice of the United States, Oliver Ellsworth, as one of the commissioners. He also nominated Patrick Henry, now sixty-three years old, but Henry turned it down. It may have been for health reasons because Henry died soon afterward, on June 6, 1799. Adams then nominated North Carolina governor William R. Davie, who had founded the University of North Carolina in 1793. Ellsworth and Davie did not depart for Paris until the end of the year. One cause of the delay was that Adams left Philadelphia in March and stayed home in Braintree for seven months, three hundred miles away, running the government by courier. It took five days for a courier on horseback to make that trip one way. In the meantime, the US Navy continued to attack French shipping as well as French warships in the West Indies, supported by and cooperating with the Royal Navy. These were the kind of arrangements that could not simply be turned on and off, and operations continued most of the year.

Adams continued to clash with Hamilton, who was still dominating Adams' cabinet and was, for all practical purpose, the commander in chief of the Army that was being raised. Adams expressed fear of Hamilton's potential as a military dictator, and this was a large factor in Adams' decision to seek peace with France. It wasn't the only one, though, as public passions against France had subsided with the end of the XYZ Affair. The raising of the Army was not going well, an indication of public apathy or even disapproval. Rumors were going around that the Army, consisting mostly of men recruited within a hundred miles of New York and Philadelphia, would be marched south to seize Florida and New Orleans. The thought in the north was that the Army ought to be recruiting Southerners for such a mission. The Republicans were speaking loudly against the Alien and Sedition Acts, which they viewed as Federalist overreach. For his part, Hamilton viewed the Republicans as willing to dismantle the federal government and return to the chaos of the Articles of Confederation.

As the year wore on, Washington became less enthusiastic about the Army that he was nominally in command of. This could have been because his health was declining or because of correspondence he was receiving from the recently freed Lafayette, confirming the desire of France for peace, or because he disapproved of going against the wishes of the sitting president. He never commented on the mental state of his surrogate son, Hamilton, but he might have started having doubts. Washington didn't resign, but it became more difficult for him to stay involved. By September, the Army had only recruited half the authorized men.

In October, Adams returned to work but not in Philadelphia. Because of a yellow fever epidemic there, the government was assembled in Trenton, New Jersey. He met with Commissioners Ellsworth and Davie to finalize the details of their instructions before they left for Paris. Murray, Ellsworth, and Davie presented themselves in Paris at the end of the year 1799 just as the coup of 18 Brumaire was putting Bonaparte in power, so it wasn't until April 1800 that negotiations began in Mortefontaine, a small town about thirty miles northeast of Paris.

Hamilton asked for an interview with Adams for the purpose of making one last effort to halt the commission to Paris before it left. The meeting lasted several hours and presumably allowed Adams to air his grievances about Hamilton, to include his foreign birth, bastardy, and adultery. The result of the meeting was the end of the relationship between Hamilton and Adams. It was also the end of the Federalist Party, which, after 1800, never produced another president or congressional majority.

The rise of New York: From the founding of the American colonies in the early 1600s, they had been dominated by Virginia, Pennsylvania, and Massachusetts. That was changing now as New York City became the largest city in the United States in 1790, and New York State was the fasting-growing state in the Union. Even in 1799, the city population was mostly foreign-born and transient. Much of the influx in 1799 was the result of the failed Irish Rebellion

THE GREAT GLOBE ITSELF

of 1798, which had led to many Irish Protestants leaving the *Auld Sod* for America. These people had mostly been followers of Wolfe Tone, which made them pro-French and therefore more likely to gravitate to the Republicans. Aaron Burr took advantage of the situation as he expended prodigious amounts of energy engaging with the immigrants in retail politics, becoming personally acquainted with thousands of people and knowing what made them tick, which is to say, who were his core supporters, who could be persuaded, and who could be bribed. As we recall, in 1792, he had practically invented Tammany Hall and Columbus Day as a way to focus immigrants on their Americanism. Now he told his constituents to hurry up and get naturalized before the new fourteen-year-residency requirement went into effect. His efforts paid off in 1800 as he was able to flip New York into the Republican column and provide the margin of victory for Thomas Jefferson over John Adams.

Over the past several years, yellow fever epidemics had struck the large cities of the northeast. This year, Aaron Burr founded the Manhattan Company to provide a clean drinking water supply, but he used his political connections to add verbiage to the charter that gave it the ability to operate as a bank. The company built some waterworks, but its banking operations helped the people who tended to be Republicans. This was very annoying to Hamilton, who had founded the Bank of New York in 1784, and it was just as annoying to the management of the New York branch of the Bank of the United States. The Manhattan Company put the New York Republicans on the same playing field as the Federalists and made them competitive politically. The Manhattan Company sold all its waterworks by 1808, although it still maintained a working water tower on the property as late as 1898, but after 1808, it was just a bank. It later evolved to become the Chase Manhattan Bank. After a series of mergers, it is part of a conglomerate known today as JP Morgan Chase, which had a revenue of $129 billion in 2022.

In March, New York passed a law providing for the gradual emancipation of slaves. The law was signed by Governor John Jay, who, as we recall, had owned slaves himself. New York had a slave population of twenty-one thousand in 1799. There were now nine slave states and seven free states, with New Jersey the only northern state where slavery was still legal, until 1804.

The death of George Washington: On December 12, 1799, Washington spent the day on horseback inspecting his farms. A sore throat he developed the next day quickly progressed to a life-threatening situation, and he was soon on his deathbed, surrounded by doctors. He died on December 17. He was not replaced as lieutenant general, and Alexander Hamilton remained senior officer in the Army for the next six months.

Washington's legend was large in his lifetime and continued to grow after his death. One of the many tributes paid to him was by Bonaparte, who had just, the previous month, taken over the government of France. He issued a proclamation, stating:

> Washington is dead! This great man has fought against tyranny and consolidated the liberty of his country. His memory will always be dear to the French people, as to all free men in both hemispheres, and especially to the French soldiers, who equally with the American soldiers fight for liberty and equality. The First Consul therefore decrees that for ten days black crepe shall be hung on the standards and colors of the Consular Guard.

One person noticeably absent from Washington's funeral was Thomas Jefferson, who had never gotten over the poor treatment he had received from him during his last year as secretary of state. After the death of Washington, people in America began making fewer excuses about slavery, and the institution was criticized more and more over the years. Attacks on slave-owning presidents grew sharper and specifically criticized them as slave owners; for example, attacking Jefferson as fathering children on Sally Hemings.

THE GREAT GLOBE ITSELF

Egypt, 1799

Two Ottoman forces were heading to Egypt against the French Army. The force coming overland through Syria came first while the amphibious force concentrating in Rhodes would take some time. The French went on the offensive and invaded Syria in February in order to engage the Ottomans there rather than in Cairo. The Ottoman force was commanded by Ahmad Pasha al-Jazzar (al-Jazzar means "the assassin"), the Syrian governor, and he had a long military résumé. The French brushed aside an Ottoman advance force and laid siege to Jaffa, which had been an important Pharisaic religious center after the destruction of the Temple of Jerusalem in AD 70 and is the reason that Tel Aviv is where it is today. Bonaparte sent an envoy in to negotiate terms of surrender, who was beheaded. I don't know if his head was catapulted over the walls, but I'm sure it would be if they made a movie out of it. The infuriated French stormed it on March 7 and executed everyone inside.

The French Army moved seventy miles north to Acre, where al-Jazzar was defending the fortress there. It had good access to the sea, and the Royal Navy, commanded by Commodore Sydney Smith, was able to provide Marines and resupply. The French blockaded the city on March 20 and called for their heavy artillery. The Ottomans spent the time reinforcing the wall and landing some of the troops from Rhodes. When the French blasted the outer wall, they were dismayed to find a thicker one behind it. In addition to the stubbornness of al-Jazzar and Smith, cases of plague were breaking out on the French side of the line. There is a lot of drama, mostly fictional in my view, because it takes on the air of people, mostly on the British side, telling incredible stories that can't be verified.

Bonaparte gave up, departing Acre on May 21 and returning to Cairo. The people of Syria danced in the streets at the news of al-Jazzar's victory, and Selim III named him "Defender of the Faith." Al-Jazzar died in 1804 at the age of seventy. When, years later, Bonaparte was exiled on Saint Helena, he mused that if he had defeated al-Jazzar, he would have marched on Constantinople and made himself emperor of the east and "returned to Paris by way of Constantinople." These sound like the words of a lunatic, but given what he actually accomplished in life, we can't completely discount it.

When Bonaparte got back to Cairo, he found that Murad Bey was descending north down the Nile, and a hundred Ottoman ships were off the coast of Alexandria, disembarking troops into nearby Aboukir Fortress. General Desaix was detached to campaign up the Nile, defeating Murad Bey and incidentally enabling the scholars to document the ancient monuments at Thebes and other places. Future marshal Louis Nicholas Davout was one of Desaix 's subordinates.

The commander of the Ottoman ships and the troops at Aboukir was Mustafa Pasha, who was the uncle of Mohammad Ali, the man who ruled Egypt from 1805 to 1848, nominally as a satrap of the sultan but independent for all practical purposes. Ali is considered the founder of modern Egypt. He did what Bonaparte probably would have ended up doing if he had stayed in Egypt: not becoming the Ottoman sultan but ruling Egypt and a large swath of territory east and west of it. This makes him a doppelgänger for Bonaparte.

Mustafa Pasha was not as fortunate as his nephew was to be. On July 25, his force emerged from the fortress and offered battle, and Bonaparte literally drove them into the sea, where many of them drowned as they attempted to swim to the transports that were two miles away. Mustafa Pasha was taken captive. And now the wheels of conspiracy start turning because Mustafa Pasha was able to provide Bonaparte with information in the form of newspapers regarding events in Europe and how the Austrians and Russians were advancing into Switzerland and Italy and that the Directory had recalled Bonaparte to France to restore the situation but that the British blockade had cut off all communication to the French expedition. At the same time that Bonaparte was reading all this, Commodore Smith lifted the blockade, stating that his bully beef was exhausted, and he was going back to Rhodes or some other port to get reprovisioned. Why he would open the door for Bonaparte's escape has been a controversial topic. The conspiracy theory is that the British military-industrial complex needed a bogeyman to maintain its funding, but it may be either that Smith just wanted Bonaparte, who, after all,

THE GREAT GLOBE ITSELF

was just another general, out of his area operations or that it was easy for a single ship to sneak its way past enemy lines.

The same month, July, some French soldiers constructing fortifications near Rosetta (known today as Rashid), a town about forty miles east of Alexandria, dug up a stone that contained Greek, Demotic, and Egyptian words. The stone was dated from 196 BC and the reign of Ptolemy V, an otherwise unremarkable Pharaoh, except he was the first one in his line to impregnate his sister with his heir. He had also just, two years previously, in 198 BC, lost Syria to the Seleucids, an important event in Jewish history because it transferred access to the Temple of Jerusalem from the Sadducees in Alexandria to the Pharisees in Babylon. The wording of the decree on the stone is what you might expect, extoling the virtues of the Pharaoh. In 1952, it enabled scholars to decipher the ancient Egyptian language, and now Rosetta Stone is a byword for a key that unlocks hidden knowledge. When the French capitulated in Egypt in 1801, they had to turn the stone and other items over to the British, and it is in the British Museum to this day.

On August 23, a French Army bulletin announced that Bonaparte had left Egypt and that command had been turned over to General Kleber, who was a good choice. The troops were dismayed, but Kleber said that Bonaparte would return with reinforcements, which, of course, he did not, but he tried often to send troops. On board with Bonaparte were Berthier, Murat, Lannes, and Marmont, along with a few scholars and painters who had been part of the scientific expedition and who were all forever loyal to Bonaparte. Kleber would be assassinated in Egypt on June 14, 1800, the same day as the Battle of Marengo, and the French Army in Egypt, by that time down to ten thousand men from the forty thousand of July 1798, would surrender to Britain in September 1801, under General Menou, who, as we remember, had been Bonaparte's predecessor in command of the Army of the Interior, which Bonaparte had used to squash the royalist mob in Paris in October 1795. The scientists were allowed to take a large part of their hoard of priceless artifacts back to France with them, where they were lovingly cared for and examined. The imperial edition of the *Description de l'Égypte* would

PETER HARDY

be published in 1809 in a dozen volumes, with another dozen published in 1820–1822.

Italy, 1799

Suvorov conquers Italy, April to September: As we recall, the Neapolitan Army, not to be confused with MacDonald's French Army of Naples, had successfully occupied Rome in November 1798. In January 1799, MacDonald launched a counterattack, captured the city of Naples, and declared the Parthenopean Republic. The royal court fled to Palermo, and the tag went around about Ferdinand IV that "he came, he saw, he fled." The French Army occupied Naples but was called away in the spring when Suvorov invaded Italy.

In February, General Scherer took command of the Army of Italy. As we recall, he had been minister of war since July 1797 and had approved the expedition to Egypt. The Army of Italy was now made a command separate from and equal to MacDonald's Army of Naples. General Joubert was under Scherer's command, still in Turin, serving as governor of the provisional Piedmont Republic. I think Scherer meant to prove that he could have done what Bonaparte did in Italy in 1796 if he hadn't been relieved for political reasons. He was about to find out that he couldn't. Suvorov was still on his way to Italy, so for now, the allied commander in Italy was General Paul Kray. Scherer must have had intel that the Russians were coming because he preemptively engaged Kray twice: on March 26 in Verona and April 4 in Magnano. Kray inflicted a defeat on Scherer in Magnano, and the French began a retreat, eventually digging in behind the Adda River, east of Milan. Kray was promoted to field marshal on April 18, but now Suvorov and his Russians arrived, along with Austrian marshal Michael von Melas, who incorporated Kray's force into his. Kray was sent to lay siege to Mantua, an important operation that lasted until July. Suvorov was in overall command, with von Melas commanding the Austrians and Peter Bagration, who would attain great fame in the 1812 invasion of Russia and also gets mentioned frequently in *War and Peace,* commanding the Russians. Prince Constantine Romanov, Paul I's second son, was twenty years old and serving on Suvorov's staff. Not much went wrong for the allies in Italy this year, but when it did, the blame was pinned on Constantine, unfairly in my opinion.

The allies advanced against the French. Scherer attempted a defense but seems to have been rattled by his defeat at Magnano and was relieved of command on April 26, the day that the allies began their assault. He was ordered to Paris to face an inquiry, where he was acquitted, and he retired. He died in 1804, aged fifty-seven. He was replaced in the middle of the battle by Moreau, who had been cleared of all royalist charges. Moreau's three division commanders were future marshals Claude Victor and John Mathieu Serurier, and another man named General Paul Grenier, who had the résumé of a marshal but became too closely associated with Moreau to become one under Bonaparte.

The day after Moreau took command, Suvorov pressed the attacks in what is known as the Battle of Cassano but what was actually a series of battles that forced the French from their positions along the Adda River. Moreau's force was driven out of Lombardy, west of the Ticino River into Piedmont. The territory of the Cisalpine Republic was now entirely in allied hands, except for Mantua. French general Serurier and half his division were taken captive. Suvorov had him over for dinner prior to him and his men being exchanged. The allies advanced to Milan and laid siege to the citadel there, which was held by 2,400 French troops, who capitulated on May 24. Suvorov consolidated his positions and prepared to force the French completely out of Italy.

Moreau could hardly be held responsible for French failures, having taken over in the middle of the battle, and so he kept his job. Most of his forces were south of the Po River, and Suvorov had established crossing points by May 16. Moreau was outnumbered and moved his forces into Genoa. The Mediterranean alpine terrain made it easily defensible. The local Piedmont officials now denounced the French occupiers. The allies laid siege to Turin from May 26, and it fell on June 20. In Genoa, Moreau received reinforcements arriving by sea.

After the Battle of Cassano, MacDonald, in Naples, had been ordered to support Moreau. MacDonald evacuated Naples, left 2,500 troops to garrison Rome, and concentrated all his forces, about 35,000 men, in Florence by May 26. He also forced the departures of the Habsburg Grand Duke of Tuscany and the Bourbon Duke of Parma, convinced they would stab him in the back when he left. The exiled Pope Pius VI, living in Florence at the time, was also forced to evacuate, and from May to August, he was transported from Florence to Parma to Piacenza to Turin to Grenoble and to Valence. Suvorov was bringing fire and sword into Piedmont at the time that the pope was traveling through there, so they kept moving. It looked like maybe the French were trying to get him to Avignon and perhaps set him up as an antipope, similar to the situation that prevailed from 1378 to 1429, but the pope died in Valence on August 29, at the age of eighty-two, worn out by his travels.

Moving north toward Mantua, on June 12, MacDonald made contact with the enemy at Modena, driving back an Austrian corps. Rather than attempt to relieve Mantua, he moved west in an attempt to link up with Moreau 's force in Liguria. Suvorov, with the forces of Bagration, Melas, and Bellegarde at his disposal, moved to meet him, and there was a three-day battle near Piacenza, known as the Battle of the Trebbia. The battle took place on July 17–20, and MacDonald's force was severely mauled. MacDonald was hoping that Moreau might fall on Suvorov's rear, but Moreau was prevented from doing so, as he was attacked by Bellegarde, whose mission was to prevent a French linkup. MacDonald retreated and moved to the west coast of Italy, later linking up with Moreau with about ten thousand troops, about a third of what he started with. MacDonald himself was wounded and replaced by future marshal Laurent Saint Cyr.

As described below, there was a coup in Paris in June 1799, with Directors Barras and Sieyes ejecting and replacing the other three directors as well as all the ministers. This was because, as we shall see,

THE GREAT GLOBE ITSELF

the war news was bad on all fronts, not just Italy and Egypt. Sieyes had been working on a new constitution that he thought needed a military man or, as he called it, a sword. General Joubert had returned from Piedmont, where he had ejected the king of Piedmont-Sardinia and proclaimed a republic. Now he was in Paris, getting married to a well-connected young woman named Mademoiselle Montholon. They could center a soap opera around her and her family, although this is not the place to list the details. With Joubert, Sieyes thought he had found Bonaparte 2.0 and recruited him for his coup, and Joubert signed on, providing the sword needed to force the resignation of the three resistant directors. Immediately after that, Joubert was appointed to replace Moreau in Italy, arriving in Genoa on July 15. Moreau agreed to stick around and advise Joubert. There was immediate bad news as the French garrison in Mantua capitulated on July 27, freeing up thousands of Austrian troops.

Joubert advanced against the allies, heading toward the town of Alessandria, where the allies had just wrapped up a siege. Four future marshals of France—Laurent Saint Cyr, Emmanuel Grouchy, Dom Perignon, and Louis Gabriel Suchet —were serving in his Army. Suvorov had Bagration, von Melas, Kray, and Bellegarde on his side. The battle took place south of Alessandria on August 15, near a town called Novi. The nature of the battle was the allies surrounding and attacking a well-entrenched French force, so it lasted all day. Joubert was killed early in the fight as he led a counterattack against an early assault. He'd probably seen Bonaparte do the same thing a hundred times in 1796 and 1797, but he didn't have Bonaparte's luck and was shot dead on the battlefield, supposedly through the heart, but I think the Austrian troops that got him were just going for center of mass. The point of the through-the-heart bit is to emphasize that the fallen hero was advancing on and facing the enemy. His widow eventually married MacDonald. It just happened to be Bonaparte's thirtieth birthday, so Joubert gave him the ultimate birthday present. Moreau assumed command. When word of Joubert's death reached Paris in September, a day of public mourning for him was decreed, and Sieyes began looking for another general.

Suvorov pressed the attacks on all sides, and the French position began to crumble in the afternoon. Grouchy and Perignon were taken prisoner. Moreau conducted the retreat to Genoa, turned command over to General Jean Championnet in September, and returned to Paris, where Sieyes attempted to recruit him for the coup. Moreau, convinced that a coup attempt would result in the destruction of both Sieyes and whichever general he talked into helping him, told him that he wasn't interested but that Bonaparte was his man. He would later regret his decision.

Just at that time, Suvorov was ordered to take his thirty thousand Russian troops to Switzerland to support operations there, and so he undertook the crossing of the Alps, this time from south to north. This was part of a shift in strategy proposed by the British and approved by Paul I, as the British were now conducting operations with the Russians in the Netherlands. This required a change in focus from Italy to Germany. The Po Valley was completely under Austrian control, thanks to Suvorov, who was given all kinds of recognition as he left from the Austrians and the Russians, and the temporarily reestablished king of Piedmont-Sardinia named him Prince of Savoy.

Melas was now commander in chief in Italy. Championnet decided to try one more offensive, possibly to gain supplies, and descended into the Po Valley in October with his Army, but he was met by Melas at a town between Genoa and Turin called Genola on November 3 and forced back into Liguria after losing eight thousand men. Championnet died of typhus on January 9, 1800, and was replaced by Massena, who, as described below, had a good year in Switzerland.

Nelson in Naples, 1799: At the beginning of 1799, General MacDonald occupied Naples, and Nelson was blockading it. He was also blockading Alexandria and Malta, while the Ottoman-Russian combined Fleet under Admiral Ushakov, who, as we recall, had ejected the French from the Ionian Islands, was very busy blockading Genoa on the west coast of Italy, Ancona on the east coast, and supporting a popular counterrevolution in southern Naples led by a man named Cardinal Ruffo. The people of Naples were devoted Catholics and feared and loathed the godless French as much as the

THE GREAT GLOBE ITSELF

Muslims of Egypt did. As stated above, MacDonald was called upon in April to reinforce Moreau up north, so he left Naples under a local republican force and left a 2,500-man garrison in Rome. This made Ruffo's mission of retaking the city of Naples much easier. He landed in Calabria, the toe of the boot, in February 1799, gathering an Army as he proceeded, and was able to lay siege to Naples in June. He was able to end the siege by promising the Neapolitan republicans immunity.

What happened next is controversial in the history books. Ruffo was either lying to the republicans, or he was overruled by Nelson, who brought his squadron in soon after the surrender. Over a hundred republicans were arrested and executed, and large-scale reprisals were conducted. Ferdinand and Maria Carolina had a long list of scores to settle, which Nelson and Acton carried out with great energy. One of the people executed was the former commander of the Neapolitan Navy, a man named Francesco Caracciolo. His story includes the line that he was refused a firing squad and was hanged, which makes me think that maybe the same Marxist writer who wrote the one about Wolfe Tone wrote this one too. Ferdinand made Nelson Duke of Bronte (no relation to the Bronte sisters), which came with an estate on Sicily, and there is a Duke of Bronte, a descendant of Nelson's brother, to this very day. During this time, Nelson continued his attentions to Emma Hamilton, and the whispering continued, getting to the ears of his wife, Fanny, in England.

Having been informed of the result of the previous attempt to lead the Neapolitan Army on a march on Rome, Nelson made no attempt to try it again, even though the French occupation force was only 2,500 men.

Admiral Jervis needed a rest and had been replaced as commander of the Mediterranean Fleet by Admiral Keith in June. The French and Spanish Fleets had reacted to the British seizure of Minorca by entering the Mediterranean, occupying their bases in Cartagena and Toulon, and conducting operations, including an attempt to relieve Malta. Keith went after them, and he sent an order to Nelson to join him, which Nelson refused as he was engaged in the Naples situation. The French and Spanish Fleets sailed out into the

Atlantic, and Keith pursued, leaving Nelson as the senior British officer in the Mediterranean. The French and Spanish Fleets made it to Brest in August 1799 and remained at anchor for the next two years. Now the Royal Navy was not only back in the Mediterranean, but they had also driven the Spanish and French out. They made contact with the king of Sardinia and made use of their ports but held off from reoccupying their old bases in Elba and Corsica. Why go someplace where you are loathed if you don't have to? Keith returned to Minorca in November, and Nelson's insubordination was forgotten. At the end of the year, Keith ordered Nelson to inspect Malta, which the British told their Neapolitan and Russian allies that they were going to turn over to Sicily but actually intended to annex.

Papal enclave, 1799–1800: Most of the cardinals of the Catholic Church had been expelled from Rome in 1798, when the pope was and were residing in the vicinity of Austrian-controlled Venice. Rome was under French occupation and unavailable for a papal enclave. Pius VI had anticipated what might happen and, before his exile, established a procedure for what to do under this circumstance, which was to conduct the enclave in the city where most of the cardinals lived, in this case the city of Venice. The conclave met from November 30, 1799 to March 14, 1800, and was certainly influenced by the fact that Bonaparte had taken over the government of France on November 9. We would expect that since they were in Austrian territory, the Austrians would rig the election to get a pope that favored their cause, but the cardinals had their own agenda, which was wanting to settle with France and get back to their homes in Rome. Austrian pressure was able to delay but not stop that desire.

The new pope, Pius VII, who was born with the name Barnaba Chiaramonti, was elected and crowned in March 1800. He was crowned with a *papier-mâché* pope hat, since the real one was with Pope Pius VI, who had died in France. In the days when Bonaparte had been marching through Lombardy and the Romagna in 1797, Pius VII had been bishop of Imola, a district of the Romagna that was incorporated into the Cisalpine Republic. He had published a letter to his flock advising them to submit to French authority and assuring them that one could be a good Catholic within a republican

THE GREAT GLOBE ITSELF

state. This gave him enough pro-republican credibility that he was able to negotiate the Concordat of 1801 with France.

Eastern and Central Europe, 1799

Operations in the Danube, 1799: Paul I sent three Armies into central and western Europe in 1799. Suvorov 's Army was the first to arrive in April in Italy as described above. The second Army to arrive was commanded by Alexander Rimsky-Korsakov. It arrived in Stockach, near Lake Constance, in August, and its operations are described in this section. Rimsky-Korsakov was related to the composer Nikolai Rimsky-Korsakov, whose most famous work is *The Tale of the Tsar Saltan,* composed in 1900 and featuring the *Flight of the Bumblebee.* The third Army to arrive was commanded by Ivan von Fersen, who was not related to the Swedish diplomat who had arranged Louis XVI's attempted escape from Paris in 1791. He and his Army were transported to Canterbury in July, and its operations in the Netherlands are described in the next section.

General Jourdan took command of the Army of Observation, which was now optimistically renamed the Army of the Danube, and crossed the Rhine at four points between Strasbourg and Basel on March 1. The purpose of his maneuver was to block the roads east and west of Lake Constance leading to Zurich and Liechtenstein, as these were primary alpine passes between Germany and Italy. Archduke Charles, commanding the Austrian force from his headquarters in Augsburg, had been told to remain on defense but to keep the passes open in order to be able to reinforce the main effort in Italy if ordered. Charles therefore deployed his forces against Jourdan and engaged him at Ostrach, north of Lake Constance, on March 21. Jourdan was outnumbered and fell back west to Stockach. Charles pursued and attacked him there on March 25. Jourdan was even more outnumbered and had to retreat all the way back to Freiburg, which is still east of the Rhine but just barely. Charles considered that he had performed his duty, as the roads to Zurich and Lichtenstein were open to the Austrians. In keeping with his orders, he did not pursue.

Charles had Jourdan's number, as he had now beaten him three times. Jourdan turned over his command to General Massena, who incorporated it into his Army of Switzerland. As a result of Jourdan's departure, Michel Ney was promoted to major general and distinguished himself in Switzerland under Massena's command. He would serve under Massena again in Portugal in 1810, when they were both marshals, and by then, he had lost his awe of Massena and was relieved for insubordination. Two other future marshals serving under Massena this year were Francois Joseph Lefebvre and Jean-de-Dieu Soult.

Jourdan returned to the Council of Five Hundred, where in November 1799, he vigorously opposed Bonaparte's coup but was soon reconciled to the new regime and, in 1800, was given important duties in Milan. He was made a marshal in 1804 and went on to serve the empire for many years in important positions.

In eastern Switzerland, von Hotze split his command in half, sending a division under Field Marshal Bellegarde into Italy while he moved into Germany to protect Charles' left flank. He was too late to take part in the battles at Ostrach and Stockach but was able to repel the French in northeast Switzerland. Austria had now secured half of Switzerland and most of Germany. Charles was authorized to pursue the French, now all under Massena, except for a force to the north, the Army of Mainz, commanded by General Muller. While Hotze and Bellegarde consolidated in Switzerland, on May 20, Charles crossed the Rhine at Schaffhausen between Lake Constance and Basel, where it runs east to west before turning north at Basel. Massena concentrated his force in front of Zurich. The First Battle of Zurich was fought on June 4, and the French had to fall back to the Gommiswald, about halfway between Zurich and Lichtenstein.

William Pitt's foreign minister since 1791 was his cousin William Grenville. As we recall, their fathers had been close political allies, and now they were too. Grenville was watching the lines on the map of Europe carefully as the Russians maneuvered across Europe. By June, Suvorov had achieved success in Italy, Fersen was on his way to England, and Rimsky-Korsakov was on his way to Germany. Grenville proposed to the Russian and Austrian emperors that Suvorov and Rimsky-Korsakov link up in Switzerland and complete the liberation of that country, while Charles would move back north to Germany, engage the small French Army of Mainz, and with any luck, establish contact with the Anglo-Russian force about to invade the Netherlands. The Russian, Austrian, and British governments all agreed to this change of strategy. The strategy was implemented in September. Charles and Suvorov, who were both doing great in their respective theaters, disagreed with these changes, but they obeyed.

By late August, Charles was able to move his forces to Germany once Rimsky-Korsakov was in place in Zurich. Charles eventually engaged General Muller on September 18 at the Battle of Mannheim, with Muller being forced back. This was fine with the French, who were happy that they had drawn Charles away from Switzerland. Muller was criticized for his performance, however, and was replaced by General Ney, who had shown a lot of energy leading a division. Muller stayed in the Army until 1814 but held no more Army commands.

Hotze also remained in Zurich. The Austrian-Russian force was small and vulnerable, but it was thought that Suvorov was on the way and would get to Zurich in time. This was not the case, as Massena had sent divisions south to block the alpine passes. While Suvorov was blocked, Massena concentrated his force on Rimsky-Korsakov, and on September 26, they fought the Second Battle of Zurich. The allies were outnumbered and had to retreat north across the Rhine. Hotze was killed in action. Rimsky-Korsakov viewed his abandonment by Charles as a great betrayal, although Charles's apologists say he delayed his departure as long as he could. When Paul I was informed, he was so enraged that he wrote a letter to the British and Austrians on October 22, terminating the alliance. Rimsky-Korsakov headed to Lindau, where he linked up with Suvorov, who had maneuvered around the French forces. Suvorov's adventures in fire and maneuver through the alpine passes have an *anabasis* quality about them. The snow had begun to fall in October. He eventually made it to Lichtenstein and headed down the Rhine Valley to Lindau, where he met up with Rimsky-Korsakov on October 25, and the Russians commenced the long march home. When Suvorov arrived in Saint Petersburg, he was promoted to generalissimo by Paul I, but he died on May 18, 1800, aged seventy.

Great Britain, 1799

Den Helder, the Anglo-Russian invasion of the Netherlands: As far as the Anglo-Russian invasion of the Netherlands, the British provided all the transport, picking up the Russian troops in Riga and ferrying them to Canterbury, then from Canterbury to the Netherlands. The Russian commander was Ivan von Fersen. The commander of the British troops was General Ralph Abercromby. The overall commander of the expedition was the Duke of York. There were about twenty thousand British and twenty thousand Russian troops. It's only fifty miles from Den Helder to Amsterdam, but the terrain was easily flooded.

On the other side of the line, Dutch general Herman Daendels commanded the Dutch forces, while General Dominique Vandamme commanded the French forces, and General William Brune exercised overall command. They had about thirty-five thousand men between them.

The plan was to land the British troops near the Dutch naval base at Den Helder and establish a beachhead at Callantsoog. Once the beachhead was secure, the Russians could be transported from Canterbury under relatively safe conditions. There was some hope that the populace would rise in revolt against the French, but as we have seen, that only happens when it's close to the end, and it's apparent that the occupiers are finished. The invasion commenced on August 27. There were Dutch warships in port at Den Helder, but they did nothing to oppose the landing. As a matter of fact, the Dutch Navy surrendered their ships and their base to the British after three days. We've already seen that there was a lot of anti-French sentiment in the Dutch Navy. Brune left it to Daendels to offer the initial resistance, while he and Vandamme mustered the French forces, who were guarding a different part of the coast. Daendels offered

THE GREAT GLOBE ITSELF

some resistance to the landing and then retreated south to Alkmaar, about halfway between Den Helder and Amsterdam.

The Dutch stadtholder William V came ashore and was ensconced at Den Helder naval station, flying his flag from the citadel. No one was inspired to rally to his cause. The British moved south to make room for the Russians, and they were met on September 10 by Brune's force of French and Dutch troops at Krabbendam, ten miles south of Callantsoog. The French were driven back. The Russians came ashore, along with the Duke of York, who established his headquarters. A straightforward scheme of maneuver for capturing Amsterdam was developed but failed the execution due to the British being delayed by flooded roads. The Russians weren't informed of the British delay, and they conducted an unsupported attack on the enemy at Bergen on September 19. The Russians were encircled and von Fersen taken prisoner. One of his division commanders, General Ivan Essen, took command. The Duke of York had to take responsibility for this failure to coordinate. The Russians suspected that their allies might be acting in bad faith. The Anglo-Russian force still had a numerical advantage, but additional French forces were on the way, so the Duke of York pressed on. On October 2, his force attacked the French and Dutch at Alkmaar and gained a slight advantage in terms of casualties and terrain. Another battle on October 6 went in favor of the French and Dutch. By now, the word was out that the Russians were going to pull the plug, feeling betrayed by Austria and Great Britain on all fronts. The Duke of York negotiated an end to the campaign on October 18, agreeing to cease hostilities, leave the Netherlands, and return all prisoners taken two years before at Camperdown. The Anglo-Russian forces were gone from the Netherlands by November 20.

Paul leaving the Second Coalition is viewed as one of the main causes that led up to his assassination. The experience of dealing with the Austrians and the British had left a bad taste in his mouth. From his point of view, Russian strategic interests had been served by Bonaparte's departure from the east, making his decision to break with them easier.

One other note unrelated to the Dutch campaign but important to the future is that at the end of 1799, the Duke of Orleans and his two brothers managed to get to London, having obtained passage from Cuba to Nova Scotia, where the Duke of Kent received them warmly, then to New York, and then to Great Britain, where they arrived in January 1800. The duke lived in Great Britain for the next fourteen years, during which his brothers both died of tuberculosis. He proposed to George III 's daughter Elizabeth, but she supposedly turned him down because he was Catholic. I don't think it was a serious proposal as she was nearly forty at the time. He got married to a daughter of Ferdinand and Maria Carolina in 1809, and they had ten children. Two of his grandsons served in the American Civil War on the side of the Union.

Aftermath of the Irish Rebellion: The Irish Rebellion had been mostly led by Irish Protestants who attempted to rally *all* Irishmen to the cause of an Irish Republic. The people who had crushed the rebellion were also Irish Protestants. Many of the rebels left for America, and the character of Ireland soon became that of a Protestant minority (10–20 percent of the population) ruling over a Catholic majority.

Over the course of 1799, the British Parliament passed an income tax, a law against trade unions, another law that outlawed clandestine radical societies, and finally a law requiring that all published material had to carry the imprimatur of a lawfully established publisher. These were all reactions to the Irish Rebellion. The laws passed by the British Parliament were binding in Ireland, but maybe there was some doubt in London as to how vigorously these laws would be executed, and so the idea of a United Kingdom of Great Britain and Ireland was seriously considered. The union of England and Scotland to form Great Britain in 1707 had been driven by a desire to prevent Scotland from being taken over by the exiled House of Stuart, and now a union of Great Britain and Ireland would hopefully have the same effect. The leader of the idea of a UK was Robert Stewart, known to history as Lord Castlereagh, who was chief secretary for Ireland, which meant that he sat in the cabinet and represented Irish interests in London, while the lord lieutenant ran the Irish government in Dublin. Castlereagh, an energetic and faith-

THE GREAT GLOBE ITSELF

ful protégé of Pitt's, argued that the benefit of British-Irish union to national security would be very great, while the Catholics, who constituted a large majority in Ireland (four million out of a population of five), would constitute a minority in a United Kingdom (four million out of seventeen) and would moderate their demands. Castlereagh argued that these moderated demands would be satisfied by parliamentary acts that would lift various restrictions on Catholics. If you look at a list of these restrictions, they seem pretty severe, but most of them were honored more in the breach than in the observance. For example, in theory, Catholics weren't allowed to serve in the military, but the recruiters never seemed to turn one away if he stumbled into their office, smudging the words in the box on the form labeled Religion.

Catholics were prevented from practicing law, or at least being officers of the court, until 1793. Many of the leaders of the Irish Rebellion, including Wolfe Tone, had been lawyers, so I'm surprised this law wasn't reenacted after 1798. Of course, he was a Protestant. The only restriction that was strictly held to was Catholic exclusion from national public office, meaning election to Parliament, obtaining rank as a general or admiral, or appointment to a high-level judicial post. The promise of rescinding these restrictions, known as Catholic emancipation, became a sticking point in British-Irish politics for the next thirty years. Looking at the small number of people these restrictions actually affected reinforces the conclusion Catholic emancipation was a code word applied to those who were getting wobbly on France.

France, 1799

The Constitution of 1795 said that the term of a director would be ended each year, and the director to be terminated would be selected by lot. In 1799, Director Rewbell drew the short straw and was turned out of office. He was replaced by none other than Abbey Sieyes, one of the heroes of 1789, who, as we recall, was the author of *What Is the Third Estate?* When asked what he had been doing the last ten years, he said, "*J'ai vécu*" (I survived). Actually, he had served quietly in the legislative bodies until 1795, then spent a few years as a diplomat. He had just returned from Berlin, where he had been the minister.

For the last two years, the Directory had annulled the spring elections, because the people had elected too many royalists or too many Jacobins. This year, they again elected too many Jacobins, but no efforts were made by the Directory to annul the election, because none of the generals wanted to back the directors up. As it turned out, Sieyes had secretly recruited General Joubert, not to disenfranchise the Jacobins but to overthrow the Directory. Joubert was supposedly in town to get married, but he was commanding the military forces in and around Paris.

Thus the Jacobins took office and formed majorities in both houses of the legislature. Lucien Bonaparte was a member of the Council of Five Hundred, while Joseph Bonaparte was a member of the Council of Ancients. Their presence in the councils was an indication of the popular discontent with how the war was going, as Suvorov was rampaging across Italy, Charles had conquered half of Switzerland, and nothing was being done to relieve General Bonaparte in Egypt. The Directory had even angered the United States to the point that they were ready to declare war on France. Not only was the war going badly, but the government's credit was at an all-time low, and the currency was worthless.

Meanwhile, at the Jelgava Palace in Latvia, Princess Marie Therese, the only surviving child of Louis and Marie Antoinette, married Louis Anthony, the eldest son of the Count of Artois, on June 10. As we recall, Paul I had given Louis XVIII use of the palace, where he and hundreds of courtiers maintained the old traditions of Versailles. Louis XVIII had urged the marriage, being worried about plots to marry her to the Archduke Charles and installing him as a regnant prince consort in Paris. It was a terrible match. Louis Anthony and Marie Therese never had any children, unlike her namesake empress grandmother, who had sixteen. From 1824 to 1830, she was Dauphiness, but she was swept out with the rest of the Bourbons in 1830.

THE GREAT GLOBE ITSELF

With no fear of military interference, in fact with confidence of military support, the councils took action to remold the Directory more to their liking. On June 18, they passed a decree invalidating the May 1798 election of Director Treilhard, citing a technical fault in his election. A man named Louis Gohier was put in his seat. The next day, the councils demanded the resignations of two more directors: Merlin and Revelliere. Directors Sieyes and Barras added their voices to those of the councils. General Joubert mobilized his troops and marched them around the city, which was enough to produce the desired resignations. They were replaced by Roger Ducos, who was soon a provisional consul with Bonaparte and Sieyes, and Jean Francois Moulin, who was a general but not a famous or ambitious one. Joubert turned over command of his troops to General Francois Joseph Lefebvre, as Joubert was on his way to Italy with the goal of duplicating Bonaparte's 1797 victories. As discussed above, he was killed in action on August 15 at the Battle of Novi.

The four new and one tenured directors began a purge of the ministries, starting with interior minister and former director Neufchateau on June 22. On July 2, the war and Navy ministers, Mureau and Bruix, were ousted. Bruix would later command the transport flotilla at Boulogne in 1803. General Bernadotte was named war minister. The other four ministers of foreign affairs, justice, finance, and police (Talleyrand, Lambrechts, Rame-Nogaret, and Bourguignon) were replaced on July 20.

Joseph Fouche was appointed as minister of police. He had been performing "diplomatic service" in Milan in 1798 and The Hague in 1799, two places that needed a man that knew how to organize a secret police force. I don't know if Fouche had spent any time in Milan while Bonaparte was there, but he may have. Now he took the big job in Paris and went after the royalists and the Jacobins (shutting down the newly opened Jacobin Club), defanging them and thus enabling Bonaparte's coup. Fouche kept his job until August 1, 1802, when he opposed the new constitution, making Bonaparte consul for life. His job was temporarily eliminated, its police functions transferred to the minister of justice, while the consular guard took responsibility for finding and catching assassins. Bonaparte conciliated Fouche by making him a senator and bestowing an estate on him. Then when the empire was declared in May 1804, the Ministry of Police was reconstituted, with Fouche, once again, at its head.

Talleyrand had a good relationship with Fouche, having been his boss the last two years, although there would be some tension over the years. Talleyrand was annoyed at being ejected from the Foreign Office by Sieyes and was the first to start talking to Bonaparte about a coup when Bonaparte got to Paris. Talleyrand had been courting Bonaparte since 1796, so Bonaparte listened. I imagine that among other things, he told Bonaparte how much he reminded him of his friends Aaron Burr and Alexander Hamilton.

In September, word came to Paris that Joubert was dead, and Bonaparte was alive. A national day of mourning for Joubert was declared by the Directory. Moreau had just returned from Italy, having turned command over to Championnet, and Sieyes asked him to be the new Joubert. Moreau refused to be a tool but said that Bernadotte or Bonaparte would be glad to fill in. Bernadotte's supreme self-confidence was, by now, apparent to the directors. Paris wasn't big enough for both Bernadotte and Bonaparte, and the directors published an article in the state newspaper that Bernadotte had resigned, which was how Bernadotte found out about it. Bernadotte's ace in the hole was his wife, Desiree, whose sister was Joseph Bonaparte 's wife, Julie. As we recall, Desiree had been engaged to Napoleon Bonaparte for a brief period in 1796. Bernadotte was persuaded to accept his subordinate position by Joseph, who promised to take care of him.

From August 23 to October 1, Bonaparte sailed the Mediterranean, hugging the North African coast to avoid detection. On October 1, he landed in Corsica, probably to congratulate them for resisting British efforts to reestablish a naval base there. He was there for five days, giving his native land a long goodbye and then departing for Metropolitan France, landing in Frejus on October 8, where he was met by jubilant crowds. The people of France had thought he had been lost to them, but now here he was! It must have been a Jesus-like experience for Bonaparte as well as the French people. He made his way to Paris over the next two weeks, greeted by cheering throngs as he went.

THE GREAT GLOBE ITSELF

On October 16, Bonaparte arrived in Paris, and it was all anyone in the city could talk about. The plot to overthrow the Directory was hatched and executed in twenty-three days. General Lefebvre was enlisted, and he enthusiastically agreed to help "throw all the lawyers in the river." That month, Lucien Bonaparte was elected as president of the Council of Five Hundred, an office that rotated every few weeks. Lucien had a prominent role in the coup, which he later regretted and eventually went into self-imposed exile.

Brune and Massena, despite their victories in the Netherlands and Switzerland, faded into the background. Bonaparte made them both marshals in 1804, but he always considered them as potential rivals at some level. Massena spent the next year commanding in the Vendee, where revolt was perking up again, and was in Genoa in 1800, where he withstood a fierce Austrian siege. Another rival, Moreau, who assisted in Bonaparte's coup by detaining the directors at the Luxembourg Palace, commanded in Germany in 1800. He also later regretted his role, becoming the focus of opposition to Bonaparte and eventually being implicated in an assassination plot, which resulted in his exile.

On November 9, 18 Brumaire on the revolutionary calendar, Barras, Sieyes, and Ducos resigned as directors. Barras was supposedly told by Talleyrand that he could take a large bribe and resign, or they could do it the hard way, but as is often the case when Talleyrand is involved, no one knows for sure who said what to who. Moreau pulled up with his troops at the Luxembourg to detain the other two directors, Moulin and Gohier, delivering Sieyes's message that their resignations were needed.

The councils were meeting at Saint Cloud because of a phony security issue declared by Lefebvre, who claimed that Paris was unsafe. Napoleon and Lucien Bonaparte addressed the Council of Five Hundred, telling them that the directors had all resigned. They requested a decree stating that Sieyes, Ducos, and General Bonaparte be made provisional consuls, that the councils adjourn for the next three months, and that a convention be held to ratify a new constitution, which Sieyes had already drafted. The council was resistant to these demands, even attempting to pass an outlaw decree on

Bonaparte. Eventually, Murat was called in with his troops, and the Bonapartes got what they wanted.

Gohier and Moulin returned to their obscurity, and Barras retired to his huge estate (later owned by Berthier) with all of his money. Bonaparte eventually had to exile him to Belgium and then Rome because he was a magnet for plotters and assassins. All the ministers were replaced except for Fouche, who had done a lot to enable the coup. Talleyrand returned as foreign minister, and Berthier was made war minister, and they both lasted until August 1807. Justice Minister Jean Jacques Cambaceres was made a consul in December, otherwise he would have kept his ministry. The famous mathematician Pierre Simon Laplace was appointed as minister of the interior, but he only lasted six weeks. Bonaparte later said that Laplace's mind was such that he overthought problems and was unable to develop solutions in a timely fashion. Lucien Bonaparte was given the job, and he commenced to organizing a plebiscite ratifying the coup.

After November 10, Bonaparte, Sieyes, and Ducos worked with the convention, which was named the Legislative Corps, to rewrite Sieyes's draft constitution into what became the Constitution of the Year VIII. About the only thing that remained of Sieyes's draft was the idea of having three consuls. Sieyes had conceived the idea of the office of grand elector as the supreme executive, having about the same level of power as the king of Great Britain, an office which Bonaparte would occupy. This idea was axed immediately in favor of the three consuls sharing all the executive power. The first consul would have all the war, Navy, police, colonial, and foreign affairs powers, and the other two would make decisions on administration, finance, and law.

The job of second consul went to former justice minister Cambaceres. Cambaceres did a lot of the heavy lifting in the codification of French law, known then as the Civil Code and today as the Napoleonic Code. The job of third consul went to Charles Francois Lebrun. Lebrun had worked for Finance Minister de Maupeou in the early 1770s and had focused on financial matters in the legislature since 1789. He must have had some solid ideas on currency reform

THE GREAT GLOBE ITSELF

because he was now plucked from relative obscurity and given his big break.

The powers of the legislature were reduced to the point that the consuls could rule by decree for all intents and purposes. Sieyes and Ducos were excluded from real power but were given money, estates, and positions in the new order as senators, with which they seemed to be satisfied, and they went into obscurity. They both protested when Bonaparte became emperor, but they didn't resign over it.

When Bonaparte was negotiating the peace of Campo Formio in 1797, he had added the stipulation that Lafayette be released from his Austrian prison. Now he showed that his use of non sequiturs in negotiations was a gift of genius, as now he had the Legislative Corps pass a law making the metric system the official measuring system of France, becoming the legal norm on November 4, 1800. The system was unpopular at first, and it didn't fully take hold until the 1850s. People liked the old names for measures, and even today, in France, a weight of five hundred grams is called a *livre*.

The Constitution of the Year VIII was ratified on December 24, 1799. It established the three-man Consulate, the Council of State, the eighty-man Senate, the hundred-man Tribunate, and the three-hundred-man Legislative Corps. The new constitution used several terms taken from the ancient Roman Republic. Bonaparte's accession caused universal satisfaction throughout France. The republicans saw the preservation of the wins of the revolution. The monarchists, Bourbon and Orleanist alike, saw the beginning of a transition back to monarchy in the style of the British Restoration of 1660. Within two years, the currency was stable, the relationship with the church was peaceful, Europe was at peace on the continent and in the colonies, and the French Academy and the Legion of Honor were established.

The next day, Christmas Day, the new government was sworn in, and Bonaparte moved into the Tuileries Palace. On December 26, Bonaparte signed letters, written by Talleyrand, to George III and Francis II expressing France's desire to end the war and proposing negotiations. Pitt's reply was that the best hope for peace was to restore the House of Bourbon. Francis II dodged the question by saying he would have to consult his allies. The diplomatic exchange was conducted by France with great ostentation and public display, so nobody could blame France for the upcoming season of campaigning.  On December 28, Bonaparte issued a warning to the Vendee and Chouan rebels to lay down their arms, or General Brune would be getting after them. This seems to have been enough to calm things down, as we don't read much about any major operations there in 1800. It seems that the real reason to have a lot of troops there was so they would be within marching distance of Paris if they were needed by the first consul.

As if to put an exclamation point on the spirit of reconciliation, as well as the "Roman-ness" of the new era, a new art display at the Louvre opened in December featuring JL David's latest painting, *The Intervention of the Sabine Women,* showing Romulus and Titus Tatius being prevented from striking each other, as Hersilia, daughter of Tatius and wife of Romulus by kidnapping, places herself and her children between them. The display was a sensation and cemented David's genius for putting his finger on the pulse, as he had earlier with *The Tennis Court Oath* and *The Death of Marat*. You can see the painting next time you're in Paris at the Louvre.

AN AFTERWORD TO PART 1

The Years of George Washington

I hope you enjoyed this look into the nooks and crannies of the past, in which I attempted to bring to life by illustrating some of the obscure details, the what-ifs of history, and the connections in the wider world between events that are usually considered in isolation. This book is the first in a series that I hope to extend to the year 1918.

As we have seen, people are born, they are important for a few years, and then they die. Yes, even George Washington. As Shakespeare writes in *The Tempest:*

> Our revels now are ended. These our actors,
> As I foretold you, were all spirits and
> Are melted into air, into thin air;
> And, like the baseless fabric of this vision,
> The cloud-capped towers, the gorgeous palaces,
> The solemn temples, the great globe itself,
> Yea, all which it inherits shall dissolve,
> And, like this insubstantial pageant faded,
> Leave not a rack behind. We are such stuff
> As dreams are made on and our little life
> Is rounded with a sleep.

The deficiency, in my humble view, of almost all writing on the time period from the mideighteenth century is that it is too busy telling its particular story to notice how it is affecting its neighbors. In 1792, the French invasion of Belgium and the Russian invasion of Poland occurred within three weeks of each other, but as far as the history books are concerned, they may as well have happened on different planets. The five-sided great power dynamic that was European politics starting in 1740 formed a unity, and one of the goals of this effort is to demonstrate the connectedness of events.

This period of history is framed by the years of George Washington. He cannot be said to have dominated world events even when he was president, but he influenced them, causing the international incident that initiated the Seven Years' War, commanding the Continental Army, being a surrogate father to Lafayette, leader of the early days of the French Revolution, the presidency, and then being the senior officer of the Amy afterward until his death. During the American Revolution, Washington was the indispensable man. Bonaparte aspired to follow his example, but when he decided that he was indispensable, his solution was to make himself a hereditary emperor. After that, there were a lot of Bonapartes and very few Washingtons. George Washington is the most important person in American history, but the writing about him verges on the same you see written for saints of the church. We can acknowledge his greatness without believing that he was without fault in every way.

Benedict Arnold is the most misunderstood historical character I know. There are few people who wouldn't have done what he did in his circumstances. People who write about him have got to stop being psychoanalysts, examining his childhood and his personal life.

William Pitt the Elder was the prototype of the demagogue who plays to the peanut gallery, and his example was useful for all the revolutionaries in France and Poland to emulate. It is one thing to say that governments derive their just power from the consent of the governed, but the demagogues took that to the extreme, asserting that the will of the people trumped all other considerations, leading to rabble-rousers like George Gordon to unleash King Mob on

THE GREAT GLOBE ITSELF

London in 1780 and the *Sans Culottes* to overthrow the monarchy in 1792.

In 1836, Louis Napoleon, the son of Hortense de Beauharnais and Louis Bonaparte, wrote:

> I believe that from time to time, men are created whom I call volunteers of providence, in whose hands are placed the destiny of their countries. I believe I am one of those men. If I am wrong, I can perish uselessly. If I am right, then providence will put me into a position to fulfill my mission.

Twelve years later, by a circuitous route, he was elected president of France and later conducted a coup to make himself Napoleon III. His career was a million-to-one shot, and we can see that the same was true for Washington, who overcame a thousand obstacles on his trip to the top. Half the obstacles were overcome by effort; half were overcome by sheer luck.

One of the things that happened a lot in this period was that battle planners who planned invasions almost always often factored into their calculations that they would be greeted as liberators, and thousands would join them. This rarely panned out, and even when it did, the people that joined up were generally of little military value. I cannot name a single incident in which this idea was a factor in a successful invasion. Yet the people who planned invasions never gave up on it. More successful were the countries who were invaded, especially by France, where the local clergy was generally able to whip their flocks into a frenzy against the demonic invaders. The flocks were also generally of little military value, but in some cases, they did slow the invaders down a little.

Since this is an attempt to look at war and battle from both sides, I don't root for one country or another. I even go out of my way to point out how much spin there is in British history. If you believe their spin, the British never lost a battle. The pages of history are not filled with angels and demons. They are filled with real human beings, including those who own slaves and those who take land from Indians and weaker countries. The surest way for a historian to fall into error is to judge people of the past by current fashions.

In addition to the current fashion of dismissing all slave owners as evil and tearing down their statues, we also project our current morality on people of the past. I don't think that Frederick the Great was a homosexual, at least not in the sense of either having erotic feelings for other men or acting on them. I think that he had better things to do with his time than that. I also disagree with the opinion (yes, opinion) that Thomas Jefferson carried on with his slaves. I remember that Bill Clinton spent the night before his inauguration in 1993 in Charlottesville, Virginia, and drove up in a motorcade to Washington from Monticello. He identified with Jefferson, and I think that Jefferson would have identified with Clinton. For one thing, I think that Jefferson might have smoked some of the hemp that he grew, but he didn't inhale.

The birth of technology occurred during this period as Boulton and Watt formed their partnership that produced hundreds of engines starting in 1775. The birth of technology was the sentence of death for slavery, as the machines were found to be able to handle the tasks performed by slaves. Freeing slaves in the North was not a major problem because there were few of them, but it was in the South where 30 percent of the population was enslaved. Jefferson considered the problem and concluded that involuntary servitude was the only solution, as neither freedom nor deportation were feasible. In the institution of black slavery, America had a wolf by its ears.

Of all the events I noted from 1649 to 1799, the greatest injustice was what happened to the Massachusetts farmers in Shays' Rebellion in 1786. People serving their country for years only to come back to the farm to learn that they were being sued by British loyalists returning from Canada for their back rent! I would have been right there standing next to Shays.

History is not made by characters in a well-plotted drama. It is messy and circuitous, so historians often edit the course of events to tell a better story. For example, you can read that in January 1793, the French General Santerre organized the execution of King Louis

THE GREAT GLOBE ITSELF

XVI and spitefully drowned out the last speech of the king by shouting for the drums to beat. Did that really happen? I don't think it did because we know what it was that Louis said before he died.

This volume introduced us to Napoleon Bonaparte, ending as he was moving his things into the Tuileries Palace. For sixteen years, he was the central figure in European and American affairs. His career would bring France to the highest highs and the lowest lows.

INDEX

Abercromby, General Ralph (Great Britain) 361, 378, 406, 428

Acton, John, Naples Minister 399

Adams, John Quincy, American Politician 267

Adams, John, US President 65, 95, 115, 133, 150, 180, 298, 304, 324, 329, 364, 410, 413

Adams, Samuel, American Revolutionary 66

Adelaide, Princess, Aunt of Louis XVI 220

Albert, General Prince of Saxony (Austria) 239, 256, 269, 353

Alexander I, Emperor of Russia, 1801 to 1825 304

Alexis I, Emperor of Russia, 1645 to 1676 11

Allen, Ethan, American Revolutionary 86

Amherst, General Jeffrey (Great Britain) 38, 46, 48

Andre, Major John (Great Britain) 112, 114

Anne, Queen of Great Britain, 1702 to 1714 23, 24

Anselme, General Jacques (France) 255

Apraksin, General Stepan (Russia) 39

Arnold, General Benedict, American Revolutionary 86, 89, 97, 105, 112, 114, 124, 389, 440

Artois, Comte de, see Charles X 191, 222, 340, 357, 432

Artois, Comte de, see Charles XCharles X, King of France 192

Augereau, Marshal Pierre 293, 314, 346, 356, 373, 375, 380, 409

Babeuf, Francois Gracchus, French Revolutionary 225, 321, 350, 359

Bailly, Jean Sylvain, French Revolutionary 186, 190, 194, 199, 227, 231, 288

Barere, Bertrand, CPS Member 338

Barnave, Antoine, French Revolutionary 223, 225

Barras, Admiral Francois (France) 121, 125, 126, 373
Barras, Paul, Director 293
Barry, Jeanne, Madame du, French Courtesan 74, 99, 288
Barthelemy, Francois, Director 345, 355, 371, 379, 386
Bayet, General Jean Baptiste du (France) 344
Beauharnais, Eugéne de 272, 307, 373
Beauharnais, Hortense de 272, 307, 372, 441
Beauharnais, Josephine. See Bonaparte, Josephine
Bernadotte, Marshal Jean 314, 343, 353
Berthier, Marshal Louis Alexander 346, 356, 372, 398, 417, 436
Bessieres, Marshal Jean Baptiste 356, 371
Bestuzhev, Alexei, Russian Prime Minister 35, 39
Bezborodko, Alexander, Russian Foreign Minister 144, 218
Billaud-Varenne, Jacques, CPS Member 279, 319, 338
Biron, General Armand (France) 239, 244, 253
Blue Jacket, Indian Chief 263, 324, 325
Bonaparte, Elise 372
Bonaparte, Joseph 24, 370, 397, 432, 434
Bonaparte, Josephine 171, 355, 362
Bonaparte, Louis 441

Bonaparte, Lucien 432, 435
Bonaparte, Pauline 405
Boone, Daniel, American Explorer 30, 327
Bouille, General Marquis de (France), French Royalist 210, 225
Bourbon, Louis Joseph de, son of the Prince of Conde, French Royalist 232
Braddock, General Edward (Great Britain) 34, 36
Bradford, William, US Attorney General 263
Brienne, Etienne Charles de, French Finance Minister 161
Brissot, Jacques, French Revolutionary 176, 223, 226, 231, 248, 273
Brune, Marshal William 400, 428, 435, 438
Burgoyne, General John (Great Britain) 53, 85, 93, 97, 104, 106, 118, 136, 159, 214
Burke, Edmund, British Writer 75, 171, 206, 216, 372
Burr, Aaron, US Vice President 89, 184, 233, 252, 260, 295, 329, 351, 364, 379, 389, 413, 434
Bute, Earl of, John Stuart, Prime Minister (Great Britain) 53, 56, 57
Byng, Admiral John (Great Britain) 36, 51, 127, 138
Callender, James, American Propagandist 151, 364

Calonne, Charles de, French Finance Minister 141, 162, 163, 174

Cambaceres, John Jacques, French Consul 436

Camden, Marquess of, Lord Lieutenant of Ireland 402, 404

Carleton, General Guy (Great Britain) 87, 126, 129

Carlyle, Thomas, British Author 171, 343

Carnot, Lazare, CPS Member, Director 232, 259, 279, 280, 282, 284, 292, 311, 316, 319, 335, 340, 345, 346, 350, 352, 379, 380

Carrier, Jean Baptiste, French Revolutionary 280, 289, 293, 305, 306, 308, 321, 322

Carteaux, General Jean Francois (France) 285

Castlereagh, Lord Robert Stewart, British Politician 430

Catherine II the Great, Empress of Russia, 1762 to 1796 54, 78, 81, 83, 102, 177, 213, 218, 262, 331, 332, 366

Cavaignac, Jean Baptiste, French Revolutionary 315

Champlain, Samuel de, French Explorer 20

Charles Albert, Holy Roman Emperor 27, 29

Charles Emmanuel III, King of Piedmont 357

Charles Emmanuel IV, King of Piedmont 357, 398

Charles, General Archduke (Austria) 353, 355, 360, 371, 409, 410, 425, 432

Charles III, King of Spain, 1759 to 1788 46, 63, 76, 83

Charles II, King of England, 1660 to 1685 21

Charles II, King of Spain, 1671 to 1700 22

Charles I, King of England, 1625 to 1649 5, 7, 61

Charles Stuart, the Young Pretender 25, 29, 30, 398

Charles VI, Holy Roman Emperor 24, 25, 26, 75

Charles XII, King of Sweden 25, 75

Charles X, King of France 10, 100, 191, 222, 340

Charlotte, Queen of the United Kingdom 51, 369

Chartres, Dukes of, heirs to the Dukes of Orleans 141

Chauvelin, Marquis de, French Minister to Great Britain 268

Chichagov, Admiral Vasily (Russia) 179

Choiseul, Etienne, French Prime Minister 1758 to 1770 41, 46, 59, 63, 66, 74, 76

Clark, William, American Explorer 325

Clary, Desiree, Wife of Jean Bernadotte 342, 395, 397

Clary, Julie, Wife of Joseph Bonaparte 434

Cleaveland, General Moses (American) 327

Clerfayt, General Francois (Austria) 312, 313, 334, 335

Clinton, General Henry (Great Britain) 85

Clinton, George, American Politician 262

Clive, General Robert (Great Britain) 36

Cobenzl, Ludwig von (Austria) 264

Cobenzl, Philip von (Austria) 253, 264

Coburg, General Prince Josias von (Austria) 179, 203, 269, 284, 312, 314

Collot de Herbois, Jean, CPS Member 277, 289, 319, 338

Conde, Prince of, French Émigré Commander 236, 239, 245, 374, 380

Constantine, Prince, Grand Duke (Russia) 418

Conway, General Thomas (American) 104

Cook, Captain James, British Explorer 158

Corday, Charlotte, Assassin of Marat 275, 286, 287, 339

Cornwallis, General Charles (Great Britain) 97, 107, 110, 114, 122, 124, 125, 128, 132, 136, 405

Cortes, Hernan, Spanish Explorer 16

Couthon, Georges, CPS Member 276, 278, 305, 318

Cromwell, Oliver, Protector of the Realm, 1649 to 1658 5, 128

Cumberland, William Duke of, General 29, 36, 38, 40

Cushing, Justice William (American) 131, 183

Custine, General Adam Philippe (France) 125, 253, 256, 257, 259, 271, 281, 284, 286, 287

Cuvier, Georges, French Paleontologist 4, 160, 339

Czartoryski, Adam Jerzy, Russian Foreign Minister 267, 305

Czartoryski, Adam, Polish Statesman 266

Danton, Georges, French Revolutionary 249, 250, 252, 257, 265, 269, 271, 275, 281, 283, 291, 305, 306, 308, 318, 319, 339

David, JL, French Painter 308, 438

Davout, Marshal Louis Nicholas 416

Day, Luke, American Revolutionary 154

Delacroix, Charles, French Foreign Minister 379, 409

Delacroix, Eugene, French Painter 379

Desaix, General Louis (France) 353, 396, 416

Desmoulins, Camille, French Revolutionary 189, 191, 222, 249, 273, 281, 291, 306, 308, 318

THE GREAT GLOBE ITSELF

Devonshire, Duke of, Prime Minister (Great Britain) 37

Dickinson, Charles, Duelist killed by Andrew Jackson 295

Dillon, General Theobald (France) 239

Drouet, Jean Baptiste, French Revolutionary 224, 350

Dugommier, General Jacques (France) 273, 285, 315, 316

Dumas, General Thomas (France) 316

Dumerbion, General Pierre (France) 316

Duncan, Admiral Adam (Great Britain) 377

Elizabeth Christine II, Queen of Prussia 369

Elizabeth Christine I, Queen of Prussia 355

Elizabeth I, Empress of Russia, 1741 to 1762 139

Elizabeth, Princess, sister of Louis XVI 307

Ellsworth, Oliver, Justice (American) 328, 411, 412

Emerson, Ralph Waldo, American Author 85

Engels, Friedrich, German Author 350

Estaing, Admiral Charles Henry de (France) 108, 110, 115

Ferdinand, Grand Duke of Tuscany 330, 420

Ferdinand IV, King of Naples 418

Ferdinand VI, King of Spain 1746 to 1759 46

Fermor, William, Russian General 40

Fersen, Axel von, Diplomat (Swedish) 224, 225

Fersen, General Ivan von (Russian) 409, 425, 428, 429

Fleury, Cardinal, Prime Minister (France) 28, 141

Fleury, Jean Francois Joly de, Finance Minister (France) 141

Forbes, General John (Great Britain) 46

Fouche, Joseph, French Revolutionary 277, 279, 289, 305, 319, 349, 433

Foullon, Joseph, French Royalist 188, 190, 195

Fouquier-Tinville, Quentin, French Revolutionary 286, 339

Fox, Charles James, British Politician 138, 206

Fox, Henry, British Politician 34

Francis I, Holy Roman Emperor 29, 78

Francis II, Holy Roman Emperor 237, 264, 312, 313, 367, 437

Franklin, Benjamin, Diplomat (American) 34, 114, 133, 135, 151, 167

Frederick Augustus II, King of Saxony 27

Frederick II, the Great, King of Prussia 26, 27, 36, 38, 39, 50, 53, 56, 78, 80, 83, 86, 101, 119, 143, 165, 166

Frederick, Prince of Wales 49
Frederick William III, King of
Prussia 357, 369
Frederick William II, King of
Prussia 79, 81, 166, 175,
188, 228, 241, 272, 312,
357, 367, 368, 369
Gage, General Thomas (Great
Britain) 65, 70
Gallatin, Albert, American
Politician 167, 301
Galves, General Bernardo de
(Spain) 110
Gates, General Horatio
(American) 70, 87, 95, 123
Genet, Edmond, French
Revolutionary 262
George III, King of the United
Kingdom 39, 48, 49, 51,
53, 57, 58, 61, 65, 67, 75,
78, 79, 89, 127, 138, 150,
158, 159, 173, 197, 216,
217, 269, 310, 317, 333,
337, 342, 358, 430, 437
George II, King of Great Britain
27, 28, 29, 30, 33, 37, 39,
49
George I, King of Great Britain
24
George IV, Prince of Wales 50
Gerry, Elbridge, American
Politician 365, 381
Gibbon, Edward, British Author
98
Godoy, Manuel de, Spanish
Prime Minister 336
Goethe, Johann Wolfgang,
German Author 256

Gordon, Lord George, British
Politician 136, 440
Grafton, Duke of, Prime
Minister 64, 65, 75
Grasse, Admiral Francois de
(France) 122, 125, 126
Greene, General Nathanael
(American) 108, 114, 124,
129, 295
Grenier, General Paul (France)
419
Grenville, George, Prime
Minister (Great Britain) 47,
51, 57
Grenville, William, Prime
Minister (Great Britain) 47,
217, 426
Guillotine, Doctor Joseph,
French Revolutionary 179,
200, 229, 235
Hamilton, Alexander, American
Revolutionary 91, 134, 149,
181, 205, 234, 252, 329,
379, 414, 434
Hamilton, Emma, Wife of
William Hamilton 399, 423
Hamilton, William, British
Diplomat 398
Hancock, John, American
Revolutionary 65, 86, 108,
149, 153, 157
Hanriot, General Francois,
French Revolutionary 274,
320
Hardy, Admiral Charles (Great
Britain) 116
Hardy, Admiral Thomas (Great
Britain) 406

THE GREAT GLOBE ITSELF

Hardy, General Jean (France) 405

Harmar, General Joseph (American) 215

Harrison, William Henry, Indian Agent 325, 390

Hastings, Warren, British Politician 172

Hawkins, Benjamin, Indian Agent 386

Haydn, Joseph, Austrian Composer 367

Hebert, Jacques, French Revolutionary 305, 307, 339, 381

Heming, Sally, Slave of Thomas Jefferson 364, 414

Henry IV, King of France. 1589 to 1610 7, 37

Henry, Patrick, American Revolutionary 61, 84

Henry Stuart, Cardinal York 25

Herault de Séchelles, Jean, CPS Member 281, 285, 306

Hillsborough, Earl of, British Politician 65, 123

Hobbes, Thomas, British Author 326

Hoche, General Lazare (France) 270, 278, 285, 292, 311, 322, 335, 338, 344, 352, 353, 354, 359, 360, 372, 374, 376, 402

Hohenlohe, General Frederick (Austrian) 312, 313

Holmes, Oliver Wendell, American Author 366

Houchard, General Jean Nicolas (France) 281, 283, 288

Howe, Admiral Richard (Great Britain) 310

Howe, General William (Great Britain) 85

Humbert, General Jean Joseph (France) 404, 405

Ibrahim Bey (Egypt) 394

Ivan III, Duke of Moscow 10

Ivan IV the Terrible, Emperor of Russia, 1533 to 1584 10

Jackson, Andrew, American Politician 17, 41, 110, 122, 123, 137, 169, 171, 205, 294, 363, 366, 391, 405

Jackson, Rachel, Wife of Andrew Jackson 171, 294

James III Stuart, the Old Pretender 22, 24, 63

James II, King of England 1685 to 1688 7, 26

James I, King of England 1603 to 1625 5

Jay, Justice John (American) 133, 146, 149, 150, 182, 183, 299, 324, 327, 413

Jeanbon, Andre, CPS Member 280

Jefferson, Thomas, US Vice President 9, 61, 90, 124, 134, 151, 193, 289, 295, 297, 329, 390, 413, 414, 442

Jervis, Admiral John, see Saint Vincent 375, 393, 396, 399, 423

John III Sobieski, King of Poland 1674 to 1696 10

451

Jones, Admiral John Paul
(American) 88, 110, 166,
178, 179

Joseph I, Holy Roman Emperor
25

Joseph II, Holy Roman Emperor
77, 79, 81, 83, 100, 119,
120, 143, 164, 165, 177,
179, 200, 202, 212

Joseph I, King of Spain.
See Bonaparte, Joseph

Joubert, General Barthelemy
371, 373, 397, 398, 418,
421, 432, 434

Jourdan, Marshal Jean Baptiste
279, 284, 292, 312, 314,
317, 319, 322, 336, 346,
352, 353, 354, 360, 426

Jourdan, Marshal Jean Baptiste
Jourdan, Marshal Jean
Baptiste 410

Karl Theodor, Elector of the
Palatine 165

Kaunitz, Wentzel von (Austria)
35, 78, 119, 144, 203, 253,
264

Kellerman, Marshal Francois
253, 255, 256, 276, 277

Kleber, General Jean Baptiste
(France) 322, 335, 353, 417

Kosciuszko, General Thaddeus
(Poland) 240, 266, 303,
305, 313

Kutuzov, General Michael
(Russia) 218

Laclos, Pierre de, Author, French
Revolutionary 176

Lacy, General Maurice, Russian
General 48

Lafayette, Marquis de General
Gilbert (France) 92, 107,
124, 125, 151, 154, 173,
186, 189, 191, 193, 194,
196, 207, 211, 212, 221,
223, 224, 227, 232

Lake, General Viscount Gerard
(Great Britain) 404

Lannes, Marshal Jean 293, 314,
356, 417

Latour, Marshal Maximilian
(Austrian) 353, 354

Laurens, John, American
Politician 107

Lawrence, James, US Naval
Officer 387

Lebrun, Charles, Consul of
France 77, 436

Leclerc, General Charles (France)
371

Leeds, Duke of, British Foreign
Minister 197, 217

Lee, General Charles (American)
70, 87, 92, 106

Lee, General Lighthorse Harry
(American) 301

Lefebvre, Marshal Francois 314,
353, 426, 433, 435

Leon, Ponce de, Spanish Explorer
16

Leopold I, Holy Roman Emperor
22

Leopold II, Holy Roman
Emperor 203, 212, 226,
235, 237, 353, 361

Lepeaux, Louis, French Director
379, 380

Lessart, Claude Antoine de,
French Royalist 232, 237

THE GREAT GLOBE ITSELF

Le Tourneur, Etienne, French
Director 345, 379
Lewis, Meriwether, American
Explorer 325
Lincoln, General Benjamin
(American) 96, 110, 121,
125, 132, 156, 262
Lindet, Robert, CPS Member
259, 280
Lisle, Rouget de, French
Revolutionary 238
Little Turtle, Indian Chief 263,
324
Longfellow, Henry Wadsworth,
American Author 85
Loudon General John Campbell,
Earl of 36, 38
Louise, Queen of Prussia 369
Louis Joseph, Dauphin, son of
Louis XVI 187
Louis Philippe, Duke of Orleans
1793 to 1830 9, 141, 142,
196, 244, 256, 270, 271,
362
Louis the Dauphin, son of Louis
XV 74
Louis XIV, King of France, 1643
to 1715 6, 7, 11, 13, 22, 25,
28, 131, 160, 185, 194, 281
Louis XVIII 100, 196, 222, 331,
335, 340, 348, 357, 369,
374, 432
Louis XVII, Louis Charles the
Dauphin 51, 226, 275, 320,
335, 340
Louis XVI, King of France, 1774
to 1792 24, 77, 89, 99, 100,
114, 116, 141, 161, 173,
184, 186, 188, 209, 217,
228, 236, 238, 242, 248,
259, 267, 280, 341, 350,
353, 443
Louis XV, King of France, 1715
to 1774 8, 28, 41, 54, 59,
63, 66, 73, 75, 77, 99, 103,
160, 288
Louverture, General Toussaint
(Saint Dominique) 309,
362, 378, 407
Luckner, Marshal Nicolas 232,
238, 239, 243, 244, 250,
253, 254, 284, 288
MacDonald, Marshal Etienne
313, 398, 399, 410, 418,
420, 423
Mack, General Karl von
(Austrian) 399
Madison, James, American
Politician 134, 167, 391
Mahan, Alfred T., American
Author 47, 117
Malesherbes, William, French
Royalist 307
Malthus, Thomas, British Author
401
Mandat, General Marquis de,
French Royalist 248
Mansfield, William Earl of, Chief
Justice (Great Britain) 66,
137
Marat, Jean Paul, French
Revolutionary 192, 241,
250, 252, 255, 273, 275,
286
Marceau, General Francois
(France) 355
Maria Carolina, Queen of Naples
360, 399, 423, 430

Maria Christina, Duchess of Belgium 202, 269, 353

Maria Feodorvna, Empress of Russia 103

Maria Theresa, Holy Roman Empress 8, 22, 25, 29, 75, 78, 81, 83, 103, 119, 143, 212

Marie Antoinette, Queen of France 9, 45, 55, 74, 78, 100, 116, 137, 140, 141, 160, 161, 163, 173, 174, 175, 193, 195, 196, 197, 210, 211, 212, 213, 217, 222, 223, 224, 225, 228, 231, 237, 244, 253, 270, 275, 276, 284, 286, 287, 288, 320, 354, 361, 432

Marie Leszczynska, Queen of France 73

Marie Louise, Princess of Lamballe 237, 252

Marie Therese, Princess of France 100, 353, 370, 432

Marmont, Marshal August 356, 417

Marshall, John, American Politician 328, 365, 381, 391

Marx, Karl, German Author 249, 350

Mary II, Queen of England and the Netherlands, 1688 to 1694 7

Massena, Marshal Andre 293, 316, 356, 371, 400, 410, 422, 426, 435

Maupeou, Rene de, French Minister 1770 to 1774 59

Maximilian III Joseph, King of Bavaria 29, 118

Menou, General Jacques (France) 339, 343, 417

Merlin, Philippe, Director 346, 347, 380, 433

Metternich, Clemens von (Austria) 408

Michael I Romanov, Emperor of Russia, 1613 to 1645 10, 418

Michaud, General Claude (France) 292, 322

Mifflin, General Thomas (American) 104

Mirabeau, Honore, French Revolutionary 186, 212, 217, 220, 223, 225, 227, 258

Mirabeau, Victor, French Author 43

Möllendorf, General Wichard von (Prussia) 312, 313

Momoro, Antoine, French Revolutionary 291, 306, 307

Momoro, Sophie, goddess of Reason 291

Moncey, Marshal Bon-Adrian 315, 337

Monroe, James, American Politician 217, 364

Montcalm General Louis (French) 36, 41, 45

Montesquieu, Charles de, French Author 13

Montgomery, General Richard (American) 89

THE GREAT GLOBE ITSELF

Montmorin, Armand de, French
Royalist 174, 211, 232

Morard de Galles, Admiral Justin
(France) 352

Moreau, General Jean (France)
293, 313, 322, 332, 333,
336, 351, 352, 353, 354,
355, 356, 359, 360, 371,
374, 379, 406, 410, 419,
420, 421, 422, 423, 434,
435

Morgan, General Daniel
(American) 96

Morris, Robert, American
Politician 90, 111, 132,
147, 149, 204, 205, 233,
363

Muller, General Jacques (France)
273, 315

Murad Bey (Egypt) 394, 396,
416

Murat, Marshal Joachim 343

Necker, Jacques, French Finance
Minister 100, 101, 132,
140, 141, 177, 184, 187,
188, 189, 190, 192, 194,
199, 201, 210, 211, 212,
213, 383

Nelson, Admiral Horatio (Great
Britain) 310, 375

Nelson, Fanny, Wife of Horatio
Nelson 423

Neufchateau, Francois, Director
282, 345, 346, 380, 410,
433

Newcastle, Duke of, Prime
Minister (Great Britain) 34,
35

Ney, Marshal Michel 270, 426

North, Lord Frederick, Prime
Minister (Great Britain) 66

Orleans, Louis I Duke of, 1723
to 1752 8, 9

Orleans, Louis Philippe II,
Philippe Egalite, Duke of,
1785 to 1793 9

Orleans, Louis Philippe I the Fat,
Duke of, 1752 to 1785 9,
44, 141

Orleans, Philippe I, Duke of,
1660 to 1701 8

Orlov, Alexei, Russian Politician
54, 366

Orlov, Gregor, Russian Politician
81

Ormesson, Henry de, Rench
Finance Minister 1783 141

Orvilliers, Admiral Louis de
(France) 115, 116

Osgood, Samuel, Postmaster
General (American) 182

Otis, James, early American
Revolutionary 62

Oudinot, Marshal Nicolas 313

Padua, San Antonio de,
namesake for San Antonio,
Texas 18

Paine, Thomas, British Author
98, 216, 381

Paleologue, Sophie, Duchess of
Moscow 10

Panin, Nikita, Russian Prime
Minister 54, 81, 102, 120,
144

Paoli, Pasquale, Corsican Leader
74

Parker, Admiral Hyde (Great
Britain) 361

Paul I, Emperor of Russia, 1796 to 1801 54, 81, 103, 136, 145, 218, 304, 331, 366, 370, 392, 393, 395, 408, 425, 427, 432

Pelham, Henry, Prime Minister (Great Britain) 34

Penn, William, American Politician 21, 111

Perignon, Marshal Dominique 293, 314, 336, 421

Perry, General Screeching Anthony (Ireland) 403

Peter III, Emperor of Russia, 1762 39, 54, 81, 366

Peter I the Great, Emperor of Russia, 1682 to 1725 11, 25, 75

Petion, Jerome, French Revolutionary 231, 243

Philip V, King of Spain 1700 to 1746 24, 28

Pichegru, General Jean Charles (France) 270

Pickering, Timothy, American Politician 109, 263, 302

Pinckney, Charles C, American Politician 151, 364, 381

Pinckney, Thomas, American Politician 300

Pitcher, Molly, American Political Symbol 107

Pitt, William the Elder, Prime Minister (Great Britain) 27, 33, 139

Pius VII, Pope 424

Pius VI, Pope 144, 209, 220, 343, 370, 393, 397, 420, 424

Pompadour, Madame, French Courtesan 54, 73, 74

Poniatowski, Marshal Joseph, Marshal of France 240, 241, 303

Pontiac, Chief 42, 56, 57

Portland, Duke of, Prime Minister (Great Britain) 138

Potemkin, Gregor, Russian Politician (Russia) 81, 101, 111, 120, 144, 145, 166, 178, 180, 218

Prieur-Duvernois, Claude, CPS Member 280

Prieur, Pierre Louis, CPS Member 280

Provence, Comte de, see Louis XVIII 222, 224, 226, 331, 340

Putnam, General Israel (American) 71, 86

Randolph, Edmund, US Attorney General 262, 299

Reed, Joseph, American Politician 112

Revere, Paul, American Revolutionary 85

Rewbell, Jean Francois, Director 332, 347, 380, 431

Rigaud, General Andre (Saint Dominique) 407

Robespierre, Augustin, French Revolutionary 316

Robespierre, Maximilian, French Revolutionary 277

Rochambeau, Marshal Jean Baptiste 121, 125, 232, 239, 284, 407

THE GREAT GLOBE ITSELF

Rockingham, Marquess of, Prime Minister (Great Britain) 61, 64, 127, 138

Roland, Jean, French Revolutionary 229, 238, 242

Roland, Manon, French Revolutionary 230, 242, 274

Ross, Betsy, American Flag Designer 90

Rousseau, Jean-Jacques, French Author 55

Ruel, General Pierre (France) 354

Rutledge, Justice John (American) 183, 328

Sade, Marquis de Donatien, French Author 190

Saint Cyr, Marshal Laurent Gouvion 259, 313, 353, 420

Saint Just, Louis de, French Revolutionary 255, 278, 281, 285, 292, 306, 309, 311, 314, 317, 319

Saint Vincent 115, 375, 378, 393

Saint Vincent, Admiral John, Earl of (Great Britain) 375

Saliceti, Antoine, French Revolutionary 285

Salm, Frederick von, French Royalist 307

Saltykov, General Peter (Russia) 40, 48, 145

Santerre, General Antoine, French Revolutionary 248, 268, 274, 442

Saxe, Maurice, Marshal of France 27, 29, 30

Scherer, General Barthelemy (France) 355, 386, 398, 410, 418, 419

Schuyler, General Philip (American) 86, 89, 96

Segur, Philip Henry, French Royalist 177

Selim III, Ottoman Sultan 395, 397, 415

Serurier, Marshal Jean Mathieu 356, 373, 419

Servan, General Joseph (France) 272, 273

Sevier, General John (American) 123, 294

Shays, Daniel, American Revolutionary 154, 157, 442

Shelburne, William, Earl of, Prime Minister 1783 (Great Britain) 138

Shippen, Peggy, Wife of Benedict Arnold 112

Sieyes, Abbey, Director 421, 431, 433, 434, 437

Silhouette, Etienne de, French Finance Minister 47

Simon, Antoine, French Revolutionary 275, 320

Smith, Adam, British Author 43, 97

Soto, Hernan de, Spanish Explorer 16

Soult, Marshal Jean-de-Dieu 259, 314, 426

Staël, Germaine de, French Author 101, 212, 351, 383

Stanislas II Poniatowski, King of Poland 80, 102, 266
Stanislas I Leszczynski, King of Poland 74, 76
Steuben, General Frederick von (American) 94, 105
Suchet, Marshal Louis Gabriel 356, 421
Suffren, Admiral Pierre (France) 118, 128, 310
Sullivan, General John (American) 108
Suvorov, General Alexander (Russia) 80, 179, 180, 203, 269, 304, 333, 355, 409, 410, 418, 420, 422, 425, 427, 432
Talleyrand, Charles Maurice, French Revolutionary 186, 192, 198, 201, 210, 212, 227, 232, 237, 244, 252, 348, 351, 353, 365, 374, 379, 382, 383, 386, 387, 390, 392, 396, 408, 411, 433, 434, 436, 437
Tallien, Jean-Lambert, French Revolutionary 308, 319, 348
Tallien, Theresa, Wife of Jean Tallien 338, 348, 355
Tamanend, Indian Chief 21
Tate, Colonel William (France), Battle of Fishguard 376
Tecumseh, Indian Chief 299, 325, 387
Thackeray, William Makepeace, British Author 32
Thugut, Johann von, Prime Minister (Austria) 264

Tierney, George, British Politician 403
Tone, Wolfe, Irish Revolutionary 352, 376, 377, 405, 406, 413, 423, 431
Townsend, Charles, British Finance Minister 53
Treilhard, Jean Baptiste, Director 346, 410, 433
Trumbull, General Joseph (American) 104, 105
Turgot, Jacques, French Finance Minister 43, 77, 99
Vergennes, Charles, French Prime Minister 77, 99, 140, 150, 163, 173, 174, 211, 365
Victor Amadeus III, King of Piedmont 357
Victoria, Princess, aunt of Louis XVI 216
Victor, Marshal Claude 314, 419
Villaret, Admiral Louis (France) 310
Voltaire, Francois, French Author 36, 73, 142
Vorontzov, Simon, Russian Prime Minister 35, 40, 219
Ward, General Artemas (American) 71
Wartensleben, General Wilhelm (Austrian) 353, 354
Washington, General George, US President 5, 32, 33, 40, 41, 43, 50, 55, 67, 70, 85, 90, 91, 104, 113, 124, 126, 152, 167, 171, 172, 180,

THE GREAT GLOBE ITSELF

183, 223, 234, 260, 293, 320, 388, 439

Washington, Lawrence, Brother of George Washington 5, 28, 32

Washington, Martha 43, 171

Washington, Mary Ball, Mother of George Washington 183

Watt, James, Inventor (Great Britain) 71

Wayne, General Mad Anthony (American) 234

Westermann, General Francois, French Revolutionary 248

Whitney, Eli, Inventor (American) 129, 295, 296

Wilkinson, General James (American) 325, 389

William III, King of England and the Netherlands, 1688 to 1702 7, 22

William I, King of Prussia 369

William I, King of the Netherlands 312

William IV, King of the United Kingdom 369

William V, Stadtholder of the Netherlands 157, 172, 175, 312, 332, 334, 360, 429

Wolcott, Oliver, American Politician 302

Wurmser, General Dagobert (Austria) 272, 292, 312, 334, 335, 359

Ximenez, Augustine, French Revolutionary 287

Zinzendorf, Karl von, Finance Minister (Austria) 164

Zubov, General Valerian (Russia) 331, 366

ABOUT THE AUTHOR

Peter Hardy has had a long career as an engineer. He has been married for over thirty years and is the father of three grown boys. He grew up in Texas, went to Texas A&M University, and served in the Navy. Peter is an amateur history buff, and this is his second publication.

www.ingramcontent.com/pod-product-compliance
Lightning Source LLC
LaVergne TN
LVHW060919301224
799994LV00062B/185